CHANGING H
ART WITHOUT RESERVATION 3

To Sally
from Susan

CHANGING HANDS: ART WITHOUT RESERVATION 3

Contemporary Native North American Art from the Northeast and Southeast

Ellen Taubman
David Revere McFadden

Museum of Arts and Design

museum of arts and design

Museum of Arts and Design
2 Columbus Circle
New York, New York 10019

Published in conjunction with the exhibition
Changing Hands: Art Without Reservation 3/Contemporary Native North American Art from the Northeast and Southeast
organized by the Museum of Arts and Design, New York

Exhibition itinerary:

Museum of Arts and Design, New York,
New York, United States
June 26, 2012–October 21, 2012

Memorial Art Gallery, University of Rochester,
Rochester, New York, United States
November 18, 2012–February 10, 2013

McMichael Canadian Art Collection,
Kleinburg, Ontario, Canada
March 10, 2013–June 2, 2013

Museum of Contemporary Native Arts,
Santa Fe, New Mexico, United States
August 15, 2013–December 31, 2013

University of Michigan Art Museum,
Ann Arbor, Michigan, United States
May 24, 2014–August 17, 2014

Changing Hands: Art Without Reservation 3/Contemporary Native North American Art from the Northeast and Southeast has been made possible by the National Endowment for the Arts. The exhibition catalogue was supported in part by a grant from the Smithsonian Institution's Indigenous Contemporary Arts Program.

ART WORKS.
arts.gov

Designed by Linda Florio, Florio Design
Edited by Martina D'Alton
Printed and bound by GHP, CT

Library of Congress Control Number: 2012940578

ISBN: 978-1-890385-26-2

All measurements: height x width x depth, unless otherwise noted.

Front cover:
Jeffrey Gibson
Everlast, 2011–12 (detail)
Wool, canvas, steel, acrylic paint, glass beads,
artificial sinew, tin jingles
68 x 14 x 14 in. (172.7 x 35.6 x 35.6 cm)
Courtesy of the artist; American Contemporary, New York;
Samsøn Projects, Boston

Back cover:
Maria Hupfield
Pocket Full of Stars, 2012 (work in progress)
Mixed media installation, including sound and projection
Dimensions variable
Courtesy of the artist; made possible through a generous
contribution from Swarovski

Frontispiece:
Kent Monkman
Emergence of a Legend, 2007
(in collaboration with Christopher Chapman and Jackie Shawn)
One of five chromogenic prints on metallic paper
4 ½ x 6 ½ in. (11.4 x 16.5 cm)
Courtesy of the artist

CONTENTS

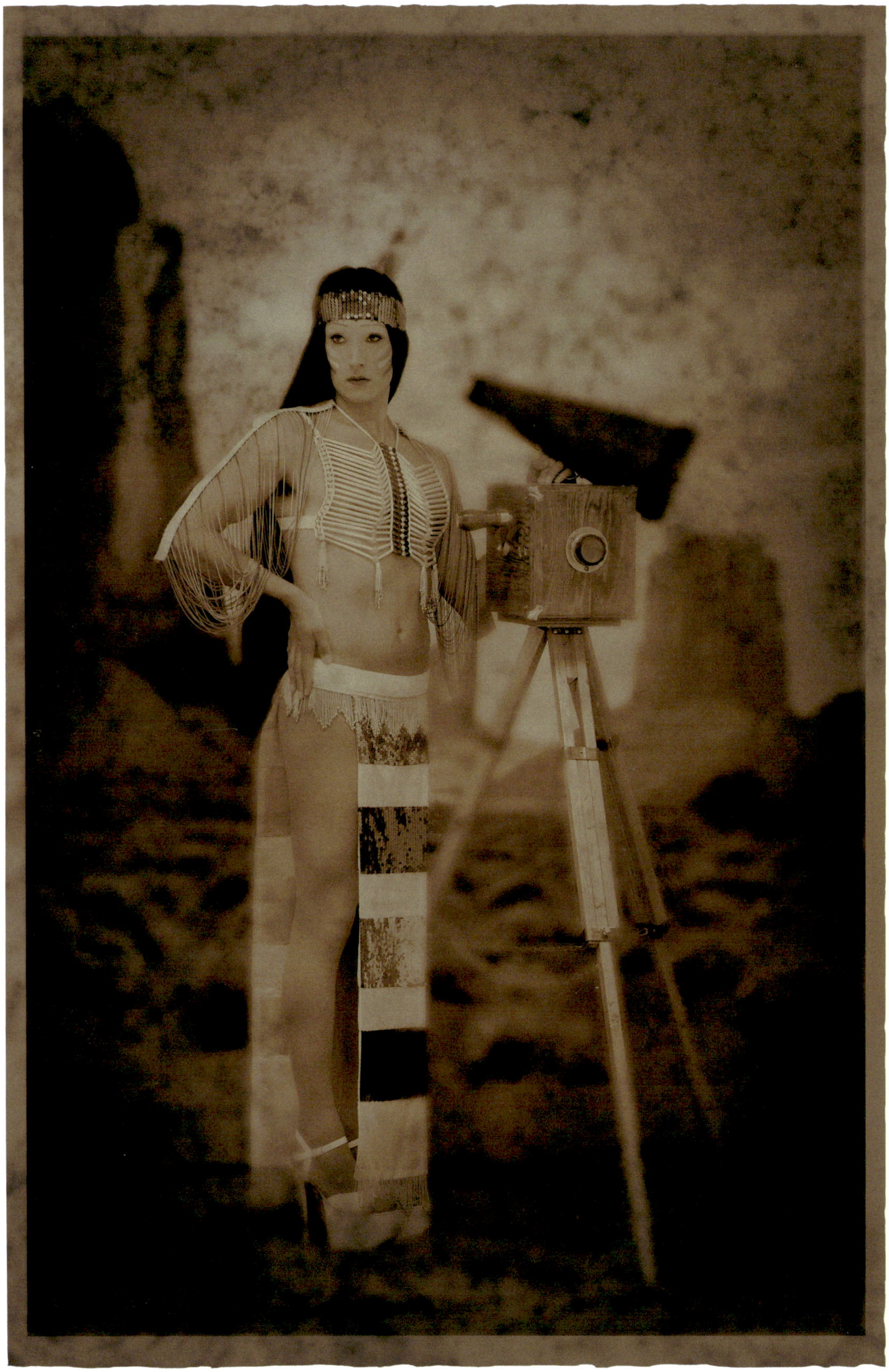

FOREWORD

The Museum of Arts and Design is proud to present *Changing Hands: Art Without Reservation 3/Contemporary Native North American Art from the Northeast and Southeast*. The exhibition, which features work by eighty-four of the most talented and influential native artists working in both the United States and Canada, is the third and final chapter in a decade-long research and exhibition initiative that has provided a unique and unprecedented survey of contemporary art by Native artists across the North American continent and Hawaii.

This ambitious series of exhibitions has presented work by many established and respected artists working in both traditional and new mediums, while also introducing the work of young, emerging, and under-recognized and often unknown artists to museum audiences. The *Changing Hands: Art Without Reservation* series documented the vitality and caliber of contemporary Native work being created today, and suggested the ideas and practices that will continue to influence artists in the coming generations. Each exhibition has contributed to public awareness and appreciation of contemporary Native art. Many of the artists who were first presented in an art museum context by way of these exhibitions have since been exhibited widely in other museums, have found collectors and patrons for their work, and have been featured in prominent art galleries. The catalogues that have accompanied each exhibition now serve as primary reference documents for the art and artists, and have influenced the exhibitions and publications of many other organizations.

When this museum was first opened over fifty years ago, a commitment was made to support innovative and experimental work by young and under-recognized artists, and I am proud that MAD continues to honor this commitment through exhibitions such as the *Changing Hands* series. This final installment in the series has been challenging to organize, not least because of the vast geographic region that the exhibition encompasses, stretching from the Great Lakes and countryside east of the Mississippi River to the metropolitan center of New York and from the coastal southeastern U.S. to the northern regions of Canada. There is a tremendous diversity of cultural groups, traditions, and practices, making this exhibition particularly memorable and profound.

The exhibition and accompanying publication came to fruition only with the generous cooperation and support of colleagues and institutions across the United States and Canada. We are grateful to the ongoing support and encouragement offered by the Museum of Arts and Design's Board of Trustees. We acknowledge the financial support of National Endowment for the Arts and the Smithsonian Institution's Indigenous Contemporary Arts Program. We are also delighted that this exhibition will be enjoyed by audiences in both the United States and Canada at host venues that include the Memorial Art Gallery, University of Rochester, Rochester, New York; the McMichael Canadian Art Collection, Kleinburg, Ontario; the Museum of Contemporary Native Arts, Santa Fe, New Mexico; and the University of Michigan Art Museum, Ann Arbor, Michigan.

I wish to thank our guest curator Ellen Taubman for her focused and intelligent work on all three exhibitions, and for sharing her passion and expertise in both historic and contemporary native arts with our audiences. I also wish to thank Ellen's collaborator, MAD Chief Curator David Revere McFadden and the team of museum curators, historians, collectors, and educators who have provided advice and guidance. Many staff members at the Museum have worked assiduously to produce this exhibition, including the registrar and staff, curatorial assistants, exhibition and installation specialists, and our educators and docents.

Holly Hotchner
Nanette L. Laitman Director

ACKNOWLEDGMENTS

The past decade has been a remarkable one in the field of contemporary art. Prices for the most important artists and significant artworks have soared, often beyond expectations, and attendance at galleries and museums has shown a dramatic increase. The same climate of unpredictability prevailed when we were conceiving of and setting the parameters for the *Changing Hands* exhibition series a decade ago: it was hard to know what responses and reactions would be generated, and this, too, has been both rewarding and inspiring.

If I have achieved anything by this series, it is my hope that they have helped to "close the gap" between contemporary Native art and the context of American art and perhaps the even broader context of contemporary art in general. I have no doubt that these exhibitions have made a difference, that they have set a new benchmark. As in the preceding exhibitions, and as Guest Curator for *Changing Hands 3*, I have had the privilege of working with a particularly remarkable group of artists without whom there would be no content. They have shared their work, their stories, histories, passions, and wisdom, all of which have provided invaluable insight that is reflected both in what is displayed in the Museum's galleries during the run of the exhibition and in this publication. Each artist's statement is as essential a component as the artworks. I have also been the humble beneficiary of the efforts so many others who have so generously given their time and provided their invaluable expertise, experience, guidance, and assistance in these endeavors. Their efforts have given *Changing Hands 3* an extraordinary depth and breadth, some of which is obvious, much of which is subtle but essential.

My more than thirty-year career in the field of Native art has continued to fuel my passion and commitment to this remarkable art represented by the *Changing Hands* exhibitions and to the ever-expanding group of artists who deserve to be recognized and acknowledged. This series would not have been possible without the support of Holly Hotchner, the Director of the Museum of Arts and Design; the invaluable assistance and guidance of David Revere McFadden, Chief Curator; and the support of the MAD Board of Trustees, with a particular thanks to collectors Eric and Barbara Dobkin, Marcia Docter, and Barbara Shuster.

To each of the artists who lent or created work for this exhibition, heartfelt gratitude is extended. I also wish to thank the many lenders who generously shared their collections with the public by way of this exhibition:

Abbe Museum, Bar Harbor, Maine
Alaska on Madison, New York
Art Mûr, Quebec
Christopher Bredt and Jamie Cameron
Richard Buckley and Tom Ford
Maura Cormack
John Cook
Marcia Docter
Dorset Fine Arts, Toronto, Ontario
Feheley Fine Arts, Toronto, Ontario
Janet and Brad Green
Charles S. King
Kitchener-Waterloo Art Gallery, Kitchener, Ontario
Drs. Steve and Shirley Kleiman, Spine and Sport Biomechanical Rehab Center, Grand Rapids, Michigan
Le Décor Français, New York
Longyear Museum of Anthropology, Colgate University, Hamilton, New York
Spirit Wrestler Gallery, Vancouver, British Columbia
National Gallery of Canada, Ottawa, Ontario
Mary Jane Laird Parks
John and Joyce Price, Mercer Island, Washington
La Fédération des coopératives du Nouveau-Québec, Baie-D'Urfe, Quebec
N. Barry Lyon

Marion Scott Gallery/Kardosh Projects, Vancouver, British Columbia
National Museum of the American Indian, Smithsonian Institution, Washington, DC
Ottawa Art Gallery, Ottawa, Ontario
PDX Contemporary Art, Portland, Oregon
Dr. and Mrs. Ari and Lea Plosker
Carolyn and Bill Pollack
Sandra Moore Riley
N. Sahs
Woodland Cultural Centre, Brantford, Ontario
Anonymous private collectors

Acknowledgement also needs to be made to the many members of the Museum of Arts and Design staff without whom this exhibition and accompanying catalogue would not have been possible: Thea Giovannini, Project Manager, for her dedication and hard work in pulling together the many loose strands that were woven to form the "tapestry" of what is *Changing Hands 3*; Dorothy Globus, Exhibitions Curator, for her uncanny ability to know how things look and where they are best placed, knowing the possibilities of the building and the art that it can hold and/or the art that can hold up in its spaces; Ellen Holdorf, Museum Registrar, and her team, for coordinating the many loans that were brought together from near and far; colleague Kathleen Ash-Milby at the National Museum of the American Indian, George Gustav Heye Center in New York for her assistance in our collaborative educational efforts; and Wanda Nanibush for her curatorial role in organizing the special film presentation.

Gratitude is extended to the many colleagues who contributed essays to the catalogue, to the skilled editor Martina D'Alton, and to Linda Florio for the memorable and engaging design of this publication. Soi Park, Sol Salgar, and Willow Holdorf, of Florio Design, also helped with the catalogue.

And I extend my thanks to the many additional artists, scholars, curators, gallerists, collectors, art professionals, colleagues and friends, who have lent their support and encouragement to my work and to this exhibition, in particular, Barry Ace; Bruce Bernstein, Southwestern Association for Indian Arts; Christina Burke, Philbrook Museum of Art; Martha Cerny; Tom Chapman, Nunavut Corporation; Dexter Cirillo; Jane Coleman; Bonnie Devine; Matthew Dipple, American Contemporary; Jimmie Durham; Pat Feheley and Jessie Newton, Feheley Fine Arts, Christina Ferki, ArtnoArt; Jeffrey Gibson; Merry Glosband, formerly of the Peabody Essex Museum; Ingo Hessel; Greg Hill and Christine Lalonde, National Gallery of Canada; Robert Houle; John and Sam Houston; Elizabeth Hutchinson; Heather Igloliorte; Judy Scott Kardosh, Robert Kardosh and Paul Conroy, Marion Scott Gallery; Professor Neal Keating; Truman Lowe; Jennifer Complo McNutt, Eiteljorg Museum of American Indians and Western Art; America Meredith, "Ahalenia Blogspot"; Lorcan O'Neill, Galeria Lorcan O'Neill; Jo Ortel; Patsy Phillips and Ryan Rice, Museum of Contemporary Native Arts; Louise Profeit-Leblanc, Canada Council; Nigel Reading, Spirit Wrestler Gallery; Susan Cohn and David Rockefeller Jr.; Debora Ryan, Everson Museum of Art; Jane Sauer, Jane Sauer Gallery; David Shultz, Home and Away Gallery; Niccolo Sprovieri, Sprovieri Gallery, London; Waylon Summers, Lovett's Gallery; Betsy and Grant Turner, Long Ago & Far Away Native Arts; John Westren, Dorset Fine Arts; Karen Wright and many others, with apologies if I have forgotten to include your name specifically.

My thanks to my closest friends, Robert Littman, Sully Bonnelly, and David Roche, who have continued to challenge me and have kept me raising the bar higher. I also wish to honor my good friend, Ruth Brand, who I had hoped would see this exhibition, but who we lost this past year. Finally, I wish to thank my husband, Bill Taubman, for his unending support in every way, and our children, Oliver and Abigail, who have grown up sharing the triumphs and disappointments of my work.

Ellen Taubman
Guest Curator

Changing Hands: At the Intersection of Past and Future

ELLEN TAUBMAN

More than thirty-five years ago, in the introduction to *Sacred Circles: Two Thousand Years of North American Indian Art*, which accompanied a landmark exhibition, art historian Ralph T. Coe wrote, "The day when American Indian Art could be dismissed as unartistic and provincial is over. It is beginning to receive world-wide attention, after centuries of neglect and much prejudice. The artistic evaluation of this art is still in its infancy, but we are just beginning to come to grips with some of its most important aspects."[1]

While admirable, this turned out to be an overly optimistic prediction that Native arts would at long last gain a place within the grand scheme of the history of art. In most museum collections today, Native American art, to a great extent, remains segregated from the mainstream, viewed more as anthropological or ethnographic artifacts than as independent works of art. This ongoing unwillingness or inability to accord Native art its deserved status has been an impediment to the careers of now several generations of Indigenous North American artists who, like other artists, seek understanding, recognition and, ideally, success in the complex and demanding world of contemporary international art. Last year, Mario A. Caro pointed out the enormous changes in the perception and appreciation of Native art, a result of increasing numbers of Native curators, critics, and scholars active in the field, along with a burgeoning number of active Native artists. However, Caro also noted that "there are still areas in which the field needs to be developed. The collecting of Native works, both by museums and private collectors, is an aspect of the art market that is still relegated to specialists in Native art and has yet to be assessed by collectors of avant-garde art."[2]

Changing Hands: Art Without Reservation 3/Contemporary Native North American Art from the Northeast and Southeast concludes a cycle of exhibitions organized under the auspices of the Museum of Arts and Design and intended to address these shortcomings. Beginning with the first installment in the series in 2002, the three exhibitions have been organized to present a comprehensive and in-depth cross section of innovative and groundbreaking work by artists who are expressing a new vitality and spirit of experimentation in Indigenous art, who are embracing tradition while moving forward and looking toward the future. Goals and parameters that were established as basic guidelines for all three exhibitions have remained fairly constant, while in contrast, the field has continued to evolve. In the last ten years, perhaps more quickly than in previous decades, we have seen a new and likely younger generation of artists emerge, stepping forward into center place. Still, over this period, the *Changing Hands* series has strived and continued to present the newest work by Native artists, viewed exclusively within the context of contemporary art, craft, and design.

In reflection, the decision to create this series was both essential and timely. Since the opening of *Changing Hands: Art Without Reservation 1/Contemporary Native American Art from the Southwest* (2002) at the American Craft Museum (now the Museum of Arts and Design), followed by *Changing Hands 2/Contemporary Native North American Art from the West, Northwest, and Pacific* (2006), revisionist wheels that were set in motion have never stopped turning. Critical thinking and writing—and rewriting—on Indigenous art and art history have also expanded tremendously since that time, likely bolstered by these two pioneering examinations of Native art and artists as a vital part of the contemporary art scene, rather than as representations of ethnographic or anthropological artifacts. Today, there is a wider range of practices among Native artists than ever before. New materials and techniques, ranging from synthetics and electronic devices to computer-generated design and rapid prototyping, have taken their place alongside traditional mediums such as clay, fiber, wood, and metal. More and more artists move comfortably in the territory of mixed media, installation art, video, and performance, and the playing field has been leveled between emerging and established artists.

Inevitably, these evolutionary and revolutionary changes have required a corresponding rethinking and significant revision of some of the "standardized" guidelines that are followed and that generally dictate the "divisions," "classifications," and other benchmarks within the more typical traditional and regionalized "Indian Markets," found throughout the United States. Equally important, if not more so, these once relatively "exclusive" marketplaces, which were almost always rigidly defined by geography, have now become more diverse, more open to featuring a wider range of artists and mediums. Today, they might include individuals not only from outside the general region, but also from outside the contiguous United States, from Canada, Alaska, and Hawaii.

Another important development has been the many exhibitions and accompanying publications that have appeared since the *Changing Hands* series was initiated. Exhibitions such as *No Reservations: Native American History and Culture in Contemporary Art* (2006–7), which was presented at the Aldrich Contemporary Art Museum, Connecticut, and the more recent *Shapeshifting: Transformations in Native American Art* (2012), at the Peabody Essex Museum, featuring a section entitled "Changing," have added to the discussion. In addition to their similar titles, these and other recent exhibitions—as well as museum reinstallations—also have begun to present works within themes or revised frameworks that relate directly to those in *Changing Hands*. Historically, contemporary Native artists featured in exhibitions were almost uniformly identified by their tribal culture, as their anonymous predecessors had been. *Changing Hands* intentionally broke with this practice by identifying artists solely by name and date and place of birth, as would be typical in more "mainstream" art presentations. Initially regarded as radical by some curators, gallerists, and collectors, and inappropriate by others, this decision was embraced and applauded for the most part by the artists, and it has been consistently applied in all three installments of *Changing Hands* and the accompanying catalogues. The artist's voice, presented as written word in catalogue texts, often articulates their tribal or cultural roots, belief systems, or more, in the statements that are solicited and accompany each work, a practice also consistent with artists in other art fields.

Undoubtedly one of the most profound changes in the Native arts scene during the past decade has been in the realm of communication. When work began in 1999 on *Changing Hands 1*, contact with artists was almost exclusively by way of the post office. While some artists were accessible at Indian Markets, generally in Santa Fe or Phoenix, there were relatively few who had work featured in exhibitions or on display at commercial galleries or who could be reached through local traders or dealers, leaving many artists often out of contact or simply unreachable. The Internet had not yet exploded, nor had the world of cell phones and digital photography as we know it today. Overnight letters (that only sometimes reached their destinations), chains of telephone calls, or as last resort, word of mouth were often the only means by which artists were reachable. In the twenty-first century, virtually every artist has her or his own cell phone, email account, and digital camera, and many also have a personal website.

Today, the Southwestern Association for Indian Arts (SWAIA) routinely records all work that is entered for judging at their annual, invitational Indian Market in Santa Fe, thus creating an accurate database of artists that had not previously existed in any formalized way. Throughout the United States and Canada, there seems to be a more generalized movement toward formalizing artistic practices, although this is still not yet universal and can vary greatly from region to region. Thus, while art is only a commodity for some, and perhaps created solely as a livelihood by others, it remains at its essence, an important visual means by which Indigenous artists are able to overtly express themselves, perhaps more articulately today than ever before.

The publication that accompanied *Changing Hands 1* helped to formalize in print the revised parameters and contexts by which we wanted viewers to consider, or perhaps reconsider, contemporary Native art within a broader framework. This exhibition was focused solely on the Southwest (primarily New Mexico and Arizona), where, generally speaking and more than in other regions in North America, collectors of "traditional" Native art have gradually moved toward an appreciation of some of the more contemporary work, acquiring art pieces by successive generations, often because of interest in a particular family. This continuity also serves as an acknowledgment of the way art, design technique, and materials are passed down or "change hands" from one generation to the next.

Changing Hands 2/Contemporary Native North American Art from the West, Northwest, and Pacific covered a much wider landscape than the first installment in the series, both geographically and culturally, making the curatorial selection process more challenging. The decision was made to include not only the continental United States and Alaska, but also the Northwest regions of Canada, as well as to consider Native artists from Hawaii. This allowed for tremendous possibilities, with a greatly expanded palette of materials and a wider selection of artists from which to choose, who varied in age, experience, and practices. The basic exhibition parameters, however, were similar to those previously established for *Changing Hands 1*: a focus on recent work (made within the last five years); a commitment to include works by both established and emerging artists, all of whom were still actively working in their studios; and an emphasis on artworks that reflected formalized traditions while also exploring new concepts and practices in both materials and techniques—works that spoke eloquently of past and present.

In contrast to the inaugural exhibition, many artists from the Pacific Northwest had good representation among a large number of regional galleries and an established collector base, as well as a presence in institutional collections. This provided a relative abundance of published material, which enhanced artists' visibility and ultimately allowed greater access to existing and new work, and to the artists' studios, all of which were vitally important resources in the selection process. Moreover, by 2004, when organization of the exhibition commenced, the Internet had grown and was having a profound impact on artists, curators, collectors, museums, and galleries. This amazing phenomenon also became one of the "key" tools in locating artwork and the artists who may not otherwise have come to our attention.

Within the continental United States, however, identifying a younger generation of Native artists and appropriate works remained a challenge, except via the more "traditional" means of regional markets and annual fairs held at museums and related institutions across the country, events at which young talent was often discovered. It is noteworthy that, even today, some of the most accomplished and inventive beadwork artists continue to compete in these same markets, submitting their work within an oddly categorized division for judging entitled "Diverse Arts." The vagueness of the title makes clear that despite all of the progress that has been made, even those who are fairly knowledgeable and who regularly consider and revise the "standards" for these juried expositions have difficulty in categorizing what has become an often highly sophisticated body of artworks. Within the regional market competitions, what has remained impressive throughout this time period are the artists who continue to challenge themselves by the materials with which they choose to engage and the parameters within which they decide to work. Even today it is often the more "unorthodox" or atypical entries that generate the most excitement among the panel of judges, as the work in question often possesses an outstanding and high level of both creativity and workmanship. More often, too, these more "cutting edge" works will generally receive the highest accolades and awards, ultimately commanding and achieving the highest prices as they also seem to attract collectors who, by nature or practice, might otherwise not consider, let alone purchase, an example of contemporary art by a Native artist.

While we worked to assemble objects for *Changing Hands 2*, American museums, which had been slow to recognize the importance of contemporary Native work, offered little in the way of collection resources. Even in what are considered the "prime" centers for collections and collectors of Native art, such as Santa Fe, there were few, if any, commercial galleries that featured examples of the type of work that we were seeking at the time. In the past decade, however, the situation has obviously changed, with more museums actively collecting or oftentimes commissioning works of contemporary art by Native artists, although public galleries have not yet seemed to follow in step. In the twenty-first century Native art is continuing to find an appropriate place in North American institutions, both in the collections of American museums and Canadian, as well as institutions worldwide.

An additional and unexpected challenge when organizing *Changing Hands 2* was the securing of loans of works in private collections. As in other art fields, the owners were often anonymous and were frequently kept at a distance by the gallerists who preferred to remain in control of the artwork, the artist, and the collectors. Unlike other fields, however, the challenge of explaining the intentions and goals of the exhibition—and all of the positive reasons behind these intentions—often seemed insurmountable. Persistence prevailed, however, and ultimately requested loans were secured from private collections, institutions, and galleries primarily in Canada and with some from the United States. In contrast, some of the youngest artists who were contacted, many of whom were just completing their graduate degrees, immediately recognized the opportunity their inclusion in the exhibition represented. In the end, *Changing Hands 2* traveled to seven venues over two years and was seen by several hundred thousand visitors. It created career paths for several of the artists who were included and was hailed as a true celebration of "form and freedom."[3] Artists—young and old, male and female—integrated traditions of technique, materials, iconography, and more, as references or focal points, creating new and exciting work and representing every corner of the broad geography covered in the exhibition

The artists featured in *Changing Hands 3*—Native American and First Nations, Métis and Inuit—also represent a wide spectrum of individuals. The regions for this exhibition begin at the Great Lakes, move north to the sub-Arctic regions of Canada, east and south to embrace the Woodlands and coastal regions, and ultimately, to the wide swath of lands between these many borders. Perhaps more overt here than in either of the preceding exhibitions has been the obvious resistance to and rejection of the concept of a one-dimensionalized "Indian" perspective. The artists and works selected for *Changing Hands 3* present a cross section of cultures, languages, lifestyles, and more, all of which may be just as easily found among any group of individuals, Indigenous or otherwise, but such diversity is rarely acknowledged within discussions of Native arts and artists. Effort has been made too, to confront some of the more romanticized notions of "Indian" or "Indianness" with the selection of works that have been included.

While organizing this exhibition, we were also compelled to reconsider the relevance and meaning of the series title *Changing Hands*, recognizing that while the selected artists were Indigenous, they come from a diversity of cultures and that traditions within these cultures were not necessarily or universally exchanged in the same manner as in the previous two exhibitions, that is, generally speaking, from one generation to the next. When the first *Changing Hands* exhibition was being organized, we used the concept of the title to reference the passing on of cultural traditions, knowledge of materials and techniques, and a visual vocabulary of forms, patterns, and motifs from one generation to another, generally within a family. This practice was particularly meaningful for (but not exclusive to) female artists. Grandmothers taught their children, while their grandchildren learned from their mothers, especially among ceramists and weavers. By contrast, most of the artists featured in this third installment of *Changing Hands* have been formally trained at accredited art schools and universities in Canada and the United States. A considerable number have achieved advanced degrees. As a result, it seemed that a reconsideration (and perhaps a redefinition) of the title *Changing Hands* was in order. Art education was no longer proscribed as family and generational issues. Many of the selected artists have also become educators, teaching at major institutions, while some are also active as curators, writers, and critics. Still others have returned to their homelands to regain a sense of their own cultural history and what has been lost as a result of displacement, marginalization, and urbanization. The goal of their quest to rediscover and revalue traditions has been to transmit experiences and insights to others, including non-Native audiences, thus adding another layer of meaning to the concept of "changing hands."

Colonization, assimilation, displacement, and the harsh realities that have an impact on individuals and families—such as the removal of children to boarding schools and the policies pursued in reservation schools—have been experienced by many Native artists from the regions in *Changing Hands 3*. This often resulted in the lack or loss, sometimes intentional, of traditions, shared histories, and shared memories. Additionally, some artists in *Changing Hands 3* are from regions where artistic "traditions" were created for economic means rather than growing out of "ceremonial" roots. Other artists in the exhibition were raised in an urbanized landscape, while still others have learned to straddle two lifestyles. The evolving circumstances for Indigenous artists in Canada, a significant number of whom are represented in *Changing Hands 3*, can also be set against the experiences of Native artists in the United States, as outlined in Sherry Farrell Racette's essay in this volume.

Changing Hands 3 has been the most challenging exhibition in the series to organize. This may be attributed to a consideration of the originating concepts and inherent meanings of the exhibition title, or perhaps to the diversity of approaches and practices followed by artists in the regions covered by this third installment. Organization demanded rigorous criteria to maintain the integrity of the original intention and to adhere to the Mission of the Museum of Arts and Design—exploring artists' engagement with the creative intersection of materials and processes, and the ways in which meaning is conveyed in the making of works of art. Within the exhibition, some works explore the use of relatively conventional mediums and applications—such as beadwork, basketry, appliqué, quilt making, and wood sculpture—but with artists taking a highly contemporary approach. Some artists have transformed what was once considered traditional handcraft mediums and practices into independent works of art, while others have chosen to work in a broader visual vocabulary that articulates traditional metaphors and meanings in new, and often, more abstracted forms that bear little resemblance to the past.

The exhibition is also the most varied of the three in the *Changing Hands* series, including significantly more installation art and videos, a greater degree of trenchant political commentary, more autobiographical narratives, and more overt content regarding issues of identity, gender, and cultural heterogeneity than the previous two exhibitions. This radical shift might suggest that the "changing hands" concept has once again expanded to become a more abstracted definition, encompassing shared insights and viewpoints that in the past had often been kept quiet or were ignored. The Indigenous or "Native" perspective is more overtly expressed in *Changing Hands 3,* with an intentional and direct interrogation of art history, the artists' view challenging the "museumification" of Native culture.[4] As Ruth Phillips has stated: "During the past two decades . . . the discourse surrounding Native art has been moving in new directions, driven by the radical reformations to art history and anthropology as disciplines and by the growing Native critique of the Western art and culture system."[5]

Changing Hands 3 does not present one voice, one language, one lifestyle, one religious belief, nor one form of artistic expression: there are many, with experiences that are equally divergent. "Indian art" or "Native American" art no longer fits within a single category or framework, just as "European" art is not clustered under one "umbrella." Indeed, even as we have endeavored to reconsider the title of the exhibition and its inherent meaning, we have still worked to maintain an "Indian" or "Native" reference point in most of the selected works. It may be suggested that this exhibition is comprised of art and artifact. Sometimes a work may be construed as a simultaneous combination of the two realms, while other works may be referenced as either art or artifact, but not both. Admittedly, with this series of exhibitions we, too, have been somewhat guilty of "grouping" or "clustering" or ethnicizing and regionalizing artists under an "umbrella," setting them apart from the "mainstream" in which we are striving to immerse them. By employing terminology such as "contemporary Native American art," we automatically impose a boundary that connotes the strand from which we are trying to help break away. There has to be, however, some basis that can be used as a starting point, and as one considers future exhibitions, re-evaluation must be part of the process.

When considering the works in this exhibition, but perhaps in all three, viewers cannot assume that the artists expect to be read only as Indian as Indigenous or somewhere between the two. For many of the artists, the experience and wisdom that is brought to bear in their creative output is from a multitude of different realities, sometimes at odds with each other, a reflection of what their lives have been. Both historically and now, Native art, like all art, is an ongoing process of change. It serves those for whom it was made and expresses an individual artist's personal "art history" within a larger world view.

---

1 Ralph T. Coe, *Sacred Circles: Two Thousand Years of North American Indian Art,* exh. cat. (Kansas City, MO: Nelson Gallery of Art, 1977), 9. The exhibition was organized by Ralph T. Coe in cooperation with the Arts Council of Great Britain, with the support of the American-British Associates, and shown at the Nelson Gallery of Art, Atkins Museum of Fine Arts, Kansas City.

2 In "Owning the Image: Indigenous Arts Since 1990," in *Manifestations: New Native Art Criticism* (Santa Fe, NM: Museum of Contemporary Native Arts, 2011), 68.

3 Form and freedom in this context were earlier analyzed in Bill Holm and Bill Reid, *Form and Freedom: A Dialogue on Northwest Coast Indian Art* (Houston: Institute for the Arts, Rice University, 1975).

4 Ruth Phillips, "Art History and the Native-made Object, New Discourses, Old Differences?" in W. Jackson Rushing III, ed., *Native American Art in the Twentieth Century: Makers, Meanings, History* (London and New York: Routledge, 1999), 97.

5 Ibid., 101.

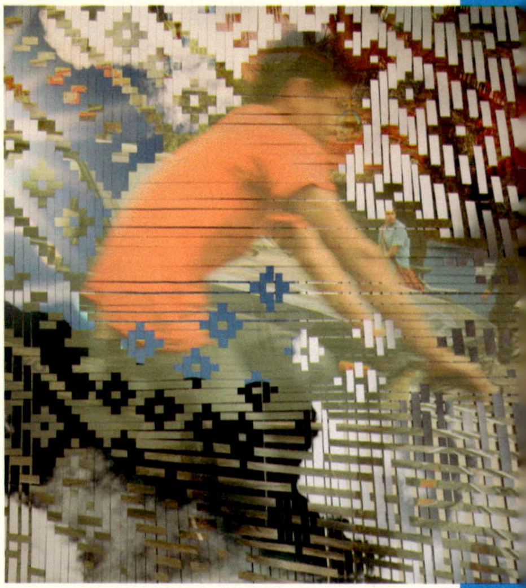

EVOLUTION AND EXPLORATION

Many Native artists create new work on a foundation of material, technical, and formal knowledge that is a profoundly important element of cultural heritage. "Evolution and Exploration" examines how Native artists are reinterpreting their cultural traditions through contemporary perspectives. These are artists for whom evolution and change are organic to their artistic vision, and the past is integral to their creative explorations. Artists may take the most traditional of materials and transform them radically; ubiquitous glass beads may be radically reinterpreted using electronic components; or traditional birch bark may be fashioned into surprisingly new forms. By embracing their own histories, these artists confirm the essential links that join past and present to the future.

BARRY ACE

b. 1958
Michigiwadinong,Maindo-minising, Ontario; lives in Ottawa, Ontario

Reaction, 2005

Found leather shoes, computer components, coated wire, paper, brass wire, rubber, metal
Each: 3 x 5 x 26 in.
(7.6 x 12.7 x 66 cm)
Courtesy of the artist

Bandolier, 2011 (full view and detail)

Cotton, velveteen, beads, computer components, digital computer screen, cotton thread, brass wire, coated wire
92 x 15 in. (233.7 x 38.1 cm)
Courtesy of the artist

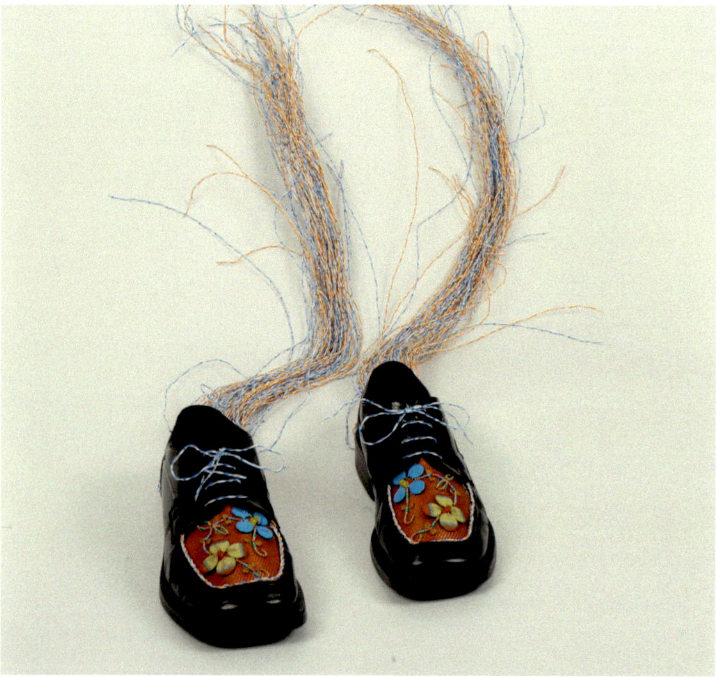

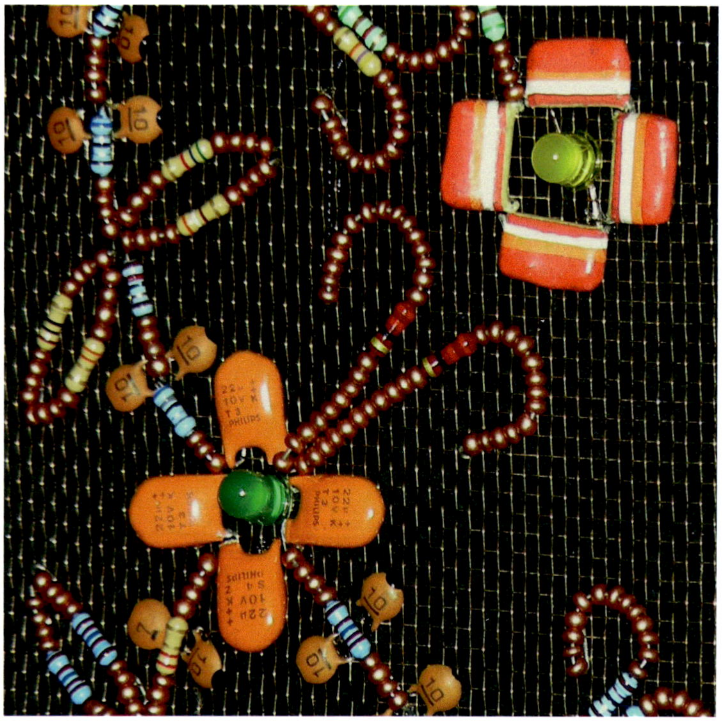

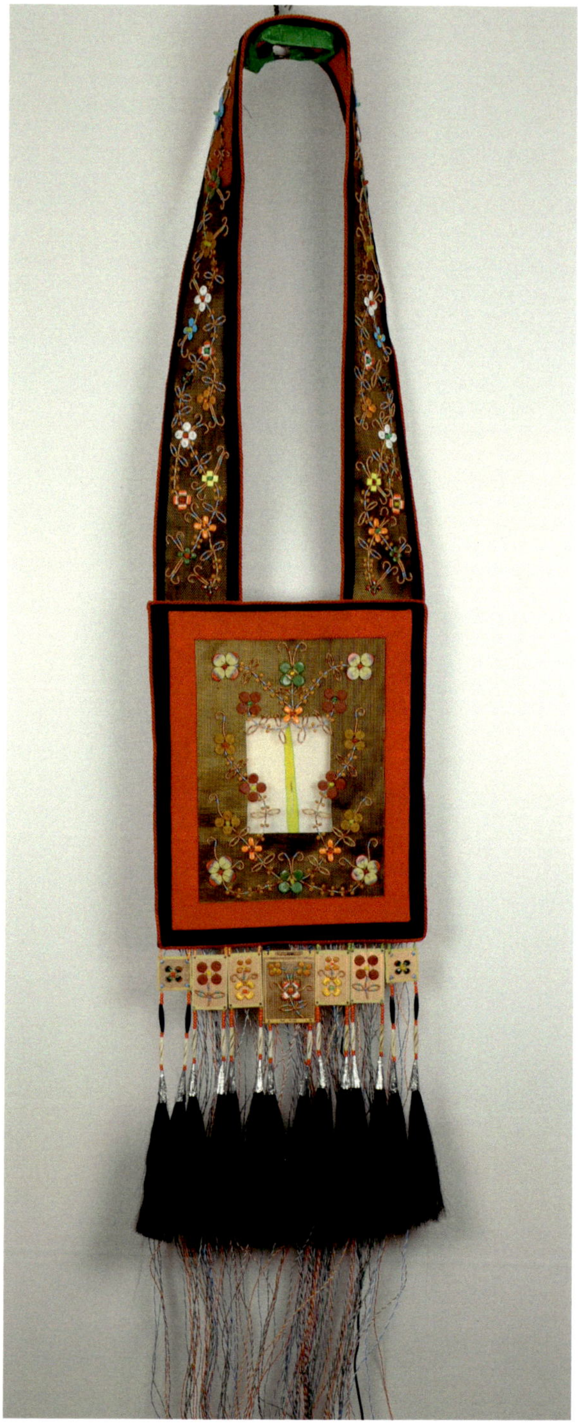

KC ADAMS

b. 1971, Yorkton, Saskatchewan;
lives in Winnipeg, Manitoba

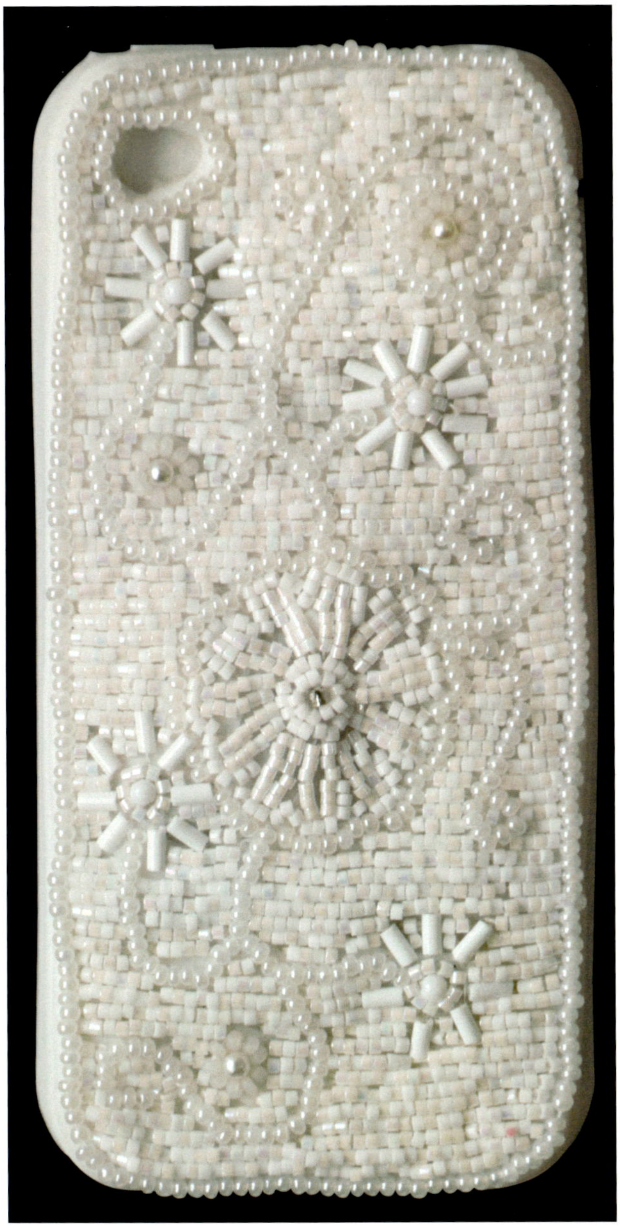

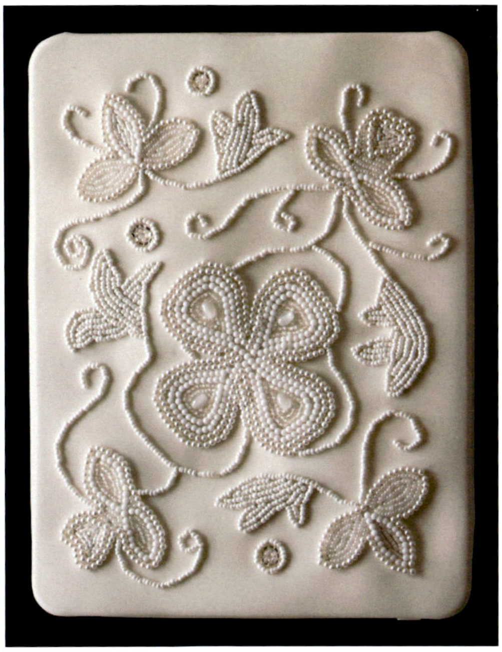

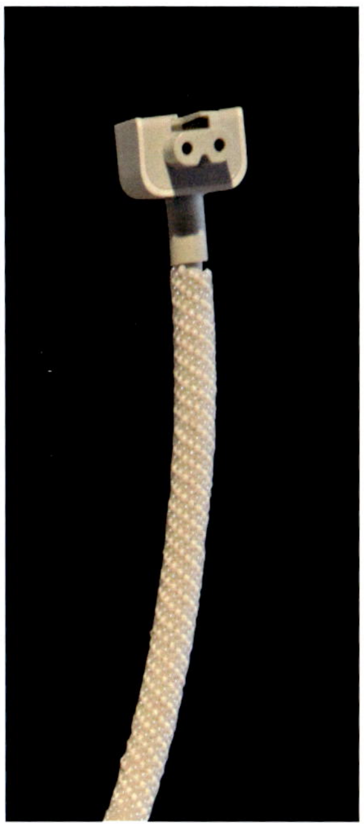

Left to right:

iPhone Communication Bytes, 2011

Glass seed beads, silicone,
cotton/polyester thread
5 x 2 ¼ x ½ in.
(12.7 x 5.7 x 1.4 cm)
Courtesy of the artist

iPad is Cree Floral, 2012

Glass and plastic seed beads, silicone,
cotton/polyester thread
9 ½ x 7 ½ x ⅜ in.
(24.1 x 19.1 x 0.8 cm)
Courtesy of the artist

Power Peyote Stitch, 2012 (detail)

MacBook Pro power cord, glass and plastic
seed beads, cotton/polyester thread
73 ½ x 1 ½ x 1 ⅛ in.
(186.7 x 3.8 x 2.7 cm)
Courtesy of the artist

ADAM ALORUT

b. 1979, Iqaliut, Nunavut;
lives in Ottawa, Ontario

Living with Sin, 2008

Stone, red pipestone, antler
10 x 3 ½ x 2 ½ in.
(25.4 x 8.9 x 6.4 cm)
Courtesy of Feheley Fine Arts,
Toronto, Ontario

She Devil, 2008

Stone, antler
10 x 5 x 5 ½ in.
(25.4 x 12.7 x 14 cm)
Courtesy of Feheley Fine Arts,
Toronto, Ontario

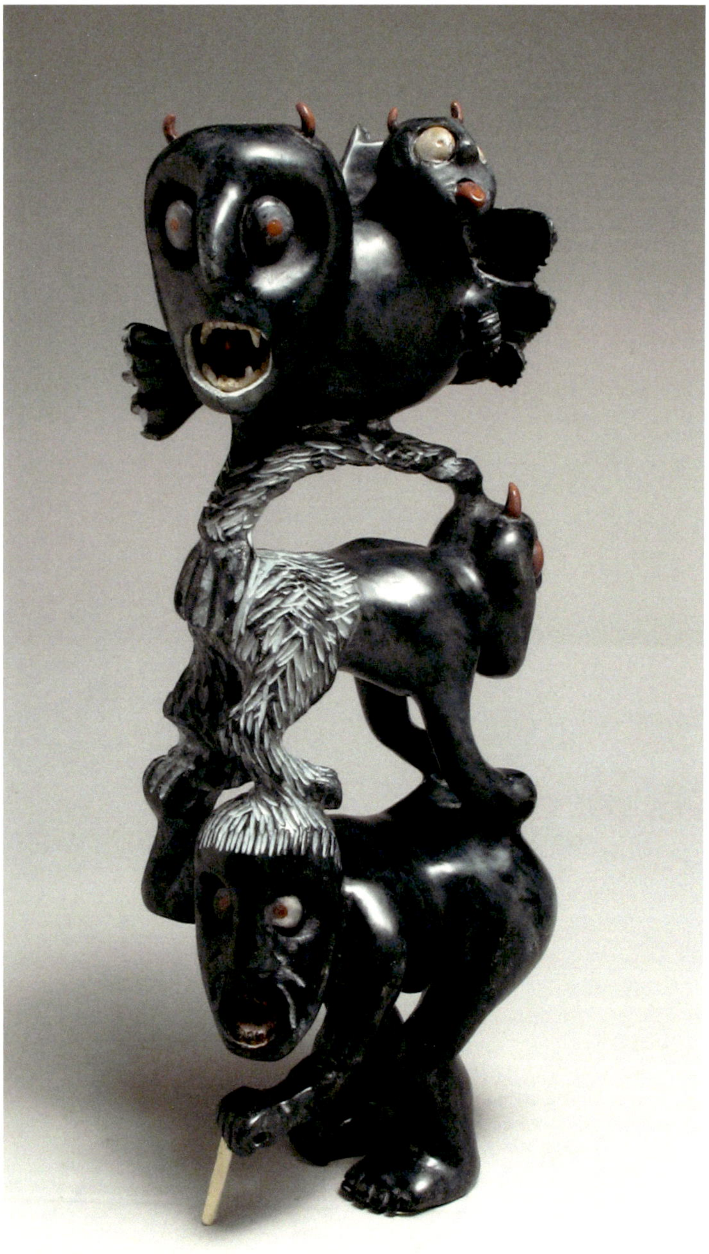

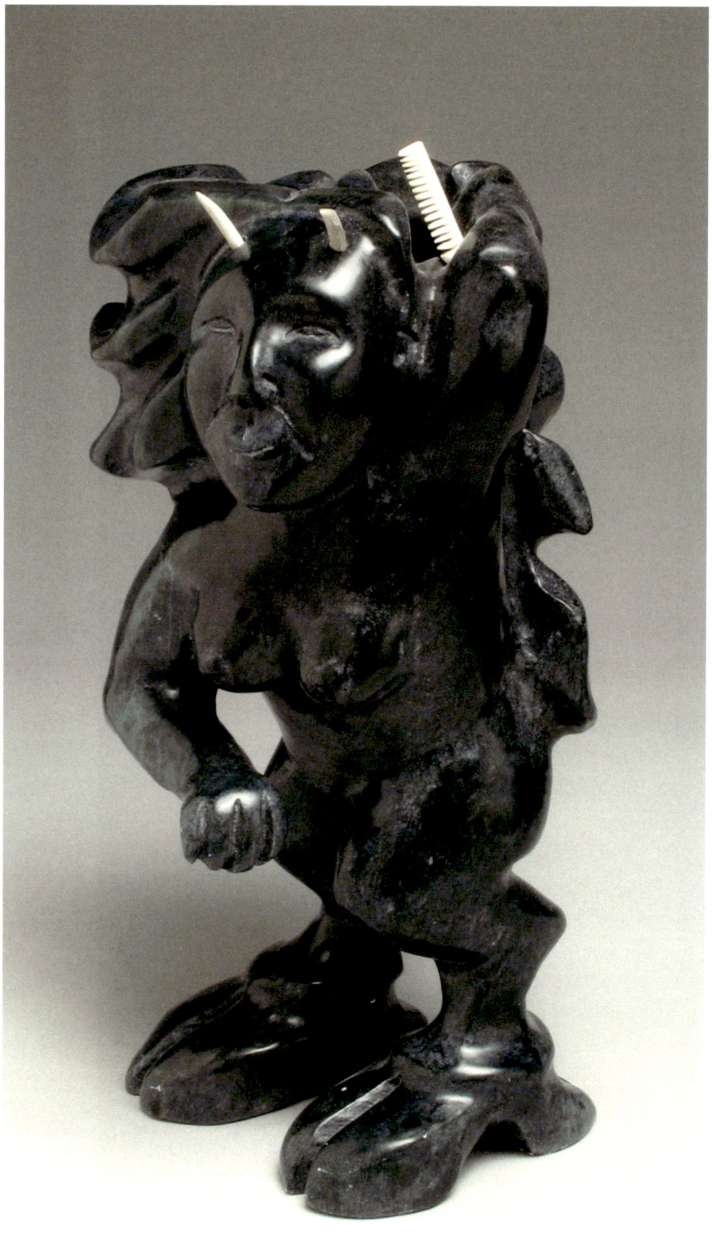

JOE BAKER

b. 1946, Bartlesville, Oklahoma;
lives in New Orleans, Louisiana

Bandolier, 2012

Wool trade cloth, glass beads, nylon thread
33 x 12 in. (83.8 x 30.5 cm)
Courtesy of the artist

Design concept for *Bandolier* pouch, 2012

Casein on paper
Proposed materials: Wool trade cloth, glass beads, nylon thread
10 x 10 in. (25.4 x 25.4 cm)
Courtesy of the artist

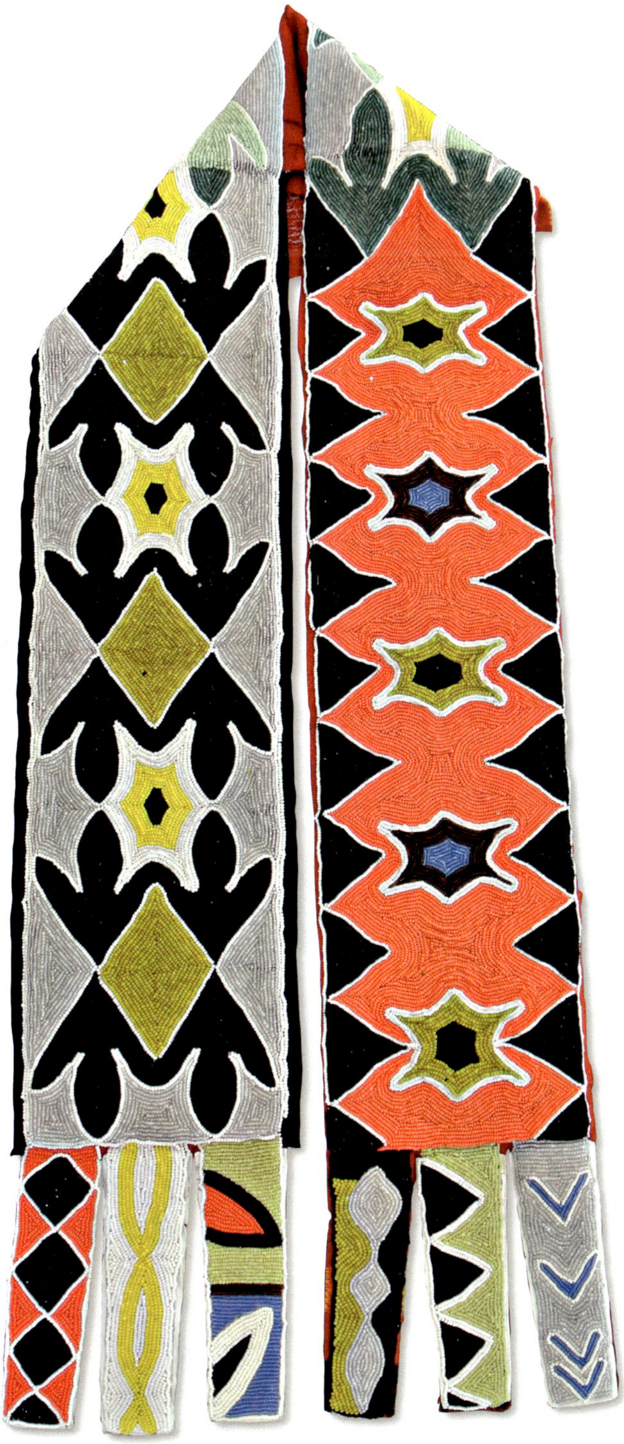

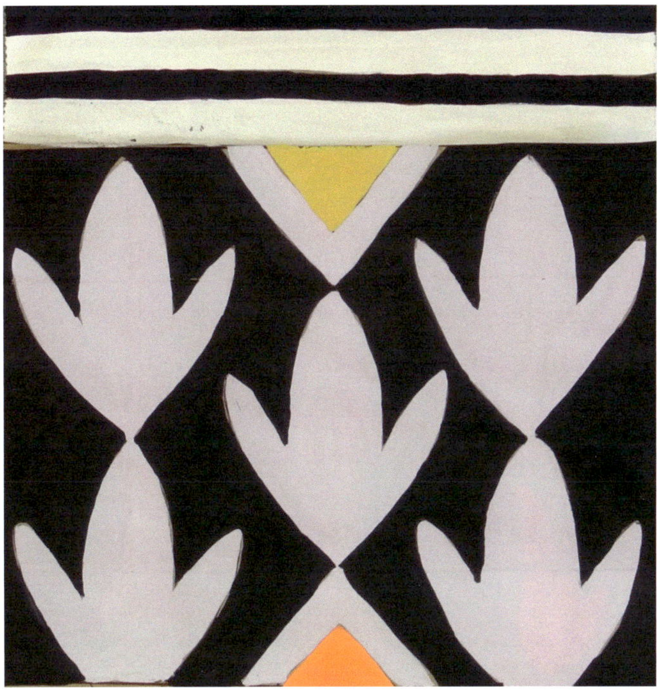

DENNIS ESQUIVEL

b. 1961, Peshawbetwown, Michigan; lives in Santa Fe, New Mexico

Design sketches for
Out of the Woodlands, 2012

Pencil on paper
Proposed materials: Bird's-eye maple, birch bark, cherry wood and quilted cherry veneer, stainless steel, porcupine quills
Each: 11 x 8 in. (27.9 x 20.3 cm)
Courtesy of the artist

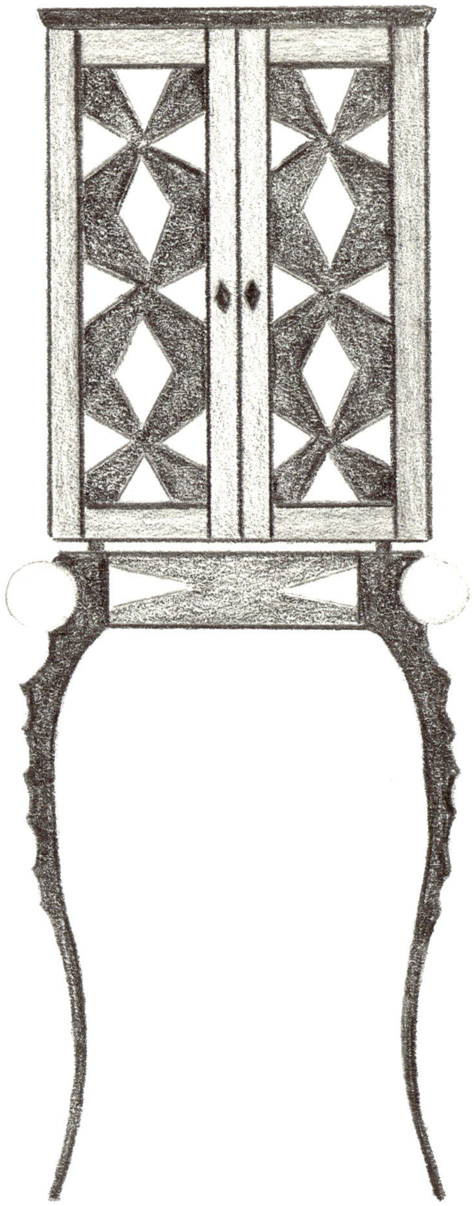

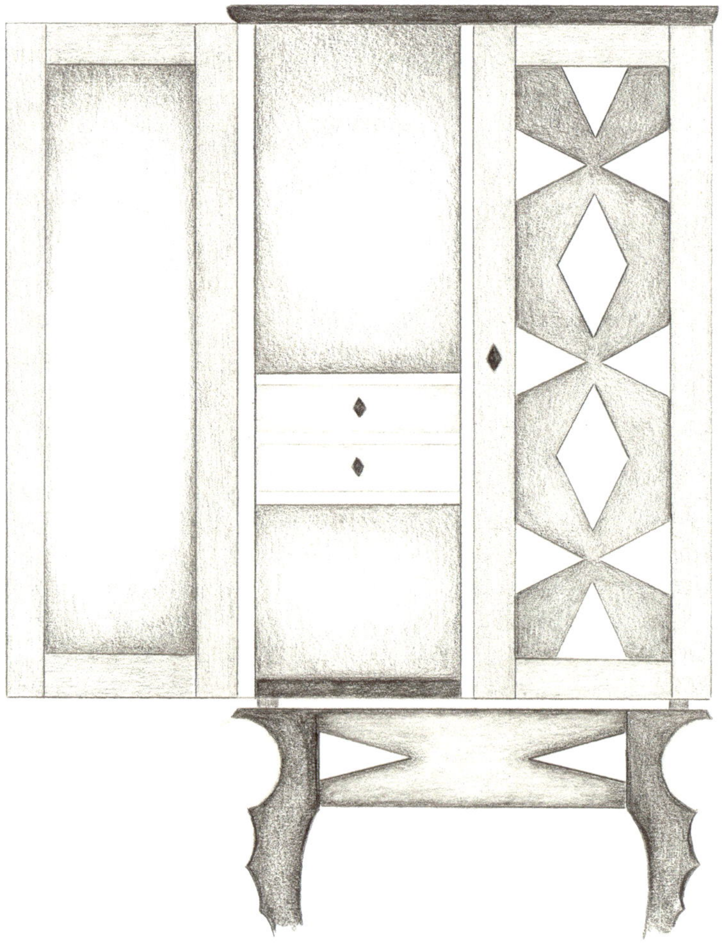

JEREMY FREY

b. 1978, Indian Township, Maine;
lives in Indian Township, Maine

Point Basket, 2011 (2 views)

Brown ash, sweet grass
Ht. 20 in. (11 cm); diam. 11 in.
(27.9 cm)
Collection of Dr. and Mrs. Ari
and Lea Plosker

Urchin, 2010

Brown ash, cedar bark
Ht. 7 in. (17.8 cm); diam. 11 in.
(27.9 cm)
Courtesy of the Abbe Museum,
Bar Harbor, Maine

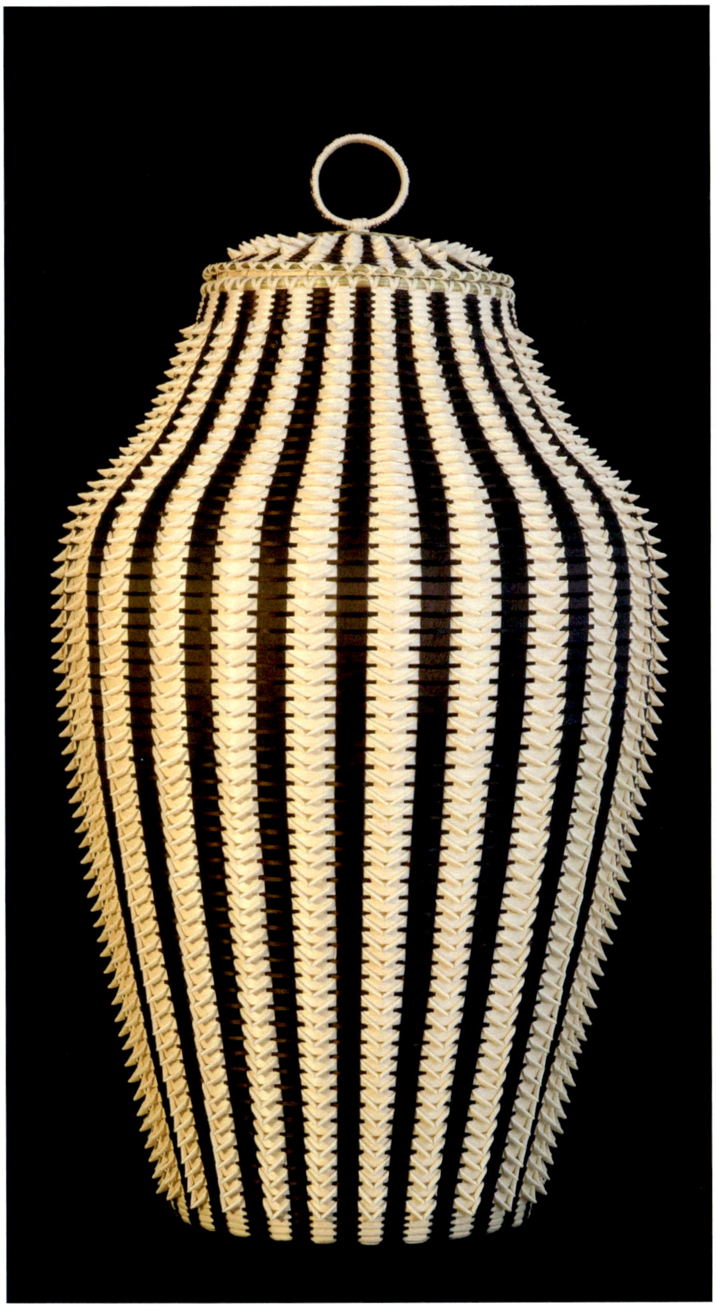

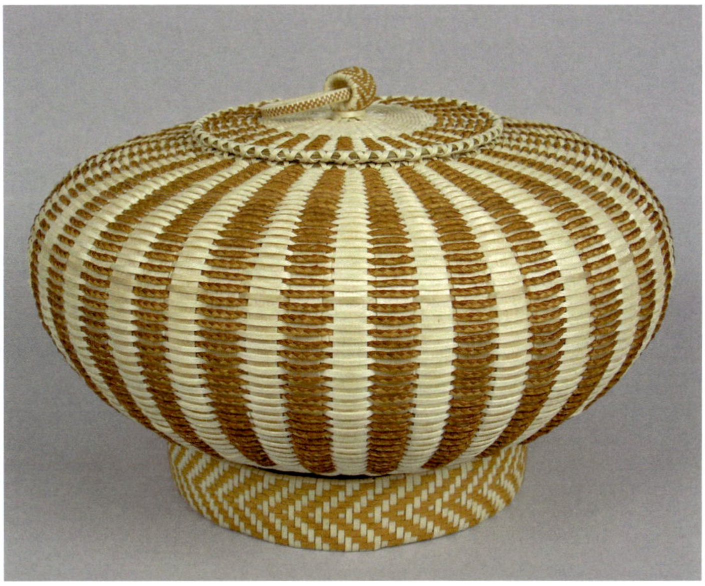

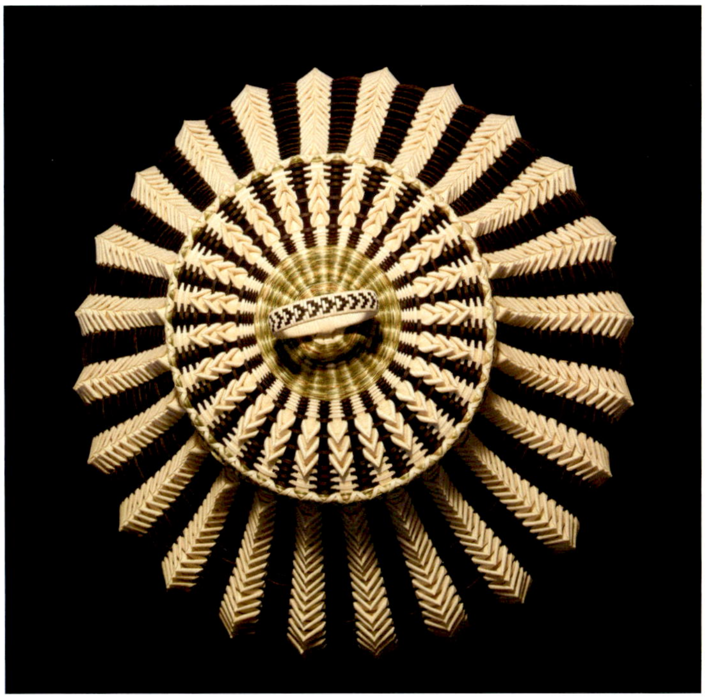

JEFFREY GIBSON

b. 1972, Colorado Springs, Colorado;
lives in Brooklyn, New York

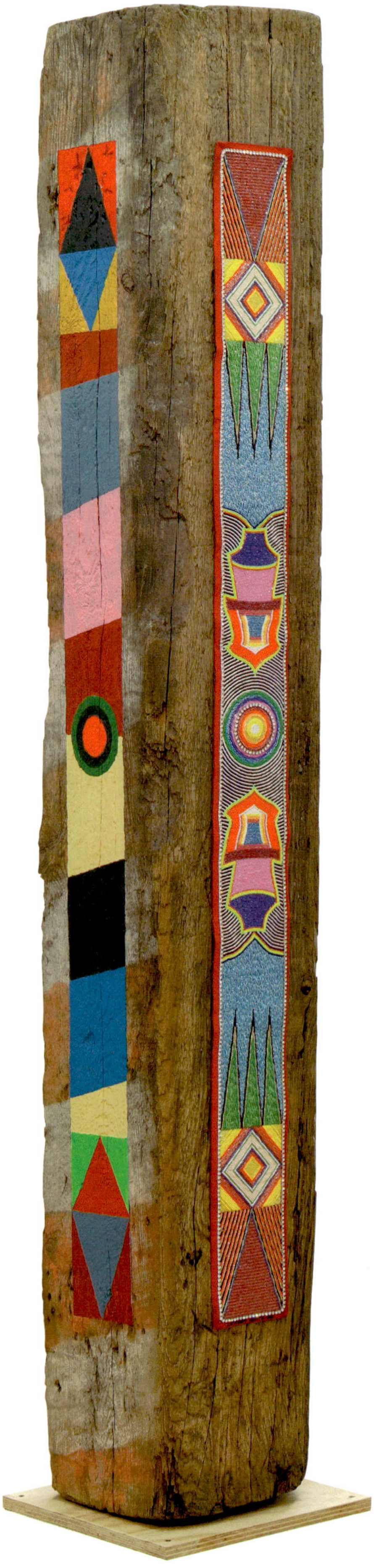

Column, 2011–12

Recycled wood construction barrier, acrylic paint, thread-sewn glass beadwork cloth panel (by Whitney Minthorn)
65 x 12 x 12 in.
(165.1 x 30.5 x 30.5 cm)
Private collection

CODY E. HARJO

b. 1981, Ada, Oklahoma;
lives in Brooklyn, New York

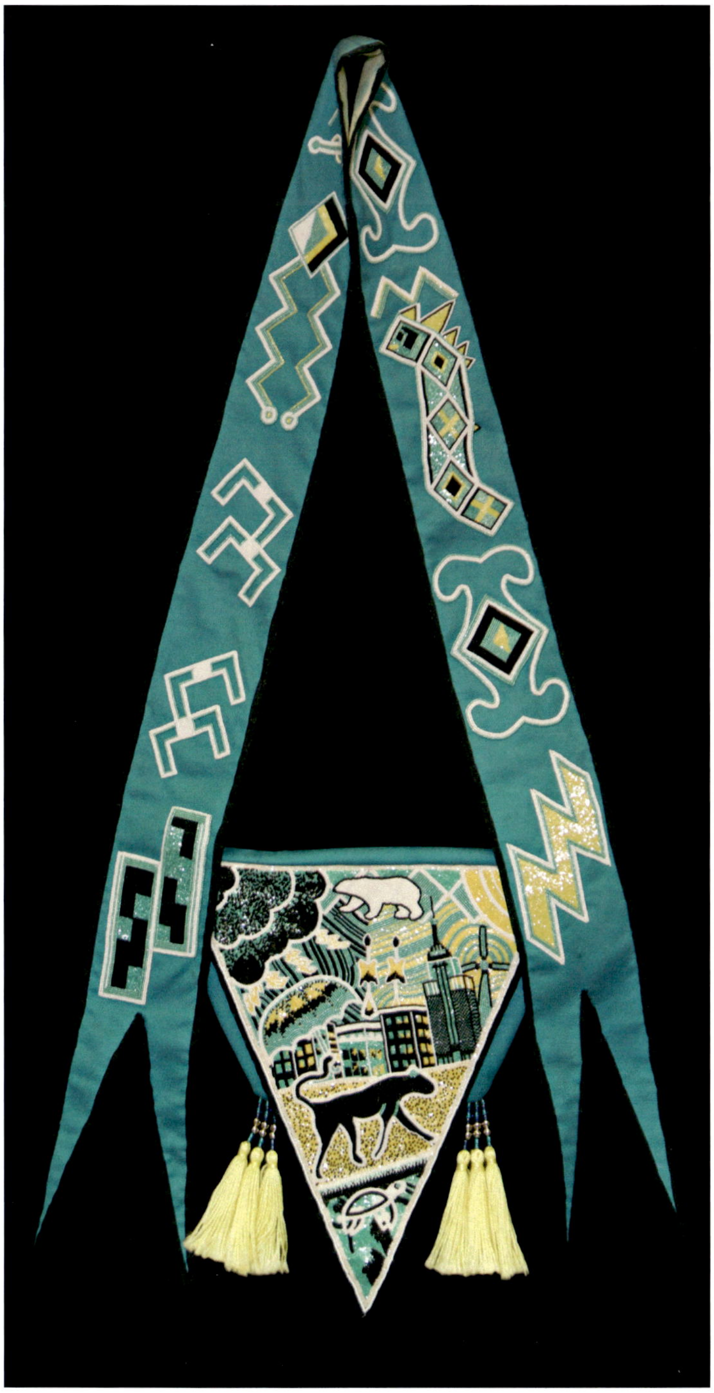

Kotcha Faces Climate Change, 2008

Italian wool, cotton, glass beads, acrylic yarn, satin ribbon, cotton thread
38 ½ x 13 ½ in. (97.8 x 34.3 cm)
Courtesy of the artist

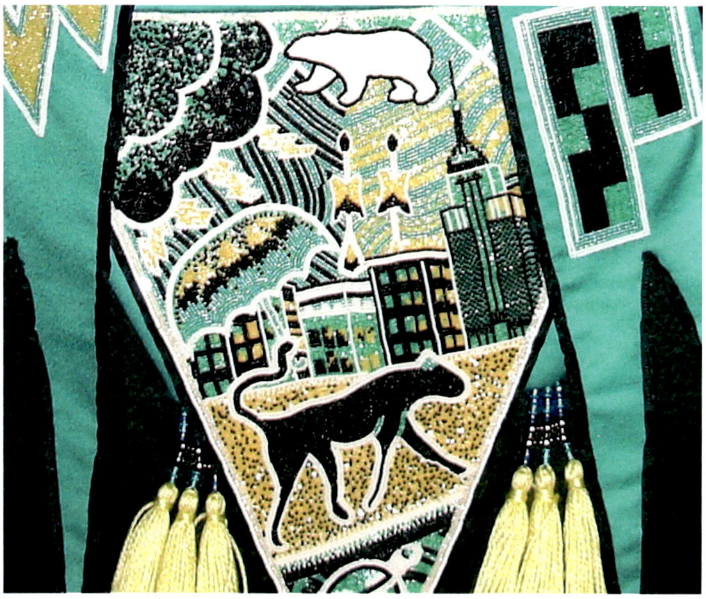

ROSEMARY RICKARD HILL

b. 1953, Niagara Falls, New York; lives at Tuscarora Reservation, New York

Four-sided European-style Vase with Elaborate Beadwork, 2008 (3 views)

Cloth, glass/crystal beads, cotton/polyester thread, glue
11 x 5 x 5 in. (27.9 x 12.7 x 12.7 cm)
Courtesy of the artist

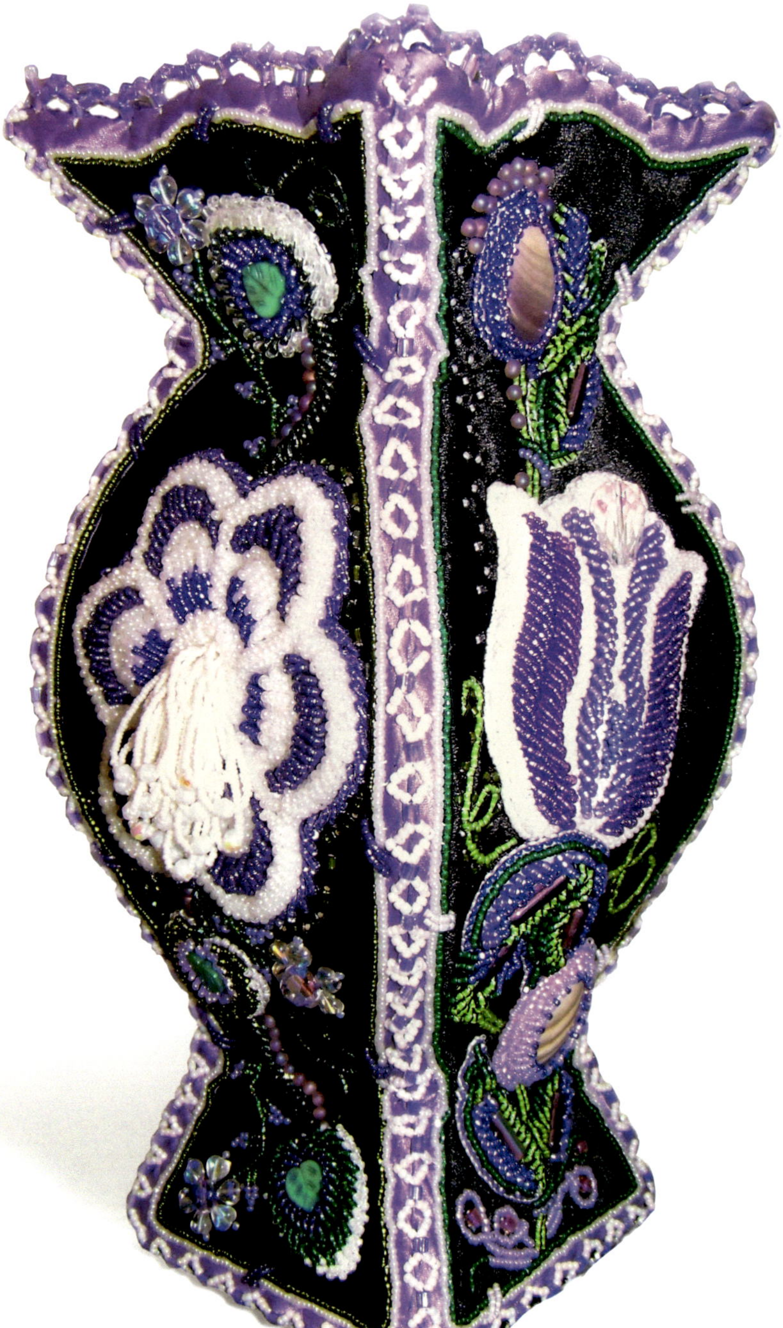

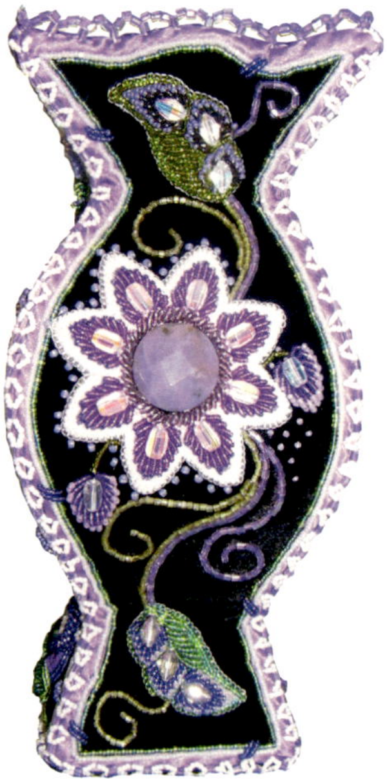

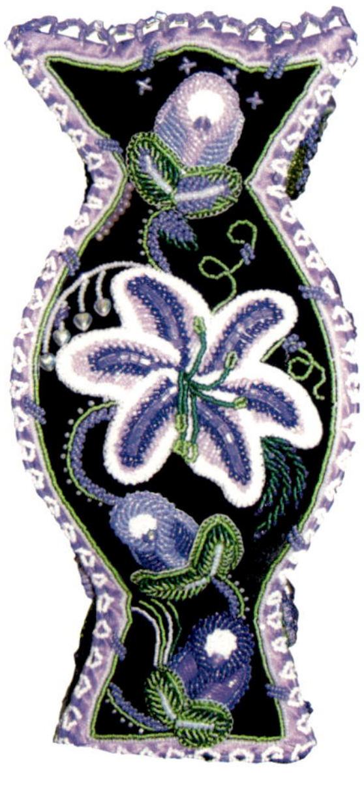

RUBEN ANTON KOMANGAPIK

b. 1976, Frobisher Bay, Northwest Territories; lives in Gaspésie, Quebec

Ujararuqtuk (Become Stone), 2011
(2 views)

Kirkidium marble
9 ½ x 5 ½ x 2 ½ in.
(24.1 x 14 x 6.4 cm)
Collection of John and Joyce Price, Mercer Island, Washington

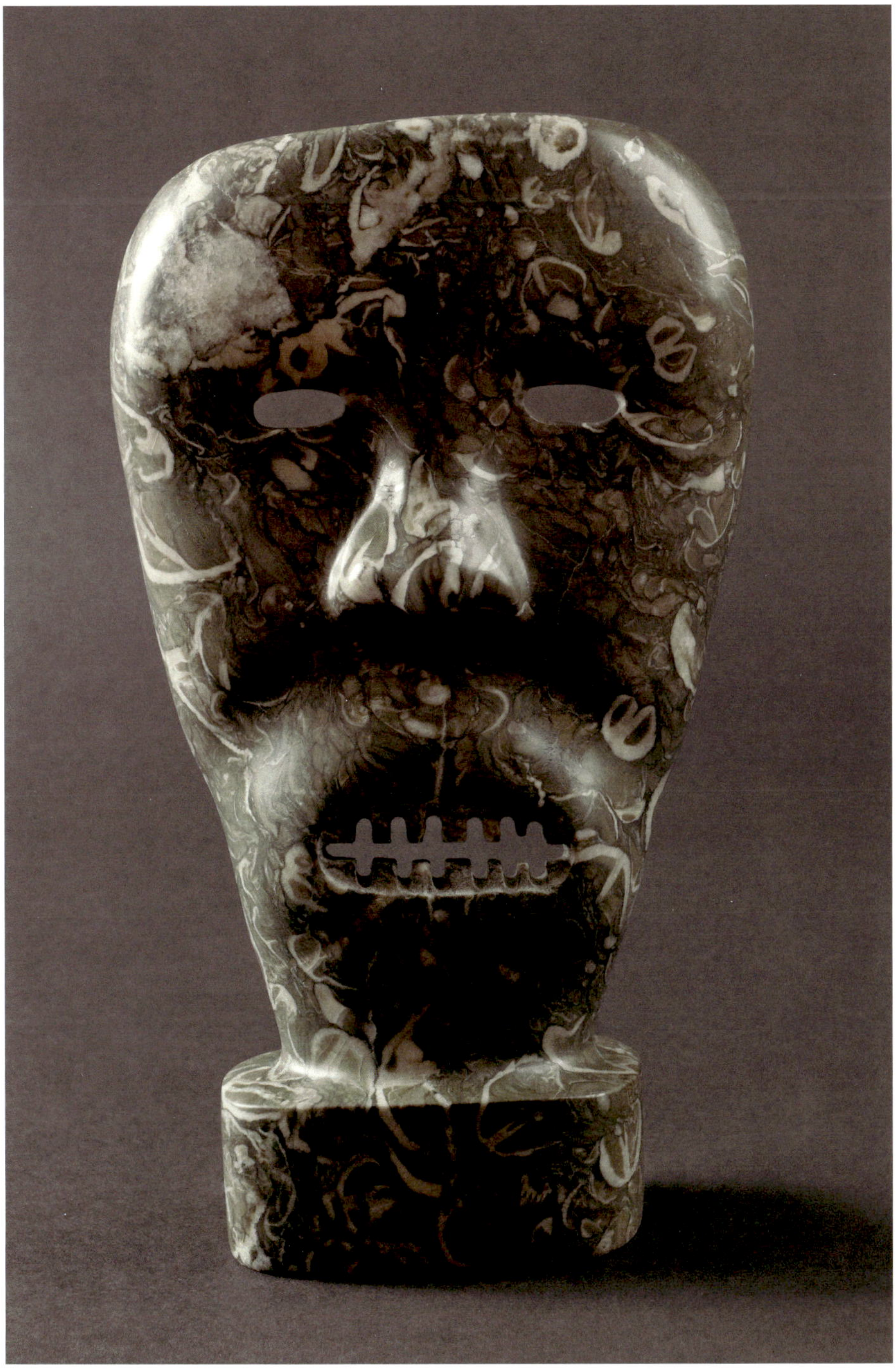

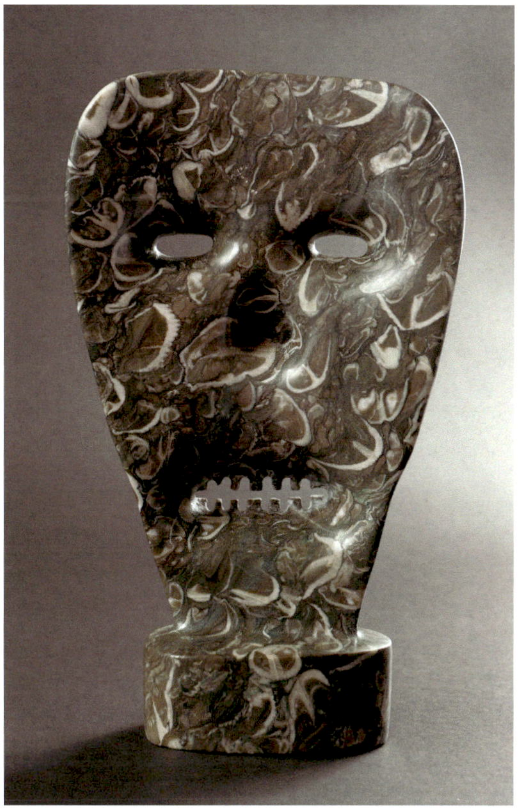

JOHN KUROK

b. 1977, Churchill, Manitoba;
lives in Rankin Inlet, Nunavut

Coat of Dreams, 2006

(in collaboration with Leo Napayok)
Clay
17 11/16 x 13 3/4 x 10 1/8 in.
(45 x 35 x 25.7 cm)
National Gallery of Canada, Ottawa
Purchased 2008 with the generous support of TD Bank Financial Group in commemoration of the National Gallery's 125th anniversary and TD's 150th anniversary

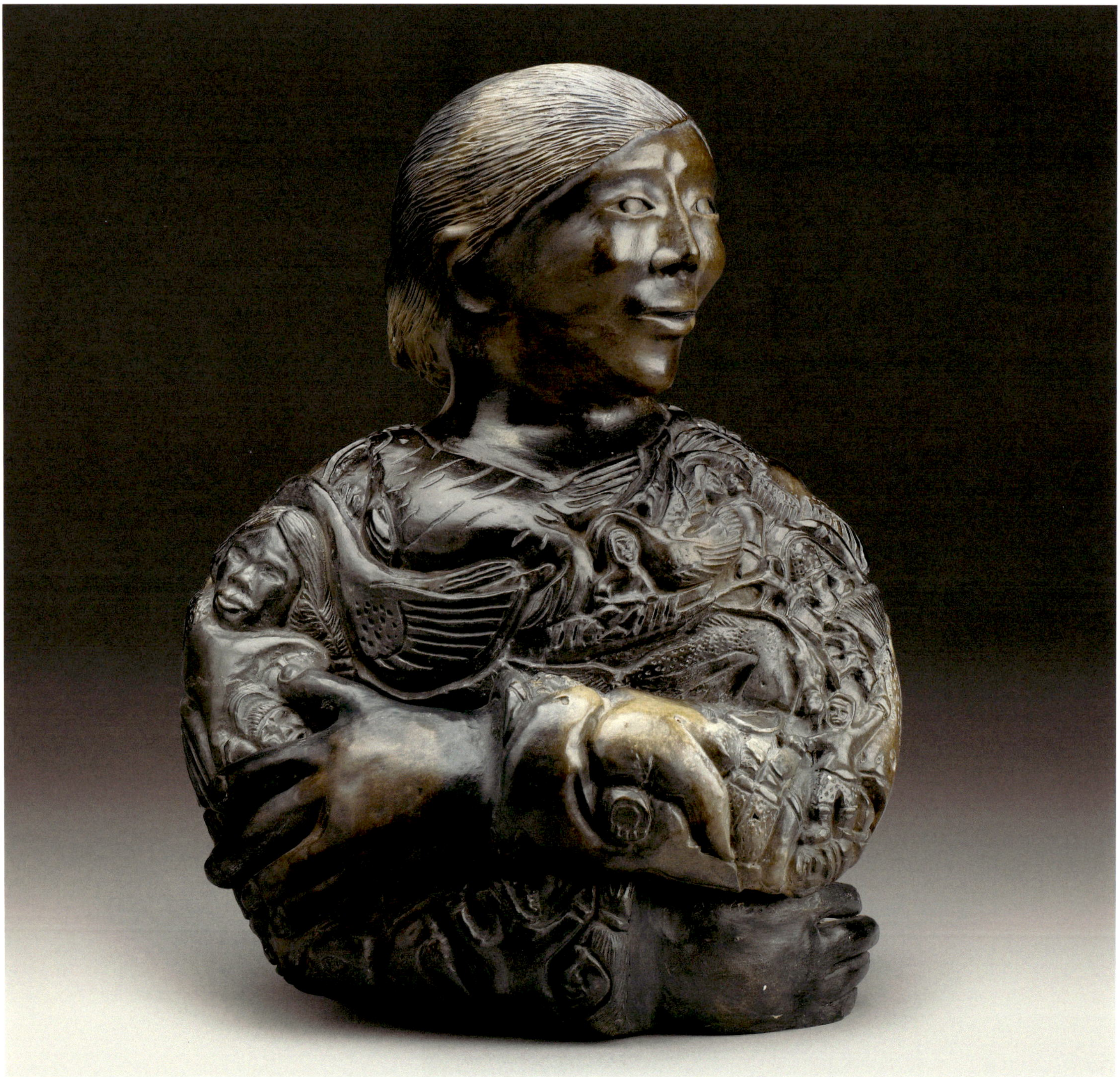

SAMUEL LaFOUNTAIN

b. 1986, Santa Fe, New Mexico,
lives in Santa Fe, New Mexico

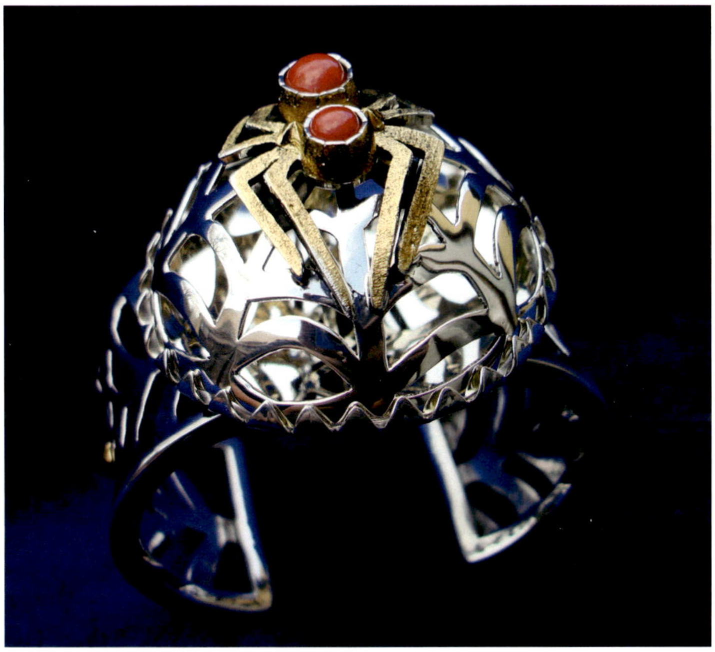

Spider Bracelet, 2012

Sterling silver, 18K gold,
Mediterranean red coral
3 x 2 x 2 ½ in.
(7.6 x 5.1 x 6.4 cm)
Courtesy of the artist

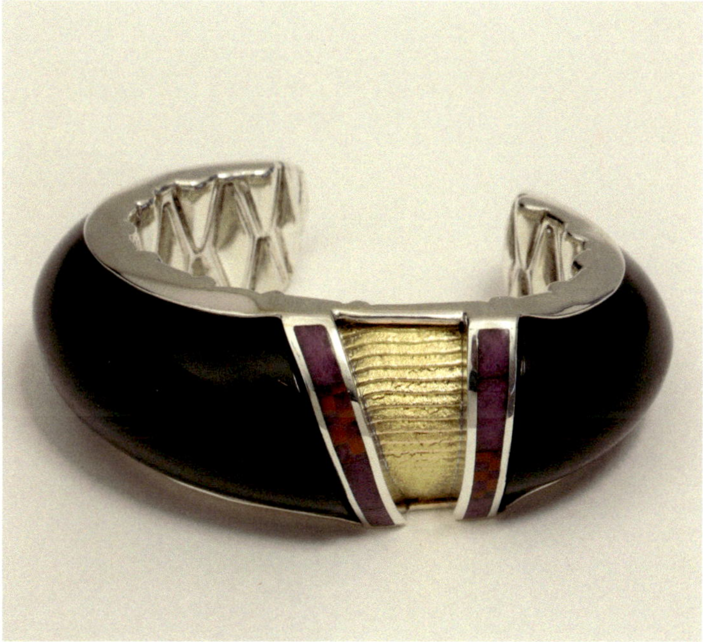

Black Jade Bracelet, 2012

Sterling silver, black jade,
sugilite, red coral, 18K gold
2 ¾ x 3 ½ x 1 ¼ in.
(7 x 8.9 x 3.2 cm)
Collection of Marcia Docter

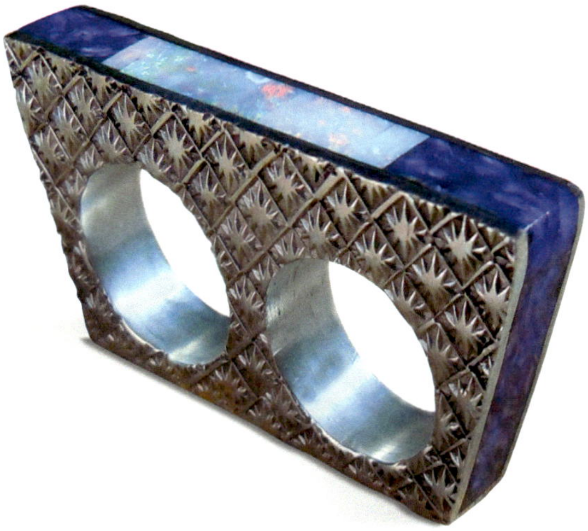

Double Ring, 2008

Sterling silver, Australian opal, charoite
1 ¼ x 2 ¼ x ⅜ in.
(3.2 x 5.7 x 1 cm)
Collection of Elizabeth Gilcrease;
courtesy of the artist

MINDY LAUREEN MAGYAR

b. 1975, Mountain Lakes, New Jersey; lives in Washington, DC

Chair, 2010

Charles Eames *Shell* chair frame, canvas, cotton and rayon thread, rubber
22 x 19 x 32 in.
(55.9 x 48.3 x 81.3 cm)
Courtesy of the artist

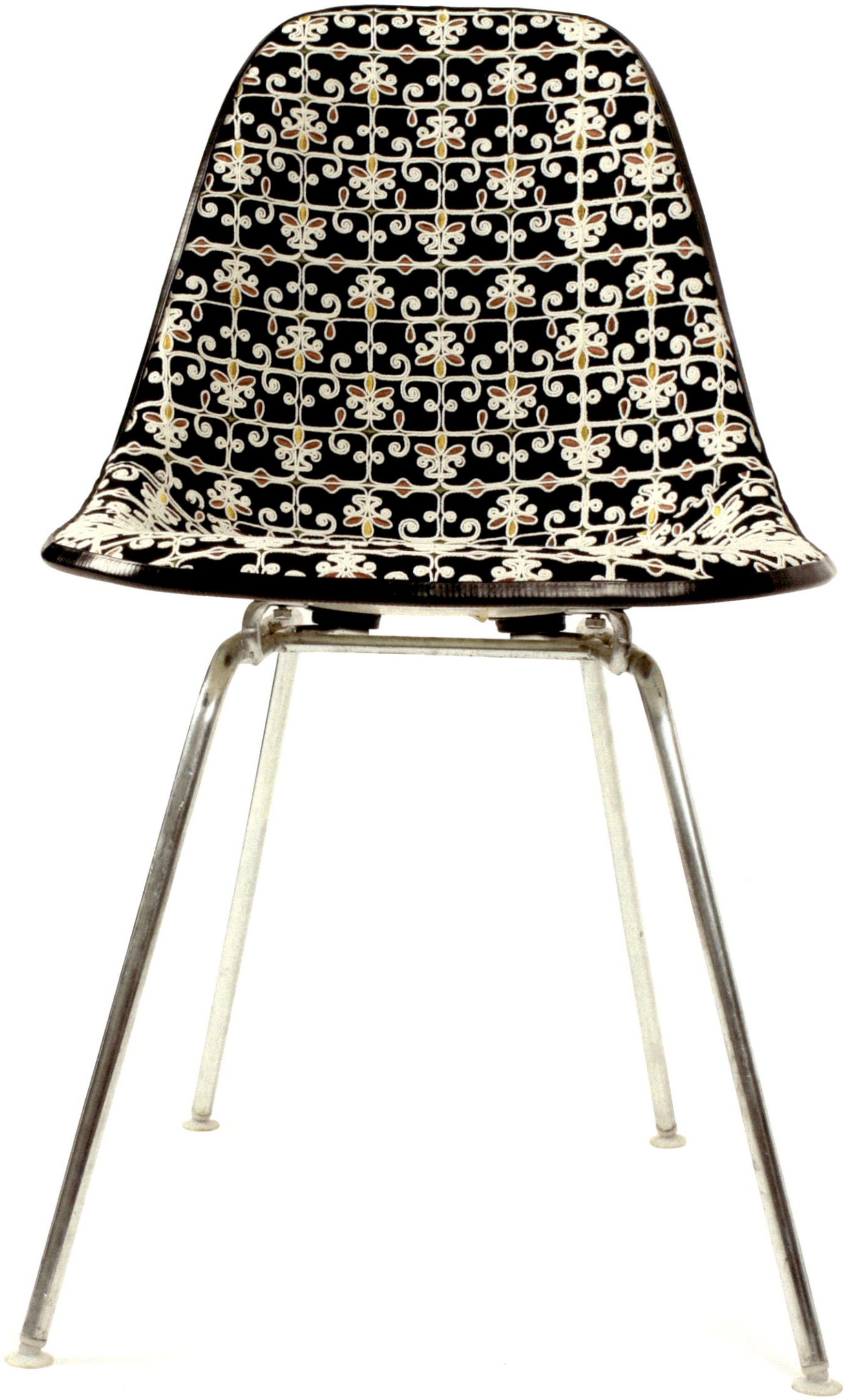

TERESA MARSHALL

b. 1962, Truro, Nova Scotia;
lives in Truro, Nova Scotia

Walk a Smile in My Shoes, aka Bitch Bark Shoes, 2012

Birch bark, glass seed beads, commercial leather, dyed porcupine quills, sinew
5 x 4 x 10 ½ in.
(12.7 x 10.2 x 26.7 cm)
Courtesy of the artist

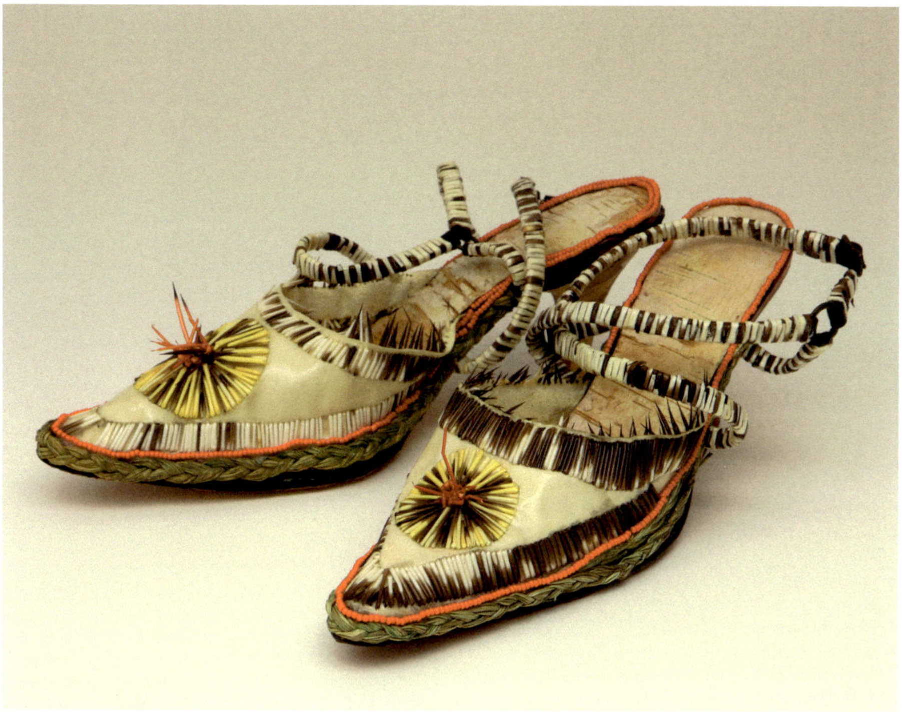

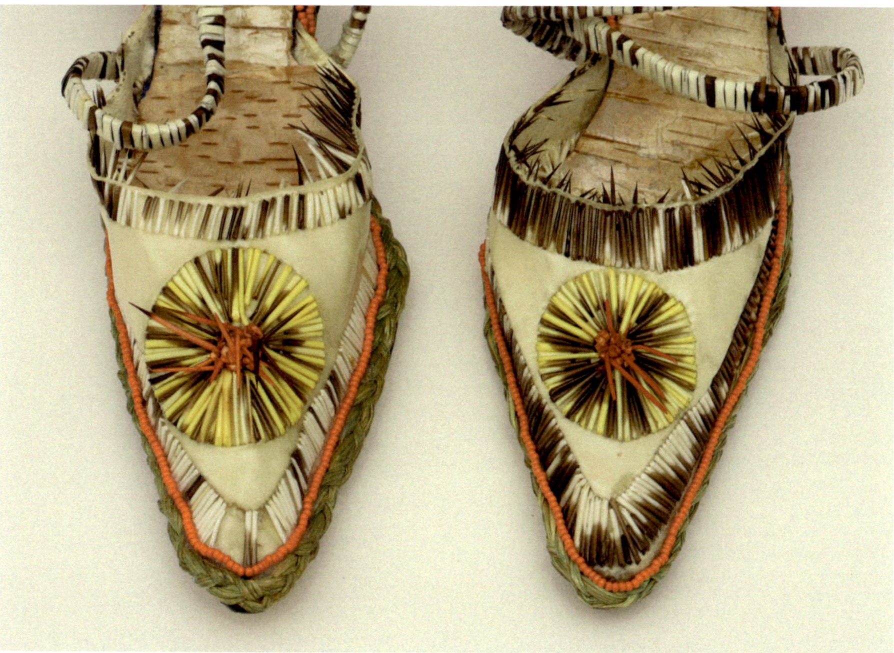

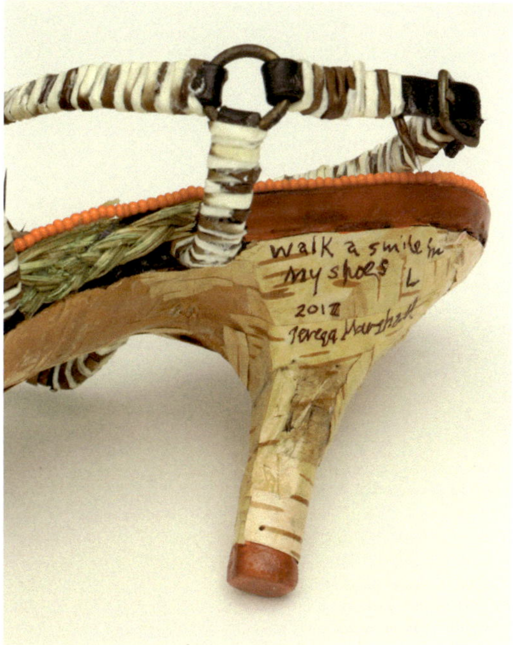

MICHAEL MASSIE

b. 1962, Happy Valley–Goose Bay, Labrador; lives in Newfoundland

they dressed for the occasion, 2011
(2 views)

Serpentine, antler, ebony, mahogany, Indian rosewood, sinew, copper
7 ½ x 15 ¾ x 12 ½ in.
(19.1 x 40 x 31.8 cm)
Courtesy of Spirit Wrestler Gallery, Vancouver, British Columbia

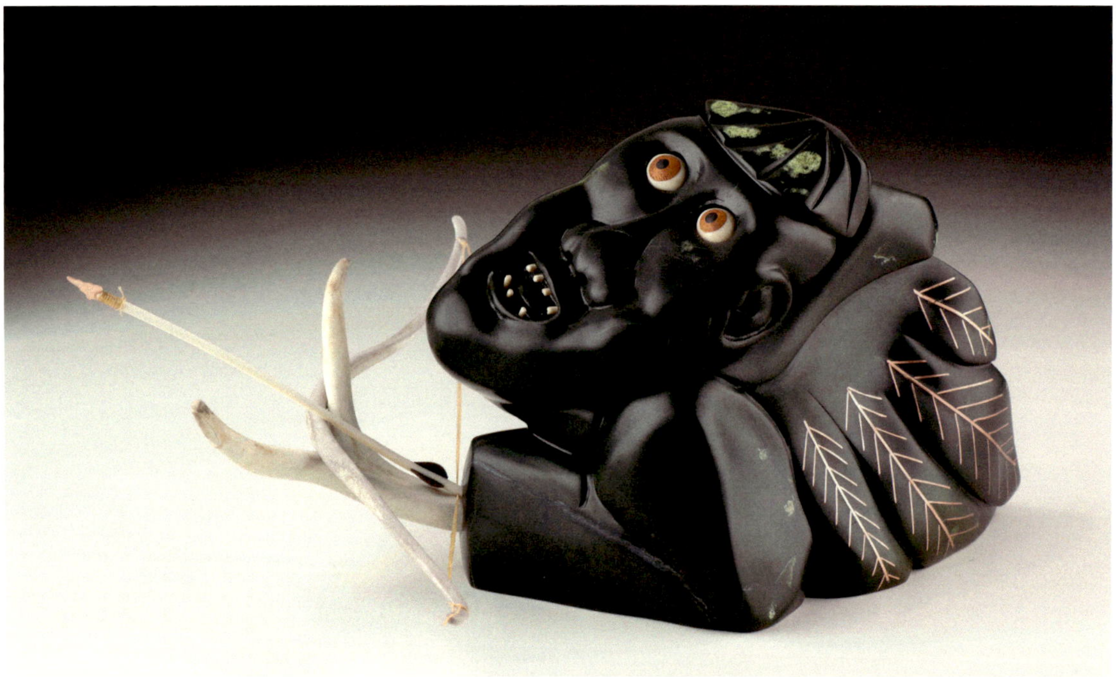

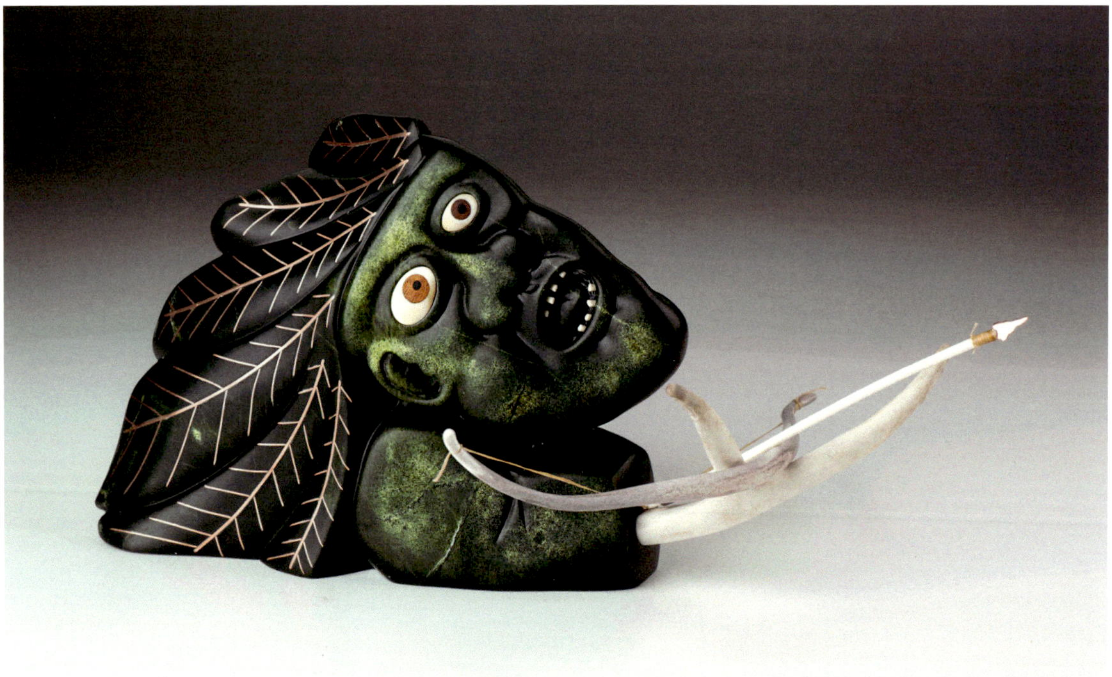

WANESIA MISQUADACE

b. 1971, Cloquet, Minnesota;
lives in Santa Fe, New Mexico

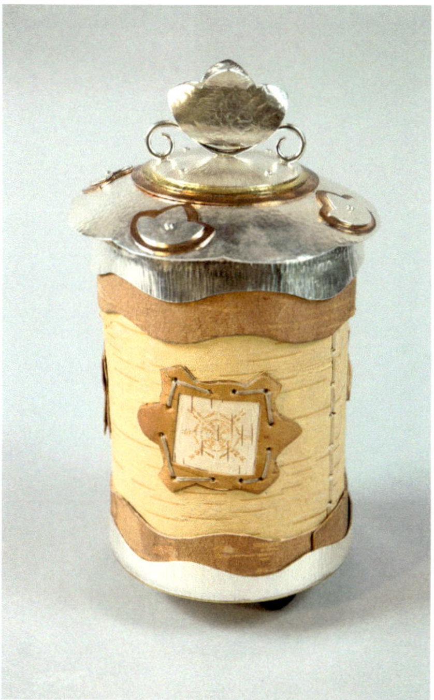

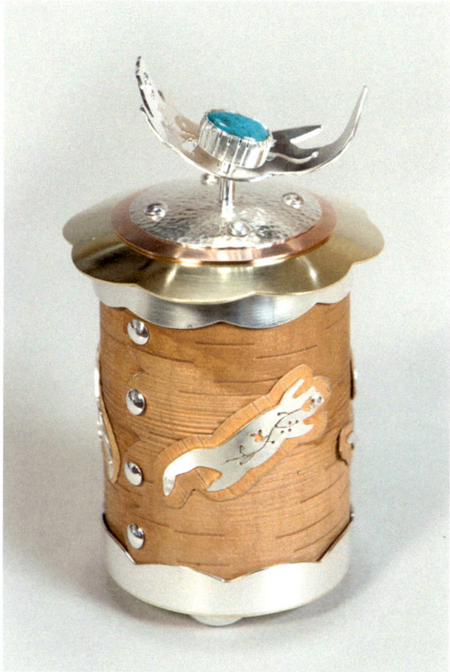

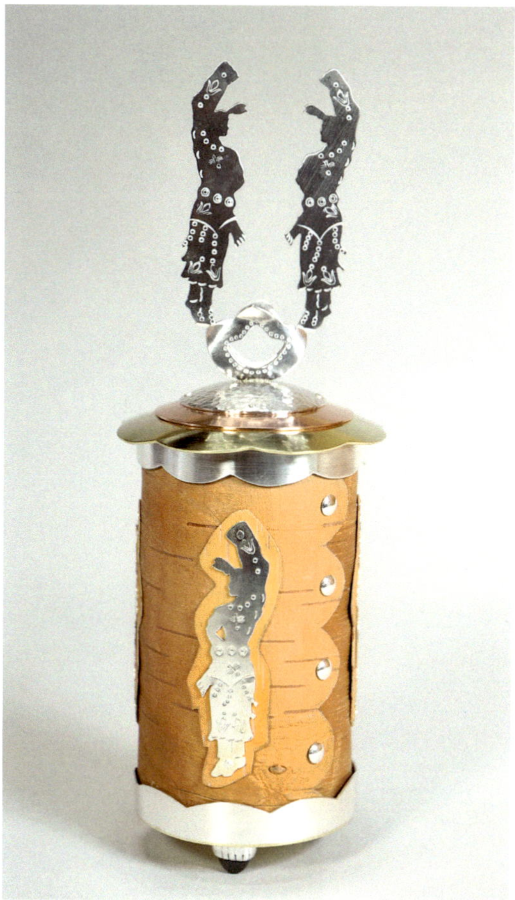

Sonny boy'z Harvest Basket, 2010

Birchbark, mixed metals,
Lake Superior pebbles, sinew
Ht. 8 ½ in. (21.6 cm); diam. 5 in. (12.7 cm)
Courtesy of the artist

One Whom Brings Earth, 2011 (top, center)

Birchbark, mixed metals, Lake Superior pebbles, turquoise
Ht. 4 ½ in. (11.4 cm); diam. 3 ½ in. (8.9 cm)
Courtesy of the artist

Earth, Water, Sky, 2011 (right)

Birchbark, mixed metals, Mediterranean coral, pink shell, tufa, 14K gold, fresh water pearl
Ht. 6 in. (15.2 cm); diam. 3 ½ in. (8.9 cm)
Courtesy of the artist

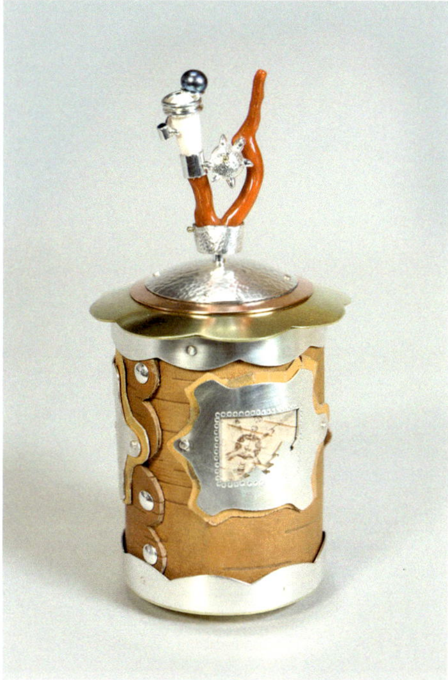

Songs For Grandfather, 2011

Birchbark, mixed metals, Lake Superior pebbles
Ht. 8 in. (20.3 cm); diam. 3 ½ in. (8.9 cm)
Courtesy of Mary Jane Laird Parks

SUMMER PETERS

b. 1977, Mount Pleasant, Michigan; lives in Chandler, Arizona

1946, 2011

Glass beads, velvet, cotton thread
17 ½ x 14 ¼ in. (44.5 x 36.2 cm)
Courtesy of the artist

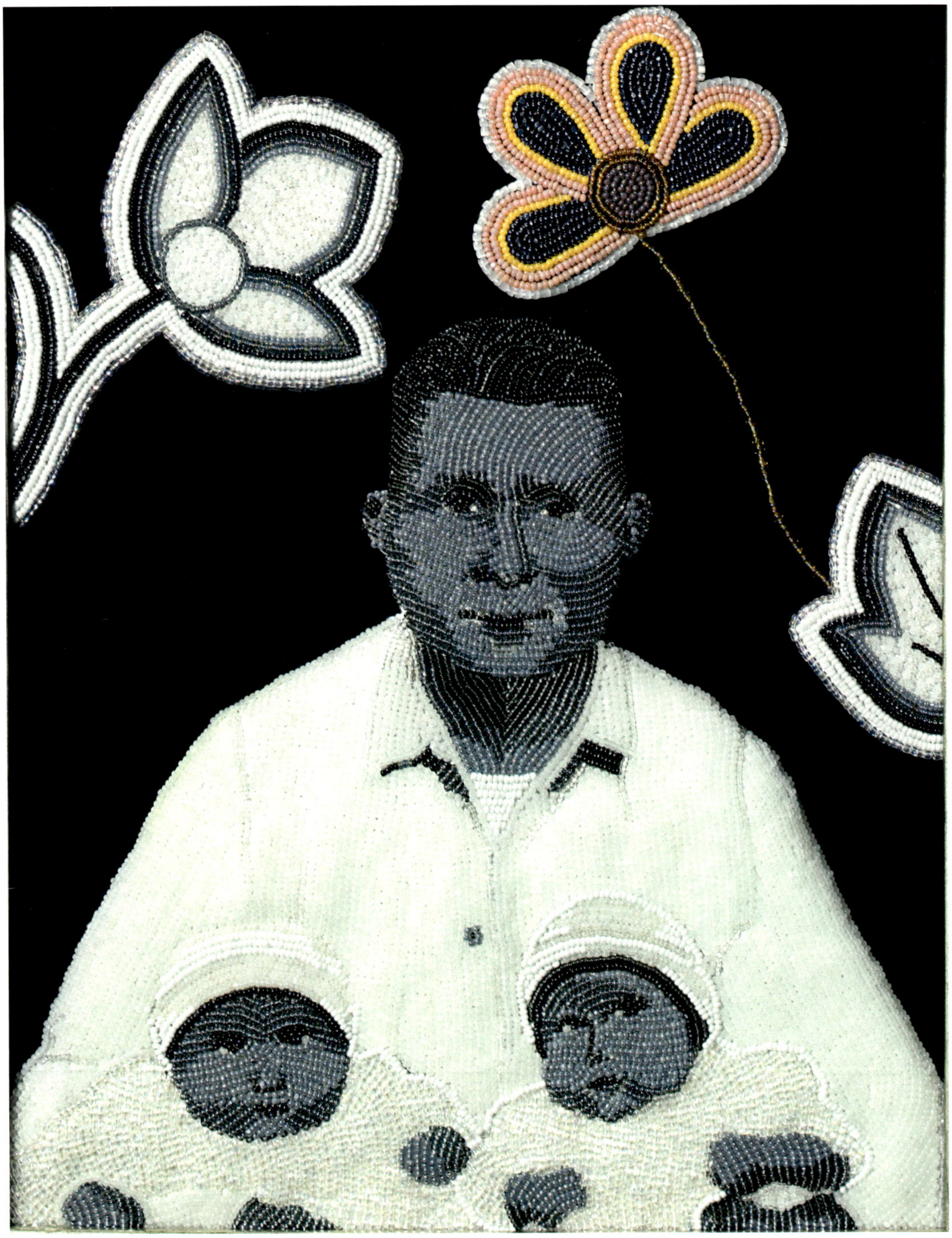

JAMASIE PITSEOLAK

b. 1968, Cape Dorset, Nunavut;
lives in Cape Dorset, Nunavut

Tiger Roars Again, 2011

Stone, antler, horn, coloring
13 x 20 ¾ x 8 in.
(33 x 52.7 x 20.3 cm)
Collection of Christopher Bredt
and Jamie Cameron

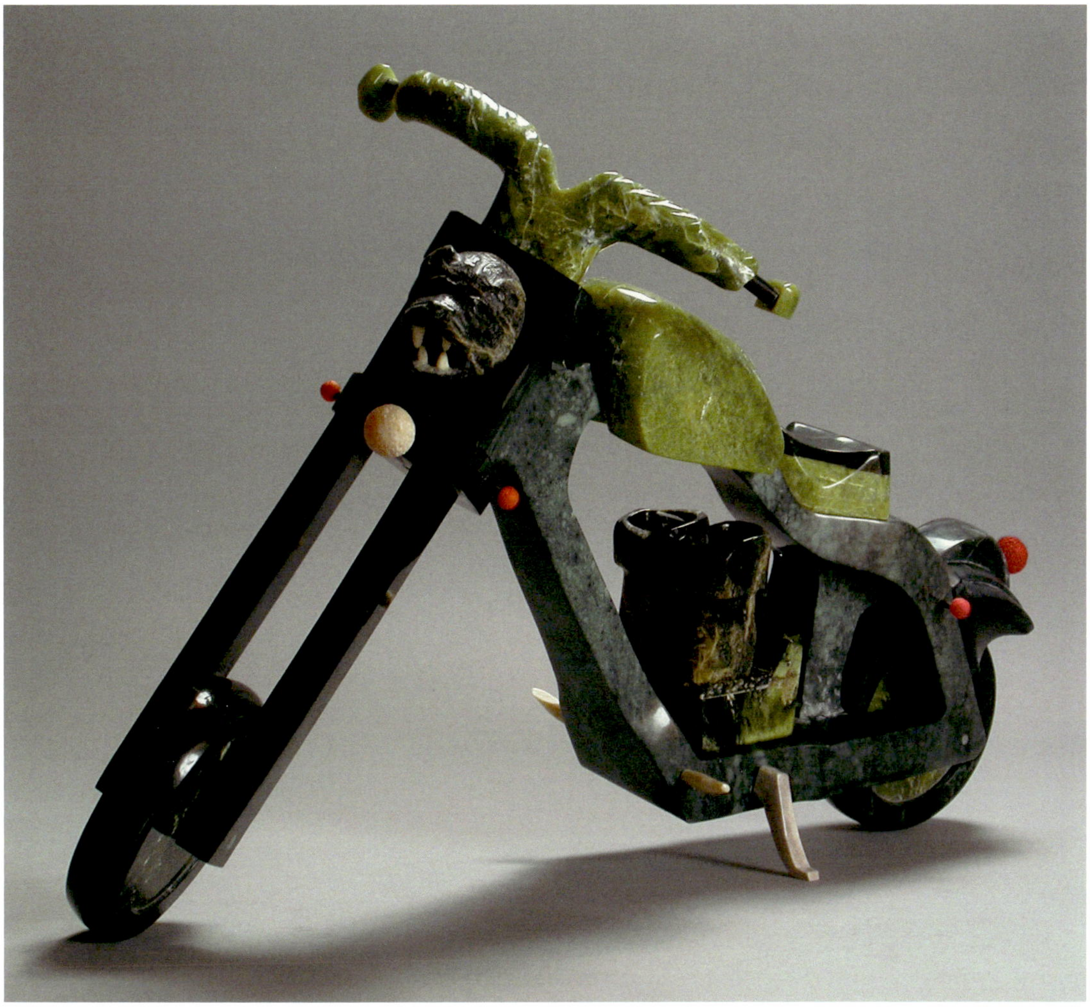

High Heel Shoe, 2011

Stone
3 ¼ x 4 ½ x 2 ½ in.
(8.3 x 11.4 x 6.4 cm)
Collection of N. Barry Lyon

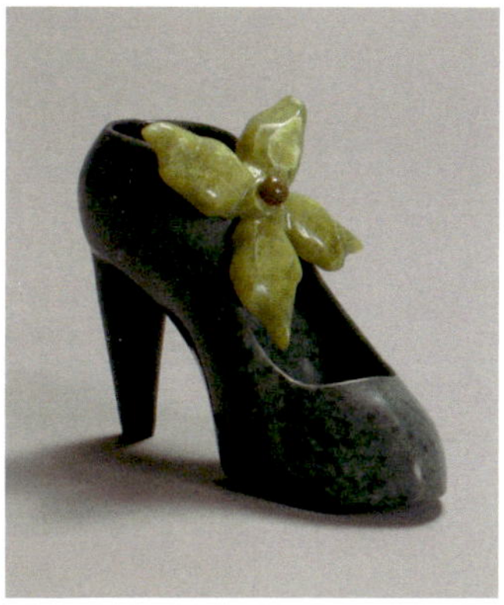

DAVID L. PRUITT

b. 1956, Adair County, Oklahoma;
lives in Stilwell, Oklahoma

Hands of the Real People—
The Past Present and Future, 2011

Clay, slip painted
21 ½ x 18 ½ x 3 ¾ in.
(54.6 x 47 x 9.5 cm)
Courtesy of the artist

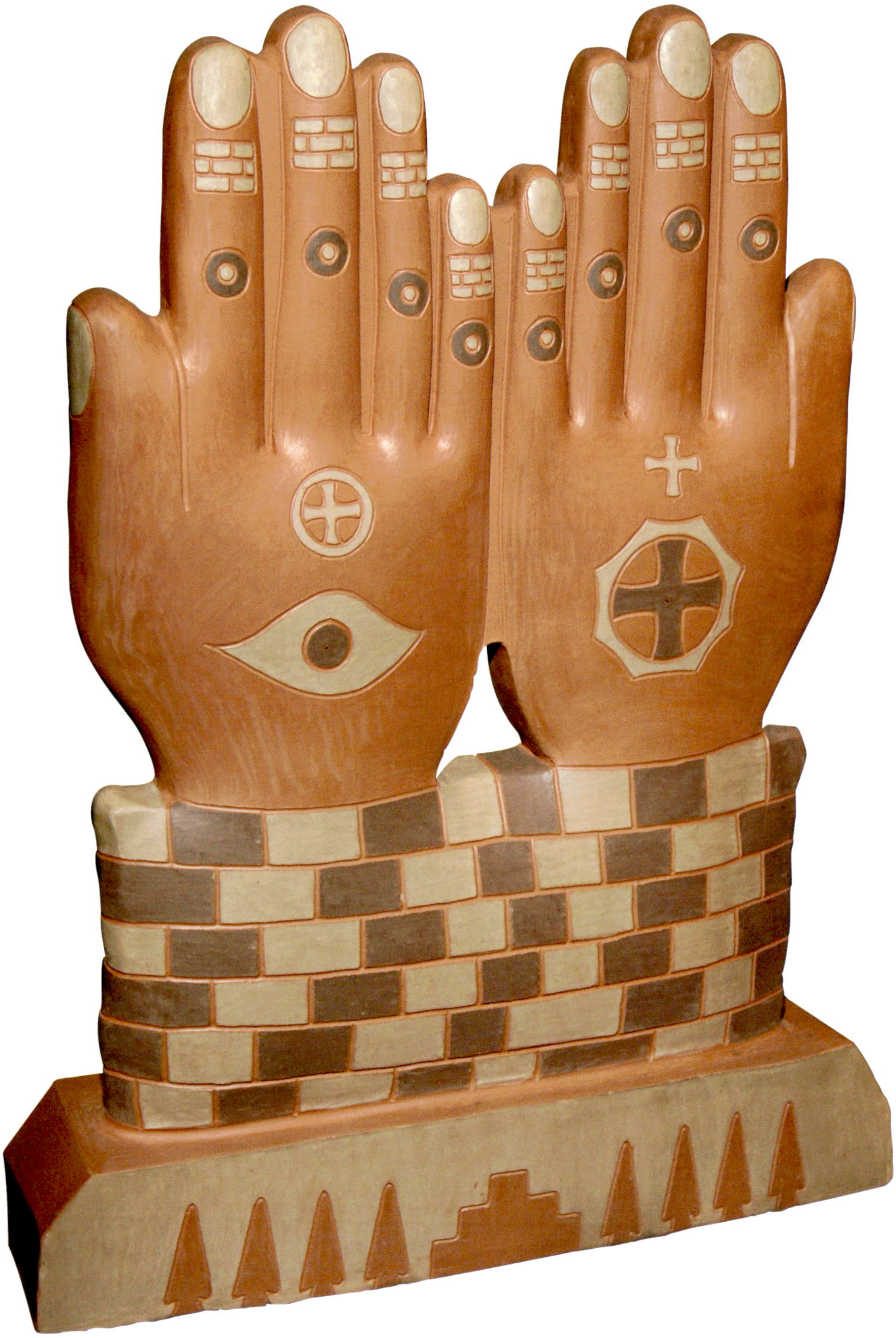

JOEL QUEEN

b. 1967, Wannesville, North Carolina;
lives in Cherokee, North Carolina

Dancing Quails, ca. 2008

Clay
Ht. 24 in. (61 cm);
diam. 15 ½ in. (39.4 cm)
Collection of Richard Buckley
and Tom Ford

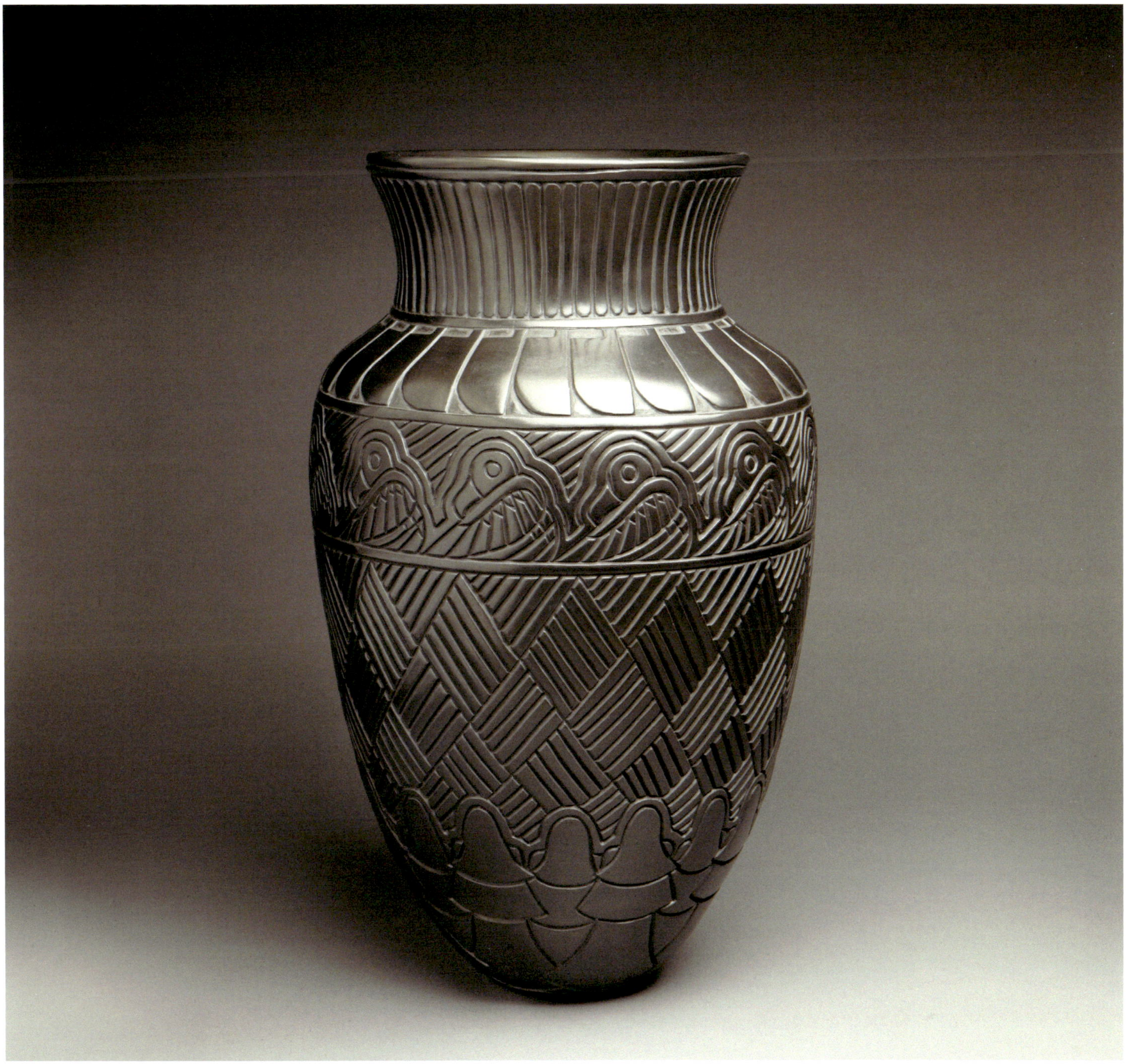

SARAH SENSE

b. 1980, Sacramento, California;
lives between Sacramento, California,
and Santiago, Chile

Weaving the Americas, Panajachel, 2011

Digital photographs, photo
silkscreen prints, tape
47 x 71 in. (119.4 x 180.3 cm)
Courtesy of the artist

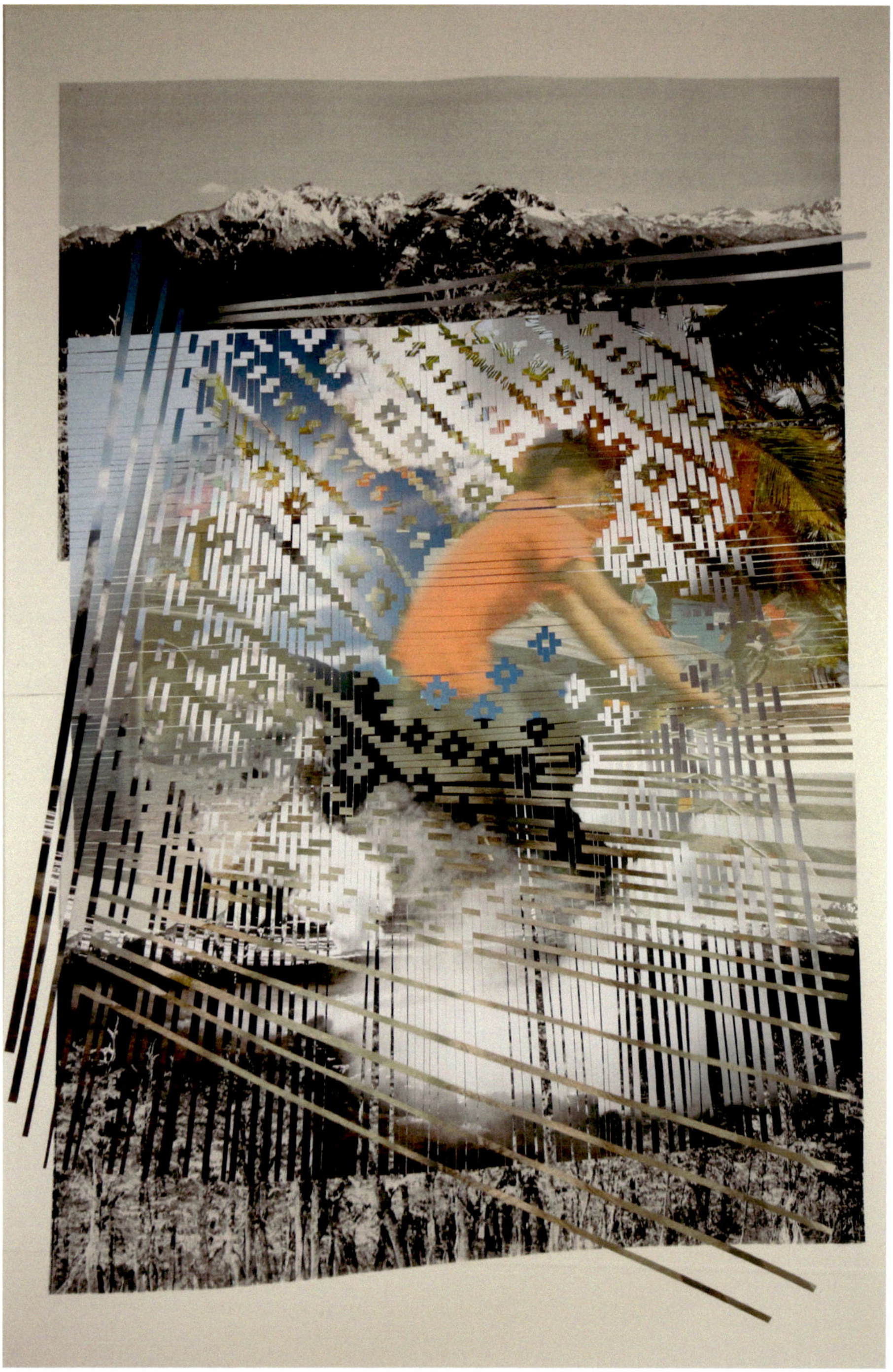

LEAH SHENANDOAH

b. 1981, Syracuse, New York;
lives in Oneida, New York

Stars in Her Hair (Headpiece), 2009

Sterling silver, feathers, porcupine quills, leather
2 ½ x 5 x 4 ½ in. (6.4 x 12.7 x 11.4 cm)
Courtesy of the artist

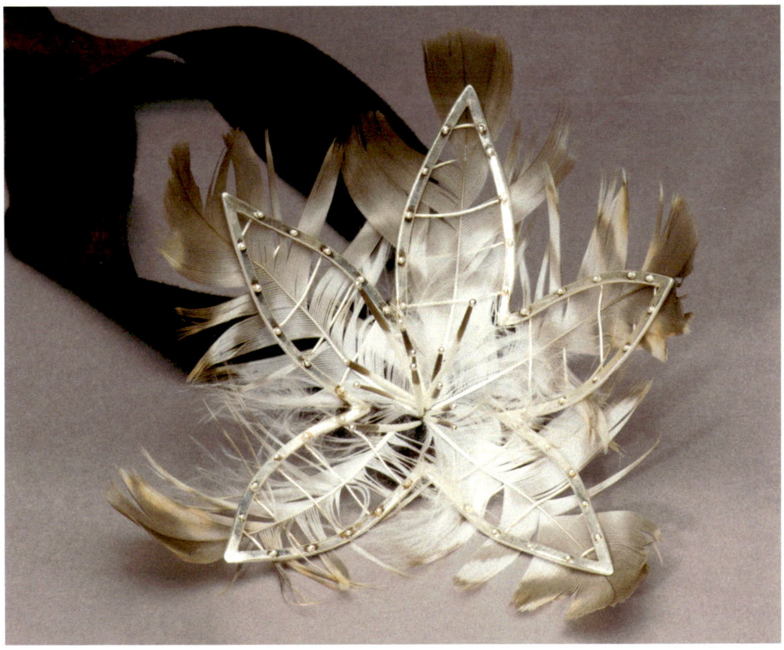

Rabbit Fur Purse, 2009

Rabbit skin and fur, satin, silver beads, satin
13 ¾ x 8 ¼ x 1 3/16 in. (35 x 21 x 3 cm)
Courtesy of the National Museum of the American Indian, Smithsonian Institution, Washington, DC
Cat. No. 26/7653

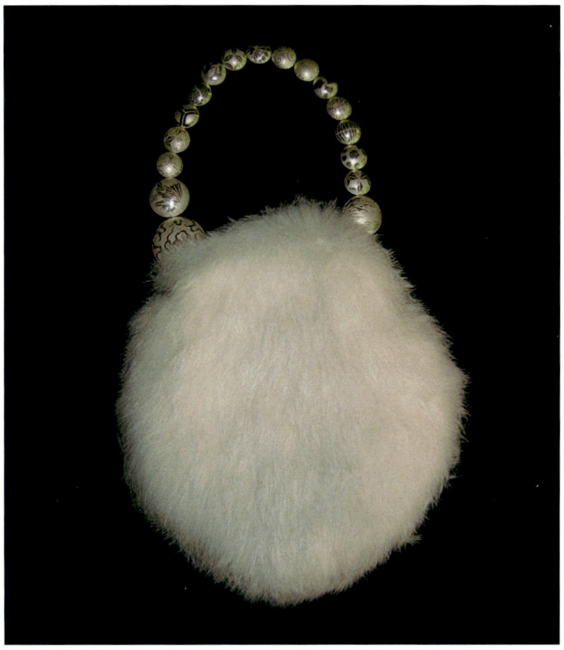

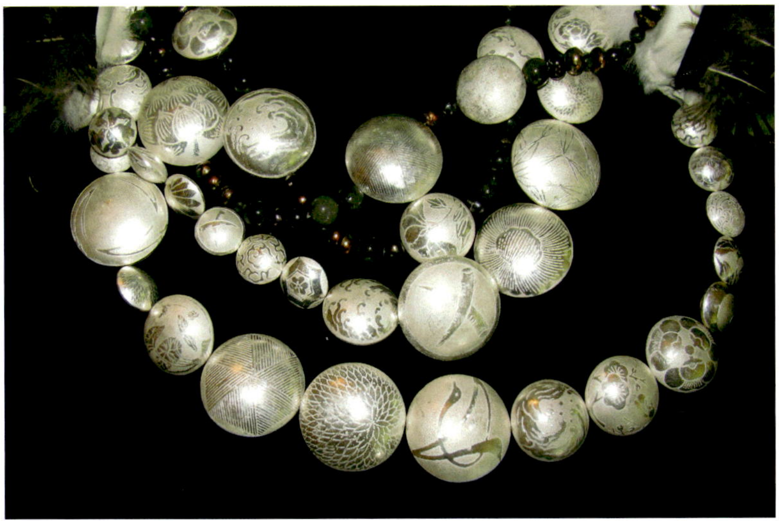

Haute Couture Hood, 2009 (detail)

Rabbit skin and fur, satin, silver beads, stone beads, pearls, feathers
21 ⅝ x 12 x 8 ¼ in. (55 x 30.5 x 21 cm)
Courtesy of the National Museum of the American Indian, Smithsonian Institution, Washington, DC
Cat. No. 26/7652

JAMIE ZANE SMITH

b. 1980, St. Louis, Missouri;
lives in Courtois, Missouri

Spiral Design, 2011

Clay, wood
Approx. ht. 14 in. (35.6 cm);
diam. 16 in. (40.6 cm)
Collection of Charles S. King

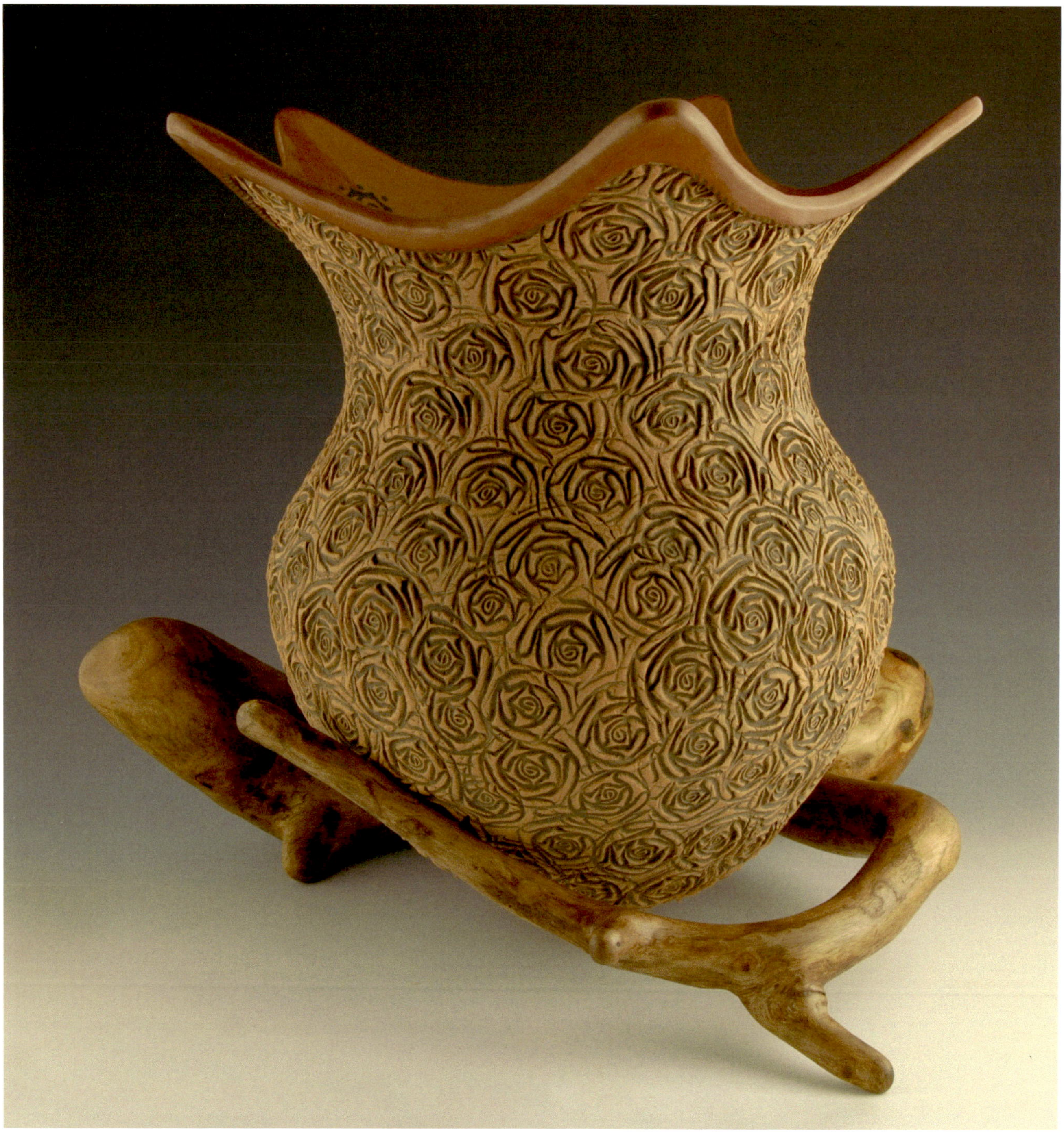

TAMMY TARBELL

b. 1950, Syracuse, New York;
lives in Syracuse, New York

Ceramic Strawberry Whimsey, 2011

Clay, glass beads, nylon thread
8 x 8 x 2 in. (20.3 x 20.3 x 5.1 cm)
Courtesy of the artist

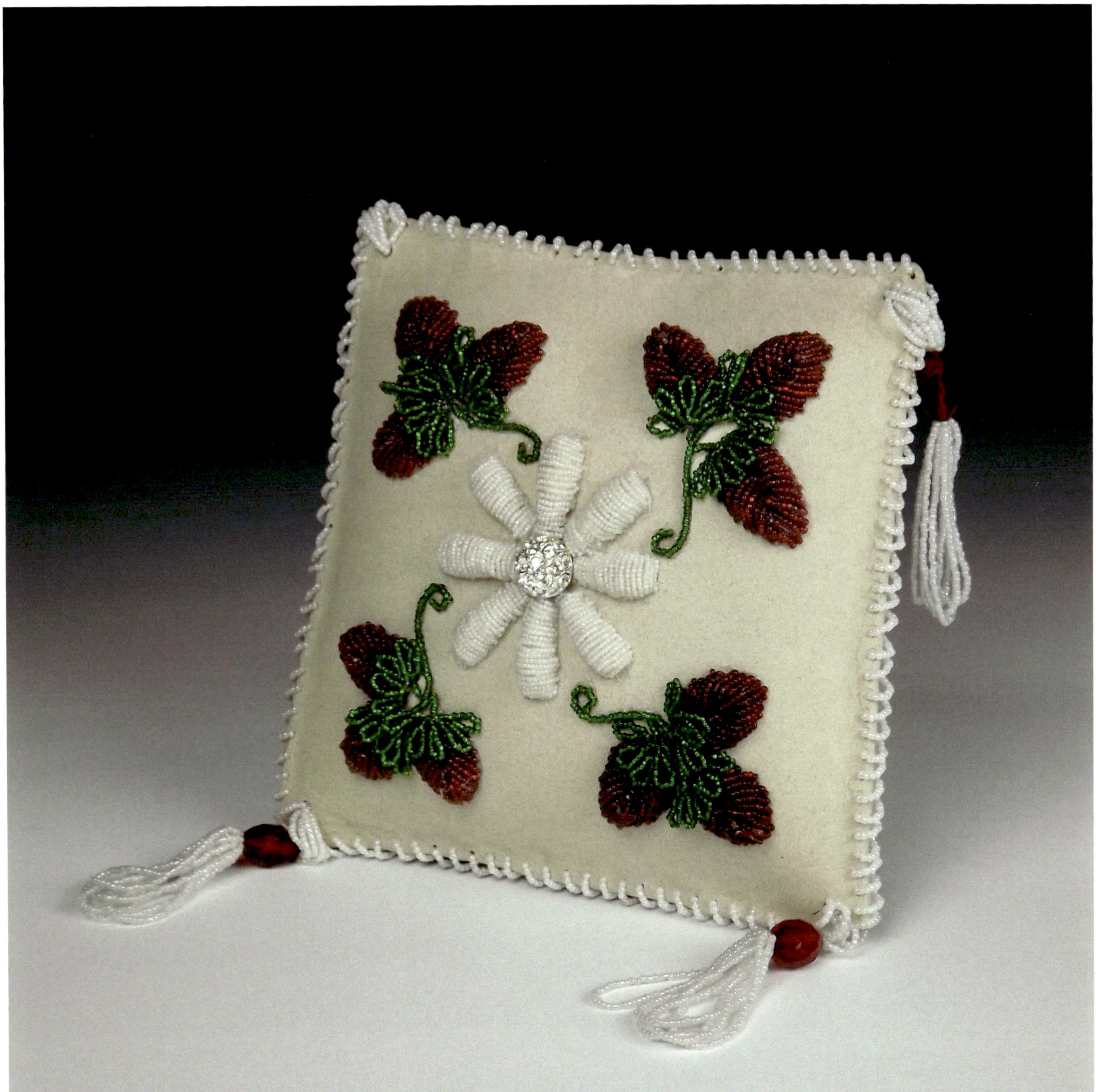

JUTAI TOONOO

b. 1959, Cape Dorset, Nunavut; lives in Cape Dorset, Nunavut

Two Guys Growing Apart, 2011

Stone
12 x 7 ½ x 3 ½ in.
(30.5 x 19.1 x 8.9 cm)
Courtesy of Dorset Fine Arts, Toronto, Ontario

In Tune with Nature, 2010

Stone
18 ½ x 9 ½ x 6 ¼ in.
(47 x 24.1 x 15.9 cm)
Courtesy of Feheley Fine Arts, Toronto, Ontario

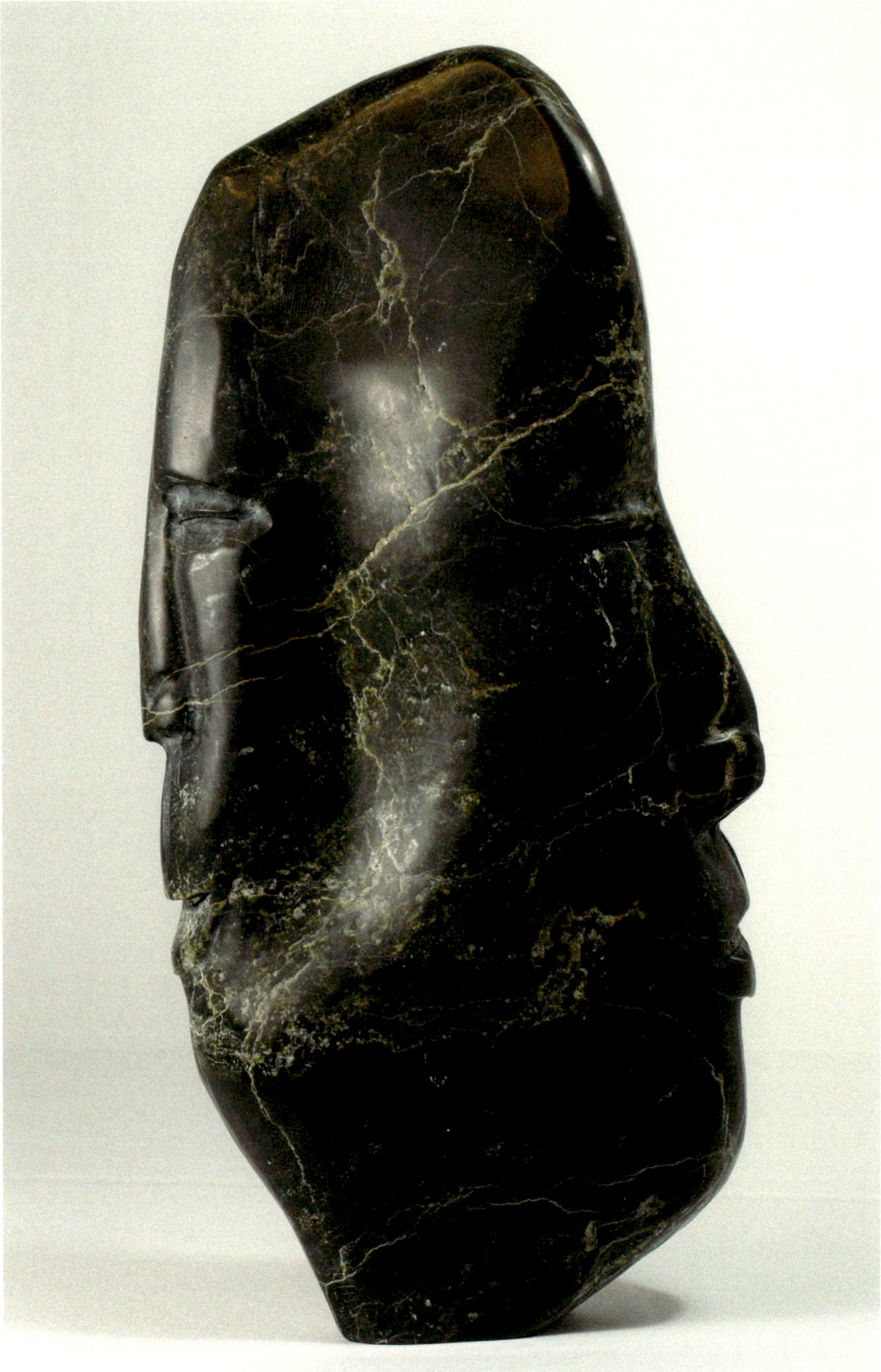

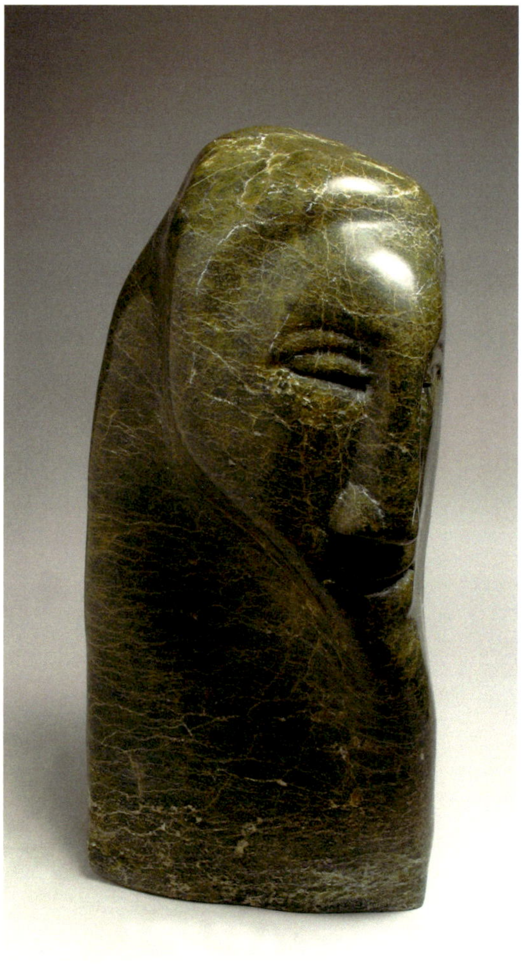

SAMONIE TOONOO

b. 1969, Cape Dorset, Nunavut; lives in Cape Dorset, Nunavut

Bow and Arrow, 2011 (2 views)

Stone, antler, sinew
12 ½ x 31 x 5 in.
(31.8 x 78.7 x 12.7 cm)
Courtesy of Dorset Fine Arts, Toronto, Ontario

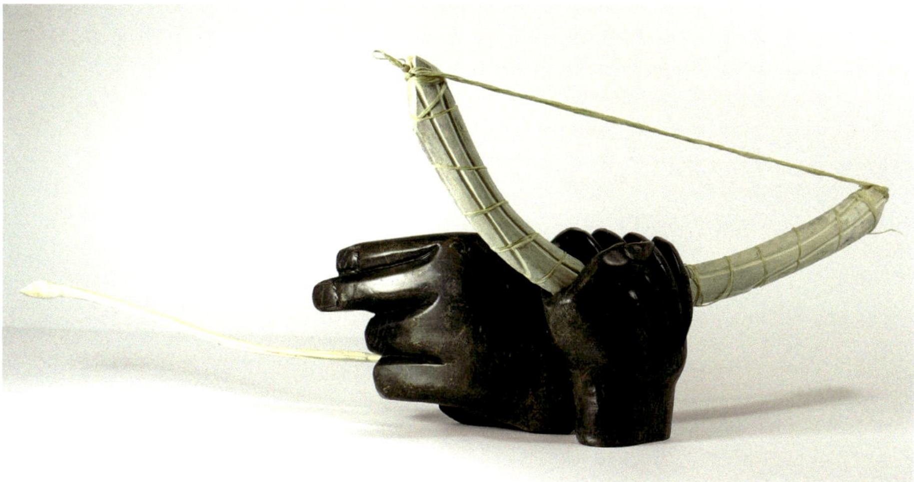

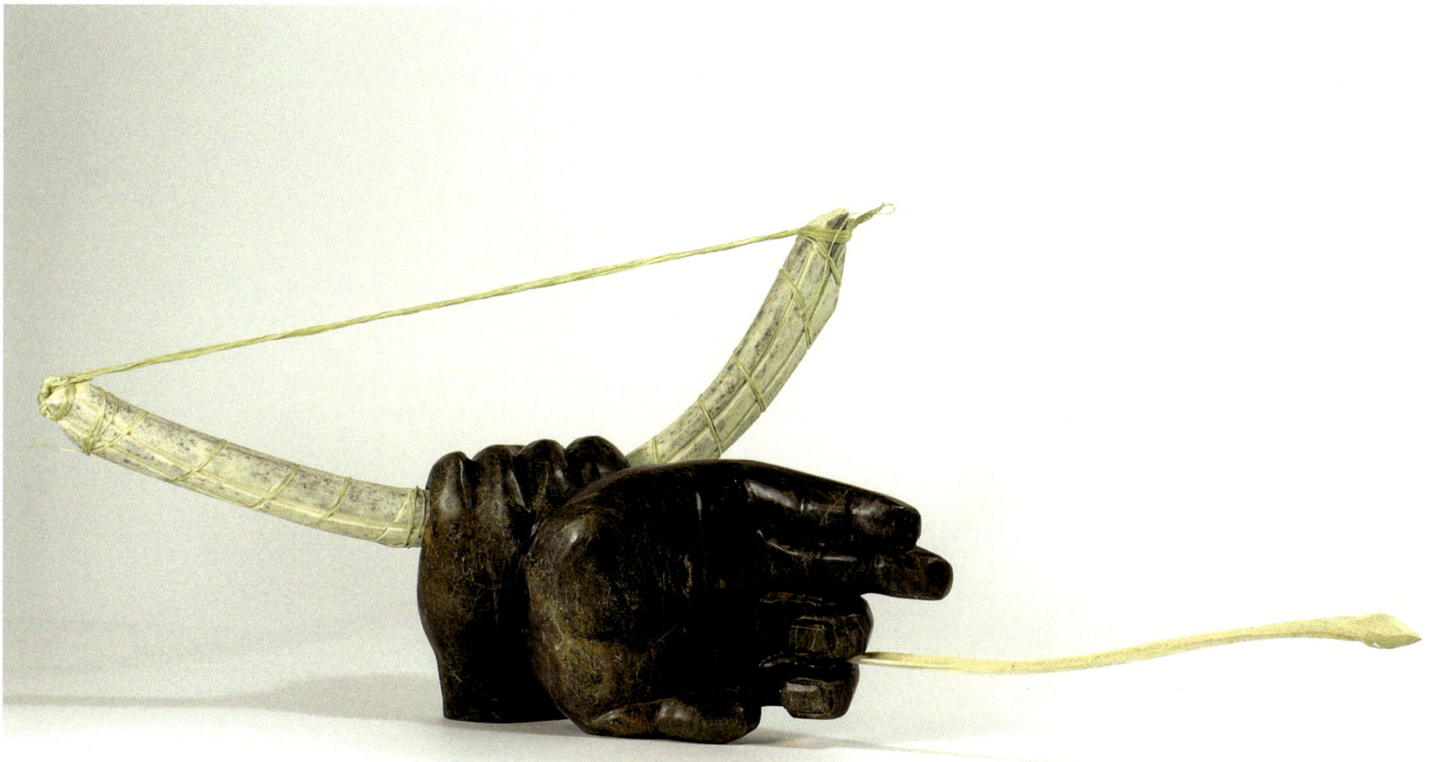

DAN TOWNSEND

b. 1957, Florida Keys, Florida; lives in Tallahassee, Florida

Speaker of the House/Warrior Society, 2009

Mother-of-pearl oyster shell, glass beads, thread
4 ½ x 5 x ⅞ in.
(11.4 x 12.7 x 2.2 cm)
Collection of Sandra Moore Riley

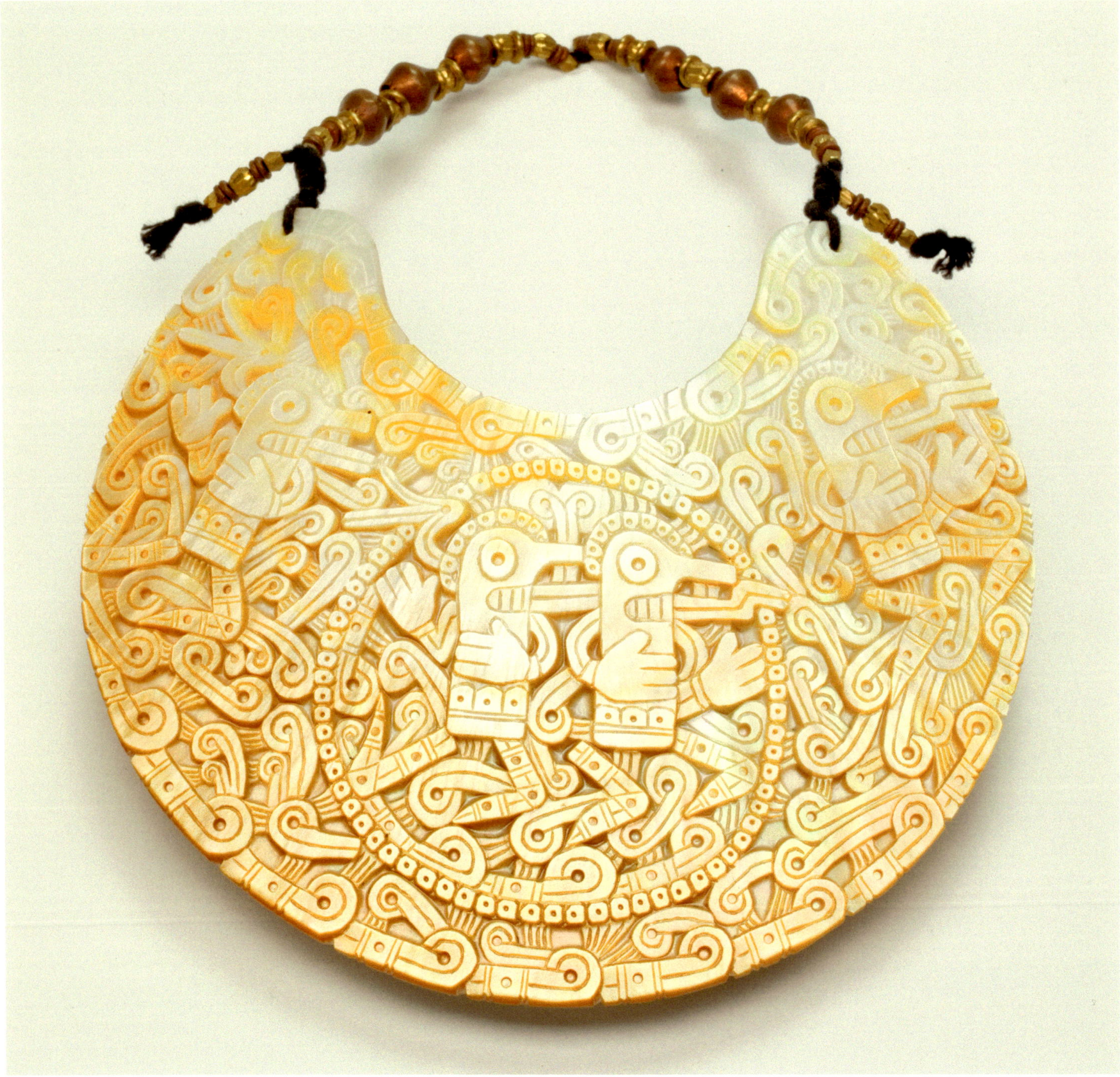

DAWN WALDEN

b. 1949, Upper Peninsula, Michigan; lives in Faithorn, Michigan

Anishinaube (First People), 2012 (work in progress, detail)

Cedar bark, bear grass, cedar roots
5 x 24 x 58 in. (12.7 x 61 x 147.3 cm)
Courtesy of the artist

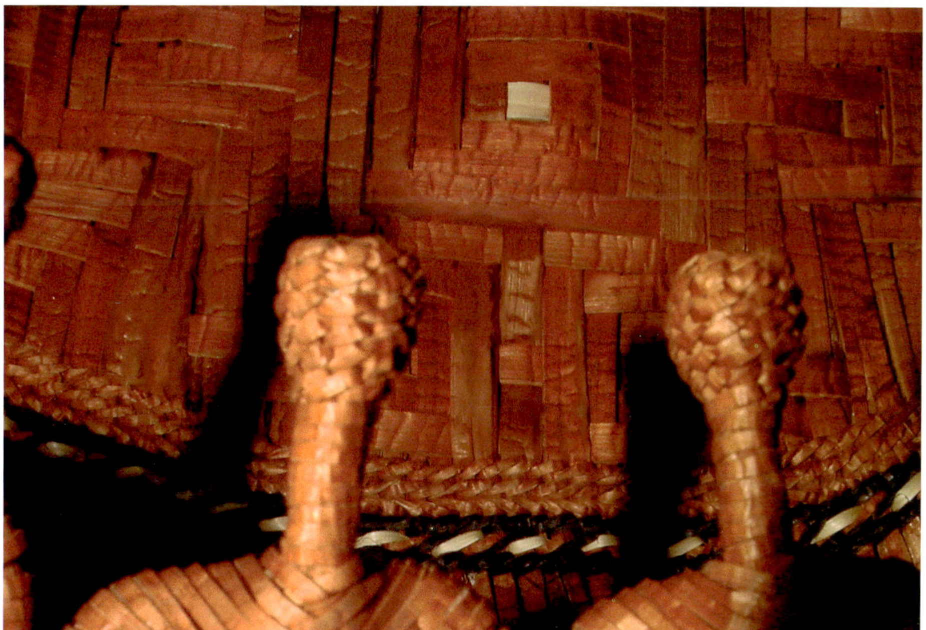

ROBIN WAYNEE

b. 1971, Mio, Michigan; lives in Santa Fe, New Mexico

Rolling Pearl Necklace, 2012

18K gold, sterling silver, Tahitian pearl, zircon, sapphires, diamonds
Pendant diam. 3 in. (7.6 cm);
L. 18 in. (45.7 cm)
Courtesy of the artist

Rolling Pearl Bracelet, 2009

18K gold, sterling silver, Tahitian pearls, sapphires, diamonds
Ht. 1 ½ in. (3.2 cm);
L. 7 ½ in. (19.1 cm)
Courtesy of the artist

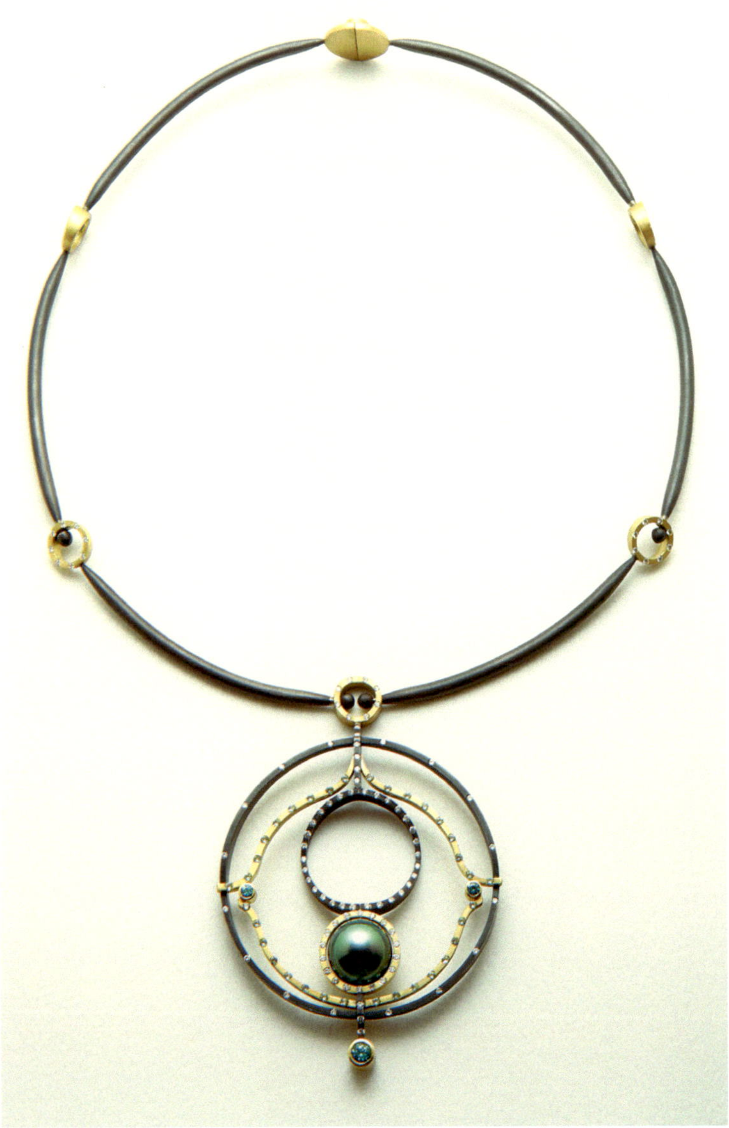

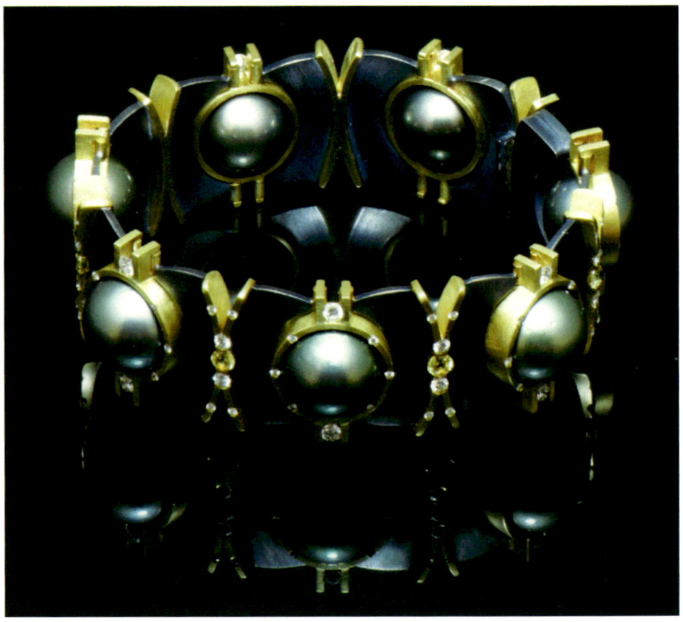

Wasp Ring, 2011

(in collaboration with
Keri Ataumbi)
18K gold, sterling silver,
Tahitian pearl, champagne
and white diamonds
Approx. 2 x 1 ¼ in.
(5.1 x 3.2 cm)
Courtesy of the artist

Wasp Earrings, 2011

(in collaboration with Keri
Ataumbi)
18K gold, sterling silver,
Tahitian pearls, sapphire,
white and black diamonds
Each: approx. 2 x ½ in.
(5.1 x 1.3 cm)
Courtesy of the artist

Wasp Necklace, 2011

(in collaboration with
Keri Ataumbi)
18K gold, sterling silver, Tahitian
pearls, sapphires, diamonds
Pendant ht. approx. 2 in. (5.1 cm);
L. 20 in. (50.8 cm)
Collection of Carolyn and Bill Pollack

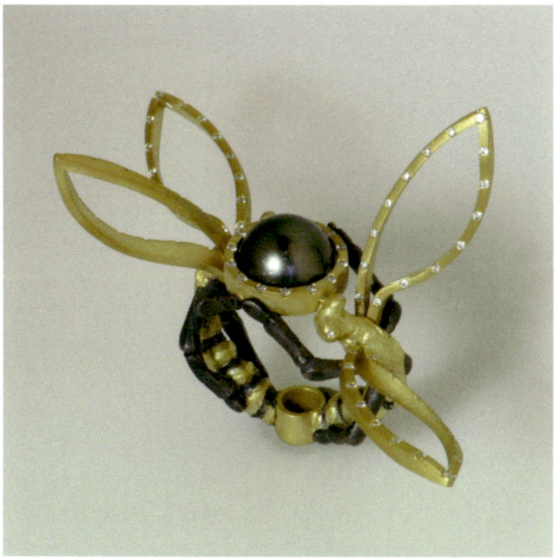

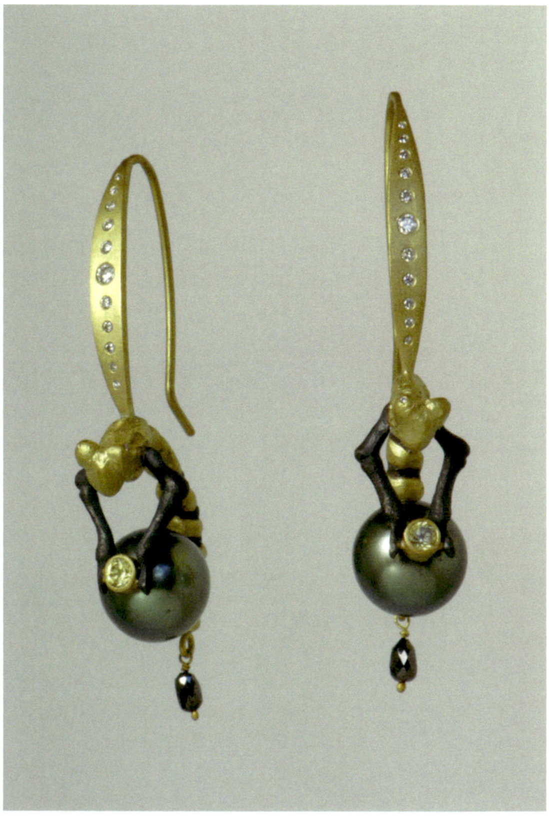

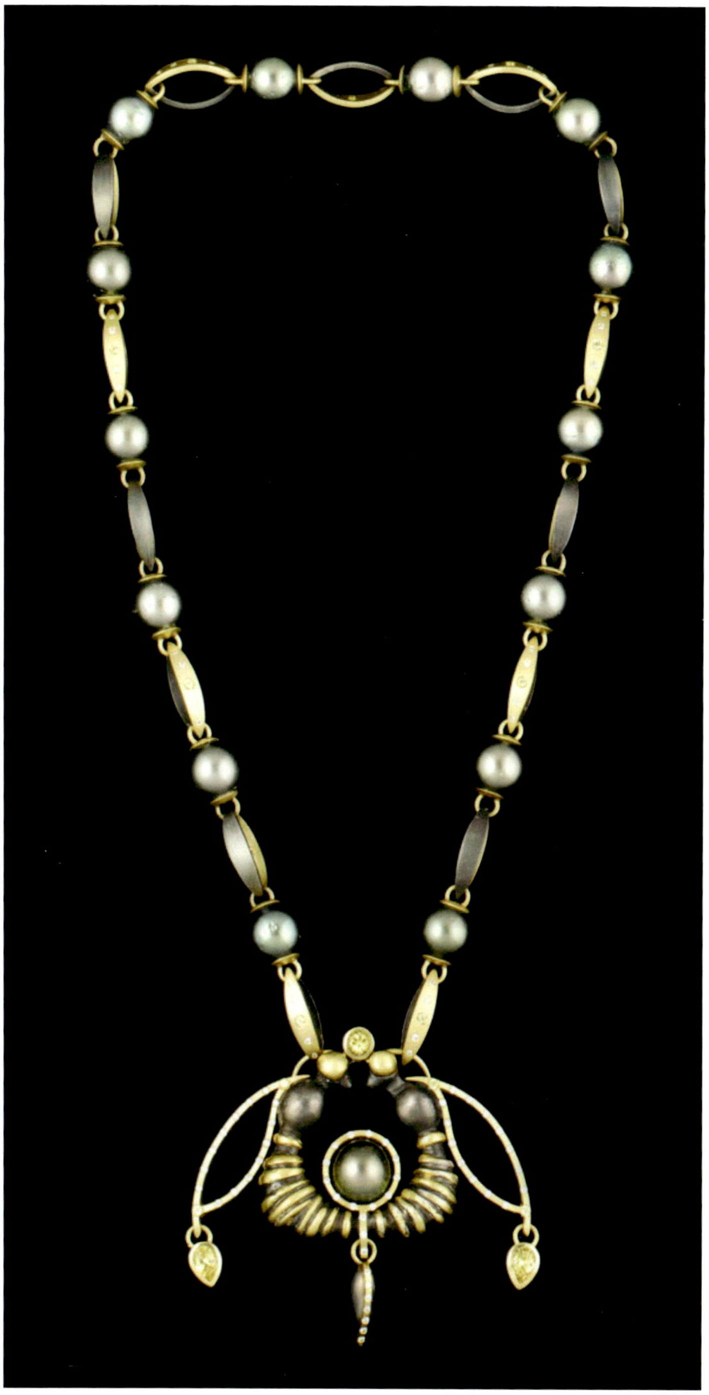

JASON WESAW

b. 1974, Kalamazoo, Michigan;
lives in Mattawan, Michigan

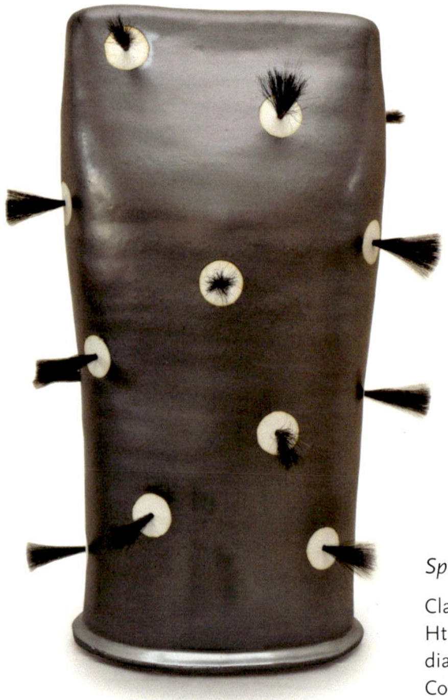

Spirit—Universal, 2011

Clay, horsehair
Ht. 34 in. (86.4 cm);
diam. 16 in. (40.6 cm)
Courtesy of the artist

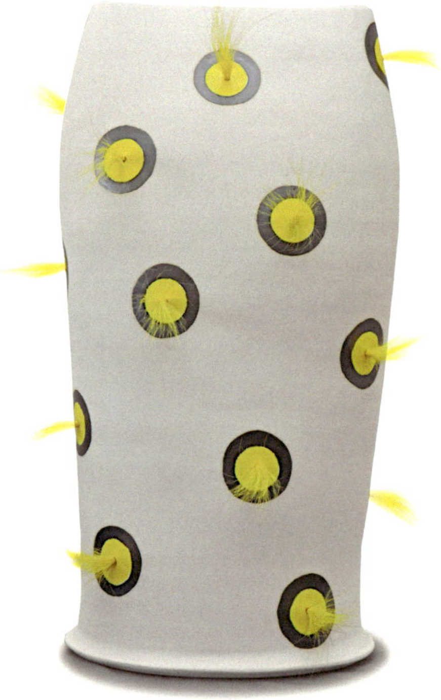

Spring—Spirit, 2011

Clay, dyed deer's tail
Ht. 34 in. (86.4 cm);
diam. 16 in. (40.6 cm)
Courtesy of the artist

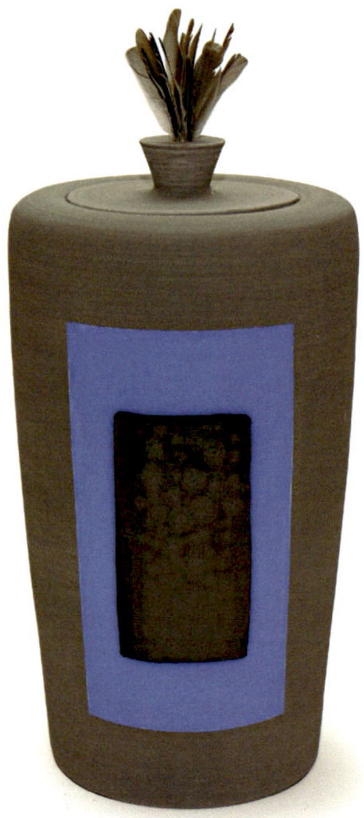

The Doorway, 2010

Clay, Indigo Bunting feathers
Ht. 17 in. (43.2 cm);
diam. 7 in. (17.8 cm)
Courtesy of the artist

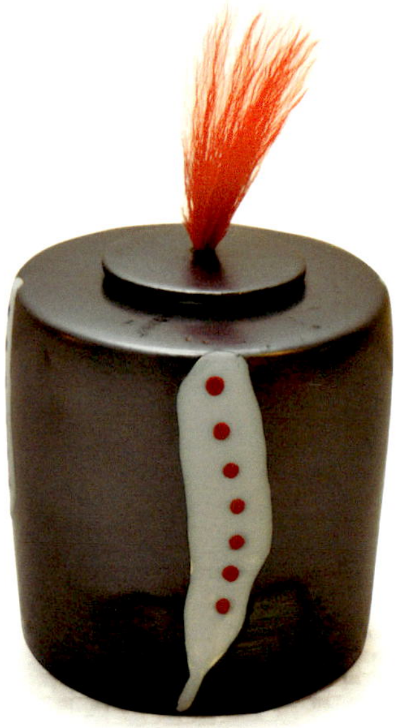

Four Directions, 2011

Clay, dyed deer's tail
Ht. 8 in. (20.3 cm);
diam. 4 in. (10.2 cm)
Courtesy of the artist

KENNETH WILLIAMS JR.

b. 1983, Provo, Utah; lives in Santa Fe, New Mexico

The Beauty of a Maiko, 2009

New and vintage glass beads, seed pearls, mabe pearl, rubies, Swarovski crystal, silk ribbon, vintage silk kimono fabric, wool broadcloth, brain tanned deerskin, hand mirror
6 ½ x 5 x ¾ in. (16.5 x 12.7 x 1.9 cm)
Private collection

The Present Beauty of the Past, 2010 (2 views)

New and vintage glass and metal beads, Swarovski crystal, brass thimbles and hawk bells, silk ribbon, human hair, dentalium shell, abalone shell, seed pearls, wool yarn, calico, nylon thread, vintage purse frame, hand mirror
18 x 8 x 1 ½ in. (45.7 x 20.3 x 3.8 cm)
Private collection

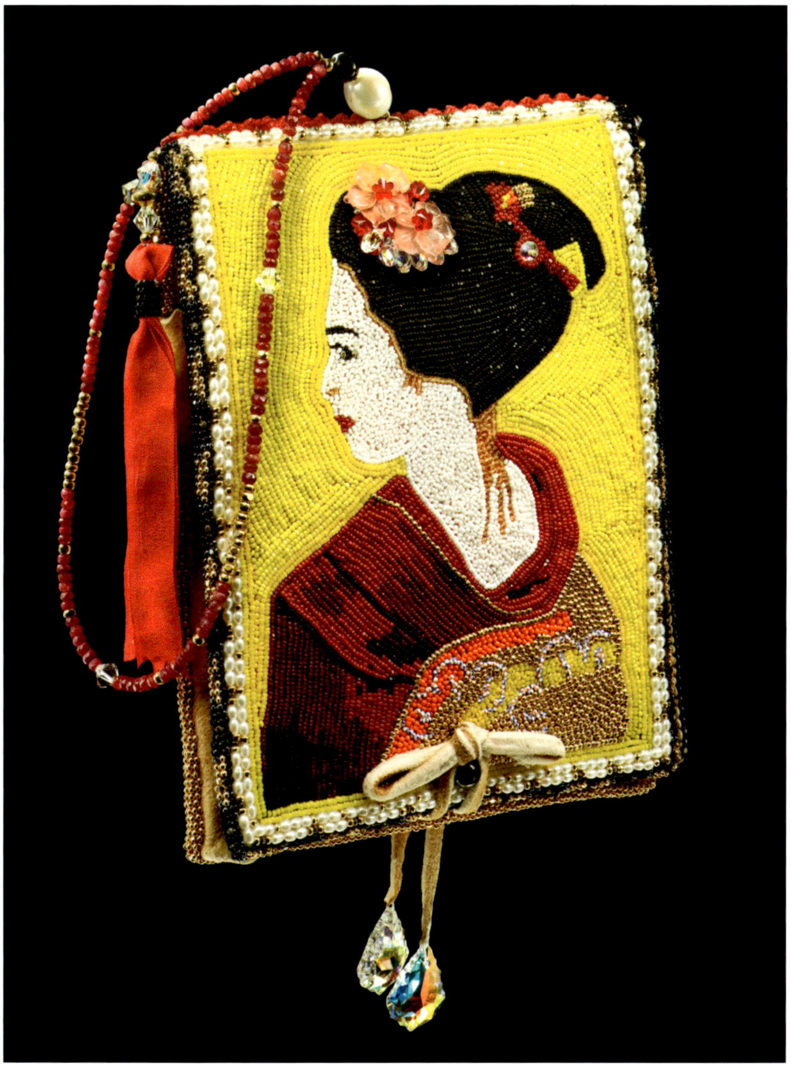

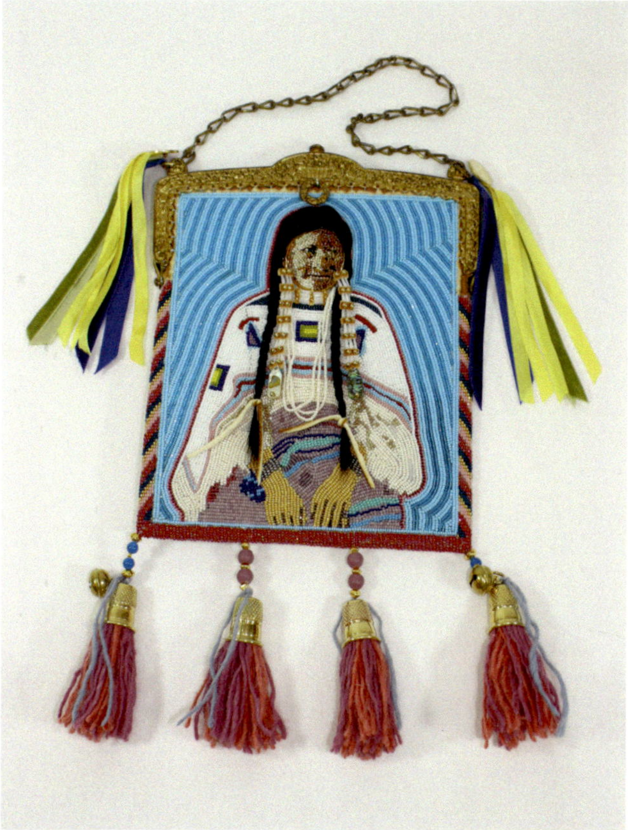

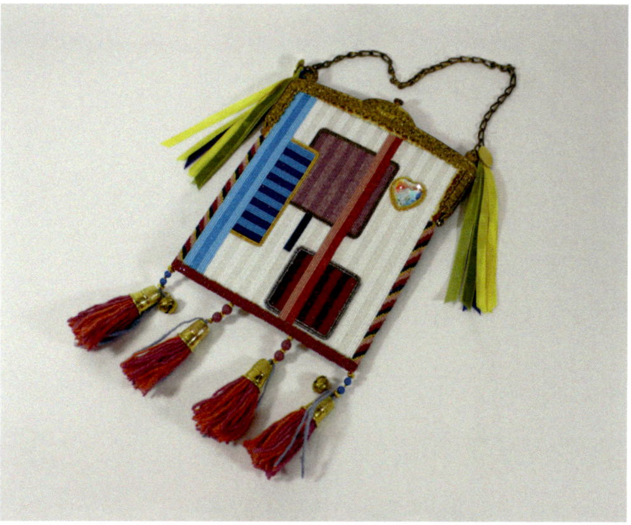

STEPHEN WOOD

b. 1980, Tahlequah, Oklahoma; lives in Parkhill, Oklahoma

A Song of Creation, 2012

Clay, acrylic paint, liquid silver leaf
38 x 16 x 23 in.
(96.5 x 40.6 x 58.4 cm)
Courtesy of the artist

Design sketch for
A Song of Creation, 2012

Pencil on paper
11 x 8 in. (27.9 x 20.3 cm)
Courtesy of the artist

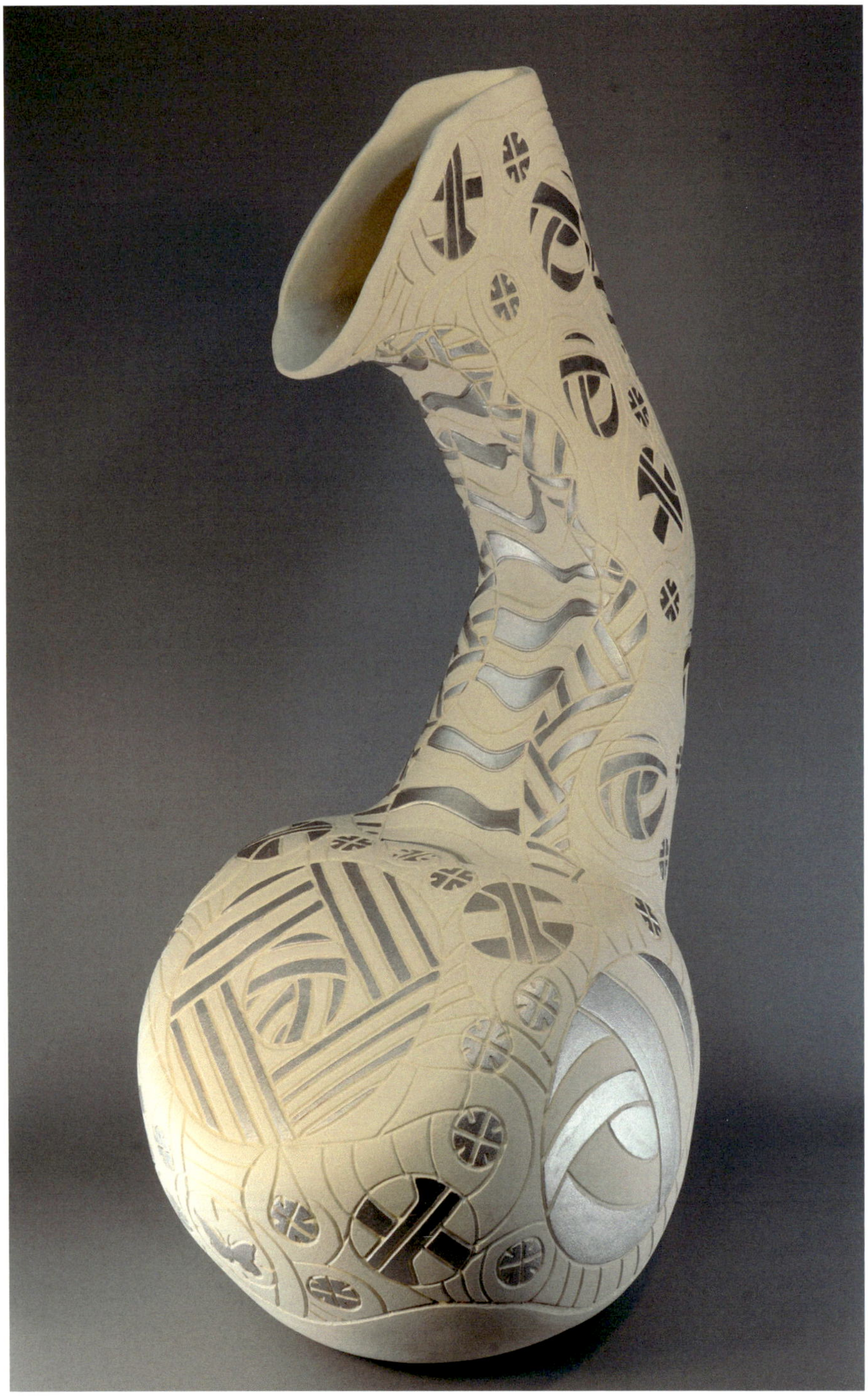

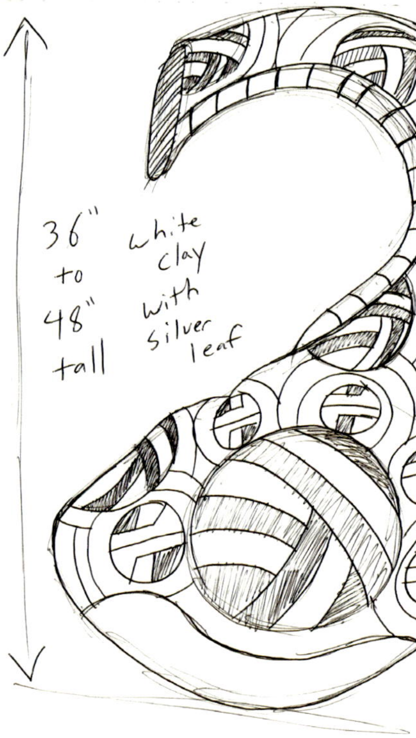

Defining Moment: What is Contemporary (NATIVE) Art?

RYAN RICE

Among Indigenous cultures, the widespread adage "there is no word for art" acknowledges a discrepancy between the dominant Western canon of art and the constructed/imposed marginalization of non-Western art practice and purpose. Traditional modes of art practice and its analysis have become woven into a foreign language that dominates art institutions with little consideration of its relevance outside Western discourse. Such semantics are limiting and presumptuous, discrediting an Indigenous worldview. By redefining categorizations and decolonizing the semantics of "artspeak," Native artists, along with critics and curators, interrogate this restricted language through the process of making, analyzing, and interpreting.

The accepted definition of "contemporary art" is art produced in the present or art produced since World War II. However, some art historians and institutions designate a stricter/linear timeframe to encompass only the past twenty to thirty years from the present. At the same time, "contemporary" as it applies to art suggests simply that this is art created during one's lifetime, meaning art that is contemporary to us. Contemporary art is exhibited worldwide in commercial galleries, corporate and private collections, and a variety of art institutions, from museums to artist-run centers. From the purview of a Western canon (of art history), contemporary art is further defined by *movements* growing out of modernity that range from the abstract expressionism of the 1950s, the pop art of the 1960s, and a multitude of other late twentieth-century art constructs, into the new millennium's shift in technologies and the succession of public/street art among other expressions.

Compelling in scope and diverse in medium, contemporary art includes painting, sculpture, photography, installation, design/architecture, video/film, and performance, which are the most commonly accessible to the public. Within this framework of contemporary art, ideas and concepts cleverly interrogate the linear, formal properties attributed to the analysis of art, thus allowing for a greater engagement/disengagement and a viable dialogue between the art and the viewer (society). Although it seems that it is:

> hard to classify emergent movements, contemporary art—collectively—is much more socially conscious than any previous era has been. A whole lot of art from the last thirty years has been connected with one issue or another: feminism, multiculturalism, globalization, bioengineering and AIDS awareness all come readily to mind as subject matter.[1]

Contemporary art parallels political and social climate changes that reflect the status quo (Western) and effects of globalization. It has slowly shifted the margins of culture to incorporate discussions on multiculturalism, whereby issues of race, gender, and class have yielded somewhat to allow African, Hispanic, Asian, the GBLT (Gay, Bisexual, Lesbian, Transgender) communities, and women artists to gain subtle recognition on their own. Even though there seems to be an increasingly fluid perception and acceptance of contemporary art as wide-ranging, the dominant institutions of art (including academia) have been criticized for regulating what is designated as (contemporary) art within their walls amid the constraints of a hierarchal Western art discourse. The shift toward inclusion of "others" has been uneven and problematic because art institutions evaluate works by their standards of cultural authenticity to fit within parameters based upon their predisposition toward history (Western canon). In contesting such a linear system of judgment, Marcia Tucker argued, "Contemporary art is always fluid and changing, its value is contingent, and it calls for research and scholarship very different from those required by historical art."[2]

The constraints placed upon contemporary Indigenous arts as determined by Western standards are apparent in a review by art critic Holland Cotter in the *New York Times*.[3] The subject was a solo traveling exhibition of the work of Annie Pootoogook, shown at the Smithsonian Institution, National Museum of the American Indian (NMAI), George Gustav Heye Center, New York. Pootoogook, a celebrated Inuit artist, an Inuk from Cape Dorset, Nunavut, received international acclaim for her work after her participation in *documenta (12)* exhibition, 2007, the international festival of contemporary art held very five years in Kassel, Germany. Additionally, she won the prestigious Canadian Sobey Art Award (2006), and her work has been widely exhibited and published. Cotter was hesitant to place Pootoogook's work in the realm of a "contemporary art" familiar to him, yet he noted that at *documenta* it had been simply presented as contemporary art. When it was exhibited under the auspices the NMAI, it changed. Hence, Cotter fell into the trope of viewing and evaluating Pootoogook's life and work through the ethnographic lens he associated with the museum. Conscious of the global shift in culture, he noted, however, that her "work offers a different model of what's traditional and authentic," but at the same time he held to a Western standard of critique and dismissal that reinforced the barriers Indigenous artists face. He stated in conclusion, "There's no question that the art that results is of this moment and that it is the genuine Inuit thing, though precisely what category you'd file it under, I don't know, and I suspect that Ms. Pootoogook, whose international presence grows by the year, is too busy to care."[4] Limited by the rigidity of art categorizations, Cotter did not really know where to place the "Inuit thing," aside from being a foreign abstraction within his experience.

The fluidity of "contemporary" is repeatedly lost among the mainstream when critiquing Indigenous art due to the parameters placed upon Indigenous culture as a thing of

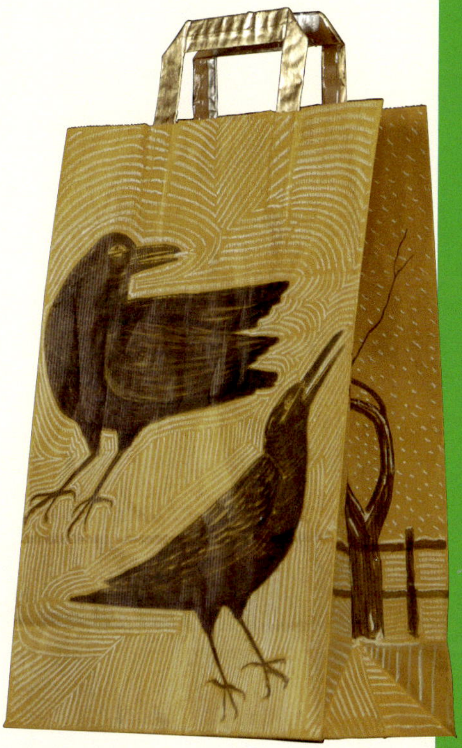

NATURAL SELECTION

Nature has remained a constant source of inspiration for artists since the beginnings of human culture. Not surprisingly, the world of nature, so closely identified with cultural and spiritual practices, appears in its rich diversity in "Natural Selection." This section features works that are comprised of unaltered natural materials, harvested and prepared by the artists themselves, ranging from reeds and branches to birch bark along with found and manmade materials. Other artists evoke the physical characteristics and psychological content of geographies in works that represent in abstract form, places, and natural phenomenon such as rivers and waterfalls. Animals are also depicted both for their visual presence and for the symbolic and mythological roles they have played over the centuries. And the human figure is prominent in many works that deal with issues of fertility and growth, as well as in memorable masks that link the tangible and spiritual worlds.

MICHAEL BELMORE

b. 1971, Thunder Bay, Ontario;
lives in Toronto, Ontario

Resistant, 2012 (detail)

Sterling silver, found stone, steel
52 x 6 x 6 in. (132.1 x 15.2 x 15.2 cm)
Courtesy of the artist

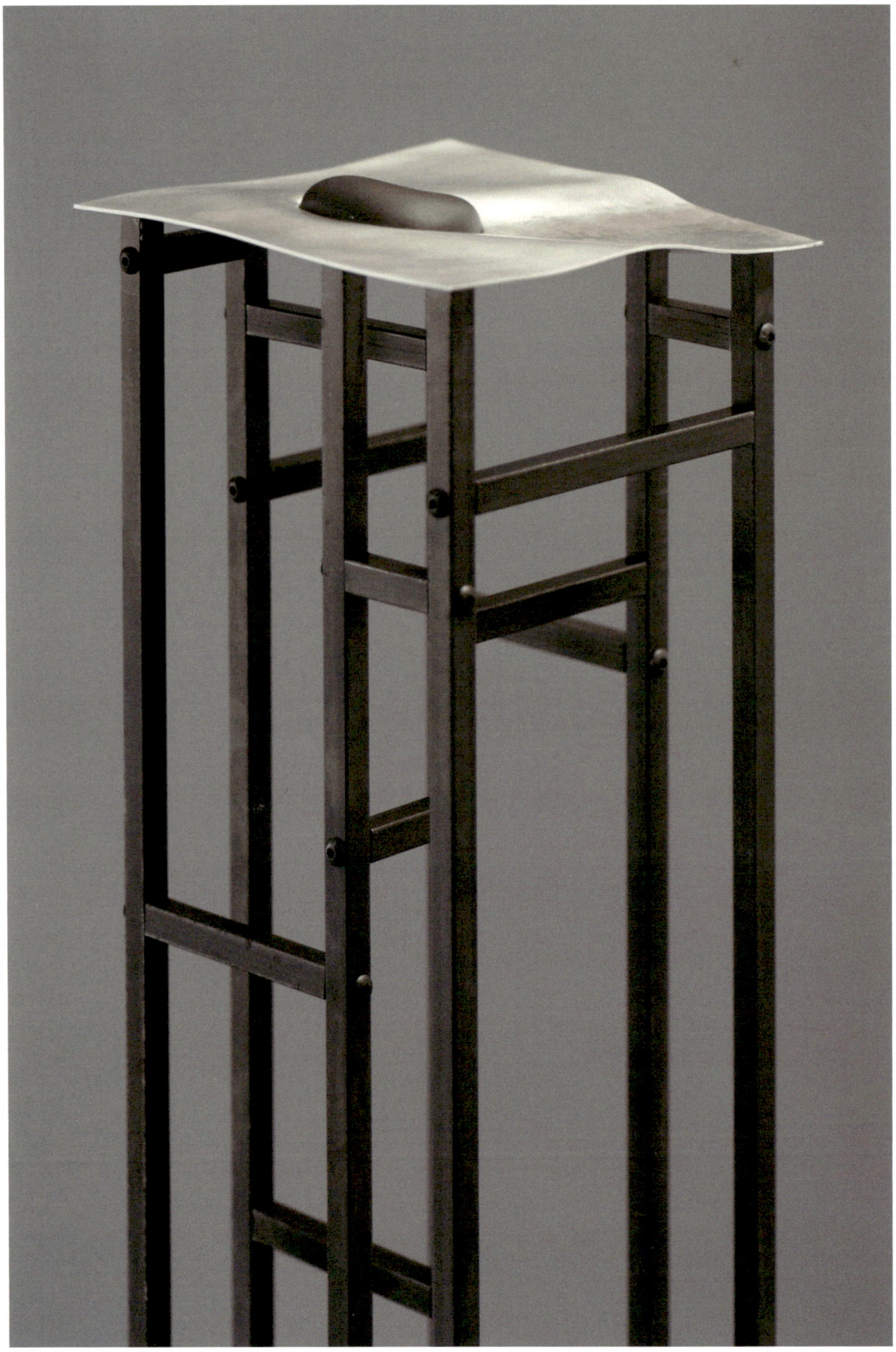

KELLY CHURCH

b. 1967, Allegan, Michigan;
lives in Hopkins, Michigan

Leap Frog: Black Ash vs. Cedar, 2010

(in collaboration with Lisa Telford)
Black ash, Rit dye, red cedar
¾ x 19 x 19 in. (1.9 x 48.3 x 48.3 cm)
Courtesy of the artists

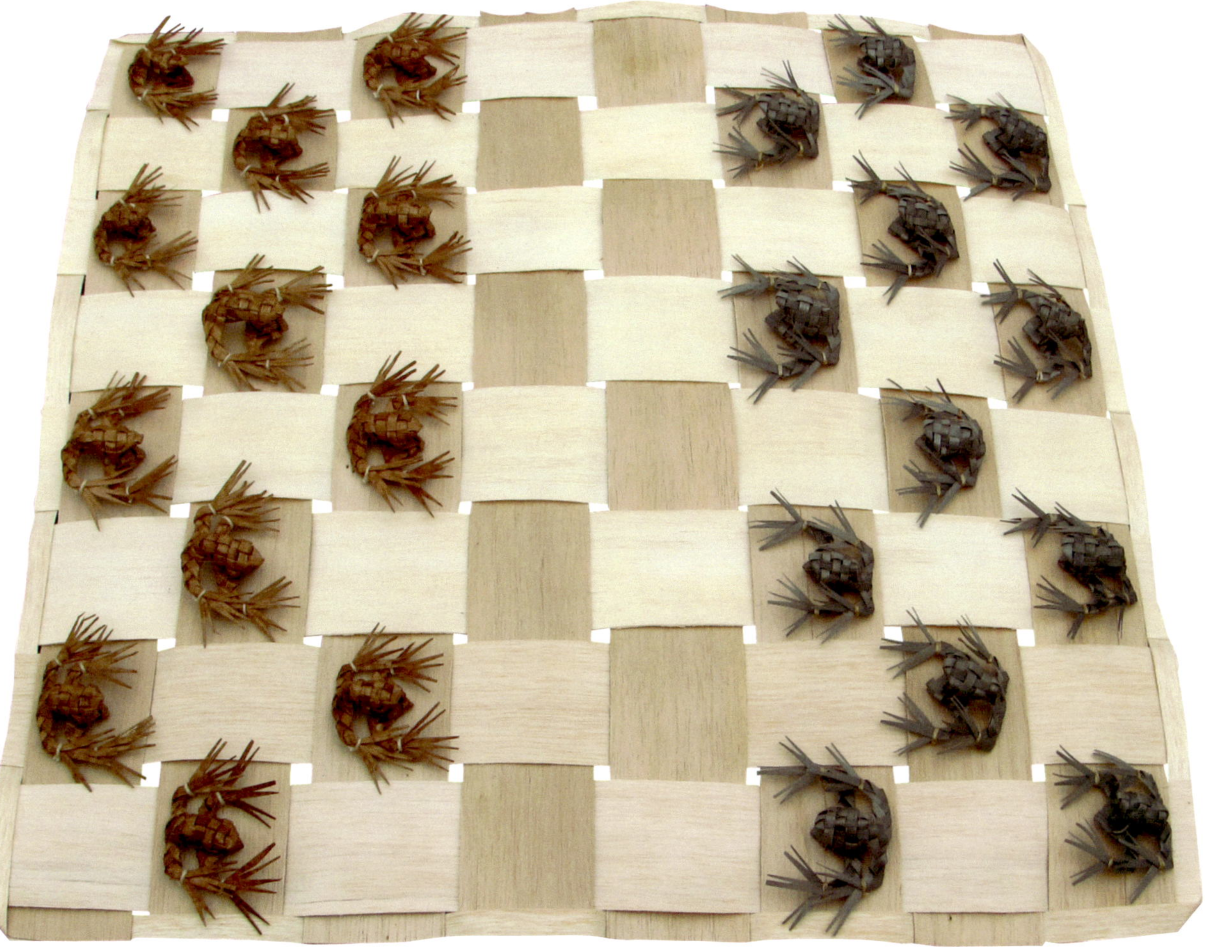

HANNAH CLAUS

b. 1969, Fredericton, New Brunswick; lives in Montreal, Quebec

Birds, 2012

Double-matte polyester film, digital photographs, cotton thread, glue, wood
64 x 48 x 48 in. (162.6 x 121.9 x 121.9 cm)
Courtesy of the artist

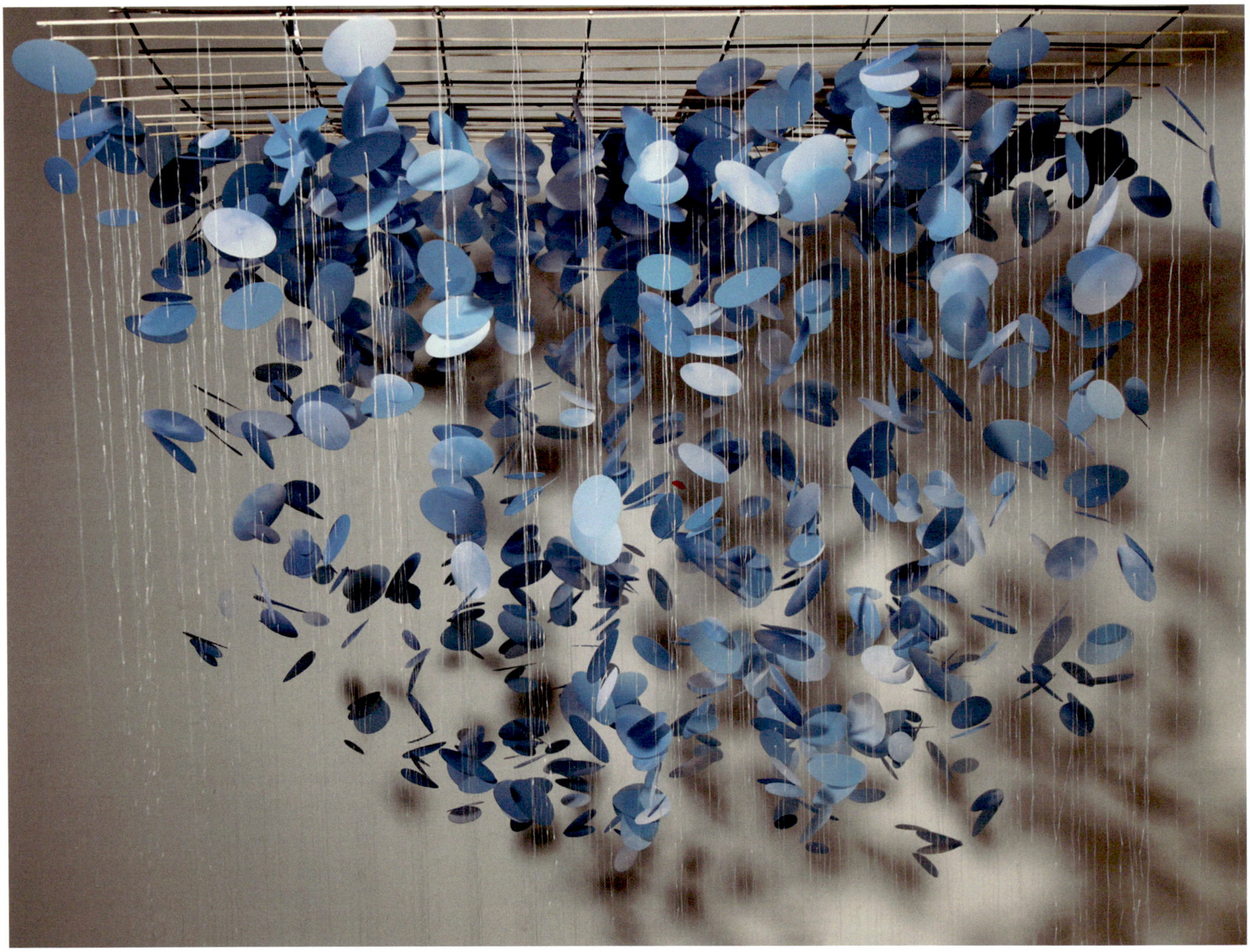

PATRICIA DEADMAN

b. 1961, Ohsweken, Ontario;
lives in Woodstock, Ontario

Cuento de Dos Jardins, 2009

Suite of 24 digital photographs
on dibond mounting
Overall: 90 x 92 in.
(228.6 x 233.7 cm)
Courtesy of the artist

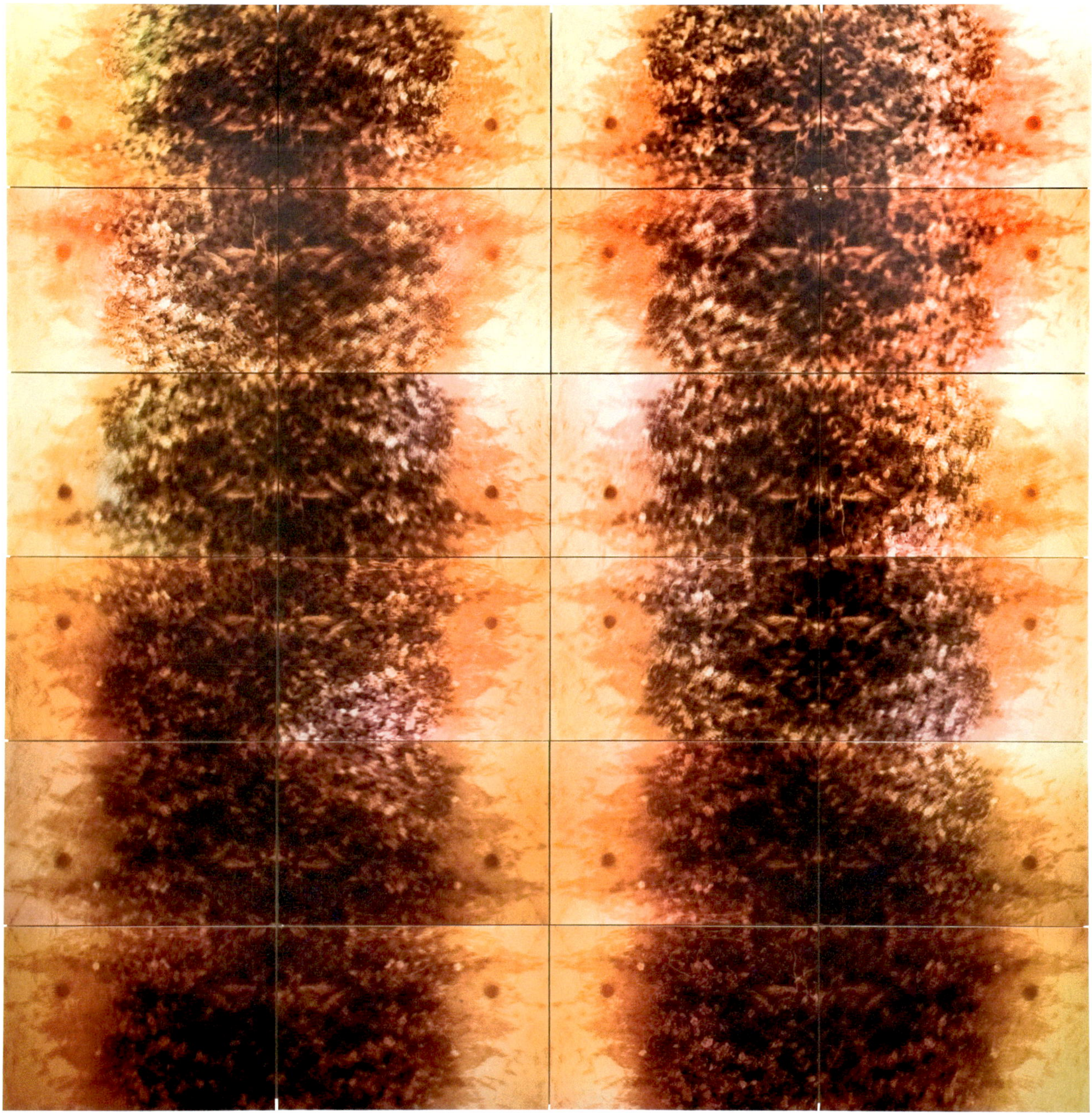

BONNIE DEVINE

b. 1952, Toronto, Ontario;
lives in Toronto, Ontario

New Earth Braid, 2009

(installed at Glenhyrst Art Gallery of Brant, Brantford, Ontario; to be re-created in exhibition as *Manhattan Braid for Lenni Lenape*)
Reeds, cardboard, paper, twine
36 x 192 in. (91 x 487 cm)
Courtesy of the artist

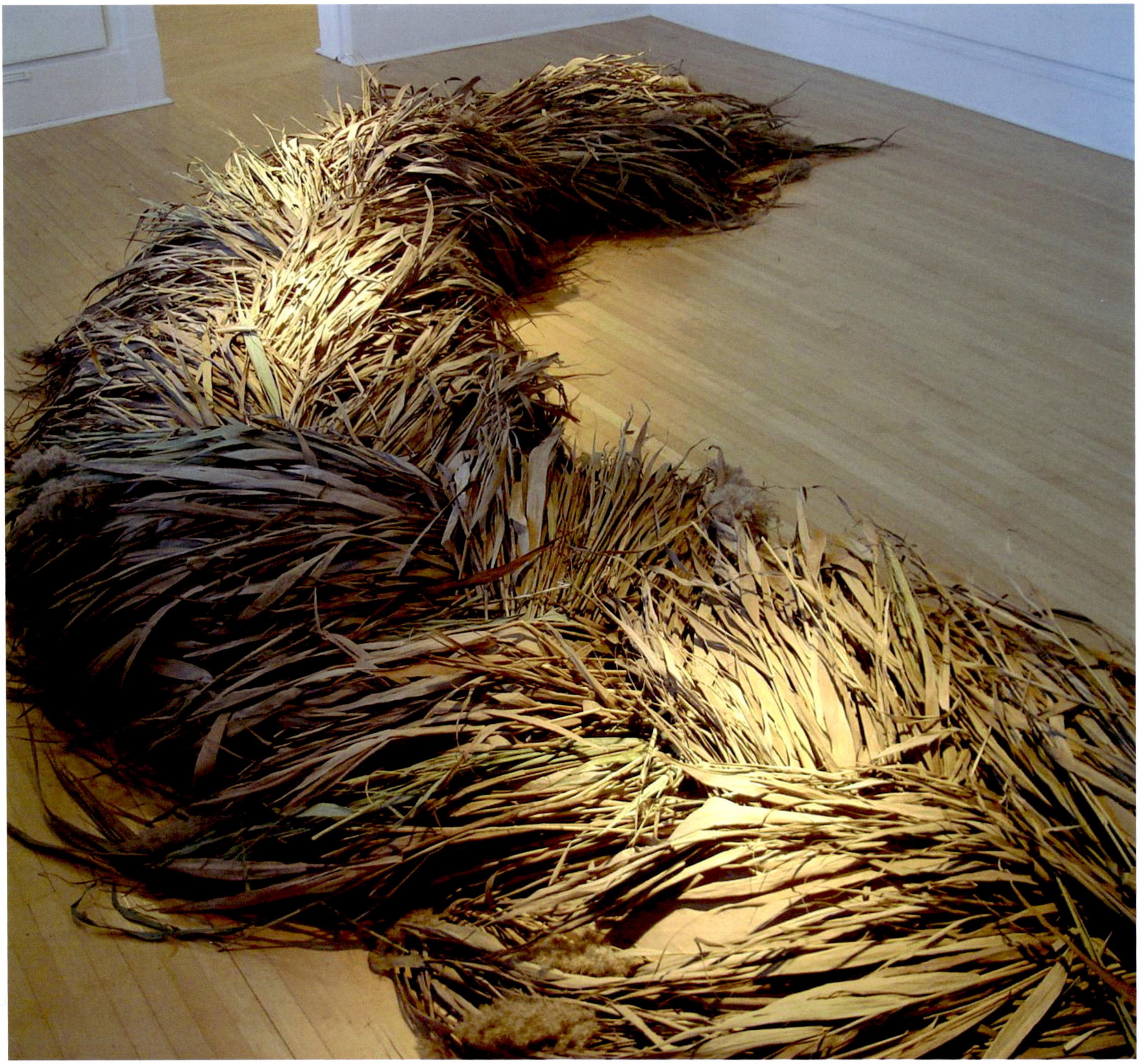

BILLY GAUTHIER

b. 1978, Happy Valley–Goose Bay, Labrador; lives in North West River, Labrador

The Flower of My Dreams, 2012
(not included in exhibition)

Serpentine, antler, bone, baleen
8 x 8 ½ x 4 ½ in.
(20.3 x 21.6 x 11.4 cm)
Courtesy of Spirit Wrestler Gallery, Vancouver, British Columbia

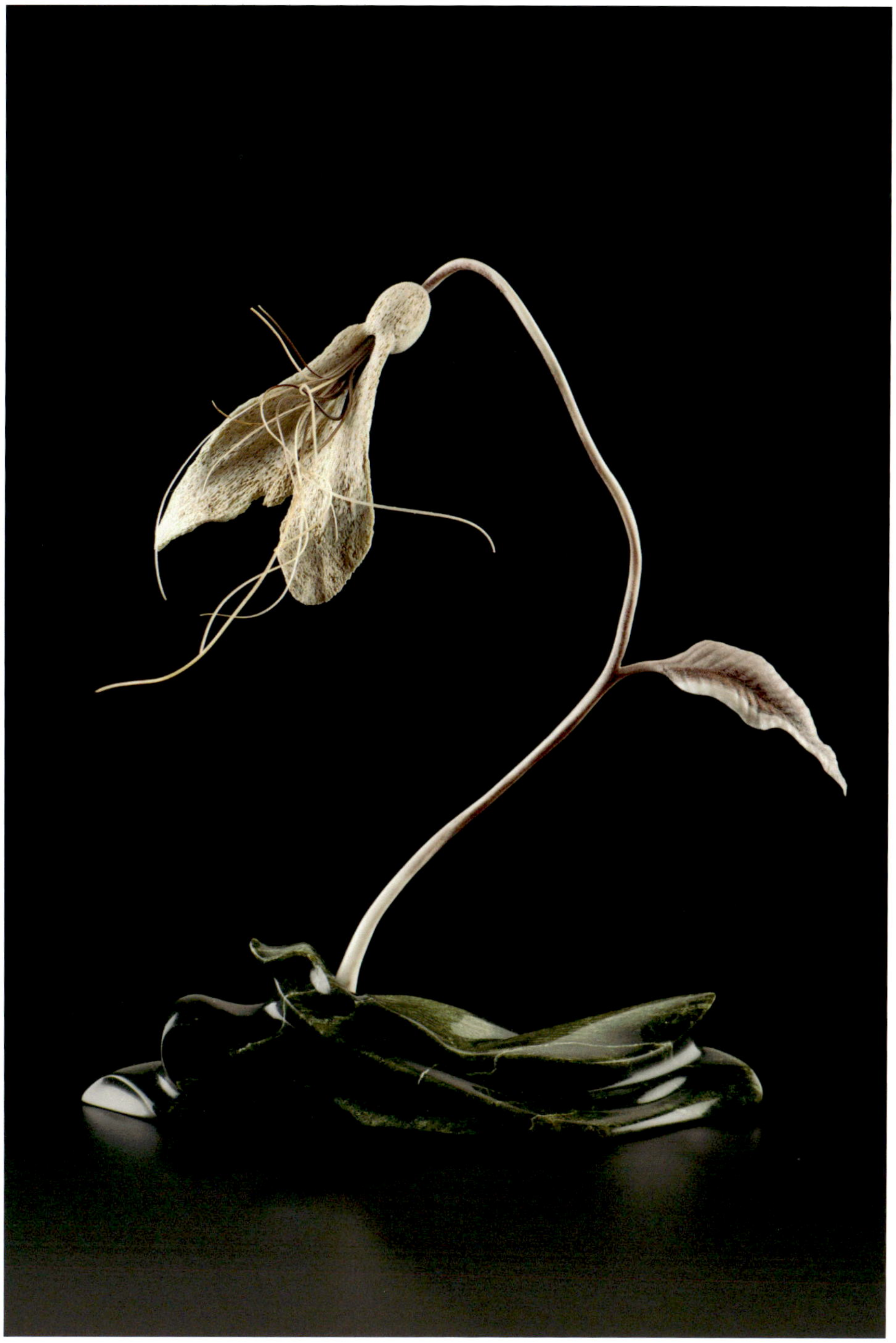

LUZENE HILL

b. 1946, Atlanta, Georgia; lives in Whittier, North Carolina

Becoming, 2011 (2 details)

Beeswax, silk
Dimensions variable
Courtesy of the artist

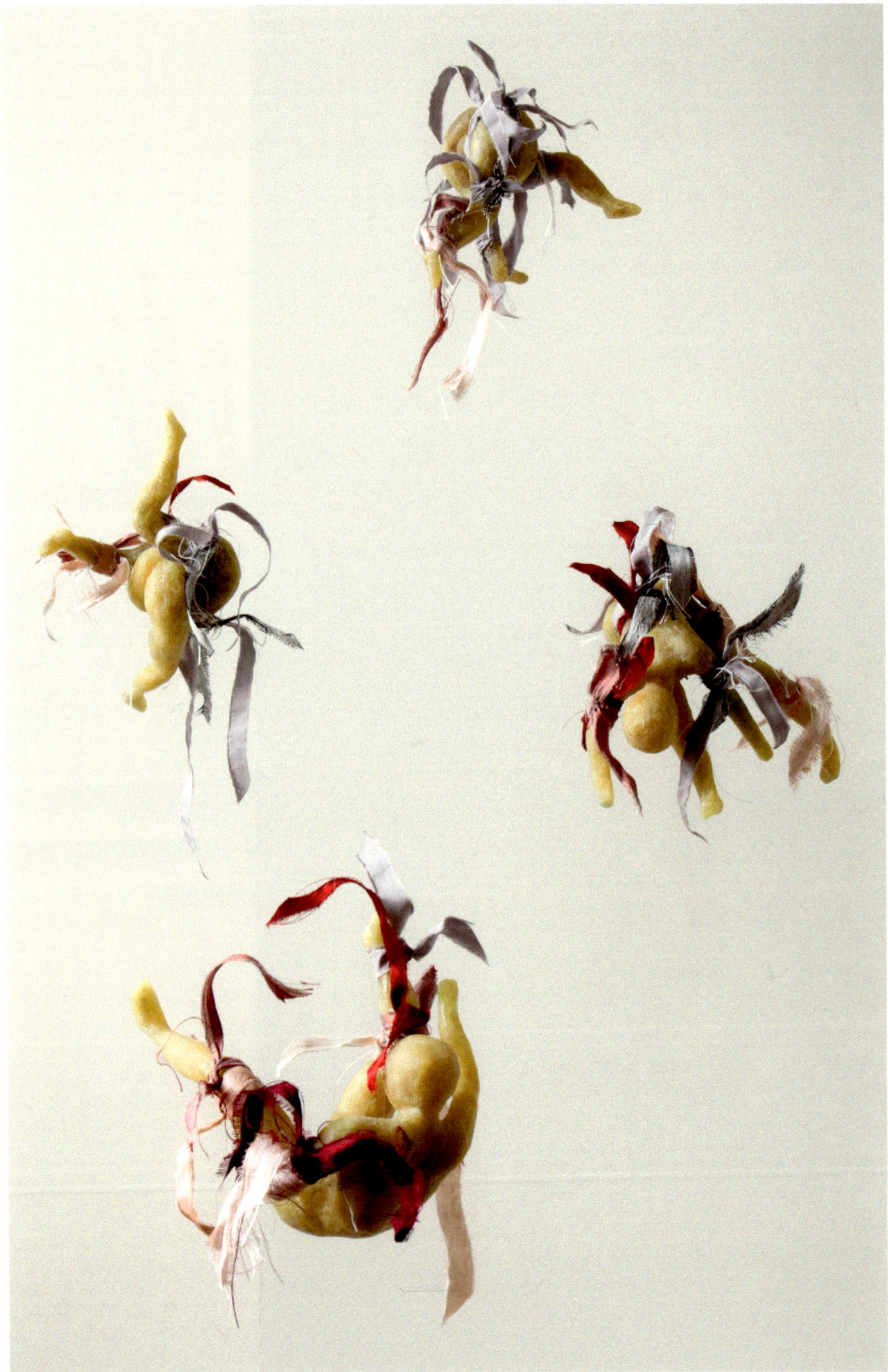

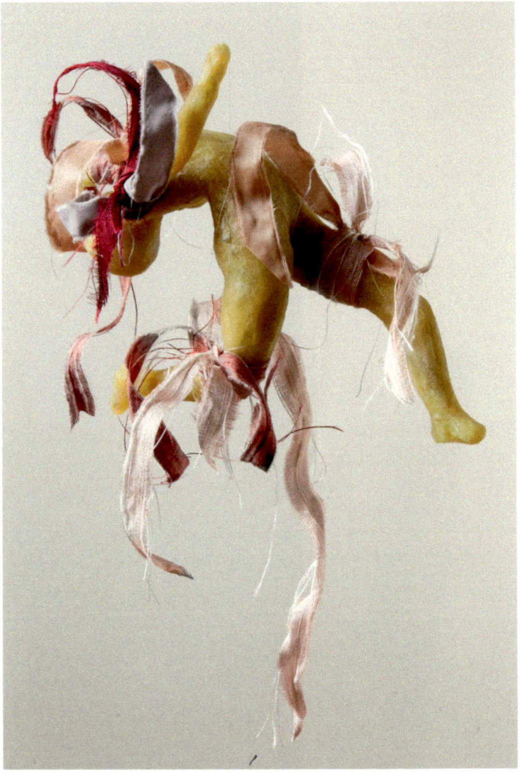

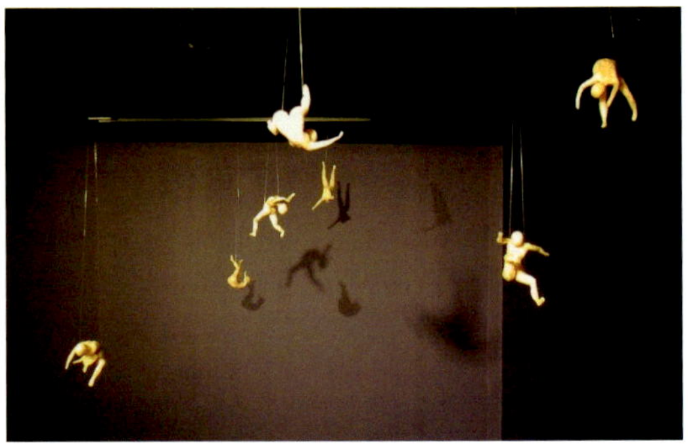

Transparent to Transcendence, 2004

(installed at LIFT Contemporary Gallery, Cherokee, North Carolina; to be re-created in exhibition as *Becoming)*

TOM HUFF

b. 1952, Silver Creek, New York; lives at Onondaga Nation, New York

The Seventh Generation, 2011
(2 views)

Brazilian soapstone
Approx. 9 x 12 x 8 in.
(22.9 x 30.5 x 20.3 cm)
Courtesy of the artist

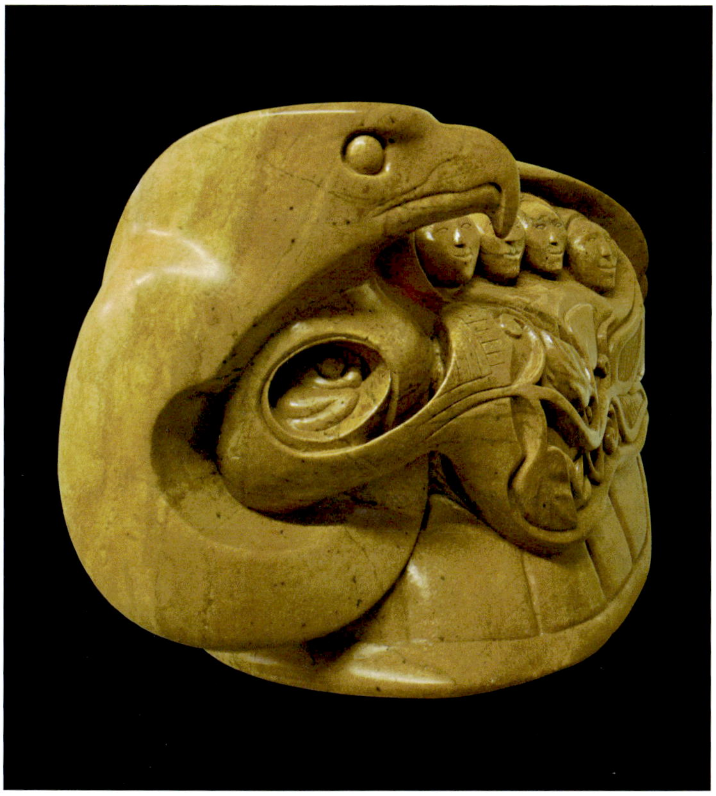

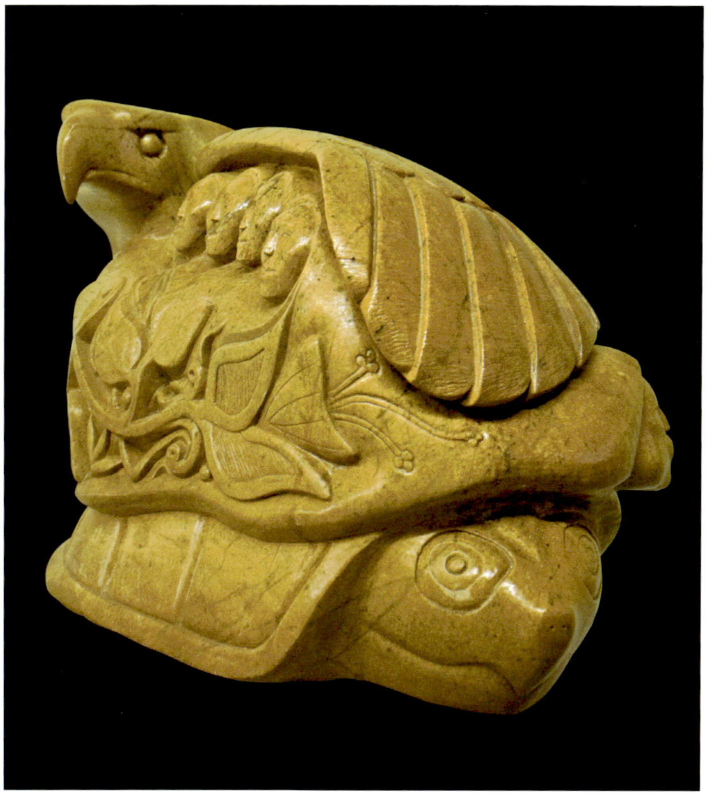

EVA IKINILIK

b. 1965, Back River region, Nunavut;
lives in Baker Lake area, Nunavut

Untitled, 2007

Felt, wool, embroidery floss
25 ½ x 27 ½ in. (64.8 x 69.9 cm)
Courtesy of Maura Cormack

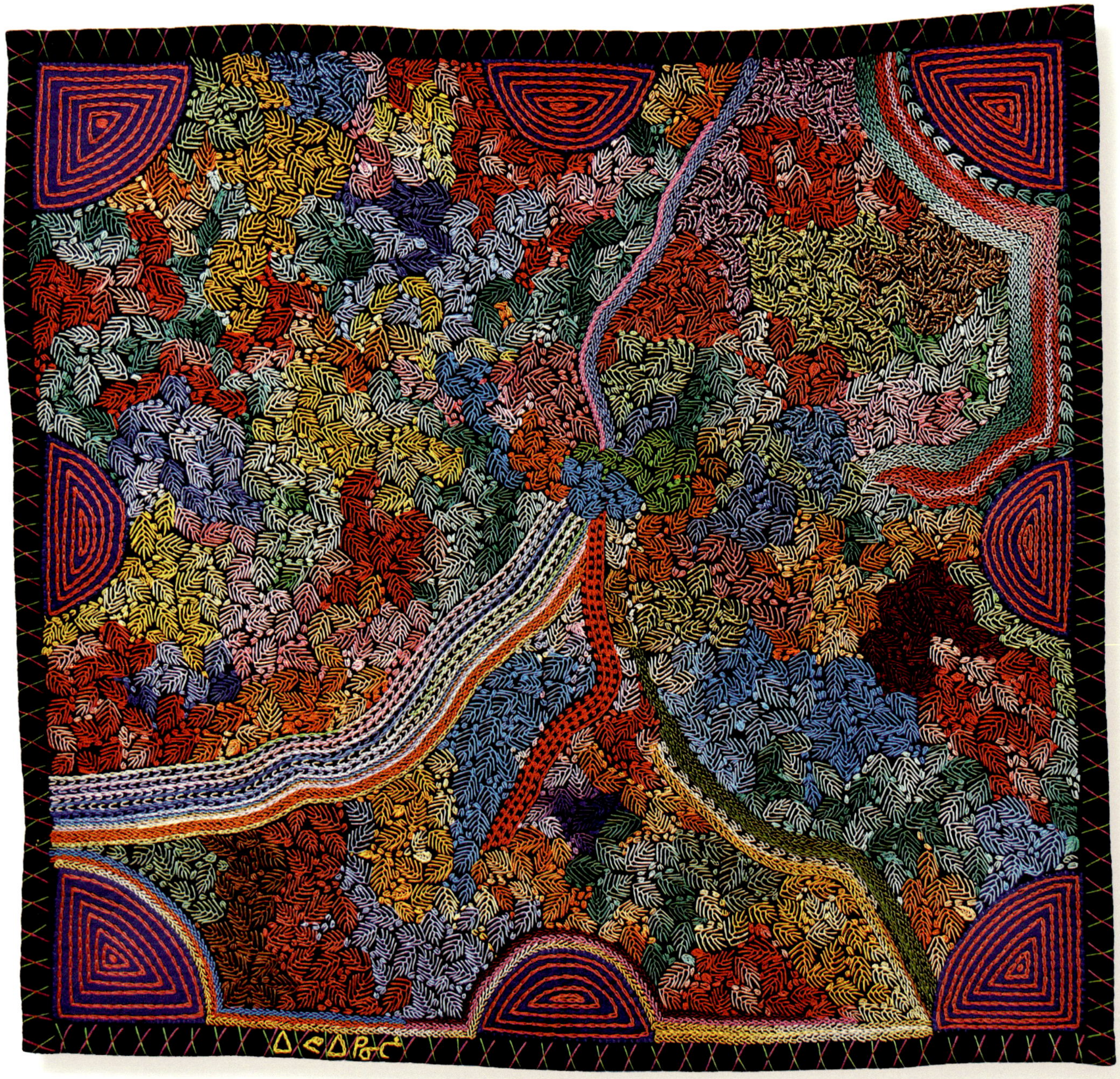

MATTIUSI IYAITUK

b. 1950, Akulivik area, Quebec;
lives in Ivujivik, Quebec

Unforgettable fantastic feeling my wife Qumaq and I experienced being near a 400 foot high iceberg in Sisimiut, Greenland

Serpentine, argillite, antler
23 x 18 x 11 in. (58.4 x 45.7 x 27.9 cm)
La Fédération des Coopératives du Nouveau-Québec, Baie-D'Urfe, Quebec

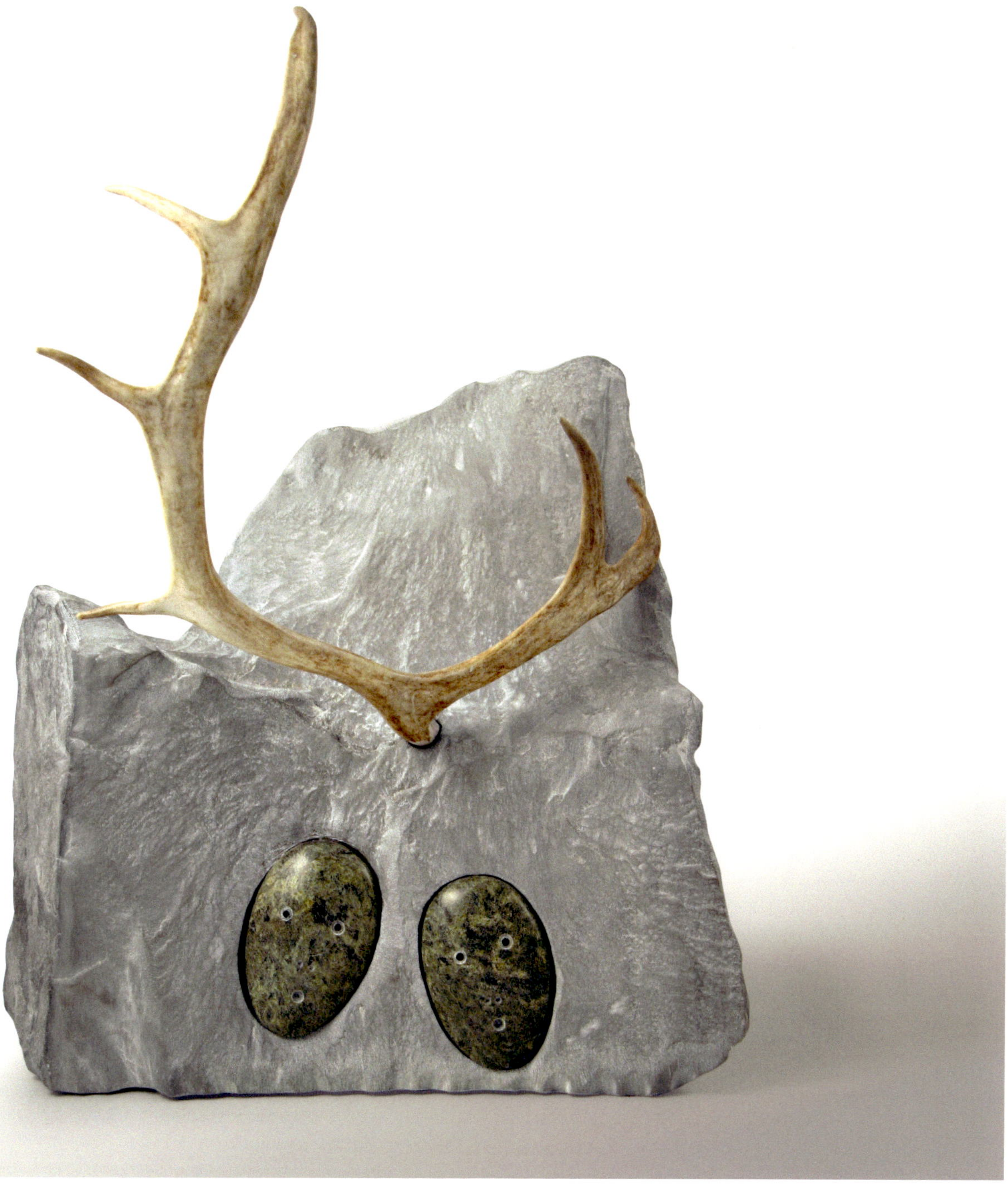

G. PETER JEMISON

b. 1945, Silver Creek, New York; lives in Victor, New York

Shadows on the Porch, 2009 (2 views)

Found paper bag, China marker, acrylic paint, colored pencil
22 ½ x 15 5/8 x 6 in.
(57.2 x 39.7 x 15.2 cm)
Courtesy of the artist

Crow in the Shadow, 2011 (2 views)

Handmade paper bag, acrylic paint, collage
23 x 12 x 6 ¼ in.
(58.4 x 30.5 x 15.9 cm)
Courtesy of the artist

Crows in Winter (Paris), 2009 (2 views)

Found paper bag, China marker, acrylic ink, foil
17 x 10 5/8 x 4 ¾ in.
(43.2 x 27 x 12.1 cm)
Courtesy of the artist

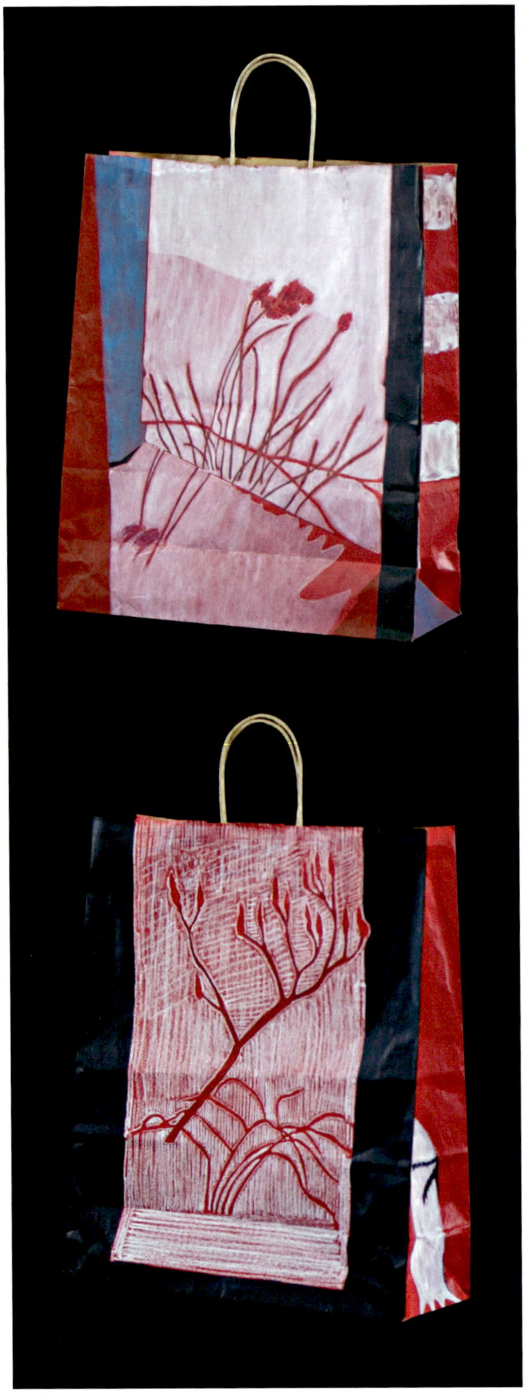

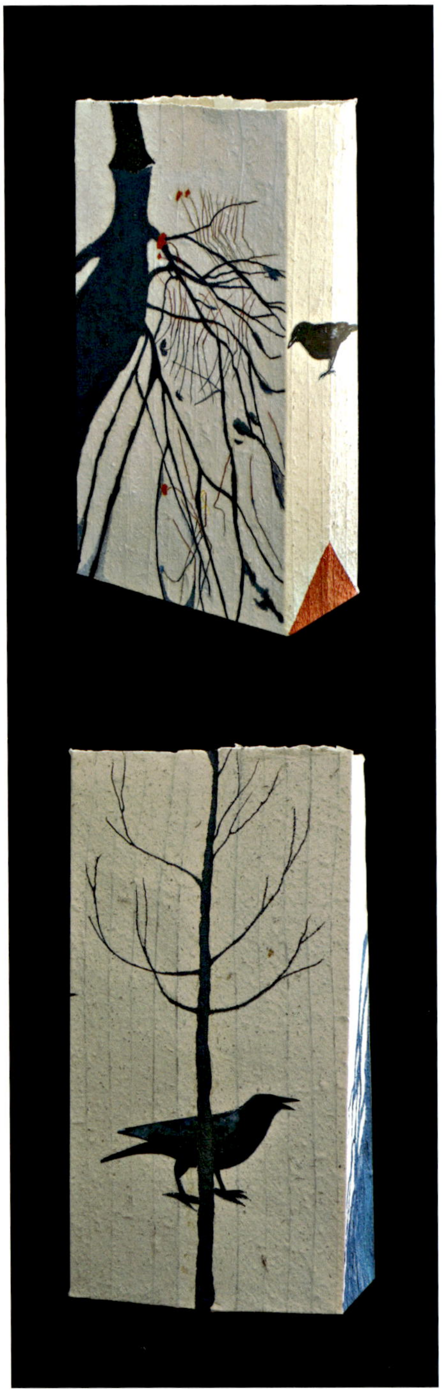

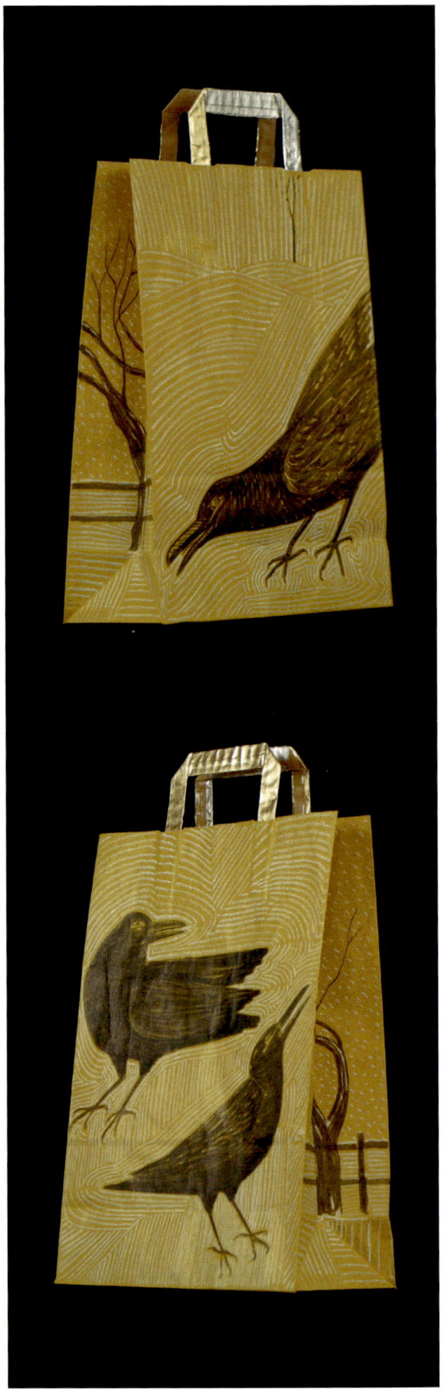

FLOYD KUPTANA

b. 1964, Cape Parry/Paulatuk, Northwest Territories; lives in Toronto, Ontario

Bear-Man Shaman Mask, 2011

Brazilian soapstone, metal, antler
34 x 19 x 10 in.
(86.4 x 48.3 x 25.4 cm)
Courtesy of Feheley Fine Arts, Toronto, Ontario

Bear Spirit Dance, 2000

Stone, antler
18 ¼ x 17 x 5 in.
(46.4 x 43.2 x 12.7 cm)
Courtesy of Feheley Fine Arts, Toronto, Ontario

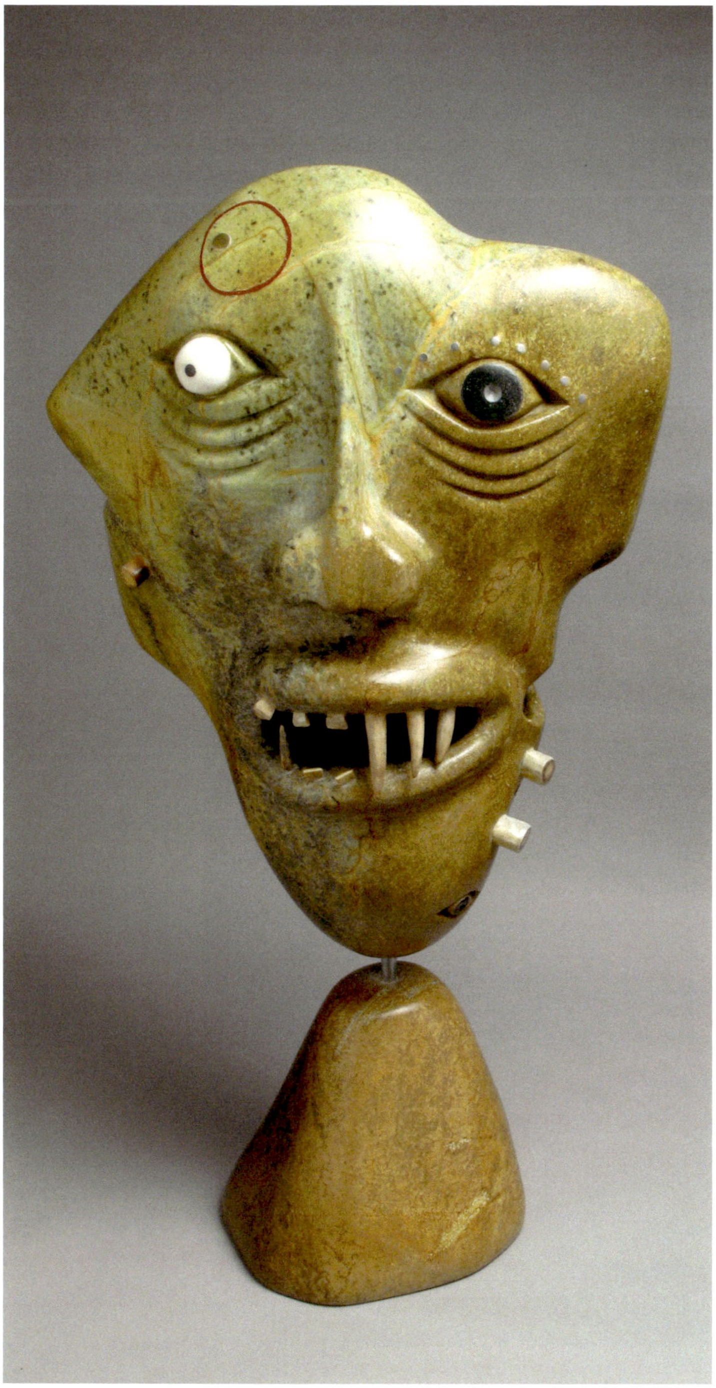

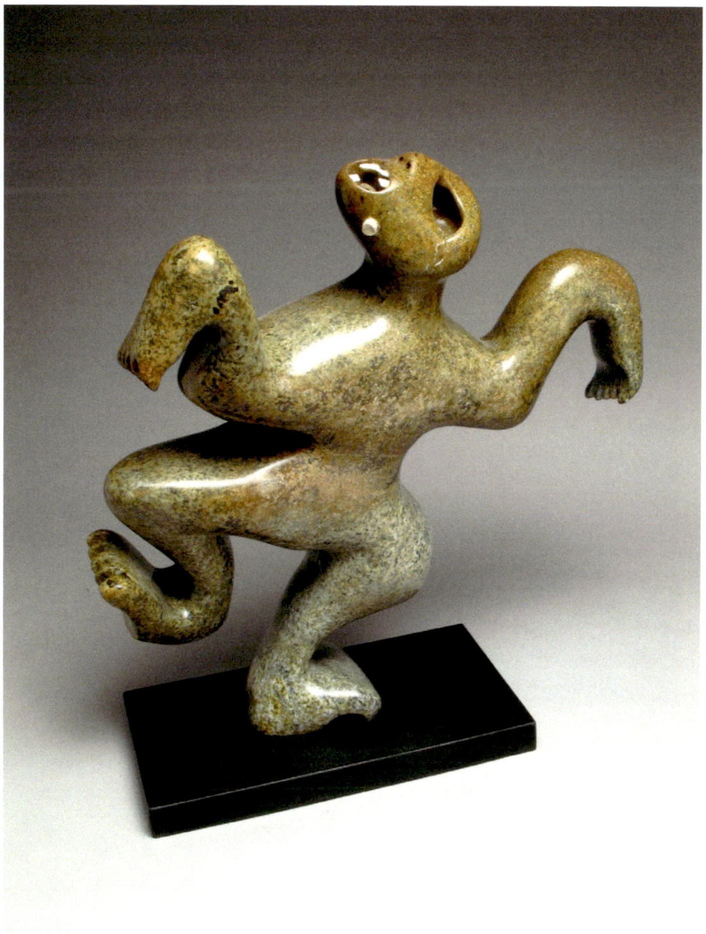

NADIA MYRE

b. 1974, Montreal, Quebec;
lives in Montreal, Quebec

Cultural, *Material*, and *Spiritual*, 2012

Photographic prints from the
Meditations on Black Lake series
44 x 44 in. (111.8 x 111.8 cm)
Courtesy of Art Mûr, Quebec

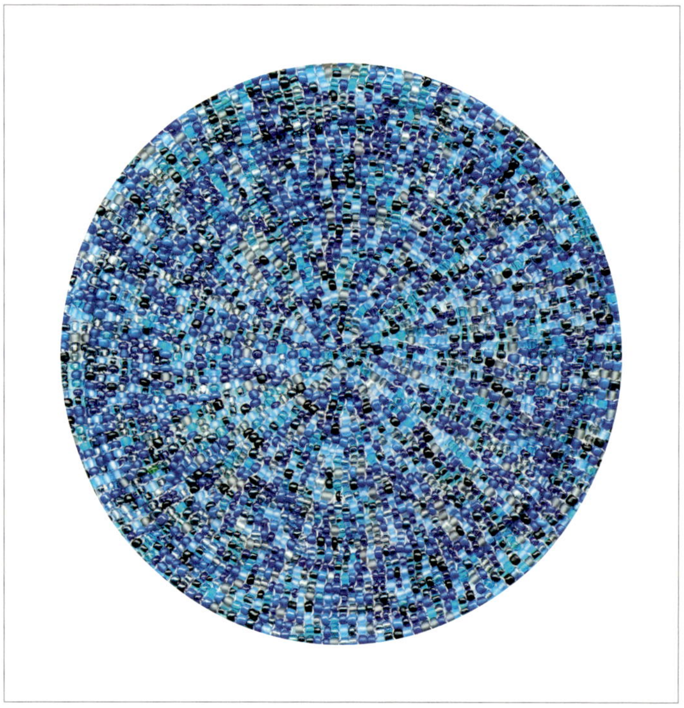

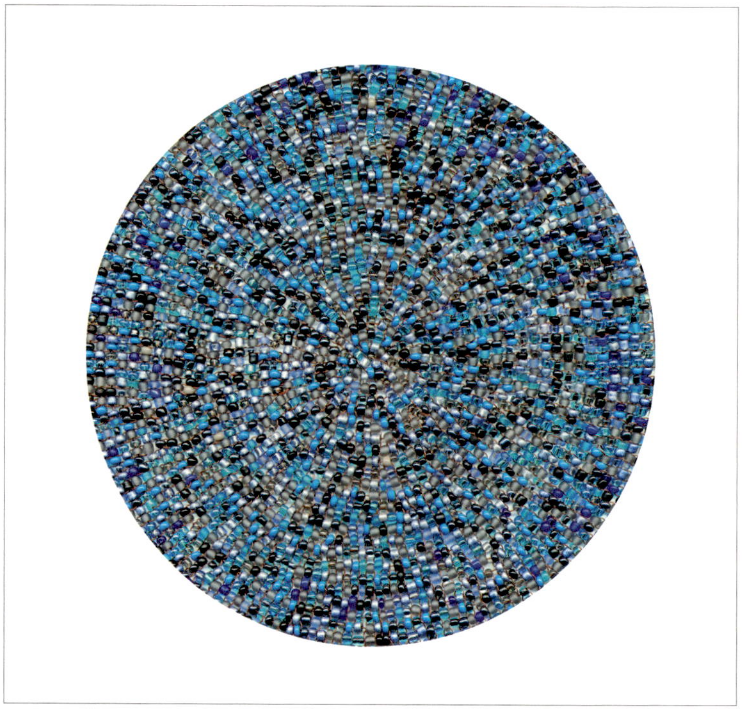

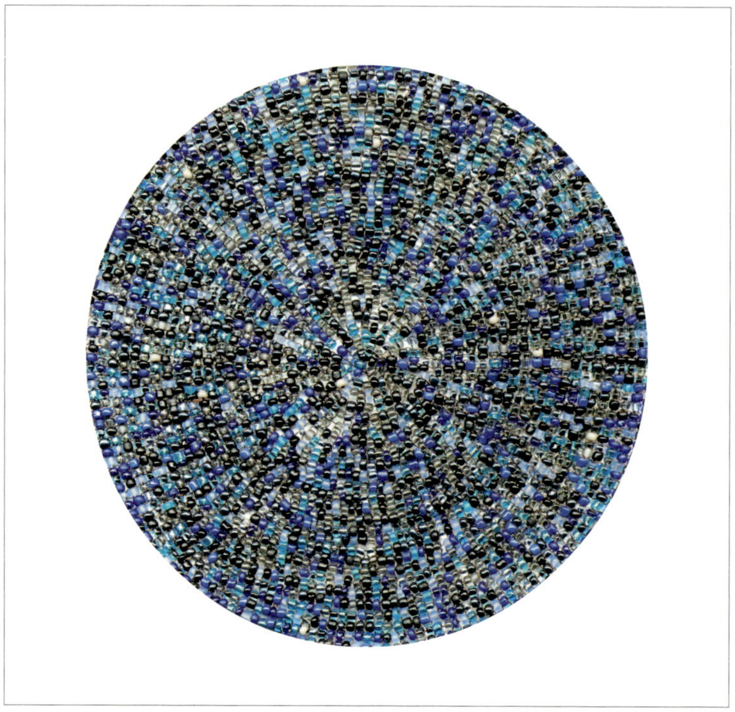

JANET NUNGNIK

b. 1954, Kivalliq region, Nunavut;
lives in Baker Lake area, Nunavut

Changes, 2004

Felt, wool, embroidery floss
23 ½ x 22 ¾ in. (59.7 x 57.8 cm)
Courtesy of Marion Scott Gallery/
Kardosh Projects, Vancouver,
British Columbia

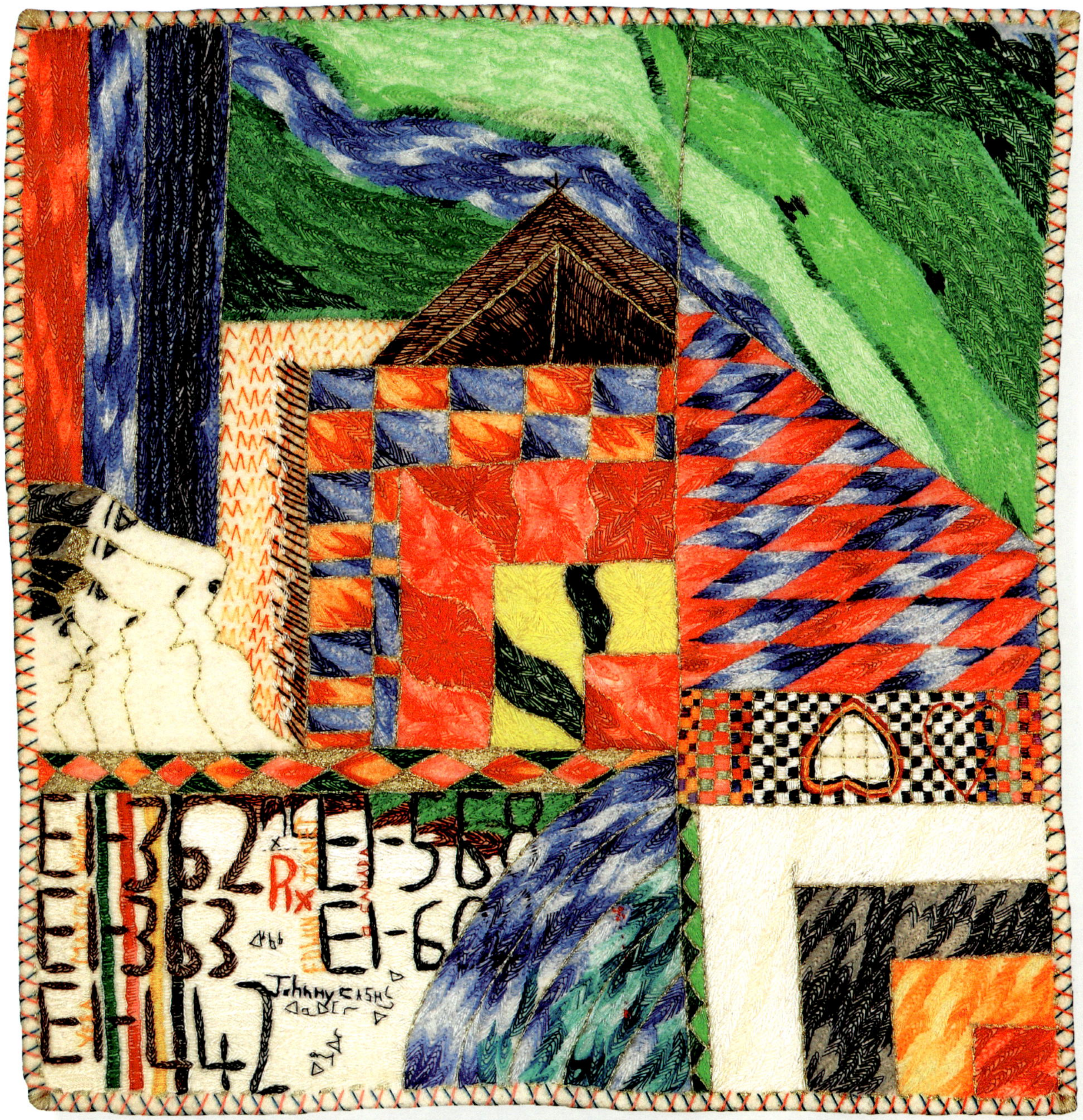

RUTH QAULLUARYUK

b. 1932, Back River area, Northwest Territories (now Nunavut); Baker Lake, Nunavut

Untitled (landscape), 2011

Felt, wool, embroidery floss
26 ½ x 17 in. (67.3 x 43.2 cm)
Courtesy of Alaska on Madison, New York

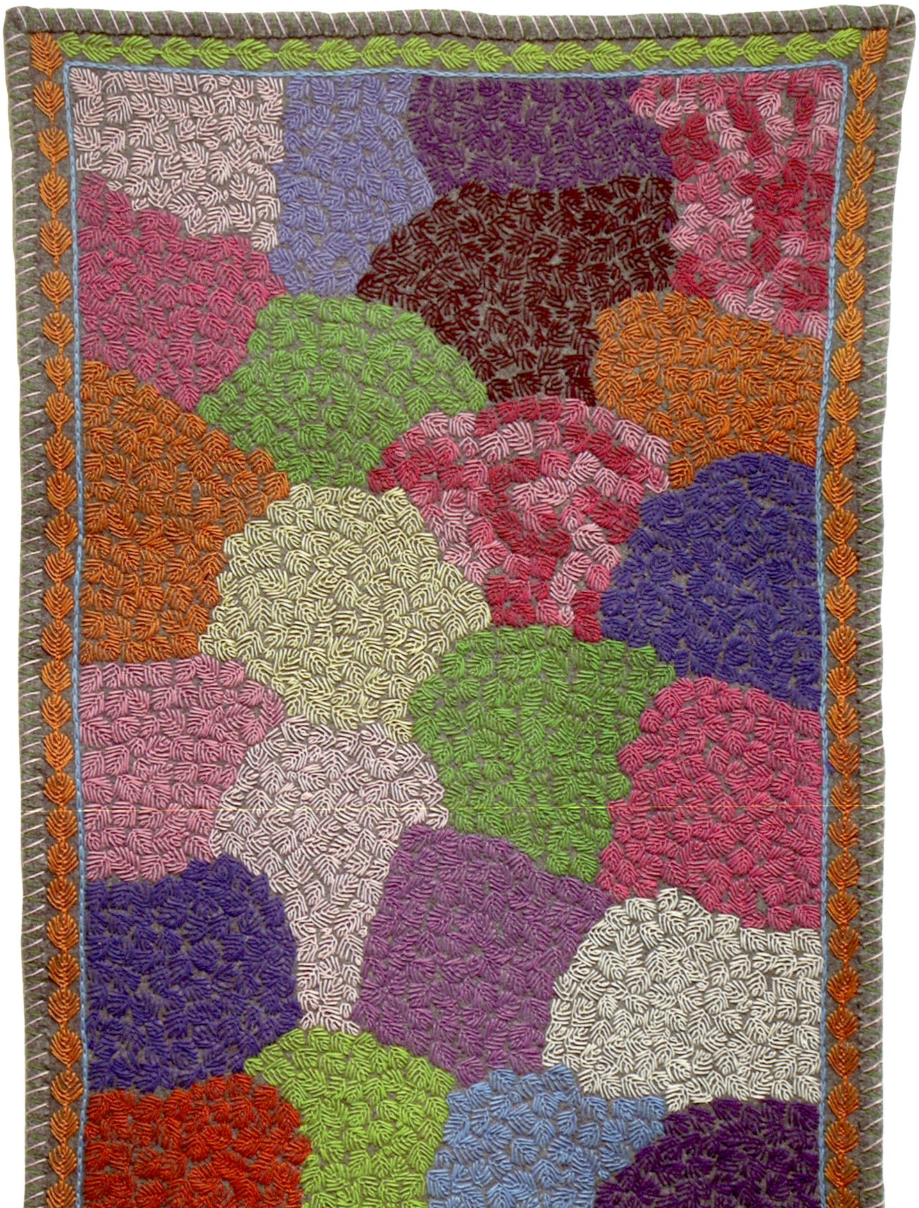

JASON QUIGNO

b. 1975, Alma, Michigan; lives in Grand Rapids, Michigan

Pillar of Tranquility, 2011

Indiana limestone
71 x 9 x 7 in. (180.3 x 22.9 x 17.8 cm)
Collection of Drs. Steve and Shirley Kleiman, Spine and Sport Biomechanical Rehab Center

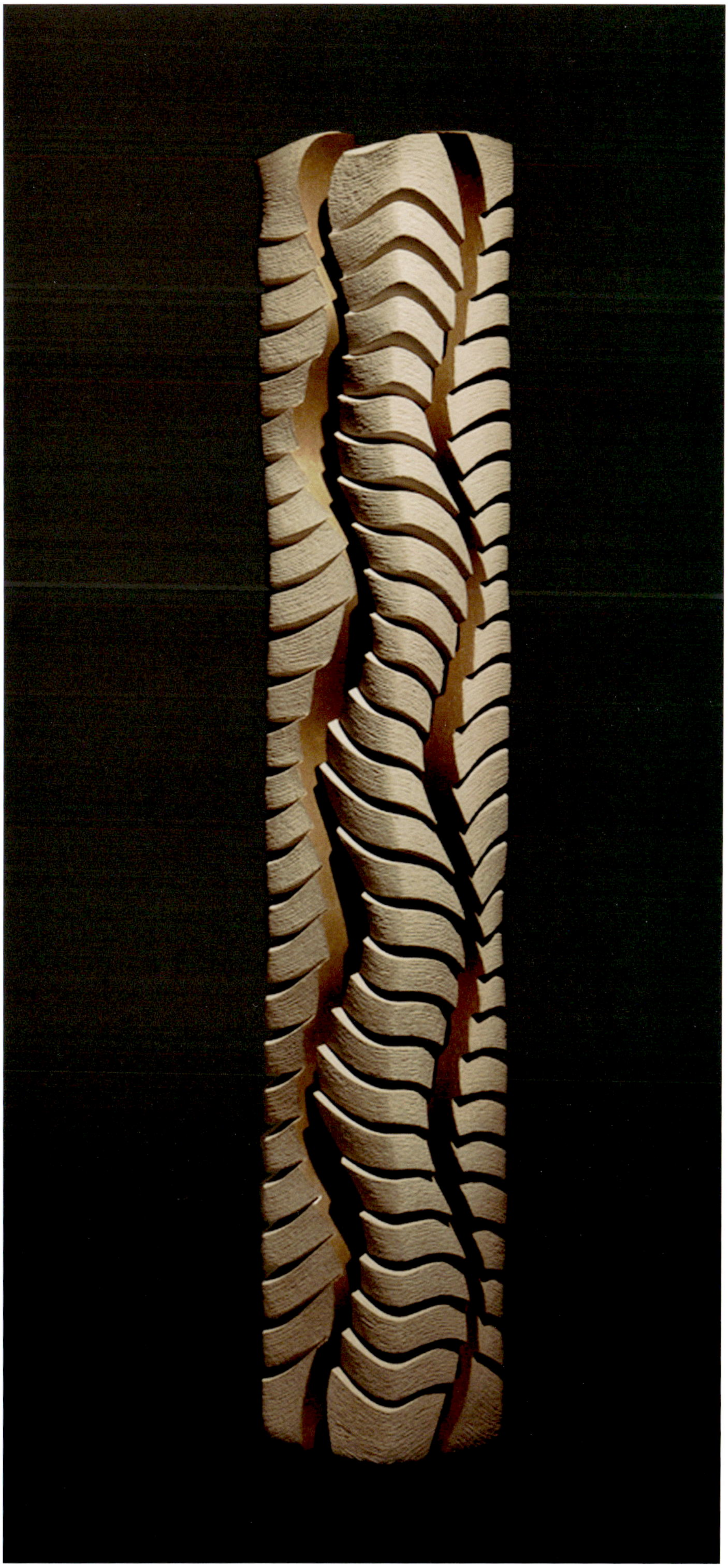

NATASHA SMOKE SANTIAGO

b. 1983, Rochester, New York;
lives in Akwesasne, New York

Calico Corn, 2010 (2 views)

Densite plaster, acrylic paint
16 x 12 x 15 in.
(40.6 x 30.5 x 38.1 cm)
Courtesy of the artist

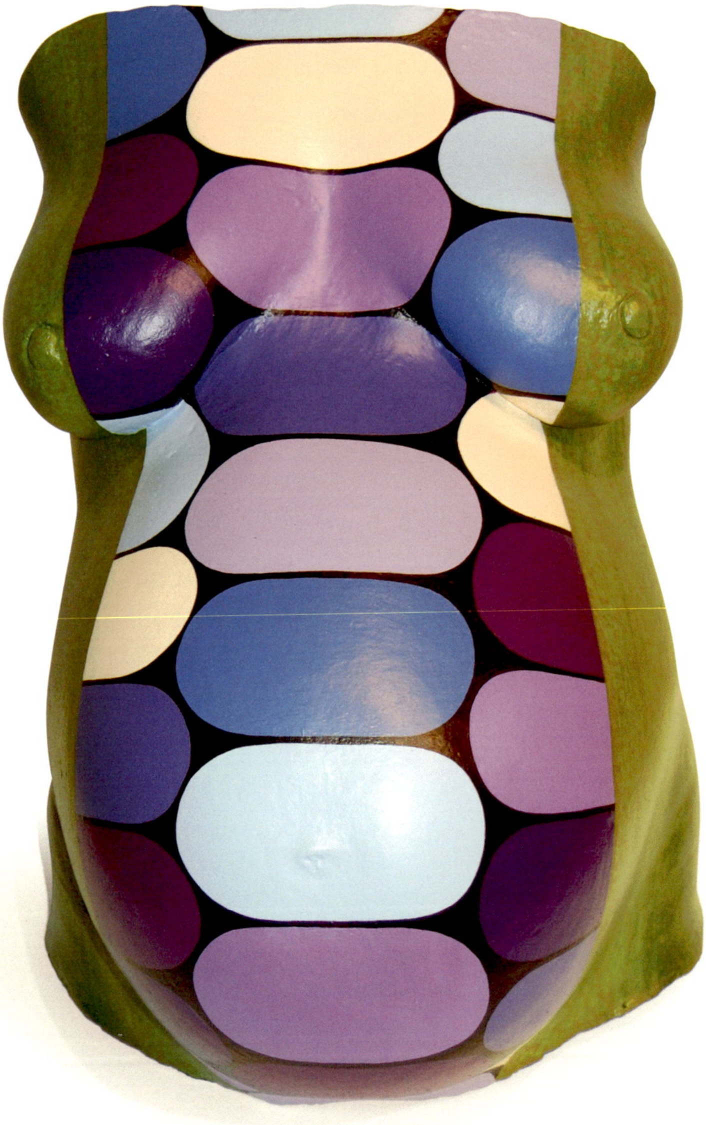

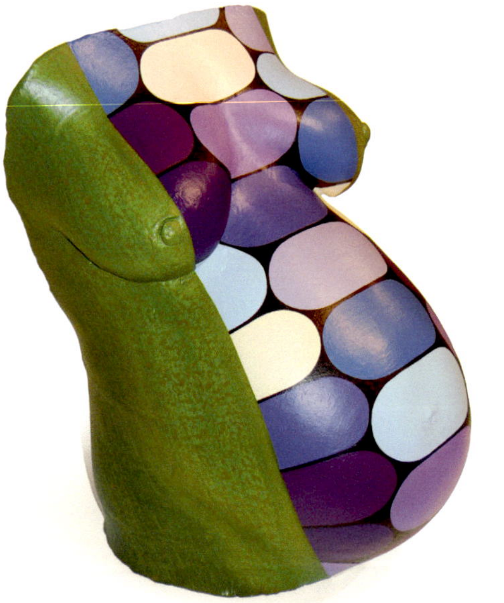

FRANK SHEBAGEGET

b. 1972, Upsala, Ontario;
lives in Ottawa, Ontario

Cell, 2010

Nylon, aluminum
96 x 96 in. (243.8 x 243.8 cm)
Courtesy of the artist

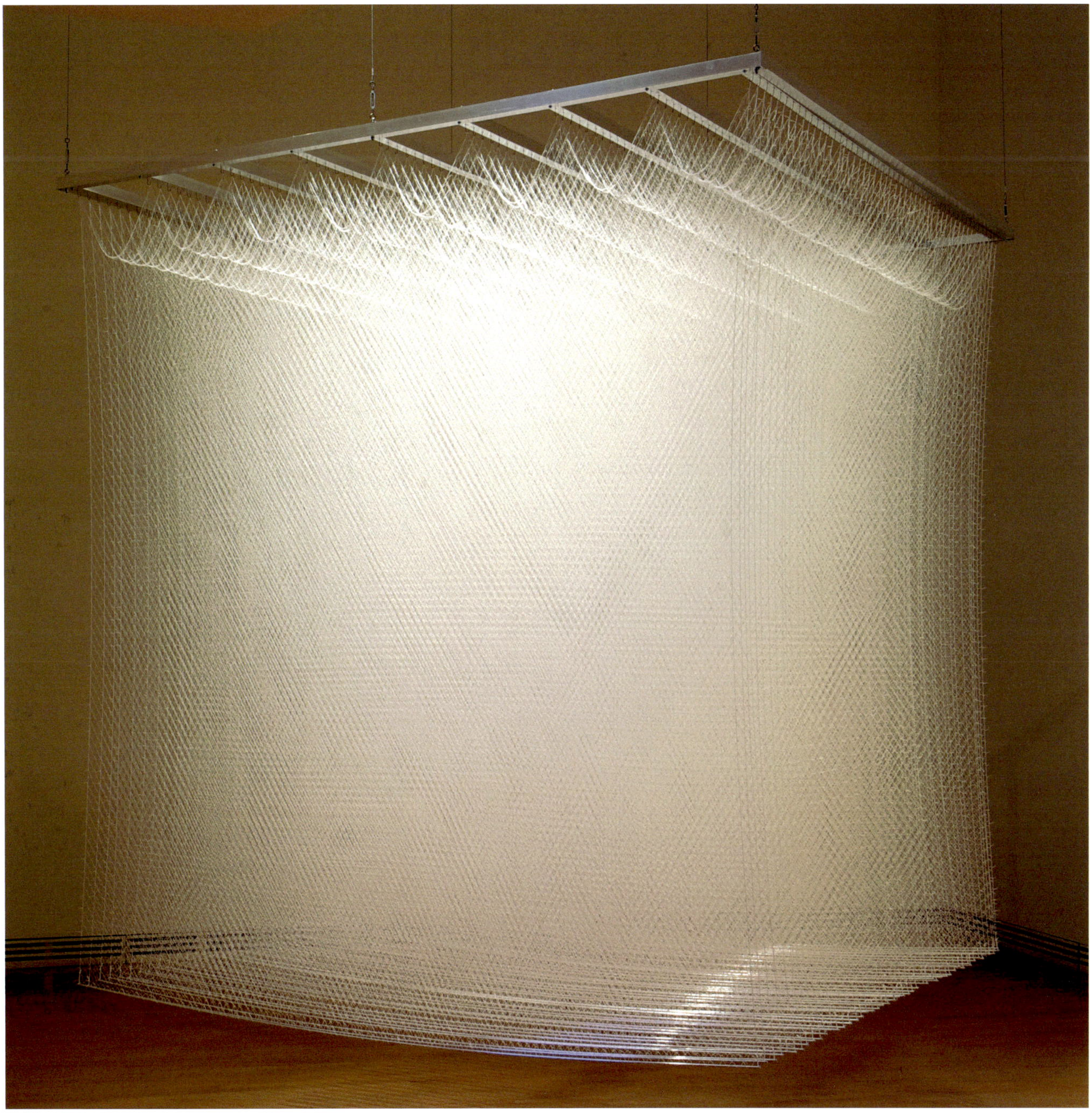

ROBERT TANNAHILL

b. 1970, Simcoe, Ontario;
lives in Simcoe, Ontario

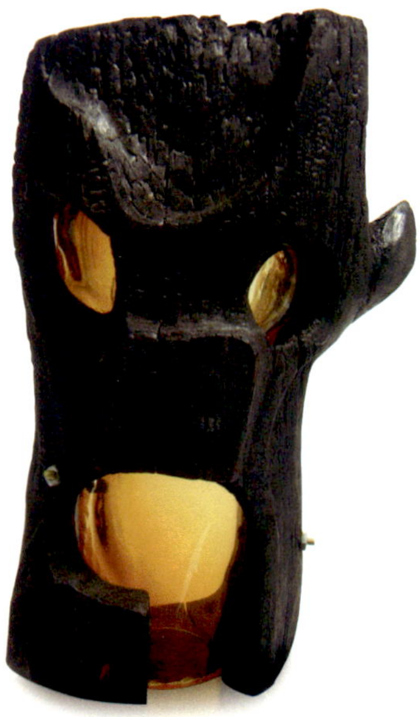

Knucklehead, 2011

Spruce wood, glass, copper wire
12 x 8 x 6 in. (30.5 x 20.3 x 15.2 cm)
Courtesy of the artist

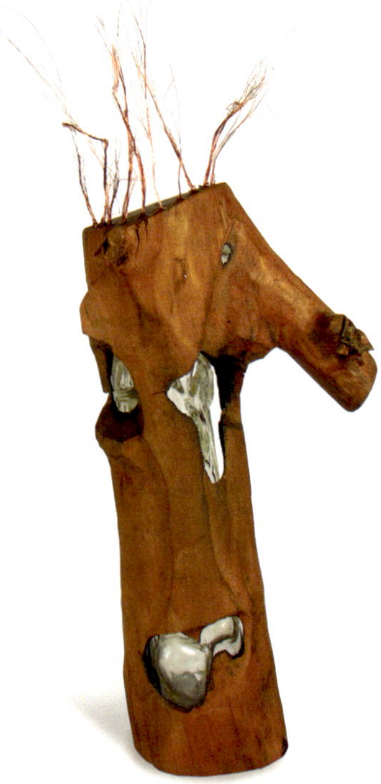

Plum Crazy, 2006

Plum wood, glass, copper wire
15 x 8 x 5 in. (38.1 x 20.3 x 12.7 cm)
Courtesy of the artist

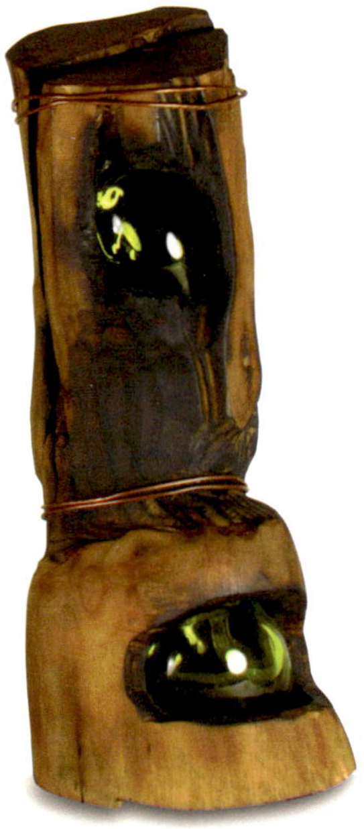

Sour Puss, 2008

Apple wood, glass, copper wire
14 x 5 x 6 in. (35.6 x 12.7 x 15.2 cm)
Courtesy of the artist

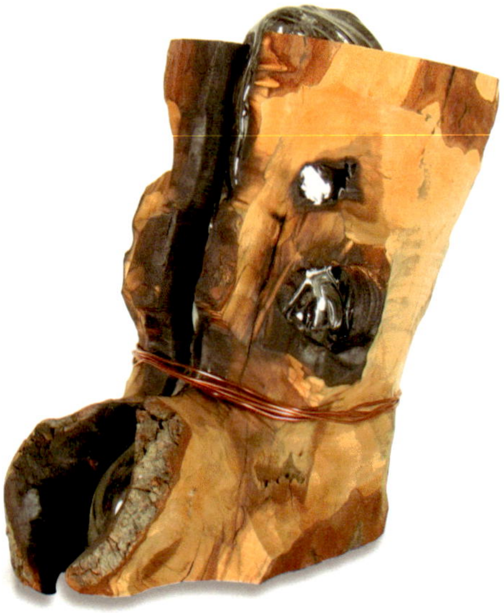

Whistleblower, 2011

Cherry wood, glass, copper wire
12 x 6 x 12 in. (30.5 x 15.2 x 30.5 cm)
Courtesy of the artist

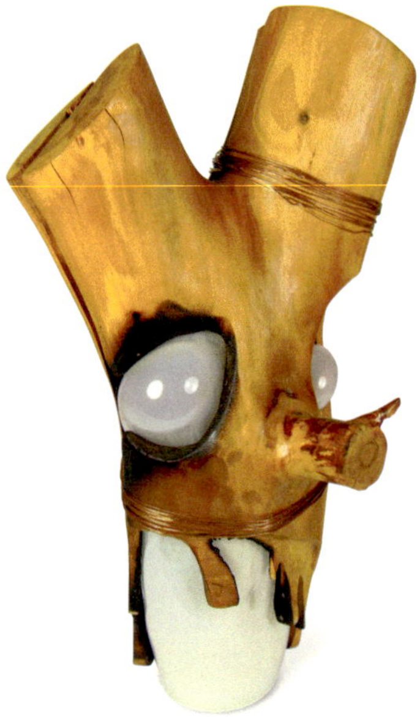

The Heckler, 2005

Plum wood, glass, copper wire
14 x 8 x 6 in. (35.6 x 20.3 x 15.2 cm)
Courtesy of the artist

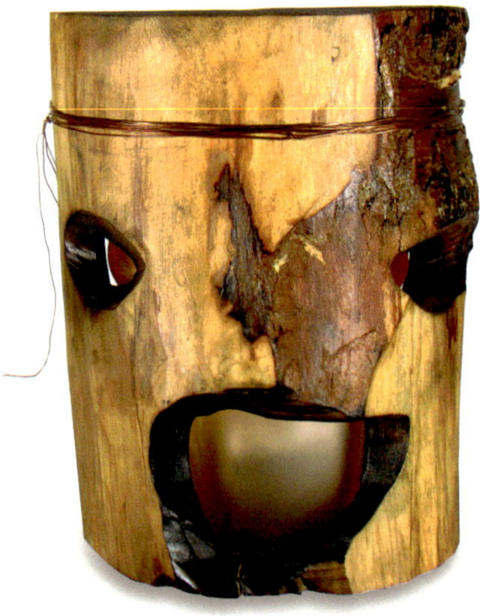

Wise Ass, 2010

Birch wood, glass, copper wire
10 x 8 x 6 in. (25.4 x 20.3 x 15.2 cm)
Courtesy of the artist

SAMUEL THOMAS

b. 1964, Six Nations of the Grand River; lives in Niagara Falls, Ontario

Prophecy II, 2012

14K gold beads, wire, Queenston shale, liquid gold leaf, liquid acrylic, nylon thread
22 x 12 x 10 in. (55.9 x 30.5 x 25.4 cm)
Courtesy of the artist

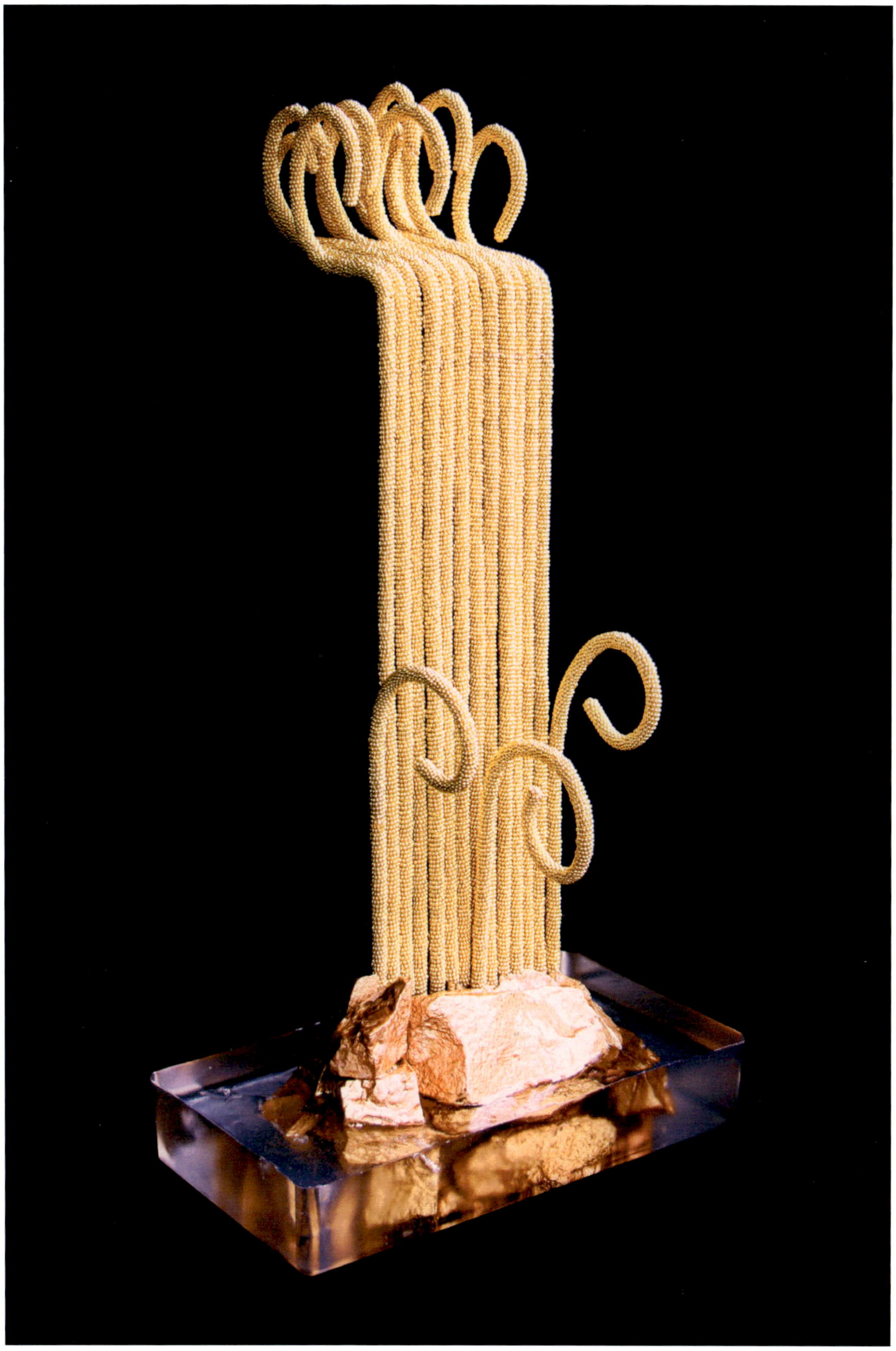

What We See When We Look: Transcending Myths and Stereotypes

JO ORTEL

Native American art made in the twentieth and twenty-first centuries is delightfully rich and diverse, yet the art world continues to marginalize Native American artists. Other artists who once might have been overlooked because of their place of origin or ethnicity are finding increased visibility on the globalized contemporary art scene—Shirin Neshat (Iranian), Rirkit Tiravanija (Thai), Kara Walker (African American), Yinka Shonibare (British Nigerian), and Cai Guo-Qiang (Chinese), to name a few. Why aren't contemporary Native American artists granted the same art-star cachet?

Whether the recent proliferation of large-scale global exhibitions and interest in non-Western artists truly indicates a radical shift in Western attitudes and not simply another form of cultural imperialism is open to question.[1] As theorist Homi Bhabha wrote in 1992, "The globe shrinks for those who own it; for the displaced or the dispossessed, the migrant or refugee, no distance is more awesome than the few feet across borders or frontiers."[2] Still, the absence of Native American artists on this stage is noteworthy.

One reason lies in demographics and, presumably, the law of averages. After all, American Indians comprise only a small portion (roughly one percent) of the U.S. population.[3] One imagines an even smaller percentage of that small population will become artists, and fewer still will rise to prominence. It could be that no Native artist working today has yet "arrived." This explanation deserves serious consideration, though it is not as straightforward as it may appear. Identity is not a simple, uncontested concept. Questions of Native American identity, and who or what determines "Nativeness," are particularly complex. The designation alone obscures the plurality and wide geographic dispersal of the sovereign nations, communities, and groups that the term encompasses.[4] The most sensible approach may be to follow groups' definitions of themselves, but, as critic and art historian Lucy Lippard has written, "There are classes and cultures *within* cultures, not to mention the infinite individual diversities that disprove both external stereotypes and group self-naming alike [emphasis hers]."[5] Consensus about communal identity within any community is never assured.

What's more, the invented Indian of American lore is in many ways more real to most than are Native people of actual existence.[6] Historian James Wilson and others have argued that the Indian of the popular imagination "belongs essentially to the past rather than to the present. He (or she) is an exotic relic of some earlier sate that we have already passed through."[7] To the extent that we hold onto stereotypic images of the Indian rooted in nineteenth-century ideology, living, breathing, twenty-first-century Native Americans seem inauthentic.[8] The effects can be devastating. Speaking strictly in terms of art, it is difficult to imagine the cinematic Indian as a Damien Hirst–like celebrity artist. And if it is difficult to imagine, how much harder will it be to materialize in reality?[9]

Then, too, intractable myths about art and creativity obscure the preconditions for art-world recognition. In the discourses on modernism, for example, and at least since the Romantic era, art transcends its material existence. Correspondingly, the "true" artist is compelled to make art not out of financial need, but out of inner necessity: she or he cannot do otherwise. Further, art is often popularly conceived as the direct personal expression of individual emotional experience; consequently, instruction is not only irrelevant but potentially lethal. These, however, are modern-day constructions, as even a cursory study of medieval or Renaissance art demonstrates. The truth of the matter is that artistic originality and success in the contemporary art world occur mainly within pre-existing parameters.

In 1971, at the height of the Women's Liberation movement, art historian Linda Nochlin wrote a seminal essay entitled "Why Have There Been No Great Women Artists?"[10] Four decades later, her conclusions about the preconditions for artistic achievement, and the ways class, gender, and access to education impact art-world recognition are surprisingly relevant to a discussion about Native American artists' visibility in the contemporary art world. Myths of artistic genius, she observed, minimize the social and institutional structures within which artists live, work, and find success.

Contrary to prevailing myths, art schools and university art programs are places where individuals aspiring to succeed in the art world learn the skills of the trade and, more importantly, absorb the values and priorities of the profession. In her recent ethnographic study of the art world, Sarah Thornton stressed the link between higher education and art-world success. Calling one representative graduate program an incubator "where students transform themselves into artists and learn the vocabulary of their trade,"[11] Thornton went on to write that since the 1960s, "MFA degrees have become the first legitimator in an artist's career, followed by awards and residencies, representation by a primary dealer, reviews and features in art magazines, inclusion in prestigious private collections, museum validation in the form of solo or group shows, international exposure at well-attended biennials. . . . More specifically, MFA degrees from name art schools have become passports of sorts. Look over the résumés of the artists under fifty in any major international museum exhibition and you will find that most of them boast an MFA from one of a couple of dozen highly selective schools."[12]

Until quite recently, there were virtually no Native American artists in these programs. The majority of Native American artists receive art training at the Institute of American Indian Art (IAIA), a federally funded two-year college founded in 1962 in Santa Fe, New Mexico.[13] Because of the spectacular failure in the twentieth century of national policies for American Indian education, Native students did not begin enrolling in "mainstream" institutions of higher learning in appreciable numbers until the late 1960s.[14] What's more, for the first generation of these formally trained artists, passion for art-making found a counterweight in dedication and commitment to education and community: by choice or circumstance, many went on to enter teaching careers in these same colleges, universities, and art schools.[15]

Rather than organizing their lives around the single-minded pursuit of personal fame, they worked to create opportunities for other aspiring artists, including many Native artists they recruited and mentored, who are now embarked on their own careers. Presumably then, if Thornton is correct, we can look forward to greater art-world recognition for Native American artists as the numbers pursuing higher education continue to increase.[16] Certainly, since the publication of Nochlin's essay in 1971, recognition of female artists has improved. A similar path may be ahead of Native American artists in the future.

And yet, neither access to education nor an abundance of talent guarantees an artist star status on the contemporary art scene. Art is made by individuals, but its valuation and visibility depend upon "the dealers, curators, critics, and collectors who 'support' the work."[17] To this list, I would add art historian–educators, myself included. Through even the most guileless choices made when curating or reviewing an exhibit, designing an academic course, or preparing a class lecture, the people on this list *determine* which works receive attention, which are marginalized, and which are passed over altogether.

At a more fundamental level, the way these art-world insiders organize the world through linguistic (and visual) representation is one way cultural values are assigned—and a crucial means by which social positions are continuously produced and policed. For example, what is meant by contemporary Native American art? Does the answer include all modes of cultural production made today by American Indians—arts *and* crafts? For that matter, what is the difference between art and craft? Is one mode intrinsically more vital than the other? According to whom?[18] The terms that are used, like the ideas they describe, are freighted with cultural bias. When the representation has the weight of institutional authority behind it, as in a college classroom or a museum exhibit, its import and influence are magnified.

Personally, I am increasingly uneasy with the courses I teach that segregate art based on the ethnicity of artists, because they perpetuate separateness and difference, a sense that these artists somehow do not belong in the modern, contemporary world. But more and more, I also worry about courses that are organized as overviews of the art of *any* group, in *any* region, at *any* particular time. "Western Art and Visual Culture Since 1300," for example, or "Art in the Twentieth Century": the survey format holds out the false promise of completeness, the reassuring illusion of totality, closure—and a certain sense of inevitability about the works of art and artists included.

Art historians will be familiar with this dilemma; the traditional, introductory art history survey course structure has been under scrutiny since at least the mid-1990s.[19] Here, however, I mean to question the ways that the "mastery" of information and the "acquisition" of knowledge, broadly construed, intersect with the maintenance of margin and center.[20] I am not calling for a prohibition on certain forms of representation in college courses, museum exhibitions, or elsewhere. Change is a process, and each of us begins from a different point of understanding.[21] Nevertheless, real consequences flow from institutional biases and oversights.

The art world is neither as inclusive nor as egalitarian as its moniker might suggest. Insofar as it acts as an intermediary between the artist and the viewer, its role is vital. Yet it is possible to overstate its importance. In thinking about the art world as a gauge of artistic achievement, rather than a means by which art finds a particular audience, it becomes easy to cede one's own critical powers of looking. No one can approach a work of art completely free of cultural baggage, but we can all try to check our biases at the door upon entering the museum, especially when encountering new and unfamiliar work. What is most important is what happens in the space between the work of art and the individual viewer. What do *we* see when we look?

Special thanks to Chris Nelson, Reference Librarian at Beloit College, for tracking information and sources, and to artist Truman Lowe, for providing invaluable feedback. Most especially, thanks to my students for their lively and fearless intelligence.—JO

1 In the 1990s, international biennial and triennial exhibitions proliferated. Western cultural interest seems to flow to those regions that hold promising economic opportunities and/or attractive natural resources. In the early 1990s, it was the former Soviet Union; in the early twenty-first century, it is China and the Middle East. In the period in which land and natural resources were taken from American Indians, European settlers also bought, stole, and collected Native American cultural objects. It may be cynical, but having acquired what was coveted, Westerners may simply have turned their cultural interests elsewhere. One theory holds that "Part of the crippling bias of ethnocentrism in this country comes from the fact that we learn geography mostly from imperialism, discovering other nations when our government chooses to interfere in their sovereignty"; Lucy R. Lippard, *Mixed Blessings: New Art in a Multicultural America* (New York: Pantheon, 1990), 156.

2 Homi K. Bhabha, "Double Visions," *Artforum* 30, no. 5 (1992): 88.

3 USA QuickFacts from the US Census Bureau, http://quickfacts.census.gov/qfd/states/00000.html.

4 Numerous scholars have discussed the fictitious and highly problematic nature of terms and labels associated with Native Americans. For one perspective, see Michael Dorris, "Indians on the Shelf," in *The American Indian and the Problem of History*, ed. Calvin Martin (New York: Oxford University Press, 1987), 98–105. Joane Nagel offers an excellent analysis of a different aspect of Native identity, historical trends pertaining to self-identification and "ethnic switching," in her study, *American Indian Ethnic Renewal: Red Power and the Resurgence of Identity and Culture* (New York and Oxford: Oxford University Press, 1996). Nagel's work raises an interesting question with regard to individual artists who may choose not to identify as Native American precisely to avoid entrenched expectations and assumptions about the art they make. The "Native American artist" was also "legislated" through the 1990 Indian Arts and Crafts Act; see U.S. Department of the Interior, Indian Arts and Crafts Board, http://www.iacb.doi.gov/act.html. Artist Jimmie Durham made

an incisive response: "I am a full-blood contemporary artist, of the sub-group (or clan) called sculptors. I am not an American Indian, nor have I ever seen or sworn loyalty to India. I am not a Native 'American,' nor do I feel that 'America' has any right to either name me or un-name me. . . . I should be considered a mixed-blood: that is, I claim to be a male but in fact only one of my parents was male"; quoted in Margaret Dubin, *Native America Collected: The Culture of an Art World* (Albuquerque: University of New Mexico Press, 2001), 40.

5 Lippard, *Mixed Blessings,* 21. For further discussion of the ongoing debate within the Indian community about what constitutes "Indian Art," see ibid., 184ff; see also Dubin, *Native America Collected.*

6 Robert Berkhofer, quoted in James H. Nottage, "Illusions and Deceptions: The Indian in Popular Culture," in *Powerful Images: Portrayals of Native America* (Seattle: Museums West in association with University of Washington Press, 1998), 75.

7 James Wilson, *The Earth Shall Weep: A History of Native America* (New York: Atlantic Monthly Press, 1999), xxii.

8 Ibid., xxv.

9 The history of anthropology and modern art provides a better understanding of the ways in which disciplinary practices shape and mutually reinforce notions of cultural and ethnic authenticity. For more on this, see esp. James Clifford, "On Collecting Art and Culture," in *The Predicament of Culture: Twentieth-Century Ethnography, Literature, and Art* (Cambridge: Harvard University Press, 1988), 215–51.

10 Linda Nochlin, "Why Have There Been No Great Women Artists?" (1971); reprint in *Art and Sexual Politics*, ed. Thomas B. Hess and Elizabeth C. Baker (New York: Macmillan, 1973), 1–39.

11 Sarah Thornton, *Seven Days in the Art World* (New York and London: W. W. Norton, 2008), xii.

12 Ibid., 45–46.

13 Many IAIA graduates became successful artists in the regional art market of the American Southwest, but this world is significantly different from the "art-world" covered in art journals. Additionally, the IAIA does not grant MFA degrees. There is in fact a separate art press for Native American art, led by *American Indian Art*, a quarterly magazine founded in 1975.

14 Many Native artists received formal art training and/or taught in institutions of higher education before the late 1960s. A small sampling includes Angel DeCora, Oscar Howe, W. Richard West, Sr., George Morrison. Many others dedicated themselves to teaching at the IAIA; these include Allan Houser and Charles Loloma. Joe Herrera received higher education, but did not pursue a teaching career.

15 Among the first generation are George Longfish (MFA, School of the Art Institute of Chicago, 1972), Truman Lowe (MFA, University of Wisconsin-Madison,1973), and Kay WalkingStick (MFA, Pratt Institute of Art, Brooklyn, 1975). Longfish taught at the University of Montana-Missoula and the University of California-Davis, retiring in 2003. Lowe spent most of his teaching career at his alma mater, retiring in 2010. He was curator of contemporary art at the National Museum of the American Indian, Smithsonian Institution (2000–2008). WalkingStick taught art at Cornell University from 1988 to 2005.

16 Tracing the parallel trajectories and effects of the Women's Liberation, Civil Rights, and Red Power movements on art-world practices is the focus of another paper in progress.

17 Thornton, *Seven Days in the Art World,* xiv. Thornton writes that the "collective belief [in an artist or work of art] is neither as simple nor as mysterious as one might imagine."

18 For a trenchant discussion of the hierarchy of the arts, see Rozsika Parker and Griselda Pollock, *Old Mistresses: Women, Art and Ideology* (London: Pandora, 1981).

19 See, for example, "Rethinking the Introductory Art History Survey," special issue, *Art Journal* 54 (Fall 1995), which was guest-edited by Bradford Collins. In 2005, *Art Journal* revisited the topic in an extended roundtable discussion.

20 I have been profoundly influenced by Maori scholar Linda Tuhiwai Smith's analysis of the inextricable link between Western systems of knowledge and European imperialism and colonialism. See, for example, Linda Tuhiwai Smith, *Decolonizing Methodologies: Research and Indigenous Peoples* (London and New York: Zed Books; Dunedin, New Zealand: University of Otago, 1999).

21 Only gradually, through sustained, intensive discussion with students in precisely these settings have I begun to feel the weight of larger ideological structures and my part in their maintenance.

Transformations: A New Era in Contemporary Inuit Art

HEATHER IGLOLIORTE

While artistic production has always figured greatly in Inuit daily life and has arguably been a mainstay of the northern economy since the 1950s, today a vibrant and unprecedented contemporary Inuit art scene is on the rise. Inuit are experiencing a cultural florescence in performance, film, literature, and art. Contemporary drum-dancing and throat-singing groups, and new media collectives have proliferated, while Inuit visual artists in Canadian and Native North American arts milieus are now a pervasive presence. A dynamic current of established Inuit visual artists and a growing pool of emerging talents are transforming the field of artistic production. Whether through the use of man-made materials and found objects or by the inclusion of critical social commentary—each rarely seen in Inuit art until recently—many artists are beginning to express themselves in ever more exciting, thoughtful, and engaging ways.

Through the introduction of daring new subject matter, experimentation with materials and techniques, and the development of individual styles and approaches, these artists are changing the field, challenging the narrow definition of "Inuit art" that has stood for decades. For Inuit artists of the twenty-first century, teapots, television, and motorcycles have become standard subject matter, just as polar bears, traditional camp life, and dog teams were in the last century. One can no longer assume that an "Inuit artist" sculpts only in stone, makes prints, or creates felt and duffel tapestries; precious metals, digital media, and oil or water-based paints are all now viable mediums. Nor is the message of Inuit art as neutral as it once was. While much work is still pictorial or narrative in scope, there is a growing tendency among artists to articulate uniquely Inuit concerns, to critique the world around them and examine their role within it. After nearly a century of prolonged contact between Inuit and Qallunaat (as non-Inuit are known[1]), artists in most Inuit regions of the north have begun to respond to the aggregate impacts of colonization and its lasting legacies in the Arctic through their work. Moreover, Inuit artists are also resisting and critiquing past epistemologies that interpreted Inuit art either as emblematic of nationalist rhetoric or as the subject of modernist/primitivist discourse. In creating works that reflect the autonomy of the artist from a multitude of perspectives—independent of Western theoretical frameworks, the demands of the art market, or expectations of style and subject matter—artists are contributing to the collective efforts of Inuit everywhere to express their cultural sovereignty and right to self-definition.

Inspired by Inuit history and strengthened by the burgeoning independence of the Inuit as self-governing peoples, these bold new works reflect the resilience of Inuit society and continuity of the culture. The precursors of this artistic movement have roots in the contemporary Inuit arts industry of the 1940s, when Inuit across the Northwest Territories and northern Quebec (today Nunavut and Nunavik) began to create large-scale sculptures in stone for a southern Canadian art market, thoroughly shaking up the small-scale ivory miniature and souvenir market in the north. Those first "master" carvers, such as Johnny Inukpuk, Joe Talirunili, and Pauta Saila, followed soon by the early printmakers and later textile artists, used the arts industry to make significant gains in a rapidly collapsing northern economy based on hunting and trapping and under strained colonial relations. Dire societal circumstances notwithstanding—and despite being mediated by government arts instructors, Hudson's Bay Company post managers, and the southern-based Canadian Guild of Crafts—a great modern art of the north emerged. The Inuit of the Arctic garnered esteem from the international modern/primitive art cognoscenti of the mid-century, developing markets and gaining avid collectors especially in Canada and the United States.[2] In the late 1950s an Inuit-owned cooperative movement began in the north with artists' collectives that blossomed into multimillion-dollar organizations.[3]

As early as the 1960s, a few artists tentatively depicted the Inuit and Qallunaat encounters in their art, while a handful of artists experimented with themes that went well beyond the typical fare of Artic wildlife, camp and hunting scenes, or depictions of shamanism. Instead, they focused on the acts of the *angakok* (shaman), such as healing, transformation, flying, and otherwise communing with the spiritual world. Pudlo Pudlat, perhaps the most prominent of these daring innovative artists, combined Inuit transformation iconography with the influx of modern transportation technologies he witnessed in the north, creating colorful, animistic helicopters, biplanes, and watercraft. While most of Pudlat's impressions of Euro-Canadian culture appear whimsical and lighthearted, he also endeavored to broach more serious subject matter, such as spirituality and religious syncretism.[4]

In the 1970s and 80s frontrunners in the graphic arts such as Napachie Pootoogook and Kananginak Pootoogook based their work on community history and autobiography, depicting the experience and impact of transcultural encounters. Interestingly, both artists became famous for their more "traditional" subject matter—Kanaginak for his lyrical bird and animal prints, and Napachie for her scenes of camp life—while creating a tandem corpus of drawings that critiqued the impacts of colonization in the north. Both artists were also celebrated later in life for their frank illustrations of events such as run-ins with police and other "officials," the introduction of alcohol and other vices to northern communities, and encounters with tourists, photojournalists, and art dealers.

By the 1980s and 90s, sculptural artists had also begun reflecting on life in the north during a critical period of transition. In *This Has Touched My Life* (1991–92), Oviloo Tunnillie was inspired by a formative experience in her childhood, when she was removed from her home to be treated for tuberculosis in a southern Canada sanatorium.[5] Likewise, Tunnillie's

Woman with Ruler (1996), a stone sculpture of a nun bent over in a menacing manner, with one hand over her mouth and the other concealing a long ruler behind her back, recalls the threat of punishment Inuit children faced for speaking their language or acting out in church-run classrooms and residential schools. Yet Tunnillie's art was also positively influenced by contact with the Western world. She frequently sculpts nudes, armless torsos, and busts in soapstone and serpentine and has referenced figures such as football players, women in high-heeled shoes, and ballet dancers. Similarly, senior Ivujivik artist Mattiusi Iyaituk has been long admired for his works that examine daily life, both as a hunter in the Arctic territory of Nunavik and as a globetrotting artist of international renown. Iyaituk has been long celebrated for his ingenious use of abstraction, and his mixed-media works often narrate moments out of his life, such as in *Unforgettable Fantastic Feeling my Wife Qumaq and I Experienced Being Near a 400-foot High Iceberg in Sisimiut, Greenland* (2011). Other exciting contemporaries of Iyaituk and Tunnillie include sculptural artists include Nick Sikkuark, Gilbert Hay, John Terriak, and Manasie Akpaliapik.[6]

In addition to examining issues of transculturation, many artists in the last decades of the twentieth century began to develop a new visual language, which set them apart from their peers. Brothers David Ruben Piqtoukun and Abraham Anghik Ruben from the Inuvialuit Settlement Region of the Northwest Territories have each articulated a style and technique so divergent from the norm that their work bears little resemblance to that of other Inuit artists. Piqtoukun has recently branched off into large-scale, abstract metal works, while Ruben focuses on the histories and mythologies of ancient Inuit and Viking-Norse explorers, who are believed to have made contact a millennia ago. Stone and mixed-media artist Michael Massie is also celebrated for his unique vision. Massie began his career as a professionally trained metalsmith, creating fanciful teapots and sculptural vessels such as *may-tea* (1991)—a play on "Métis"[7]—and *I'm a little teapot* (2001). Today he works across a wide expanse of media including stones, precious metals, and exotic woods, and his subject matter ranges from the narrative (*grandfather, I have something to tell you*, 2004; *they dressed for the occasion*, 2011) to transformation-based figures and animals (*a momentary lapse in transformation*, 2002). However, he never strays far from his longtime muse, tea and its significance within Inuit culture, finding ever-inspiring and amusing ways to reinvent his subject matter, from the surrealist, Dali-inspired *enigmas of a teapot* (2002) to his continuing love of puns and witticisms, as in *pompositea* (2011).

Throughout the contemporary arts movement, women artists have experimented with and expanded the definition of "wall-hanging," an art form traversing the boundary between two-dimensional and three-dimensional form and confounding the Western dialectic of art/craft. Irene Avaalaaqiaq was among the earliest artists of this medium to gain popular recognition—along with Baker Lake artists Jessie Oonark, Victoria Mamnguqsualuk, and Sarah Inukpuk. Avaalaaqiaq's stark red and yellow on black felt images of demons, spirits, animals, and faces have become iconic within the genre. Today embroidered and appliquéd works make up a small but significant part of contemporary Inuit art, and those artists who practice it, such as Eva Ikinilik, Ruth Qaulluaryuk, and Janet Nungnik, are recognized for their incredible vision and exquisite craftsmanship. Nungnik's piece (*Untitled*, 2005) daringly incorporates Hudson's Bay blanket iconography and Eskimo Identification Disc numbers, making a provocative statement on intercultural encounters.[8] Outside the Baker Lake region, Nunatsiavut artist Shirley Moorhouse is another wall-hanging artist, but one who has departed from working solely in textiles. She incorporates beads, wire, keys, and other objects into her postmodern wall-hangings and uses grounds made of such diverse materials as stroud (coarse wool), canvas, and even layers of wire screen-door mesh. Likewise, the Rankin Inlet ceramics project of the 1960s introduced an exciting new medium into the expanding field of Inuit artistic production. In the late 1980s and early 1990s the program was revived by the Matchbox Gallery in Rankin Inlet, and today virtuoso young artists like John Kurok, Jack Nuviyak, and Leo Napayok work alongside senior ceramicist Yvo Samgushak, producing both traditional ceramic vessels and sculptural forms in clay.

The experimentation and social commentary by the early generation of artists have been taken up by today's emerging and mid-career artists. They share a number of innovative perspectives on the transformation of the north. Several prominent new artists evince an even greater awareness (and skepticism) of Quallunaat influences and often demonstrate a new identity that reflects their contemporary reality. By fostering self-definition and facilitating a north–south dialogue on the reality of life in the Arctic, Inuit artists today express with increasing clarity a unique worldview that includes the whole of Inuit experience, not just the traditions and practices of the past.

Bolstered by increasing social, political, and economic independence, Inuit artists openly debate the entanglements of nearly a century of contact, colonization, and religious conversion. Kinngait (Cape Dorset) graphic artists Shuvinai Ashoona and her cousin Annie Pootoogook have established international reputations.[9] Pootoogook presents a courageous and sensitive view of the colonial legacy, the attendant substance abuse, and women's rights, as well as making subtle commentary on the insidious influence of trashy television like *The Jerry Springer Show* and sensational newscasts. Ashoona creates fantastic and grotesque drawings of surrealist spaces and images in the Arctic. Other graphic artists of note include Toonoo Sharkey, Arnaqu Ashevak, and Jutai Toonoo. Like many artists working in two-dimensional forms, Toonoo is not only a talented printmaker but also a gifted sculptor, whose introspective oeuvre often examines themes of the self in relation to religion, spirituality, and interpersonal relationships. Jutai's younger brother Samonie Toonoo, a talented sculptor in his own right, began by carving naturalistic forms but has recently introduced works that explore the possibilities of abstraction as well as issues of social critique. Also in the sculptural arts, impressive new talents include Floyd Kuptana, who works within traditional themes yet frequently comments on climate change and environmental issues in his work; Adam Alorut, whose fantastic amalgams of Inuit mythology and Christian demons are both beautiful and grotesque; and jewelry, metalwork, and carving artist Ruben Anton Komangapik (fig. 1), whose challenging pieces reflect both a prodigious talent and a fearless approach to medium and subject matter.

At the opposite end of the spectrum but equally groundbreaking for their style and technical skill are the young Inuit sculptors Billy Gauthier and Jamasie Pitseolak. Gauthier and Pitseolak create highly detailed and complex work, yet of divergent subject matter. Gauthier's intricate, mixed-media sculptural works often feature delicate lines, miniscule details, and an almost unimaginable precision. He chooses to work with "traditional" materials such as soapstone, bone, and antler, and to create scenes populated by Arctic animals or to visualize the pre-contact way of life. Gauthier pushes the materials to their limits and finds surprising ways to finish the work, melding the disparate elements into a cohesive whole. Similarly, Pitseolak is a master craftsman who sculpts in stone and incorporates natural materials into his art, clearly working within a contemporary carving tradition but taking a very different approach to his choice of subject. His childhood fascination with motorcycles may explain his predilection for modern machinery in his work—sewing machines, cars, guitars, and his famed "Choppers."[10] Rather than carving away to a finished product, Pitseolak is one of the few stone sculptors who creates and assembles his pieces, choosing to work extensively with inlay and tiny pegs and frequently employing experimental techniques. Many of his pieces have moving parts: wheels that spin and handlebars that turn. This kind of assiduousness and attention to detail—in some ways predicated on a respectful disregard for expectations or art market demands—has led to success for Gauthier and Pitseolak in this new phase of contemporary Inuit art.

In an era of globalization, Inuit artists have begun to question why "Inuit art" has been so narrowly defined in the past. Why should the arts of a culture be known primarily by its recognizable iconography or a through a limited visual language? As artist Michael Massie said in his 2006 catalogue, *Silver and Stone*, "I wish people would focus on the art in 'Inuit art.' Art can be anything and that is true of Inuit art as well. It isn't limited to hunks of stone or prints. That's why I call myself a contemporary Inuit artist."[11] This new approach to Inuit art, which reflects the multitude of Inuit experience in the contemporary world, is just beginning to gain recognition and acceptance in the artistic community and global art market. The movement toward aesthetic independence and artistic self-definition today allows for "the Indigenous visual voice to become a critical and social tool for critiquing and negotiating the boundaries imposed by the Western canon."[12] These practices foster and support Inuit efforts toward cultural sovereignty and self-determination in the twenty-first century, and indicate an exciting future in this new era of contemporary Inuit art.

---

1 Qallunaat is the Inuit name given to Europeans and later to Euro-Canadians and other non-Inuit that came to the Arctic. Interestingly, the word does not translate to "light skinned people" or "strangers" as one might expect, but rather, it could mean either "people with beautiful eyebrows" or "people with beautiful manufactured material." Minnie Aodla Freeman, introduction to Odette Leroux, ed., *Inuit Women Artists: Voices from Cape Dorset* (Gatineau: Canadian Museum of Civilization, 1995), 15–16.

2 Heather Igloliorte, "Sanajatsarq: Reactions, Productions, and the Transformation of Promotional Practice," *Inuit Art Quarterly* 11, no. 4 (Winter 2007): 30–36.

3 Marybelle Mitchell, *From Talking Chiefs to Native Corporate Elite: The Birth of Class and Nationalism Among Canadian Inuit* (Toronto: McGill – Queens Press, 1996).

4 Jennifer Gibson, "Christianity, Syncretism, and Inuit Art in the Central Canadian Arctic," master's thesis, Carleton University, Ottawa, 1998.

5 The disease, which devastated many northern communities in the mid-twentieth century, often led to people who tested positive being sent away, sometimes without their consent or notice to their families. It continues to be an issue today, as infection rates in Nunavut are reported at 185 times greater than elsewhere in Canada. Canada's four main Inuit regions have a TB incidence rate of 157.5 for every 100,000 people, according to the first national analysis of 2008 data by the Public Health Agency of Canada. The rate in southern Canada is 0.8 per 100,000. The problem is exacerbated by overcrowded living conditions, substandard housing, and poor food security.

6 In 1991, Akpaliapik created his groundbreaking work, *Untitled* (1991), a commentary on substance abuse, depicting a beer bottle emerging from a shattered skull. It brought him national attention—he was on the cover of *Inuit Art Quarterly* (Winter 1993)—and it made him a standard-bearer of the avant-garde in contemporary Inuit art. The work remains exemplary for its directness.

7 Massie has part-Inuit, part-settler ancestry going back several generations on the coast of Labrador. In Nunatsiavut (northern Labrador), those who intermarried and their descendants were known as "Labrador Métis" after the Métis peoples of southern Canada, who are of First Nations and settler descent. Today, the Labrador Métis are known as the NunatuKavut and have their own land claims organization in Labrador.

8 Eskimo Identification Tags—also known as E-numbers, Disc numbers, and Eskimo Tags—were developed by the government of Canada in the 1940s and 50s as a means of identifying Inuit and for census purposes. Inuit of the central Canadian Arctic traditionally had a single name, which created confusion for government officials and census developers, especially if Inuit were identified as having the same name as another community member. Furthermore, Inuit names were considered difficult to write and pronounce. The Eskimo Identification Tag system allowed the government to classify, record, and number the Inuit. Inuit people either wore or had to memorize their Eskimo Identification number. Inuit even signed their names with their numbers, and Inuit artists often carved their numbers, instead of their names, into stone sculptures. This practice of identifying Inuit by their number continued until 1969, when government officials decided that the E-number system was not working and instituted Project Surname instead (which had its own problems and challenges). Nunatsiavut photographic artist Barry Pottle also recently addressed the Eskimo Identification Tag system in his *Awareness Series* (2009–11).

9 Like many avant-garde Inuit artists, Shuvinai Ashoona and Annie Pootoogook are heirs to an artistic legacy going back through several generations in their family. The women are granddaughters to acclaimed first-generation artist Pitseolak Ashoona, and niece and daughter (respectively) of Napachie Pootoogook.

10 Jamasie described the origins of this fascination in a 2008 interview with Norman Vorano: "When my mother moved to Kimmirut, we had family there and one day I was visiting a cousin and he had a battery-operated motorcycle. I really liked it; that was almost 30 years ago. I really liked it so I kept visiting him. Come Christmas, his mother decided that I should have it." Norman Vorano, "Jamasie Pitseolak: Coming from Today," *Inuit Art Quarterly* 23, no. 1 (Spring 2008): 10–16.

11 Gloria Hickey, *Silver & Stone: The Art of Michael Massie* (St. John's: Rooms Provincial Art Gallery, 2006).

12 Ryan Rice, "Defining Moment: What is Contemporary (NATIVE) Art?" in this volume.

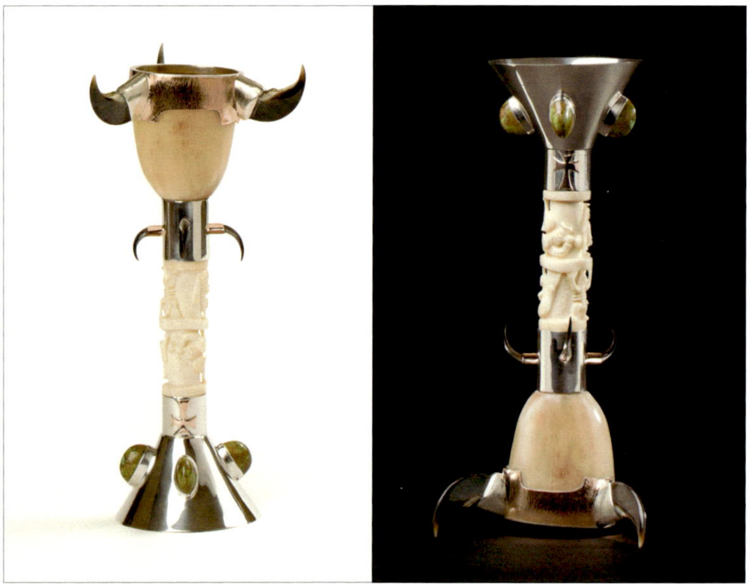

Fig. 1. Ruben Anton Komangapik. *S.I.N.S. (Shamanism Is Not Satanism)*, 2010 (not included in exhibition). Sterling silver, gaspeite, 14K red gold, ivory, horn, animal claws. 11 x 3 ¾ x 4 in. (27.9 x 9.5 x 10.2 cm). Courtesy of the artist

Notes on the Critical Practice of Native American Art

LIBBY LUMPKIN

Over the last two decades, Western avant-garde practices have been adopted so widely that they have come to constitute a universal language of contemporary art. The formal aspects of critique, which originate with French Modernism and incorporate ever-evolving varieties of styles and techniques, have come to be embraced by a global generation of artists of diverse ethnicities. Many of those working in non-Western countries do so in the face of rigid enforcement of cultural, political, and religious conformity, and too often, suffer confinement or exile. This reality is troubling in liberal North America, where many of the experimental and innovative practices adopted by the international art community were developed, and where the idea of artistic freedom is not merely taken for granted, but is exalted. It is thus all the more ironic that North America's Native artists find themselves hemmed in by a pervasive, sentimental cultural discourse that hinders their ability to speak in the contemporary visual language of dissent.

Progressive Native American artists enjoy the same freedoms of expression as all other North American artists, at least in terms of public policy and the law. Where public reception is concerned, however, invisible fences enclose them in ways that affect no other ethnic group. For the North American cultural mainstream, and too many art-world sophisticates, a critically informed contemporary Native American art is usually as welcome a prospect as Indian casinos; it is perfectly legal and fully engaging, but represents the dissolution of nationally cherished ideas of Native traditions. To North American and Native mainstream cultures, Native progressive art feels, and looks, like assimilation.

In essence, Native American artists find themselves bound by a pervasive desire to preserve Native American cultures, and Native creative productions, in their original forms. For Indigenous peoples, conformity to tradition is an enduring cause born out of the epic struggle against the official U.S. and Canadian assimilation policies of the nineteenth and early twentieth centuries that were designed to divorce "savage Indians" from their religions, languages, and traditional ways of life and, through education, to convert them to Christianity and "civilized" Western-style customs and commerce. For non-Native Americans, preservation sentiment stems less from inherited guilt, than the desire to create for themselves a myth of American freedom tied to American soil. Distressed by urban-industrial growth and divorced from democratic national origins, they created a new model of freedom as an idyllic Native American way of life on the pre-contact American continent. With Native American cultures benignly "protected" from Euro-American sins, their virtues and wisdom were taken to heart and appropriated as the heritage of all American citizens—a kind of assimilation in reverse.

Consequently, the sentiment of preservation fostered by the new concept of freedom casts a pall over progressive Native American artists, whose critical practices have the power to challenge cultural constructs. At the same time, it burnishes to a high sheen the Native American artisanal industry, which constitutes the vast majority of Native art production. The idea that the bowls, baskets, jewelry, weavings, and thematic paintings and sculptures constitute a direct link to pre-contact American cultures—and to the idyllic way of life they purportedly enjoyed—has wrapped a cozy blanket around handcraft-based industries. The growth of modern Pueblo crafts, in particular, has benefited enormously from this rhetoric despite the fact that this industry's origin is clouded by assimilation controversy. In the1930s, Pueblo handcrafts were promoted by many artists, writers, anthropologists, and social activists who settled in Taos and Santa Fe, and who embraced European-style notions of primitivist aesthetics. The structure of the industry was based on British and American Arts and Crafts models. The forms, themes, and styles of the works produced by Pueblo artists were heavily influenced by Anglo-American art instructor Dorothy Dunn and her followers at the Santa Fe Indian School. Dunn herself arbitrated the "authenticity" of the students' expressions of ethnic traditions, and her classes produced some of the industry's earliest masters. The commercial market for Native arts and craft then, as today, was made up primarily of non-Native collectors and tourists. This history of the industry has lately been the subject of considerable academic criticism, and, as early as the 1960s, the debate prompted Native Americans in Santa Fe to take control of the ways in which their artists are schooled.

Although the rhetoric of freedom that surrounds Native American art, craft, and, design in the twenty-first century boosts its popularity with mainstream consumers, it greatly diminishes the industry's reputation within the global art community. Native art may not embody untainted continuity with pre-contact Native cultures, but, taken as a whole, it effectively promotes the idea of ethnic integrity. This idea needed to be fortified—and marketed externally—as Native Americans struggled to emerge from the earlier periods of assimilation policies, and it remains a salient message for a contemporary minority culture still dealing with the long-term effects of conquest and abuse.

As the works in earlier installments of the *Changing Hands: Art Without Reservation* amply demonstrate, the evolution of the Native artisanal industry since the 1930s is studded with brilliant moments of innovation and insight. When this industry is taken for what it is—a unique, enduring, and economically successful nonutilitarian design arts industry—its luster shines the brightest. Unencumbered by the rhetoric of freedom and authenticity, this industry weathers ideological scrutiny unscathed, and the abyss that separates progressive and traditional Native art practices narrows dramatically.

That distance, however, will never be entirely bridged. A practice that criticizes policies and rhetoric, whether imposed

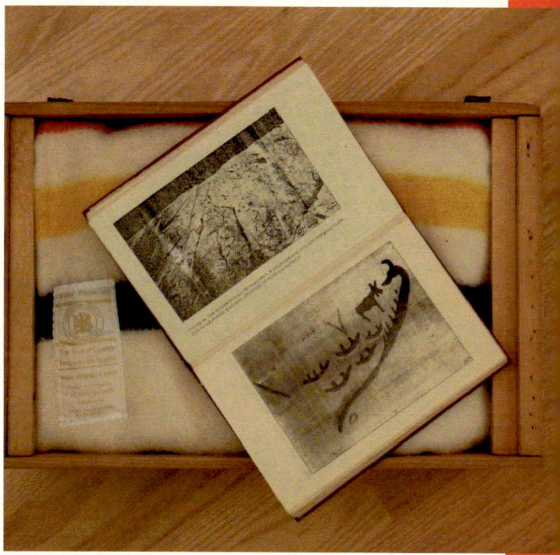

HISTORICAL PROVOCATION/ DECODING HISTORY

The works presented in the section "Historical Provocation/Decoding History" are often politically nuanced to contrast the realities of Indigenous history with the mythology of cultural assimilation that has marginalized much Indigenous art. A number of the artists examine issues of cultural identity through the lens of contemporary societal and political values and imperatives. Other artists have focused their creative energy on communicating intensely personal narratives and autobiographies based on the hopes, dreams, fears, and angst of growing up as an Indigenous individual in a pluralistic culture. Gender roles and stereotypes, sexual diversity, and the power relationships that they manifest are addressed in these works, as well as the inescapable pressures of contemporary life in realms such as communications and new technologies. Finally, many of the works are presented with an unmistakable sensitivity to the pervasive power of wit and humor. Overall, the works in this section record, but also expand and challenge, the definition of what is means to be a contemporary human being.

JORDAN A. BENNETT

b. 1986, Stephenville Crossing, Newfoundland; lives in Corner Brook, Newfoundland and Labrador

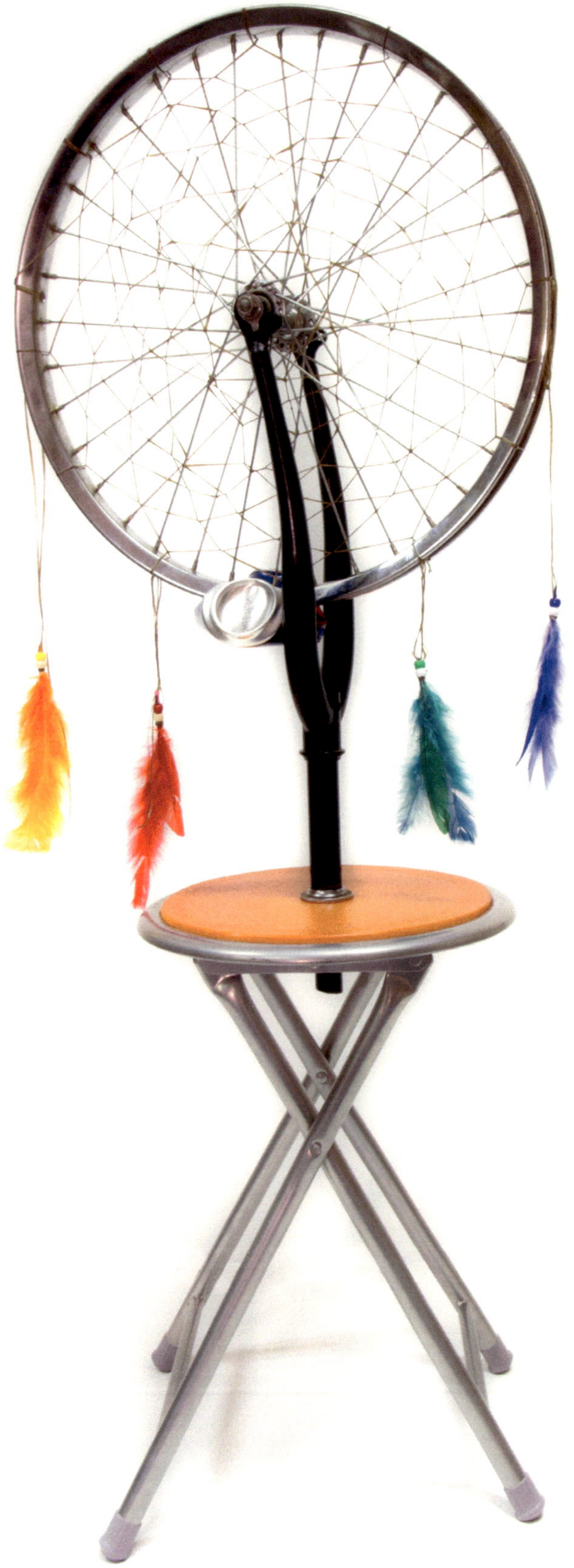

Re:Appropriating the Wheel, 2012

Mixed media, including found objects and audio
43 x 17 x 12 in. (109.2 x 43.2 x 30.5 cm)
Courtesy of the artist

KATSITSIONNI FOX

b. 1968, Sudbury, Ontario;
lives in Akwesasne, New York

Two Row Wampum, 2010

(in collaboration with Edward Burnam Jr.)
Encaustic on panel, video projection
Dimensions variable
Courtesy of Edward Burnam Jr.

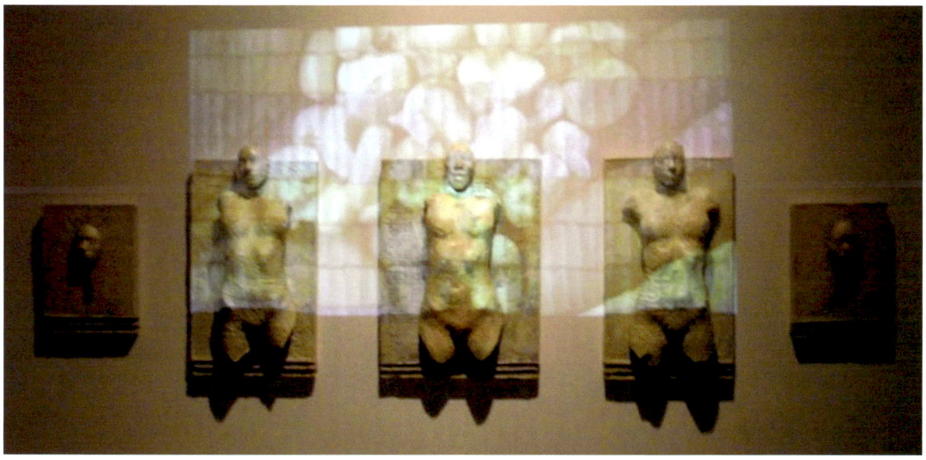

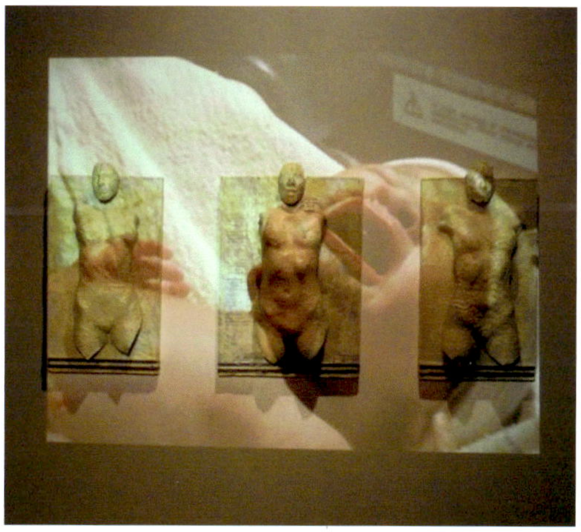

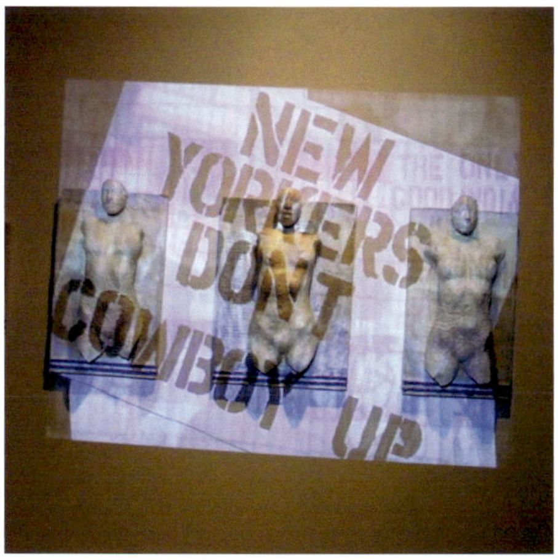

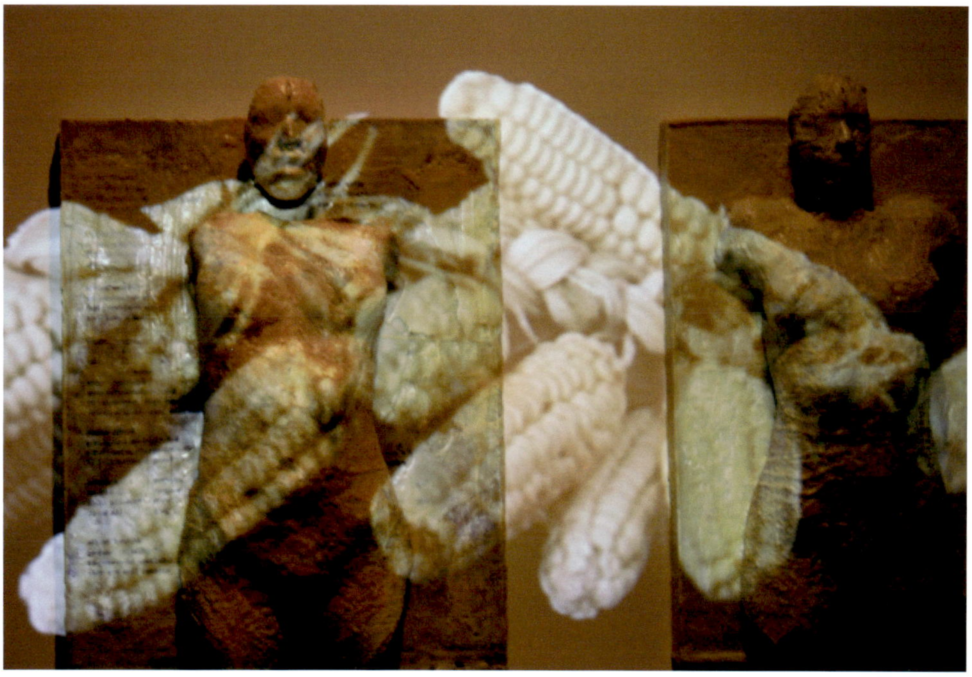

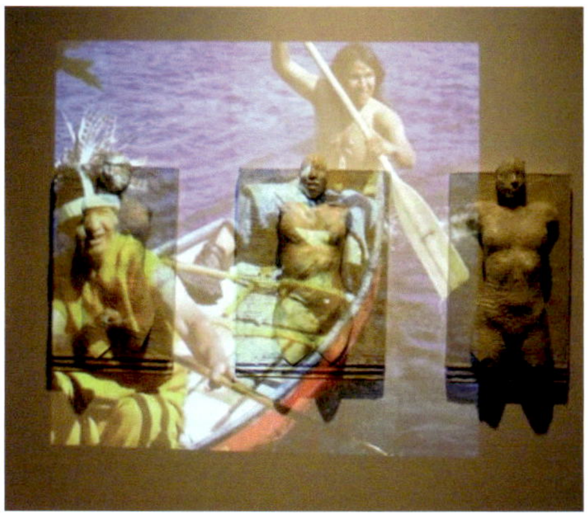

BILLY GAUTHIER

b. 1978, Happy Valley–Goose Bay, Labrador; lives in North West River, Labrador

Northern Fridgidaire Diet, 2012

Moose antler, serpentine, horn, ink
3 ½ x 3 x 3 in. (8.9 x 7.6 x 7.6 cm)
Courtesy of Spirit Wrestler Gallery, Vancouver, British Columbia

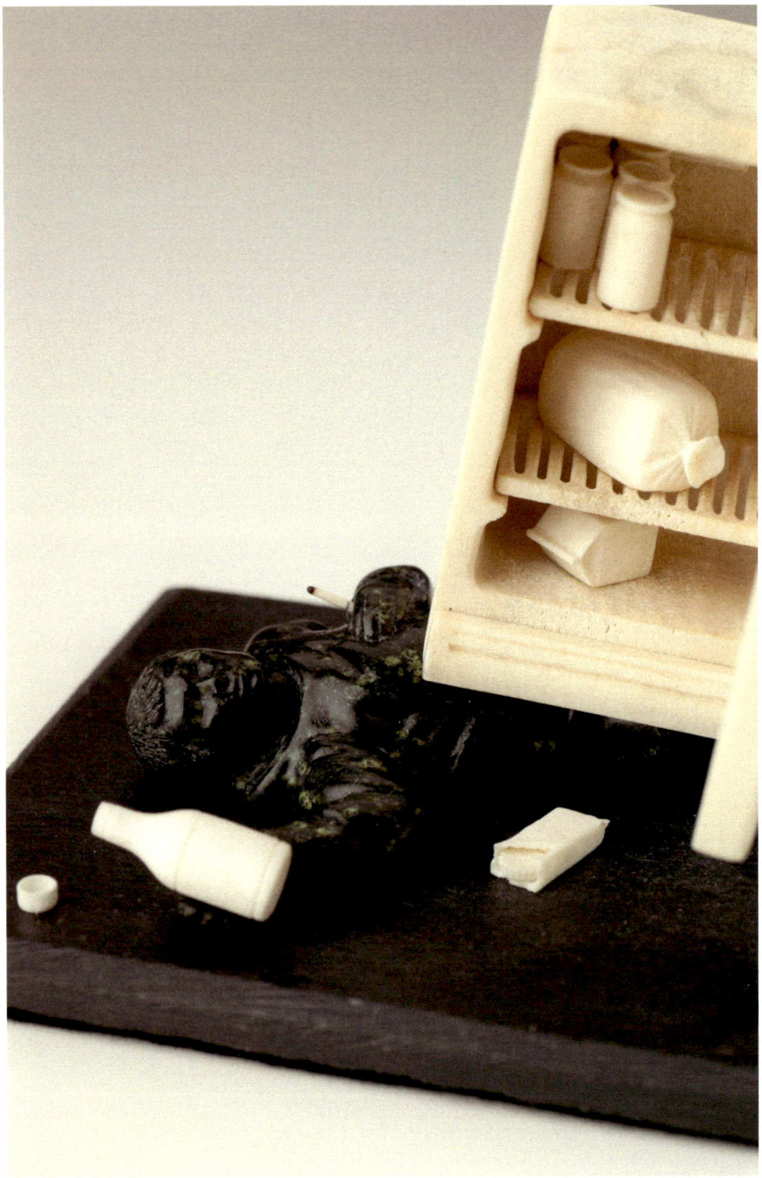

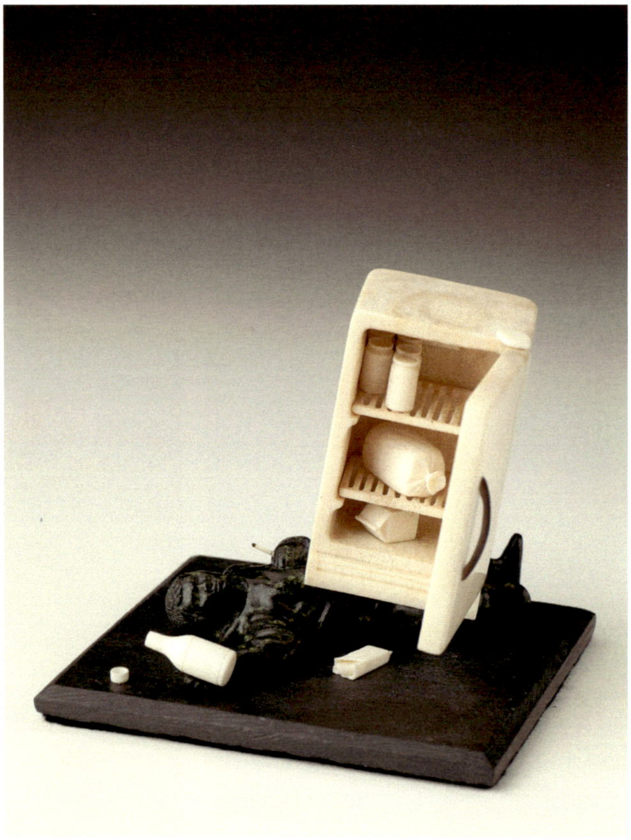

JEFFREY GIBSON

b. 1972, Colorado Springs, Colorado; lives in Brooklyn, New York

Everlast, 2011–12

Wool, canvas, steel, acrylic paint, glass beads, artificial sinew, tin jingles
Ht. 68 in. (172.7 cm); diam. 14 in. (35.6 cm)
Courtesy of the artist; American Contemporary, New York; Samsøn Projects, Boston

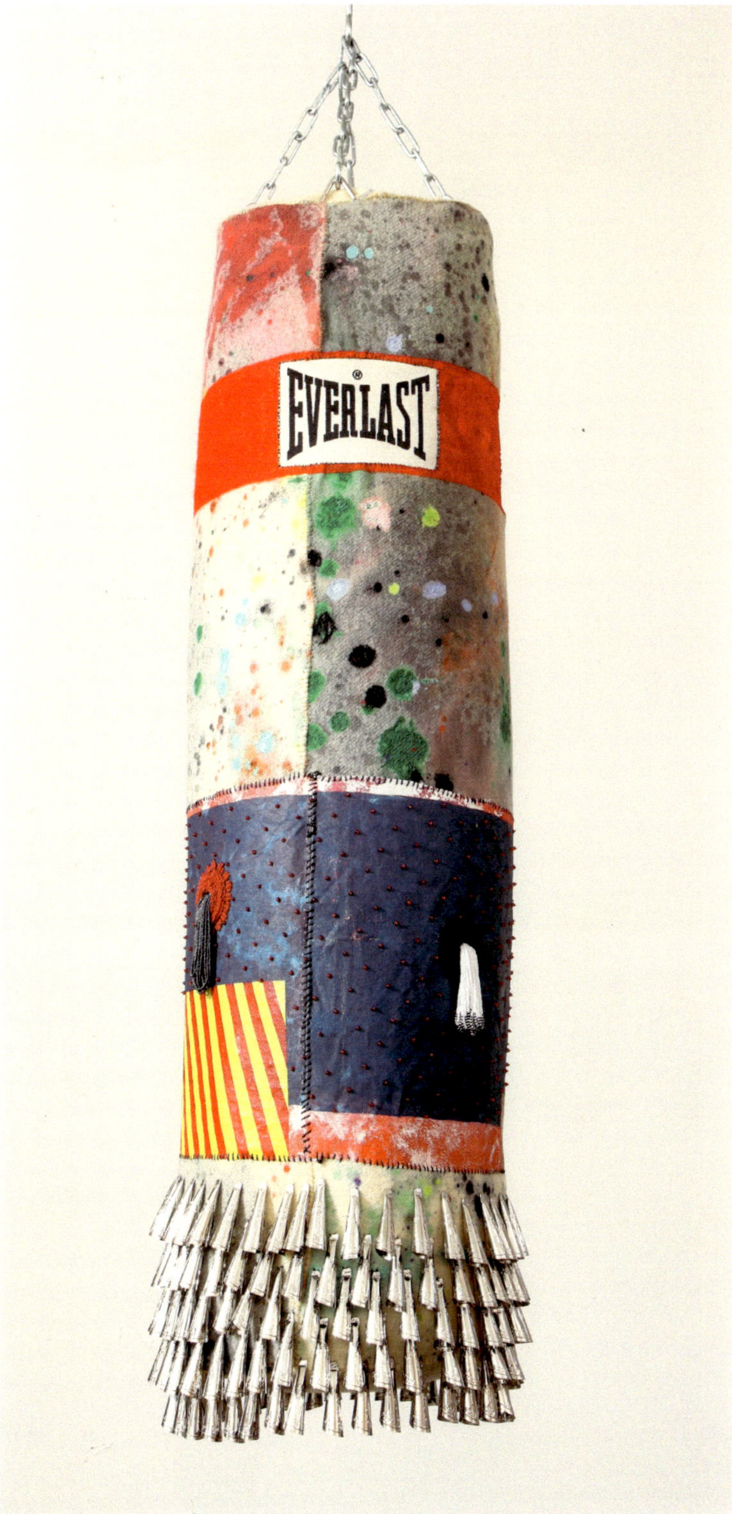

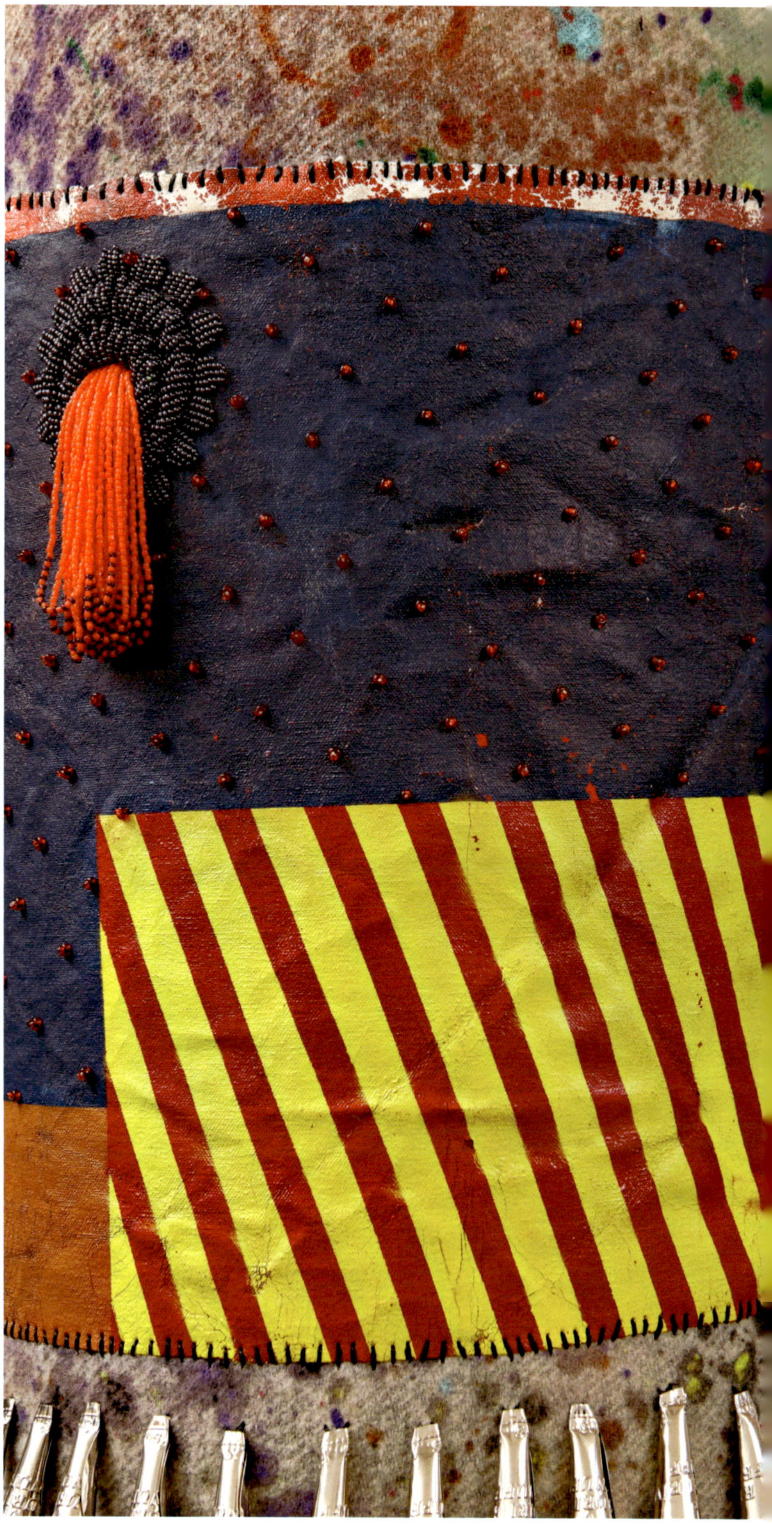

RICHARD GLAZER-DANAY

b. 1942, Coney Island, New York;
lives in Corona, California

Crazy Horse War Bonnet, 2009

Hard hat, mixed media
12 ½ x 10 ¼ x 17 in.
(31.8 x 26 x 43.2 cm)
Courtesy of the artist

Foxwoods War Bonnet, 2008

Hard hat, mixed media
11 ¾ x 9 x 12 ¾ in.
(29.8 x 22.9 x 32.4 cm)
Courtesy of the artist

Lincoln Hard Hat, 2007

Hard hat, mixed media
Approx. 11 x 9 x 12 in.
(27.9 x 22.9 x 30.5 cm)
Collection of Dr. Gerald Fecht;
courtesy of the artist

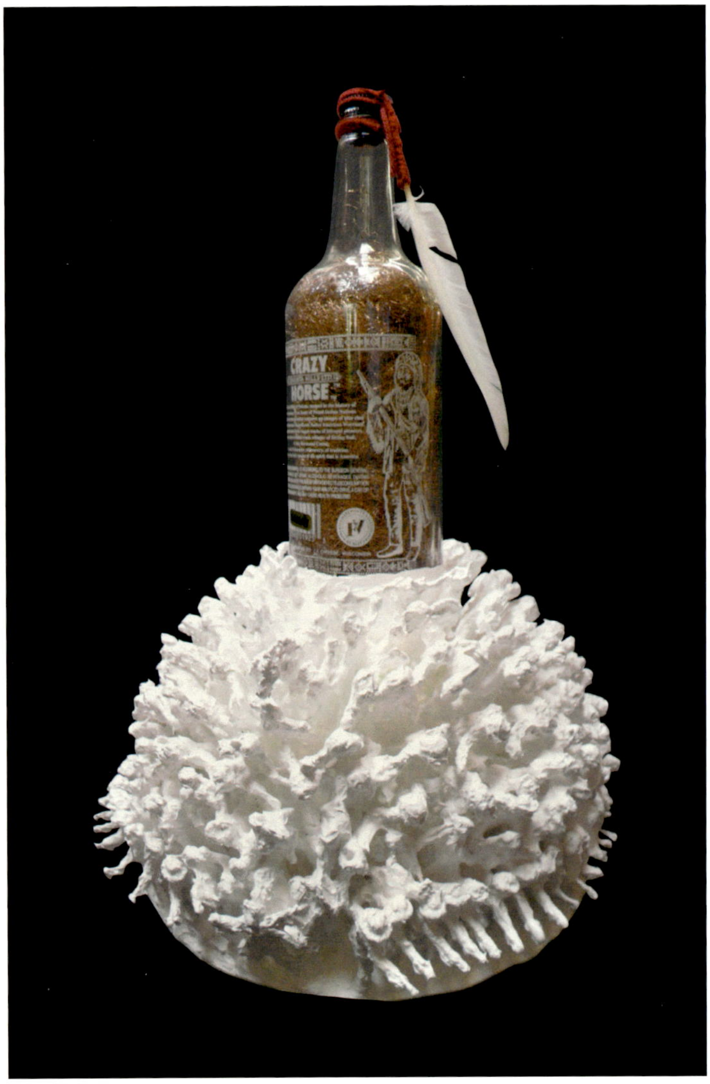

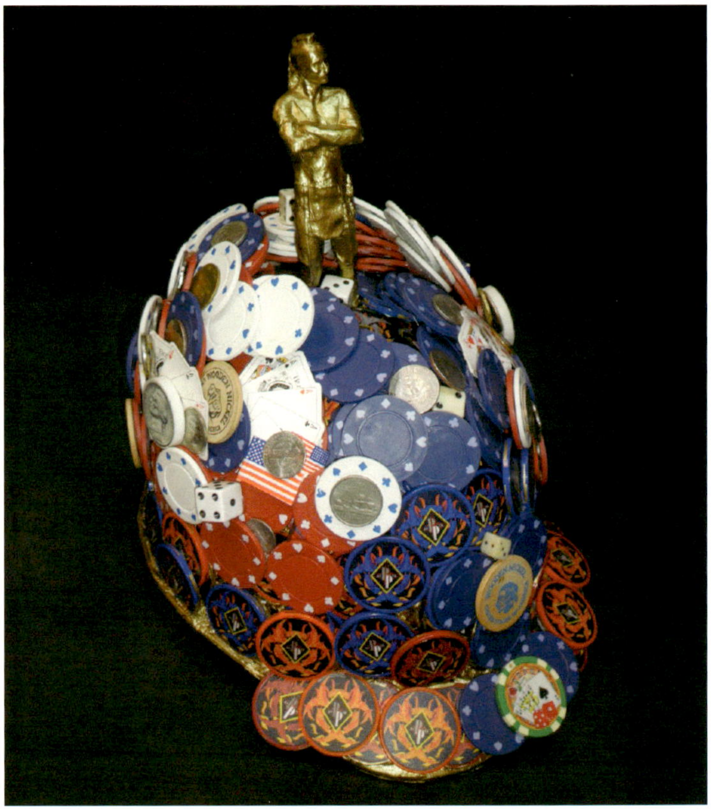

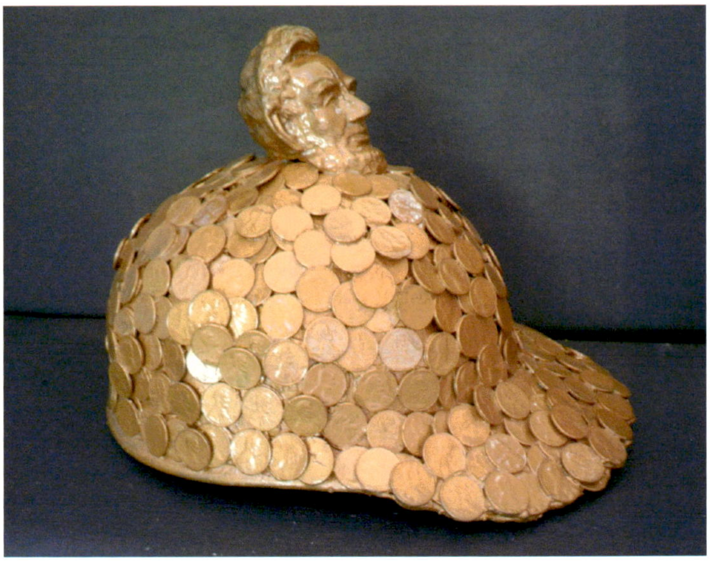

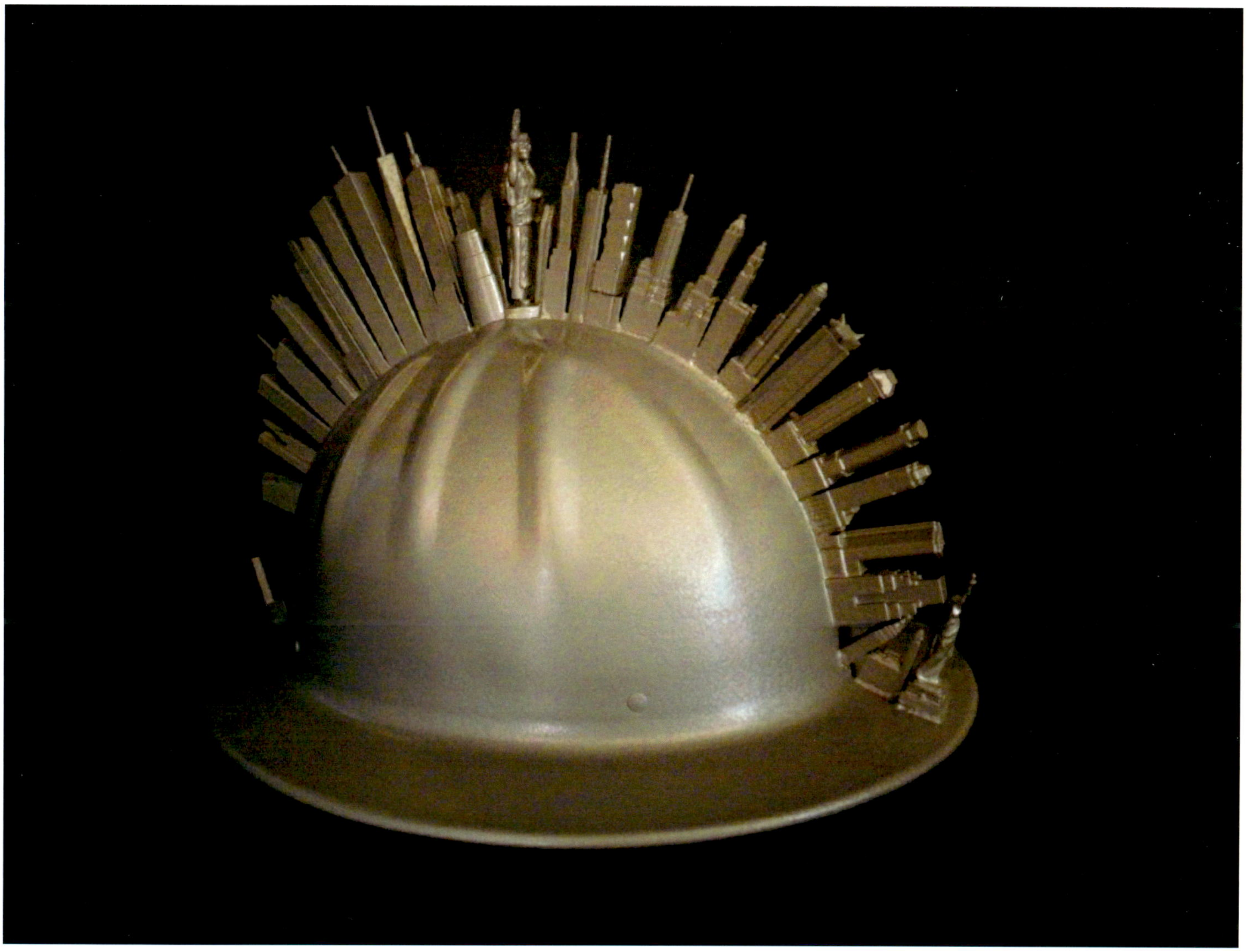

Mohawk Headdress for NYC, 2011

Hard hat, mixed media
9 x 11 ¾ x 12 ½ in.
(22.9 x 29.8 x 31.8 cm)
Courtesy of the artist

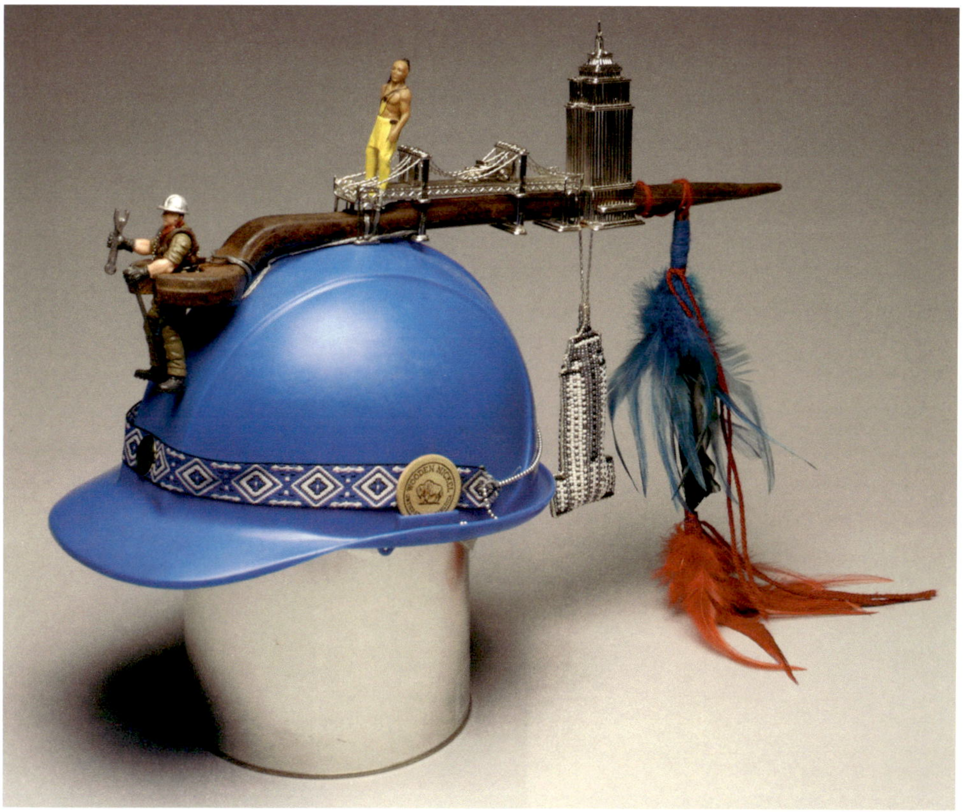

Mohawk Worker's Headdress, 2007

Hard hat, mixed media
18 ⅛ x 15 ⅜ in. (46 x 39 cm)
Courtesy of the Woodland Cultural Centre,
Brantford, Ontario

SHAN GOSHORN

b. 1957, Baltimore, Maryland;
lives in Tulsa, Oklahoma

Educational Genocide: The Legacy of the Carlisle Indian Boarding School, 2011 (details, opposite)

Wood pulp splints, archival commercial ink
12 x 20 x 12 in. (30.5 x 50.8 x 30.5 cm)
Courtesy of the artist

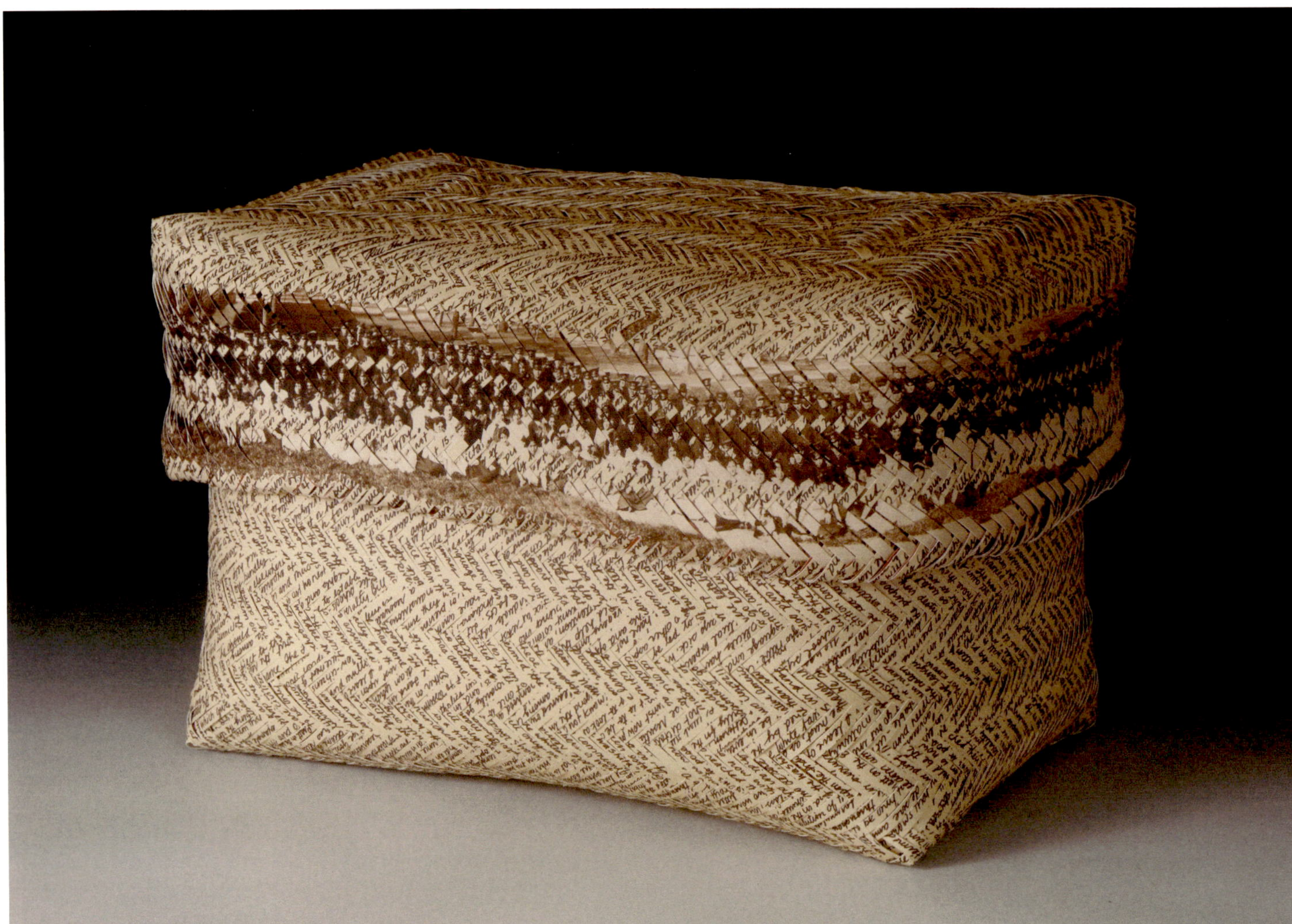

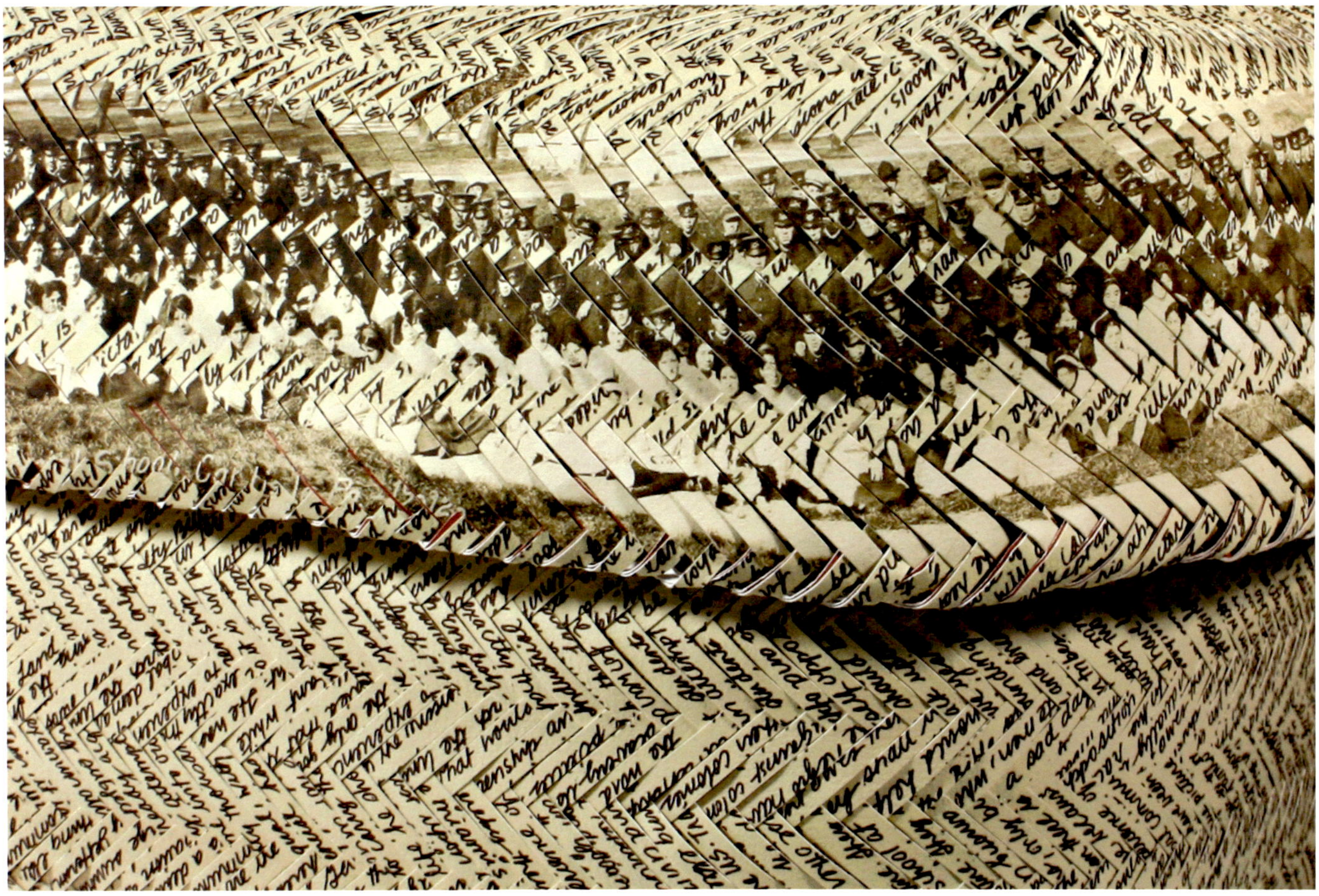

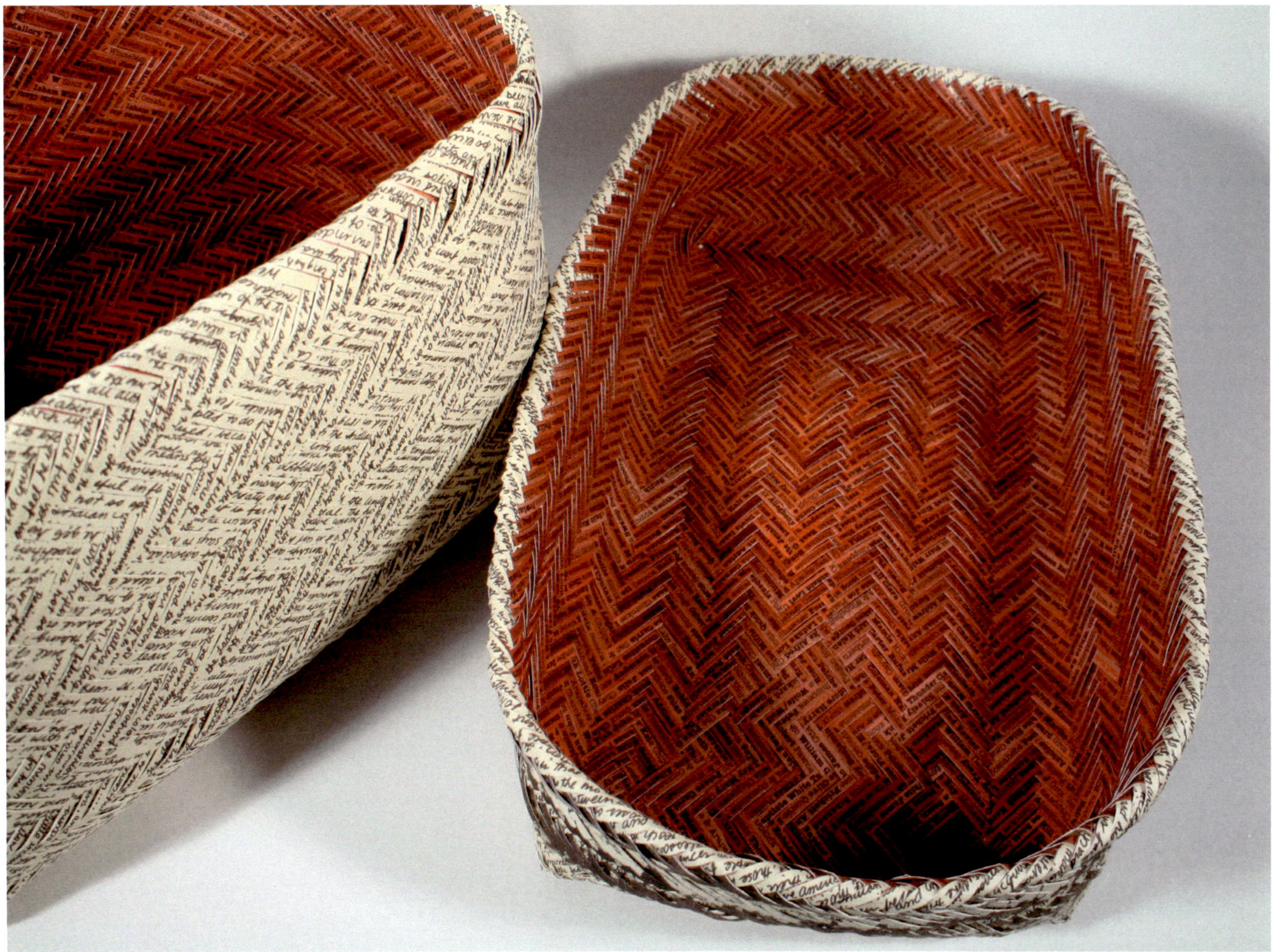

CARLA HEMLOCK

b. 1961, Kahnawake Mohawk Territory, Quebec; lives in Kahnawake Mohawk Territory, Quebec

Tribute to the Mohawk Ironworkers, 2008

Cotton cloth, glass beads, sequins, cotton/nylon threads
62 3/8 x 49 3/4 in. (158.4 x 126.3 cm)
Courtesy of the National Museum of the American Indian, Smithsonian Institution, Washington, DC
Cat. No. 26/7164

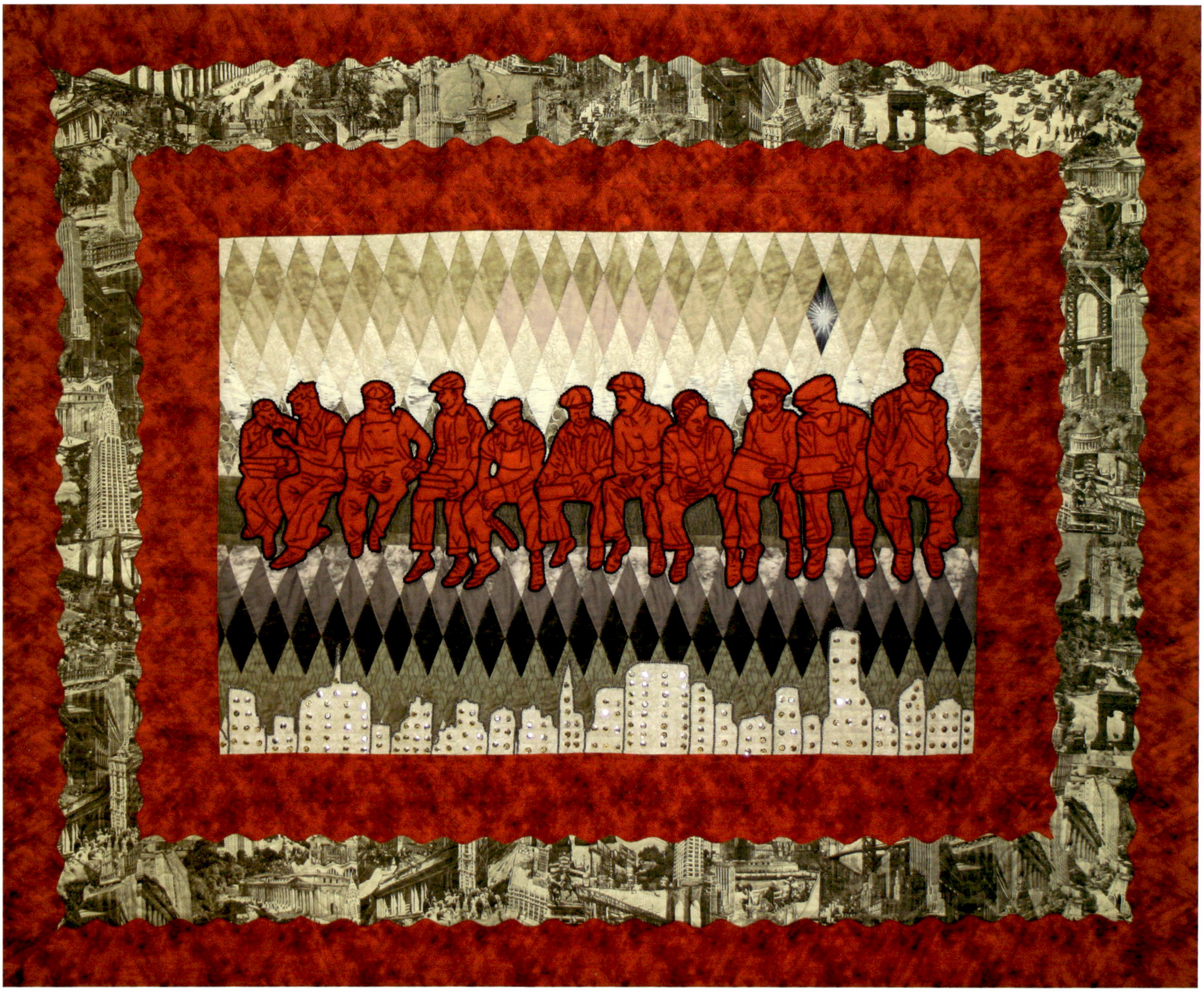

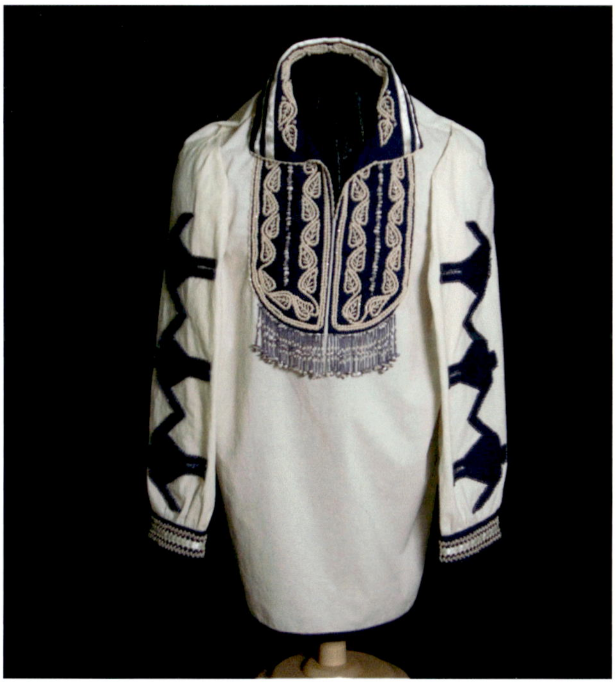

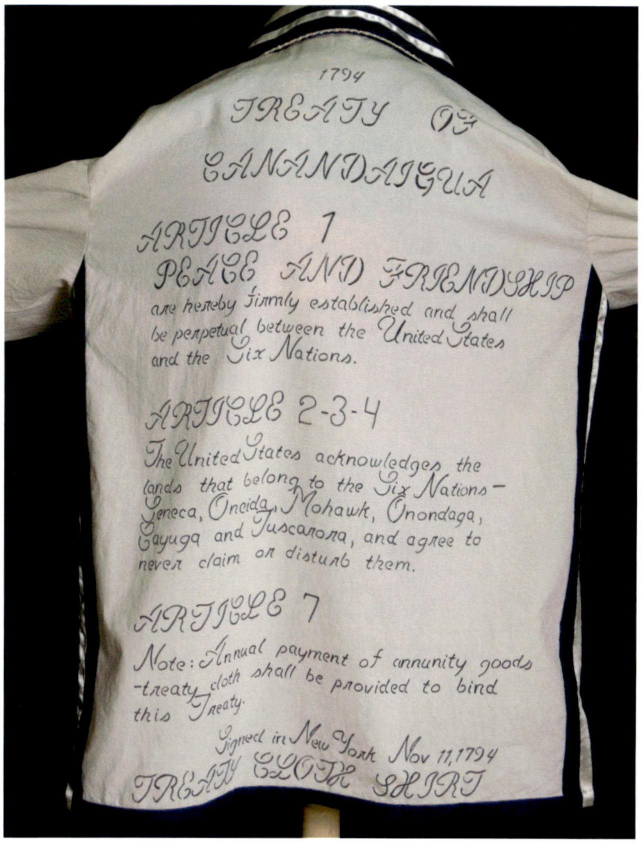

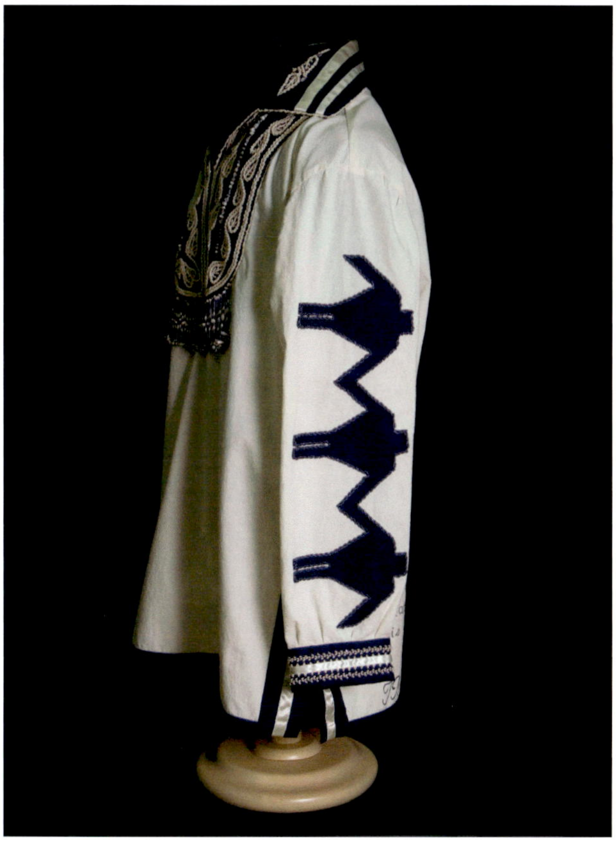

Treaty Cloth Shirt, 2012

Cotton treaty cloth, broadcloth appliqué, glass beads, shell wampum, silk ribbon, stencil, cotton thread
Dimensions variable
Courtesy of the artist

DONALD "BABE" HEMLOCK

b. 1961, Brooklyn, New York; lives in Kahnawake Mohawk Territory, Quebec

Ironworker Cradleboard, 2011

Maple, pine, and ash woods, paint pigment, animal fur, hide, and gut/intestine
29 1/8 x 16 9/16 x 9 13/16 in.
(74 x 42 x 25 cm)
Courtesy of the National Museum of the American Indian, Smithsonian Institution, Washington, DC
Cat. No. 26/8062

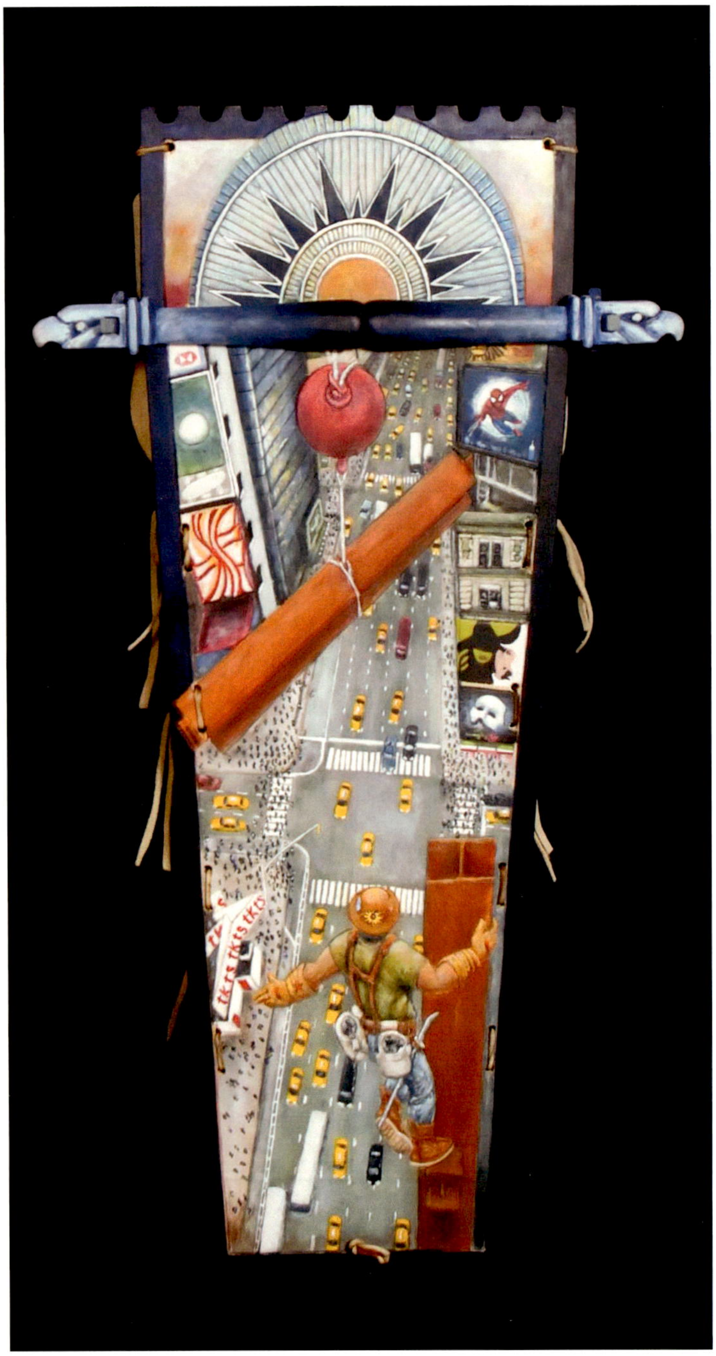

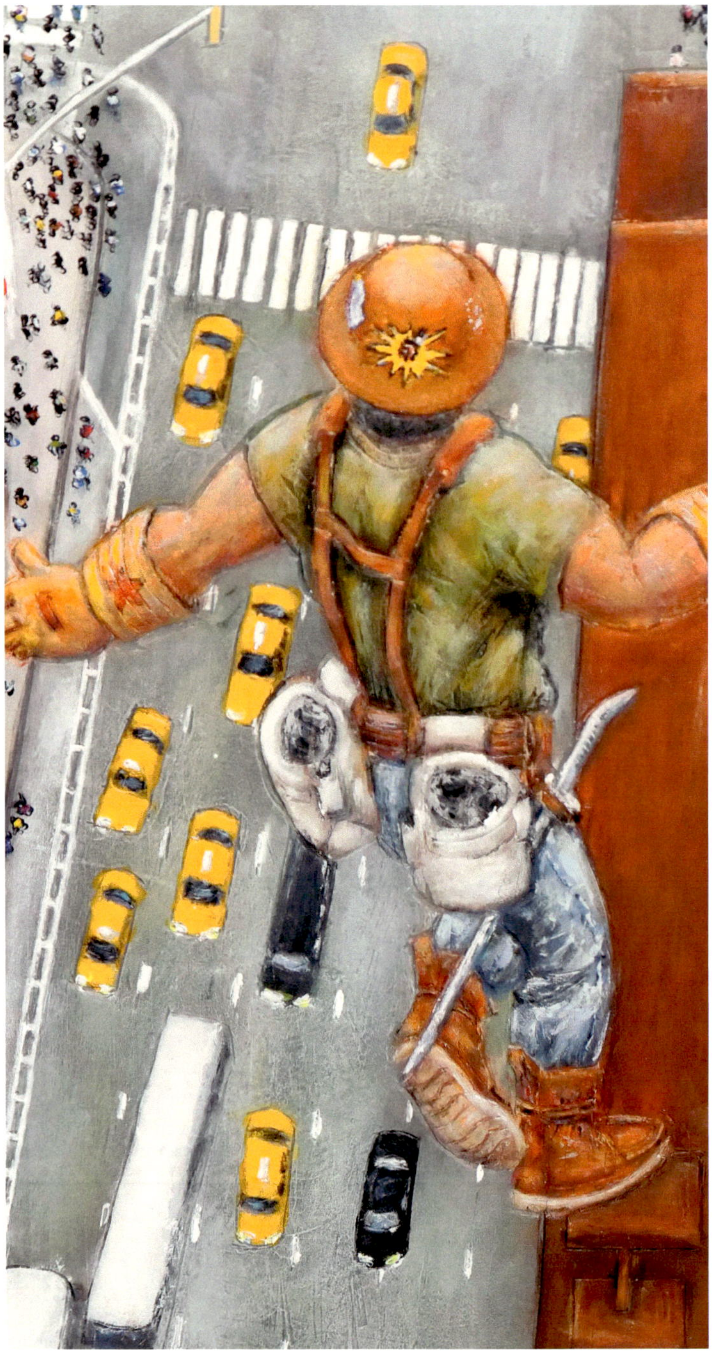

GREG A. HILL

b. 1967, Fort Erie, Ontario;
lives in Chelsea, Quebec

Cereal Box Canoe, 2000, and *Portaging Rideau, Paddling the Ottawa to Kanata,* 2005 (installed at Ottawa Art Gallery, Ottawa, Ontario)

Canoe: paperboard, wood, tar, polypropylene twine, urethane; *Portaging Rideau:* digital video; 3:28 minutes
Dimensions variable
Collection of the Ottawa Art Gallery; Purchased with the support of the Canada Council for the Arts Acquisition Program and the Ottawa Art Gallery's Art Rental and Sales Committee, 2005

Moccasins, 2012

Paperboard, felt, nylon
2 3/8 x 4 3/4 x 11 7/8 in.
(6 x 12 x 30 cm)
Courtesy of the artist

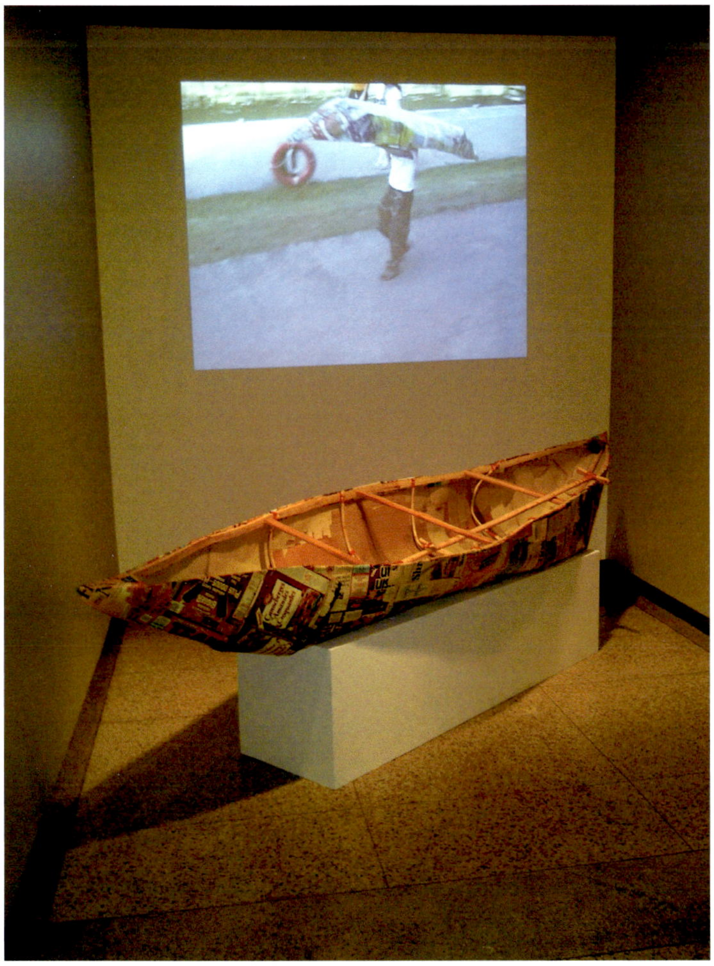

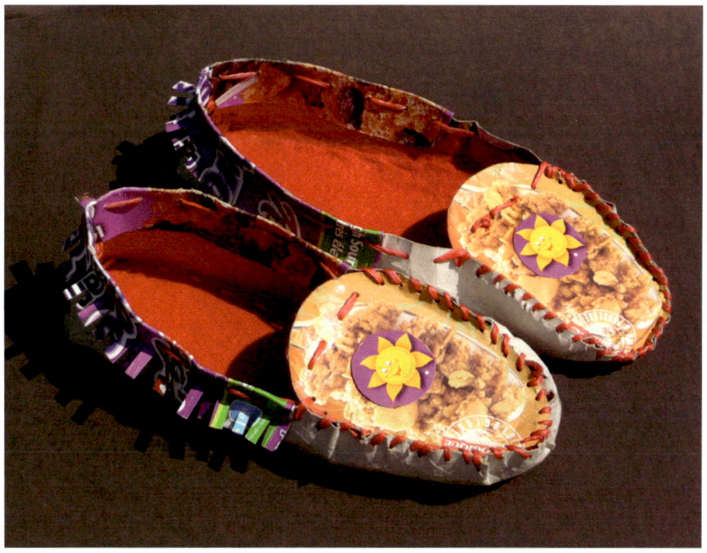

ROBERT HOULE

b. 1947, Sandy Bay First Nation Reserve, St. Boniface, Manitoba; lives in Toronto, Ontario

Sandy Bay Indian Residential School, 2010–12 (installation view)

Oil on canvas, watercolor, graphite, vinyl text
Overall: 77 x 133 in. (195.6 x 337.8 cm)
Collection of the artist

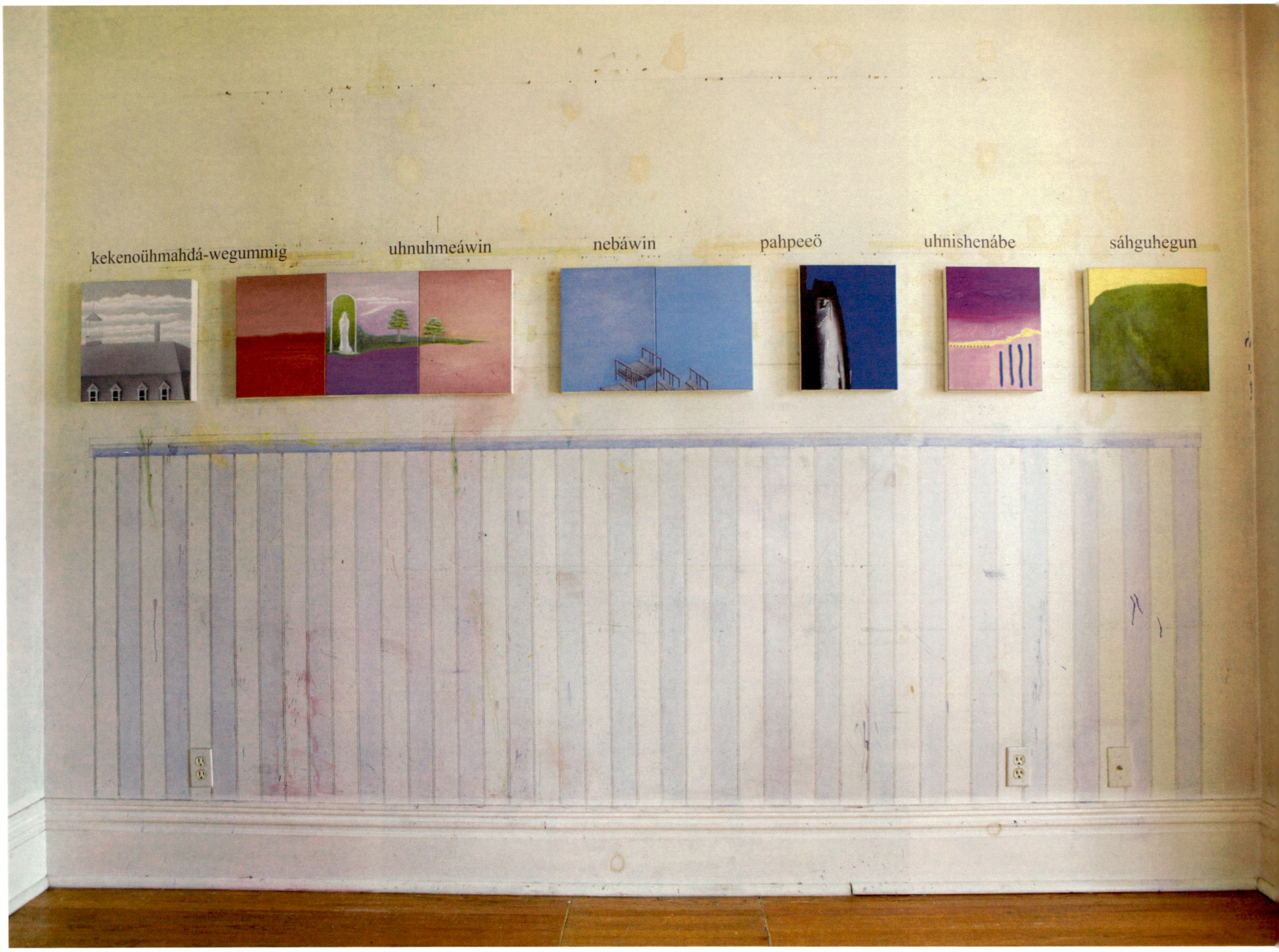

kekenoühmahdá-wegummig (school)

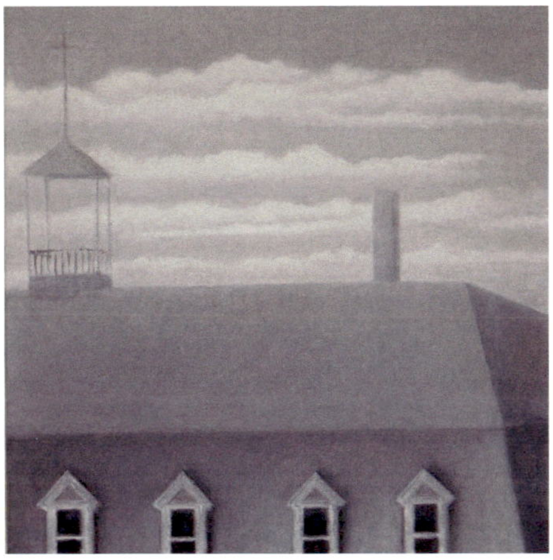

uhnuhmeáwin (praying)

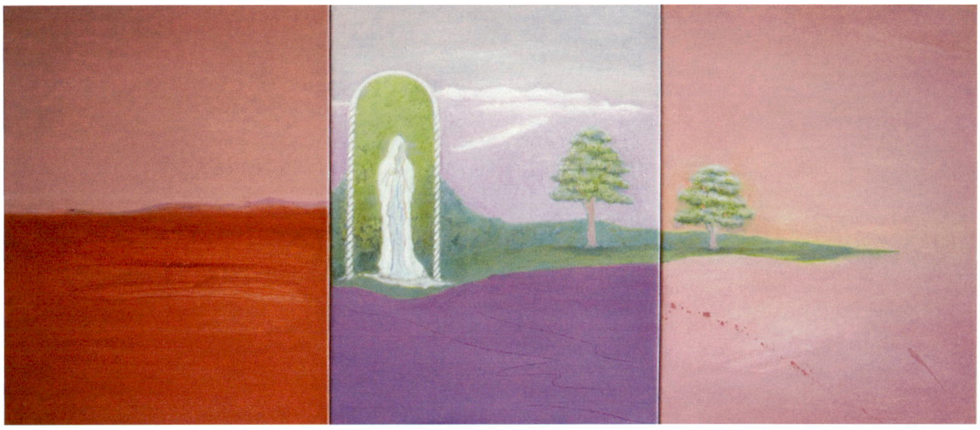

nebáwin (sleeping)

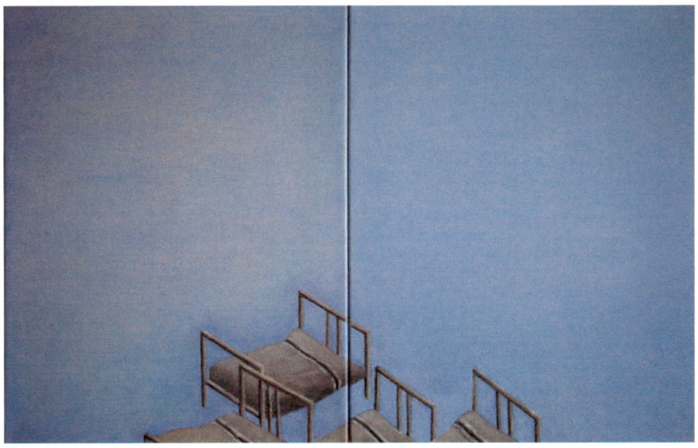

pahpeeö (waiting)

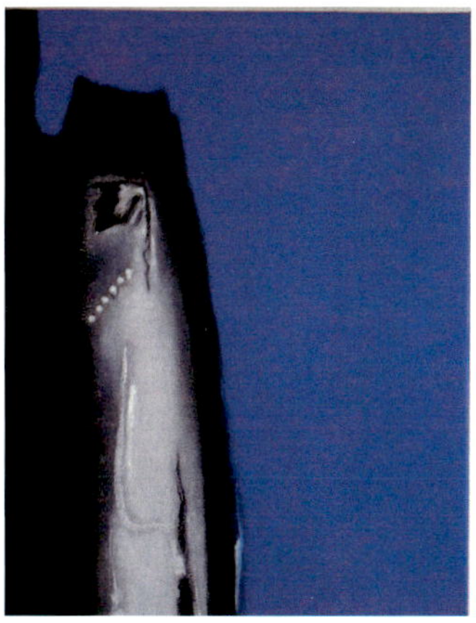

uhnishenábe (person)

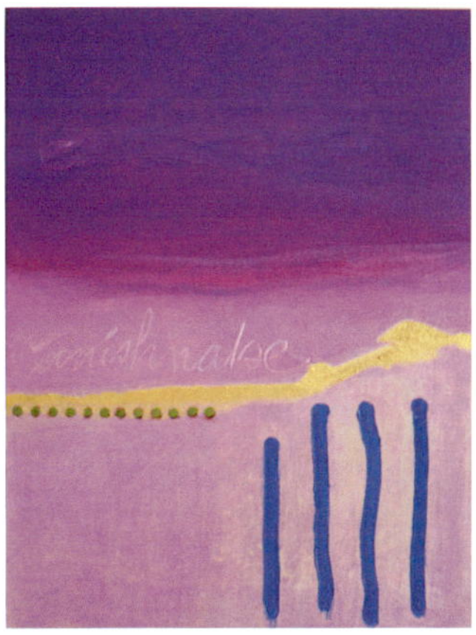

sáhguhegun (lake)

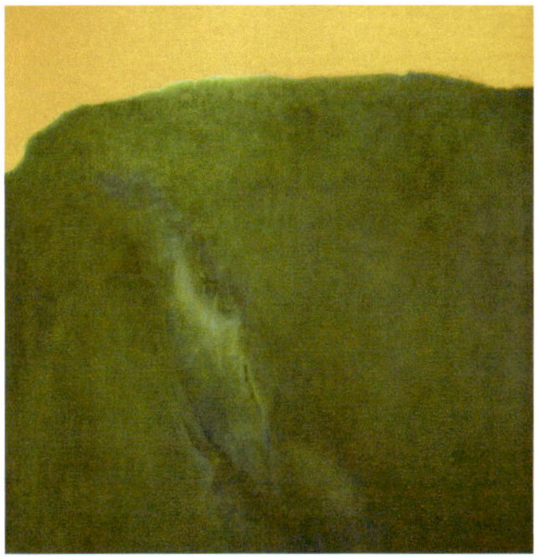

MARIA HUPFIELD

b. 1975, Parry Sound, Ontario;
lives in Brooklyn, New York

Pocket Full of Stars, 2012
(work in progress)

Mixed media installation,
including sound and projection
Dimensions variable
Courtesy of the artist; made possible
through a generous contribution
from Swarovski

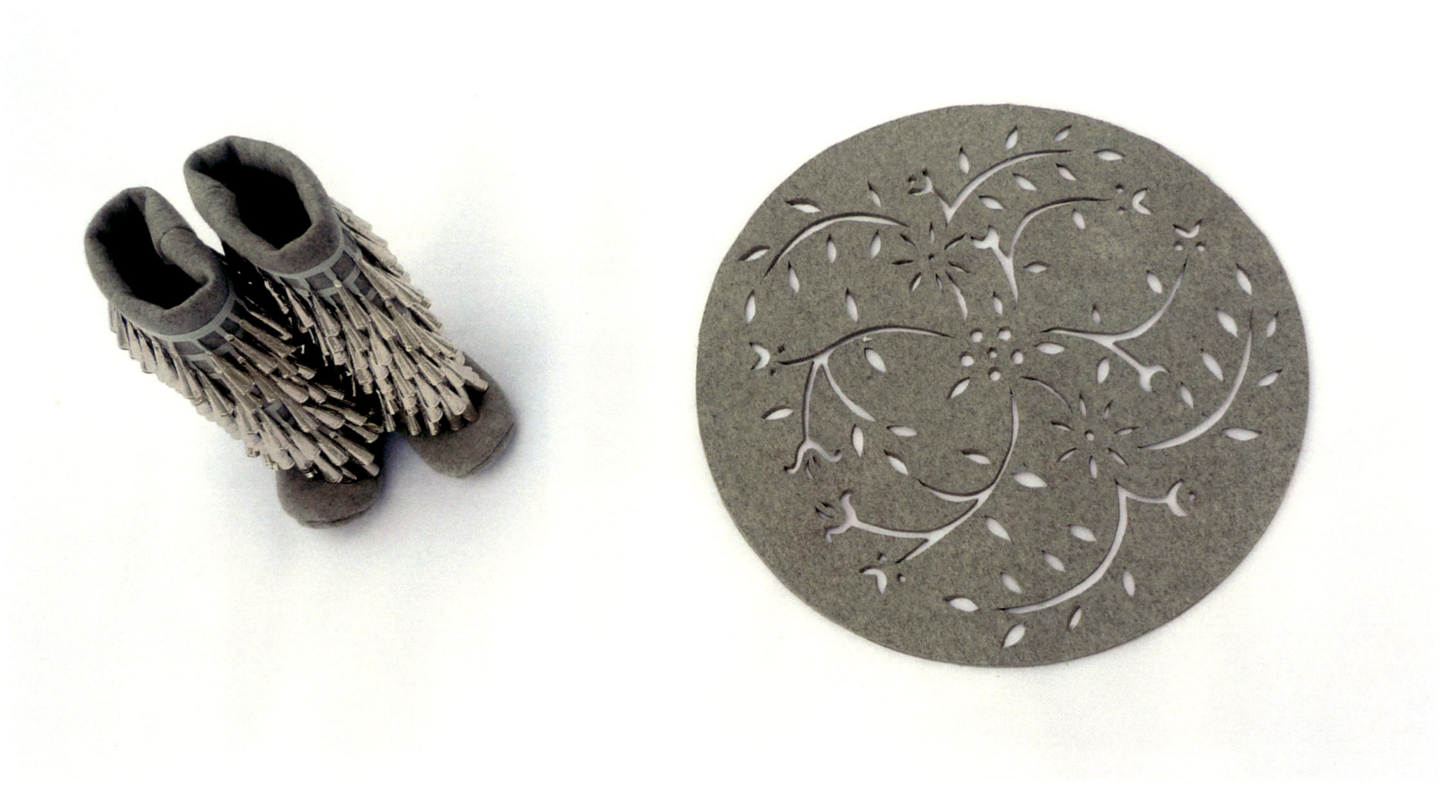

TROY JACKSON

b. 1955, Tahlequah, Oklahoma;
lives in Tahlequah, Oklahoma

Putting the Pieces Together, 2011

Clay, mixed media
15 ½ x 10 in. (39.4 x 25.4 cm)
Courtesy of the artist

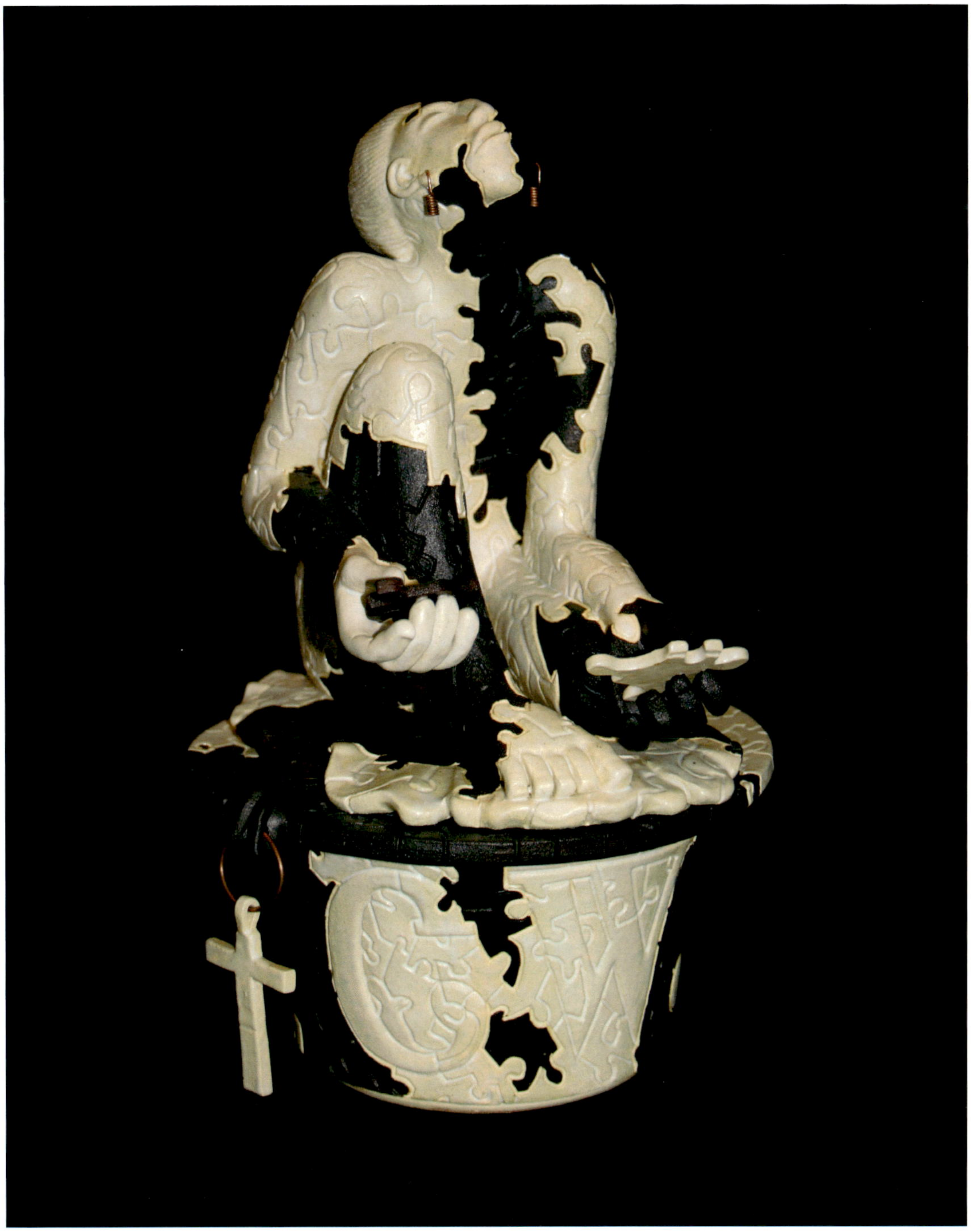

ALEX JACOBS

b. 1953, Akwesasne Mohawk Nation,
New York; lives in Santa Fe, New Mexico

My Father at the River, 2010

Fabric collage, acrylic medium,
varnish, birch board veneer
16 x 20 x 1 in. (40.6 x 50.8 x 2.5 cm)
Courtesy of the artist

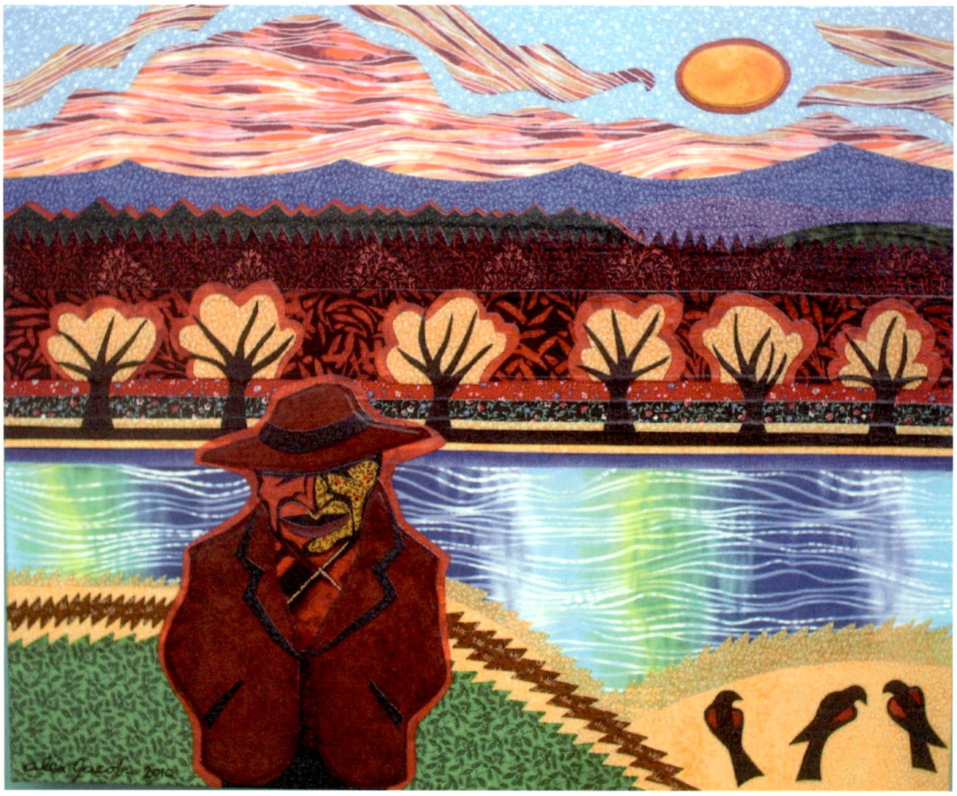

G. PETER JEMISON

b. 1945, Silver Creek, New York;
lives in Victor, New York

Treaty Indians, 2010 (2 views)

Found paper bag, collage, acrylic ink, gold foil
20 x 12 x 6 ¾ in.
(50.8 x 30.5 x 17.1 cm)
Courtesy of the artist

Fur Trade III, 2012 (2 views)

Handmade paper bag, collage, acrylic paint, copper, China marker
18 ¾ x 10 ½ x 6 ½ in.
(47.6 x 26.7 x 16.5 cm)
Courtesy of the artist

Ganondaman, ca. 2010 (2 views)

Found paper bag, collage, acrylic ink
12 ¼ x 12 x 6 ¾ in.
(31.1 x 30.5 x 17.1 cm)
Courtesy of the artist

All Hallow's Night, 2005 (2 views)

Handmade paper bag, ink, tempera, China marker, crayon, acrylic paint
17 ½ x 8 ¼ x 4 ½ in.
(44.5 x 21 x 11.4 cm)
Courtesy of the artist

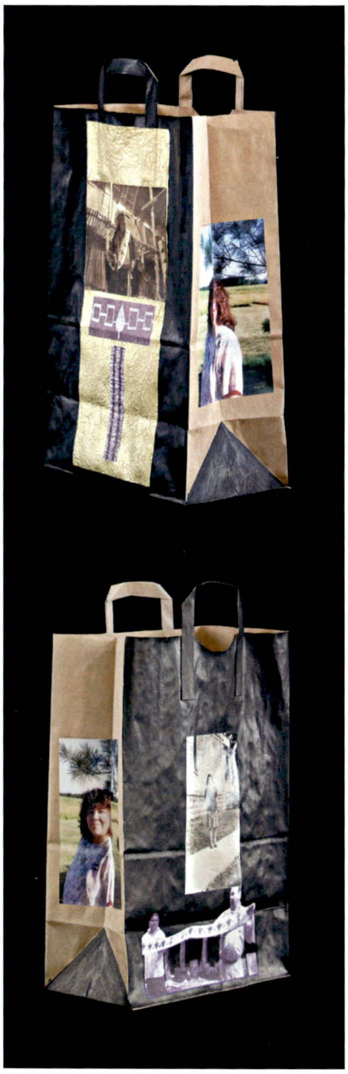

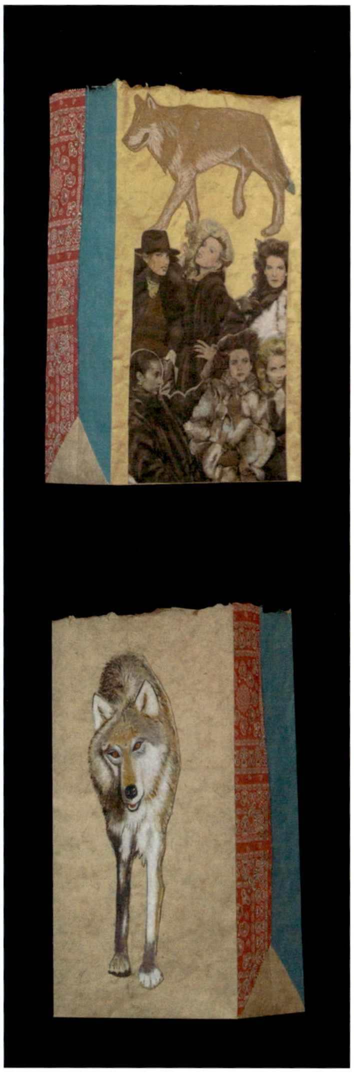

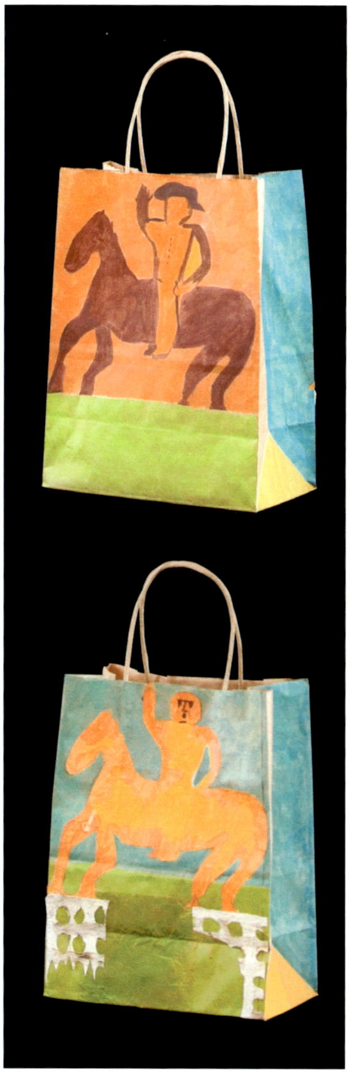

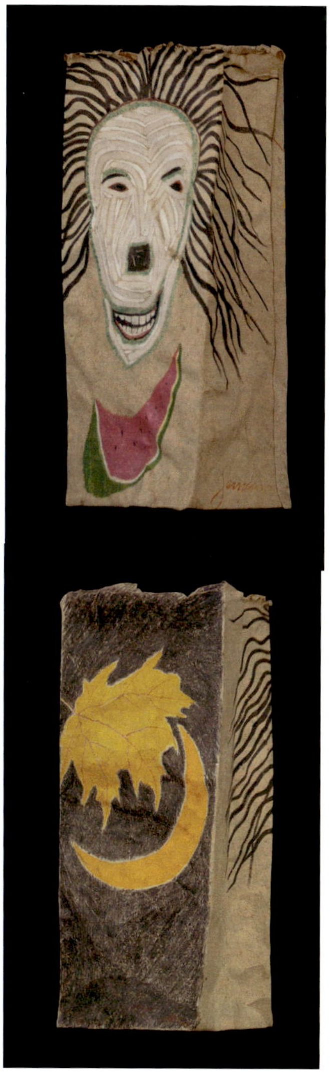

PETER B. JONES

b. 1947, Cattaraugus Reservation, New York; lives at Cattaraugus Reservation, New York

Portrait Jar—New Indian, 2010

Clay, mixed media
15 x 7 ½ x 7 ½ in.
(38.1 x 19.1 x 19.1 cm)
Courtesy of the Longyear Museum of Anthropology, Colgate University, Hamilton, New York

Red Moon, 2009

Clay, mixed media
11 x 5 ½ x 4 ½ in.
(27.9 x 14 x 11.4 cm)
Collection of N. Sahs

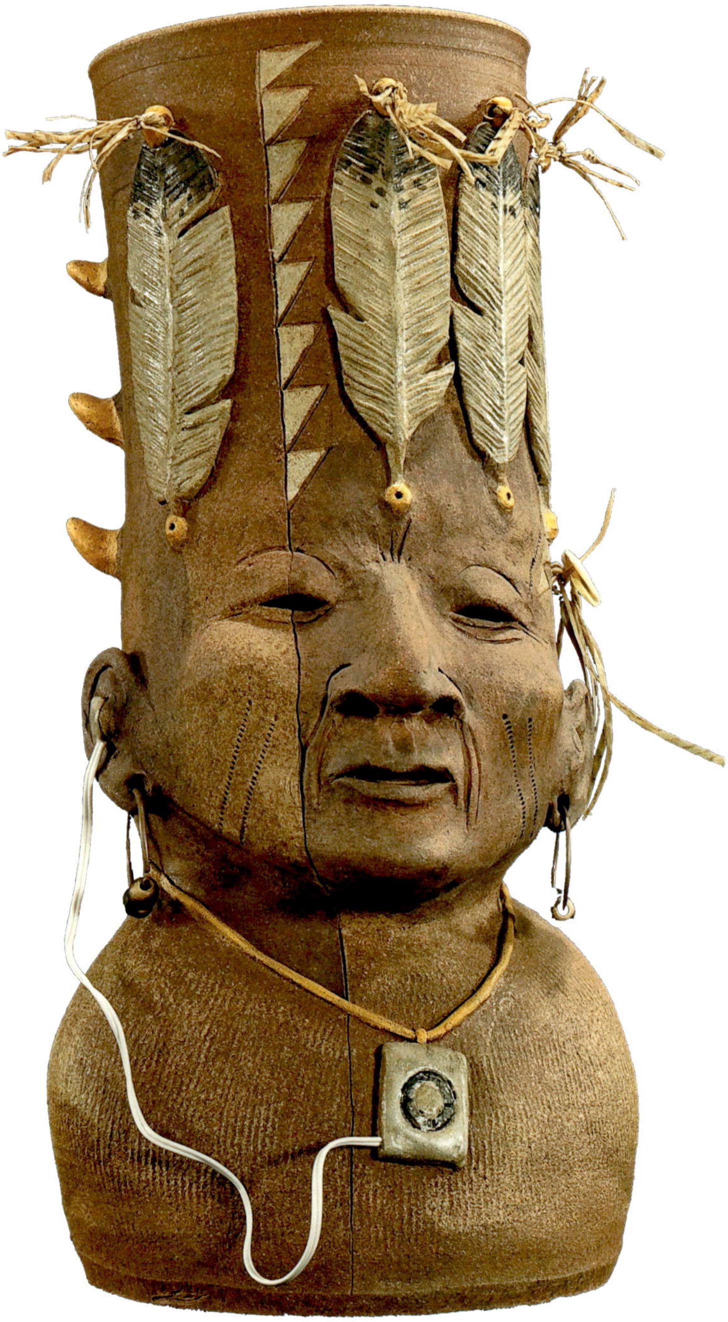

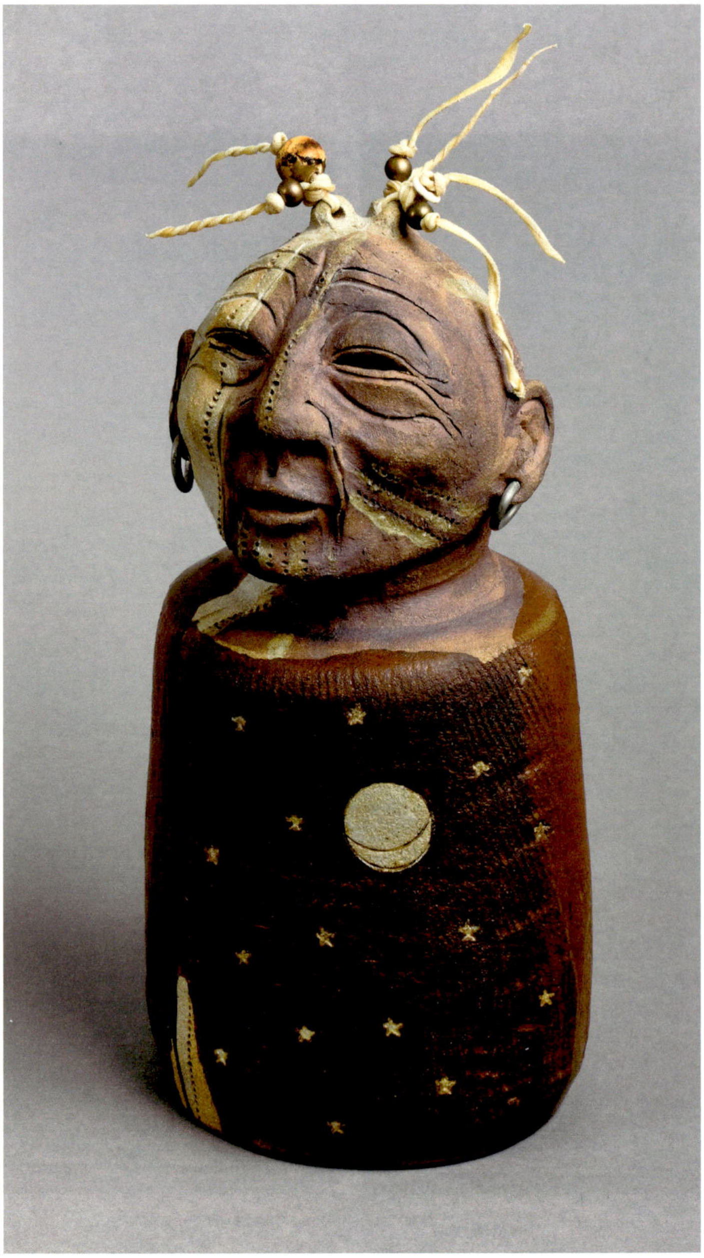

TOM JONES

b. 1964, Charlotte, North Carolina;
lives in Madison, Wisconsin

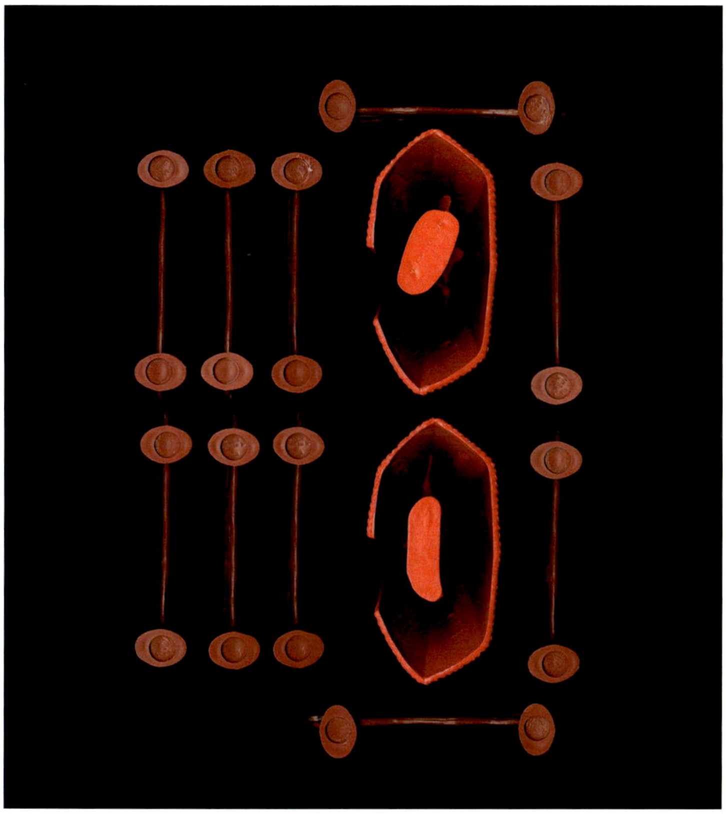

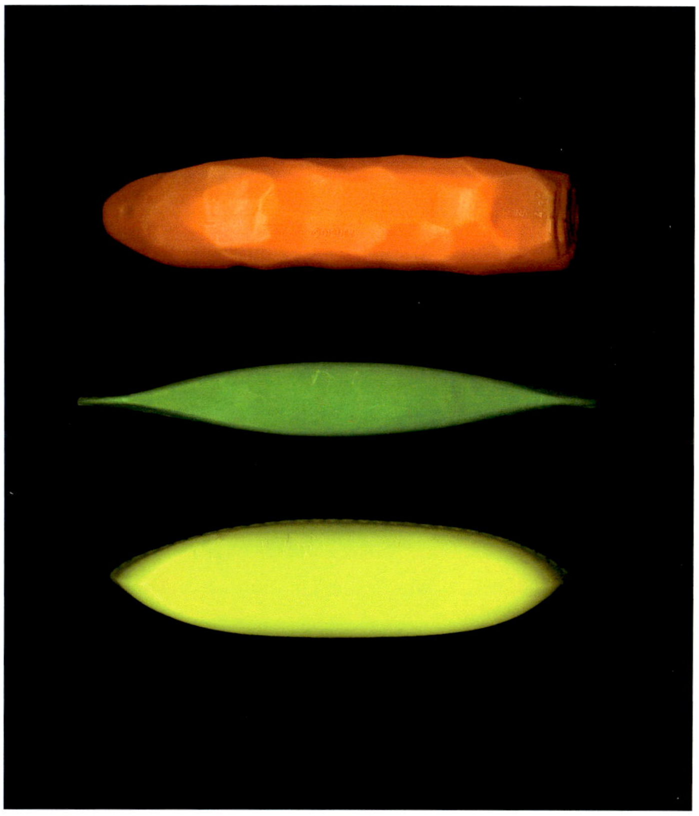

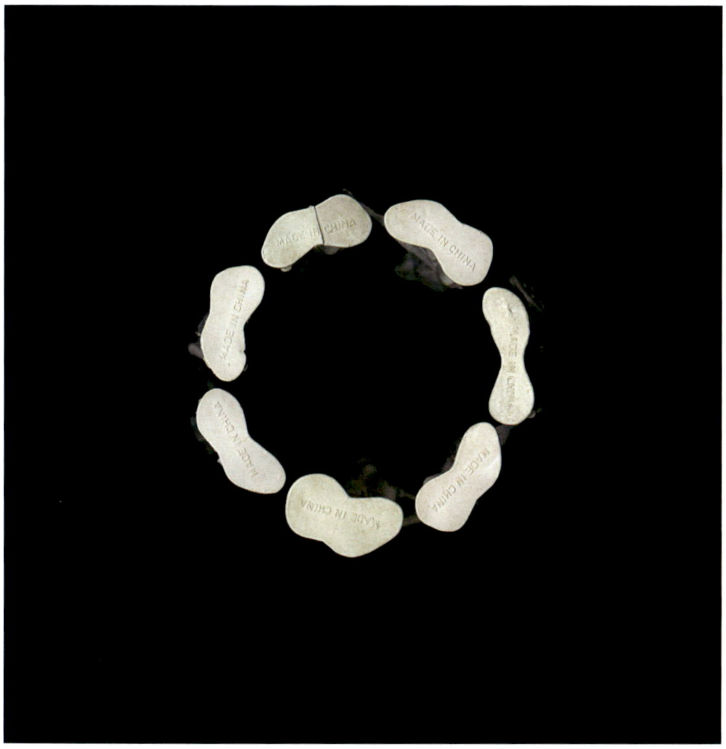

They Faced Their Homes to the West and Put Up Fences, 2011 (top left)

Archival digital print
40 x 50 in. (101.6 x 127 cm)
Courtesy of Sherry Leedy Contemporary Art, Kansas City, Missouri

Disney, 2011 (top right)

Archival digital print
40 x 50 in. (101.6 x 127 cm)
Courtesy of Sherry Leedy Contemporary Art, Kansas City, Missouri

White Circle, 2011

Archival digital print
40 x 40 in. (101.6 x 101.6 cm)
Courtesy of Sherry Leedy Contemporary Art, Kansas City, Missouri

MICHELLE LaVALLEE

b. 1977, Newmarket, Ontario;
lives in Regina, Saskatchewan

Final Proof, 2007 (installed at Mendel Art Gallery, Saskatoon, Saskatchewan)

Mixed media installation, including found materials, recycled books, wood crates, Hudson Bay Pointe blankets and ephemera
Dimensions variable
Courtesy of the artist

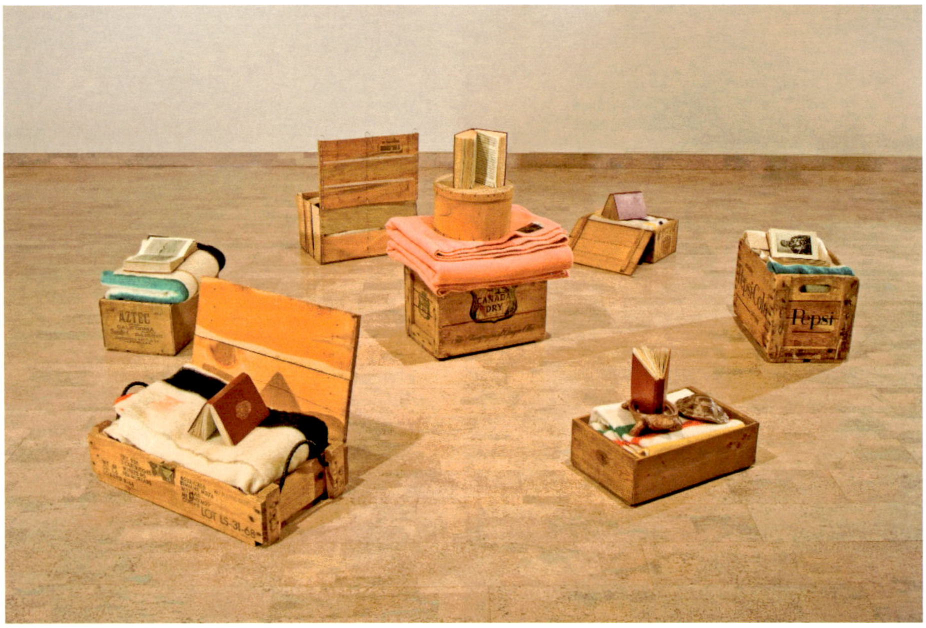

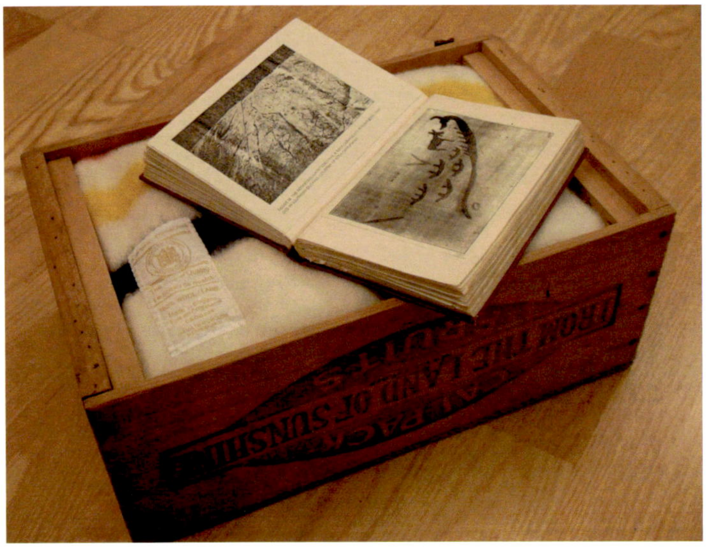

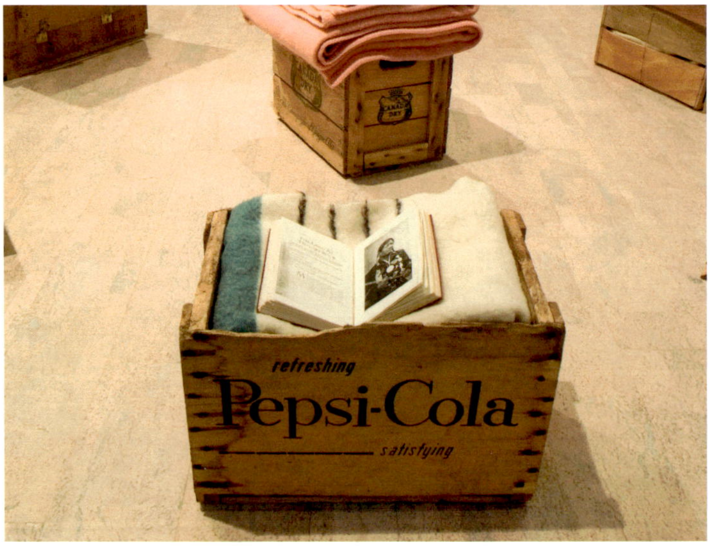

COURTNEY M. LEONARD

b. 1980, Nashua, New Hampshire;
lives in Santa Fe, New Mexico

Contact 1,609, 2009

Clay, canvas, brass, sinew
72 x 72 x 3 in.
(182.9 x 182.9 x 7.6 cm)
Courtesy of the artist

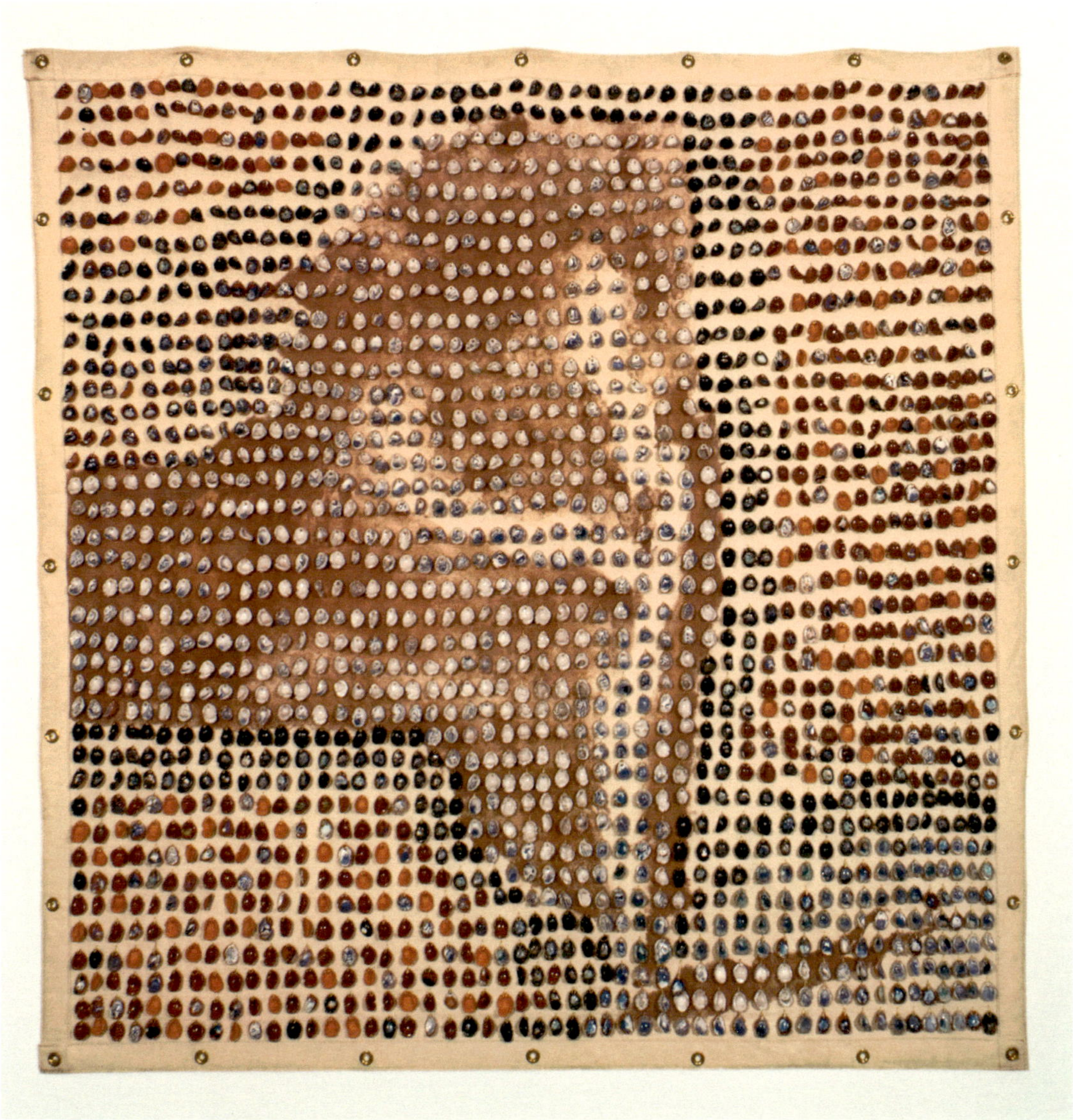

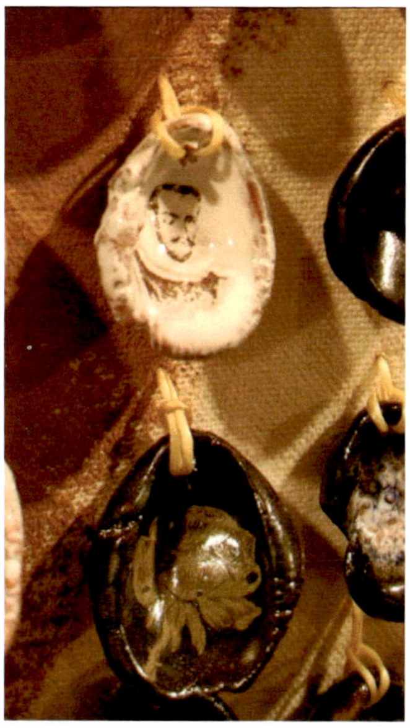

FAYE LONE

b. 1958, Buffalo, New York;
lives in Alexandria, Virginia

Constructed Indian, 2010

Cotton fabrics, cotton/polyester threads, leather, fake fur, found object
49 x 44 ½ in. (124.5 x 113 cm)
Courtesy of the artist

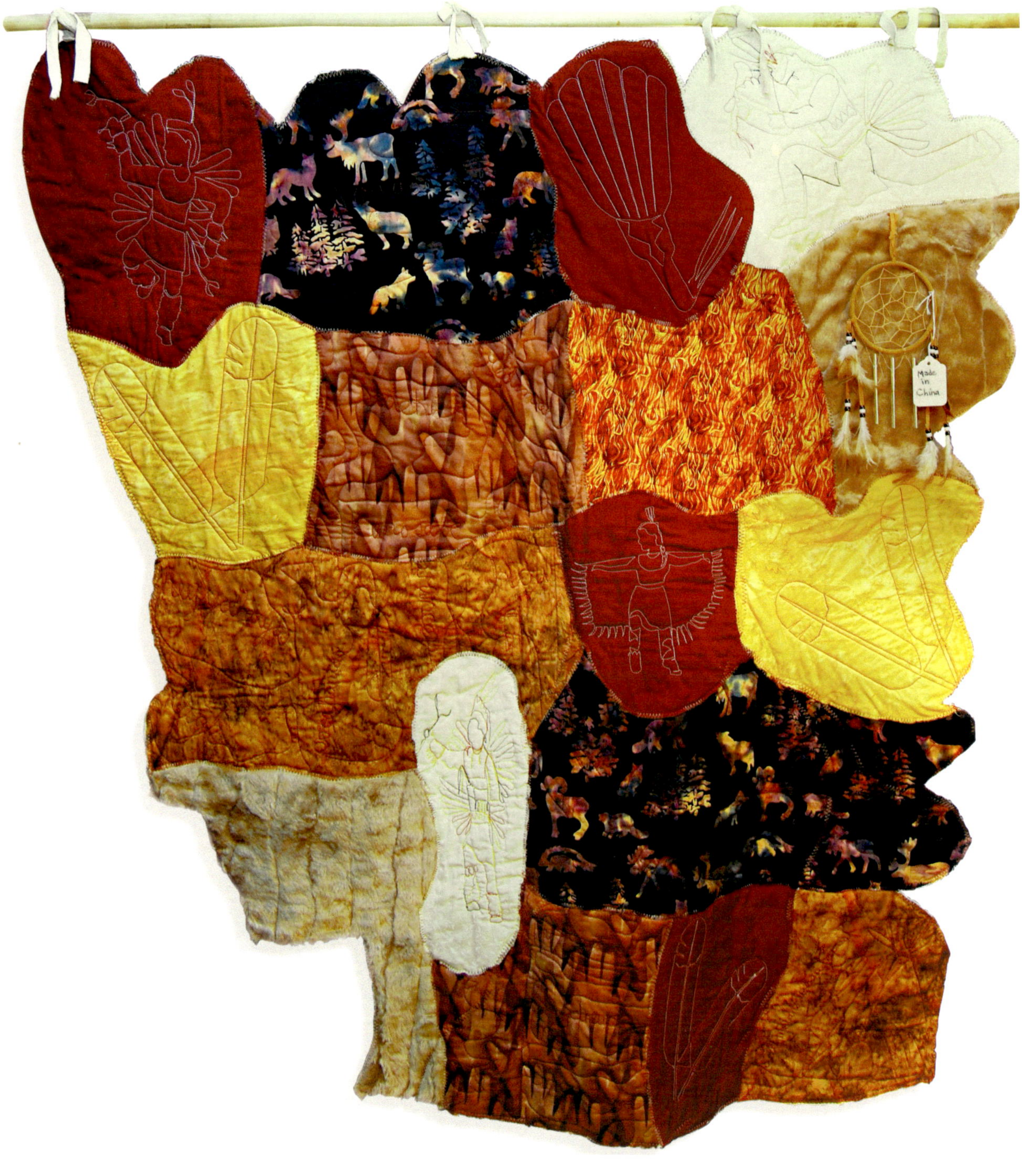

GEORGE LONGFISH

b. 1942, Oshweken, Ontario;
lives in South Berwick, Maine

Buffalo Grass, 1, 2, 3, 2010

Acrylic and glitter on wood
Each: 12 x 96 x 2 in.
(30.5 x 243.8 x 5.1 cm)
Courtesy of the artist

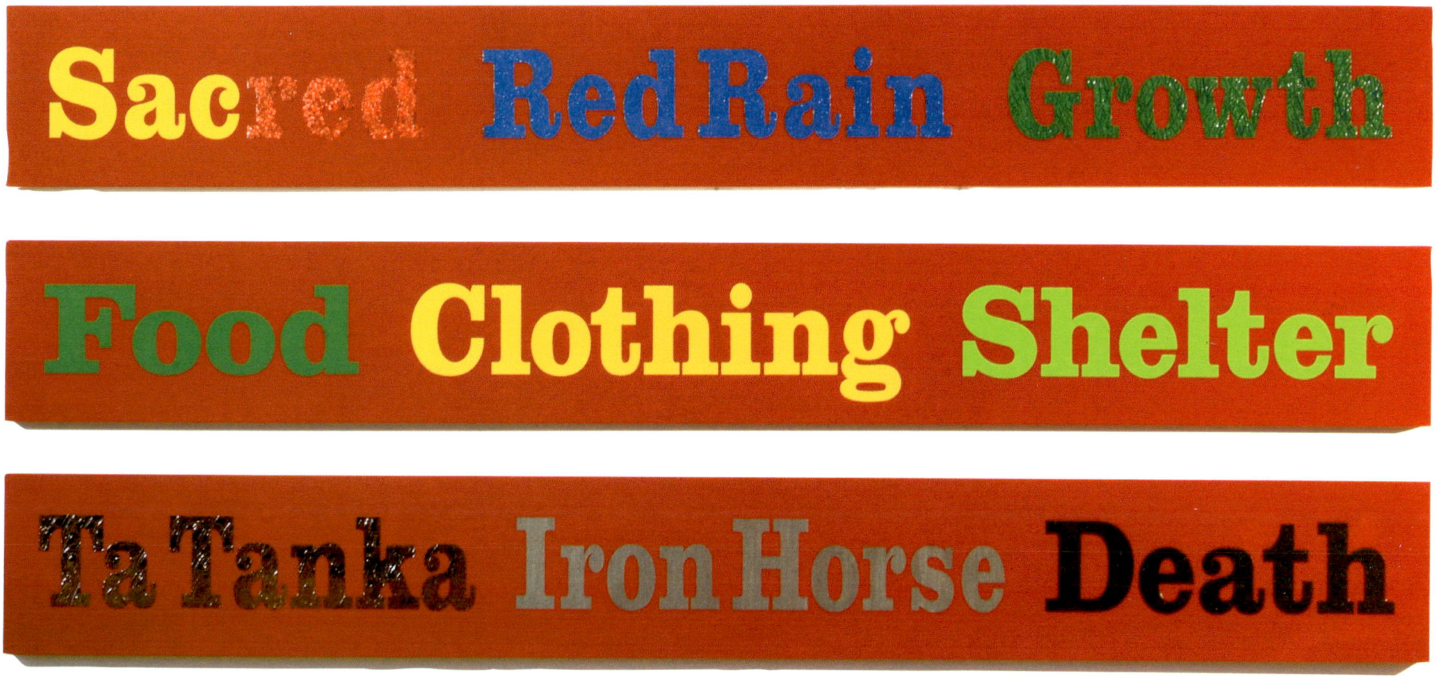

ALAN MICHELSON

b. 1953, Buffalo, New York;
lives in New York, New York

Phoenix, 2012

Handmade paper, archival board and ink, wood
19 x 17 ¼ x 31 ½ in.
(48.3 x 43.8 x 80 cm)
Courtesy of the artist

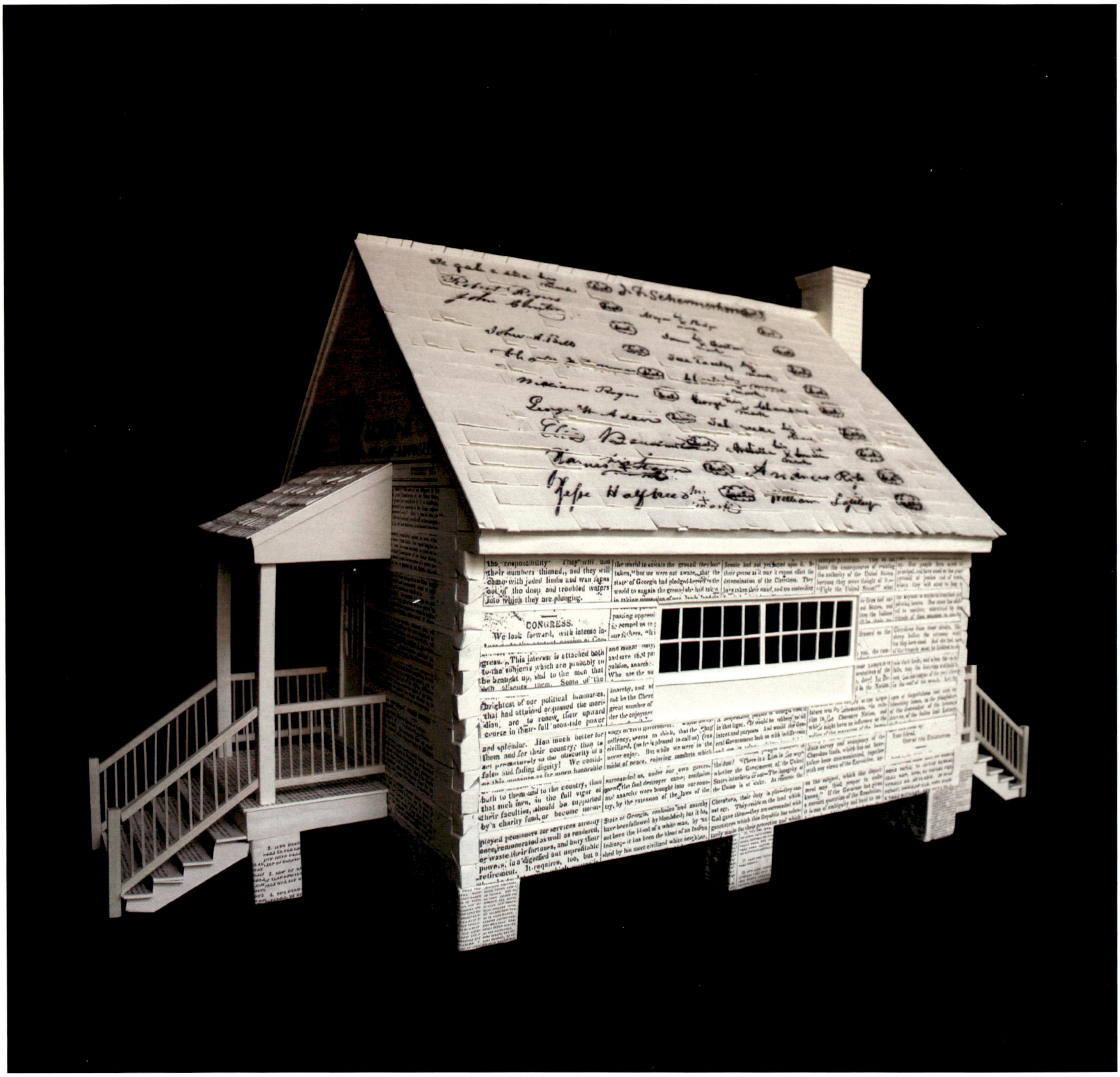

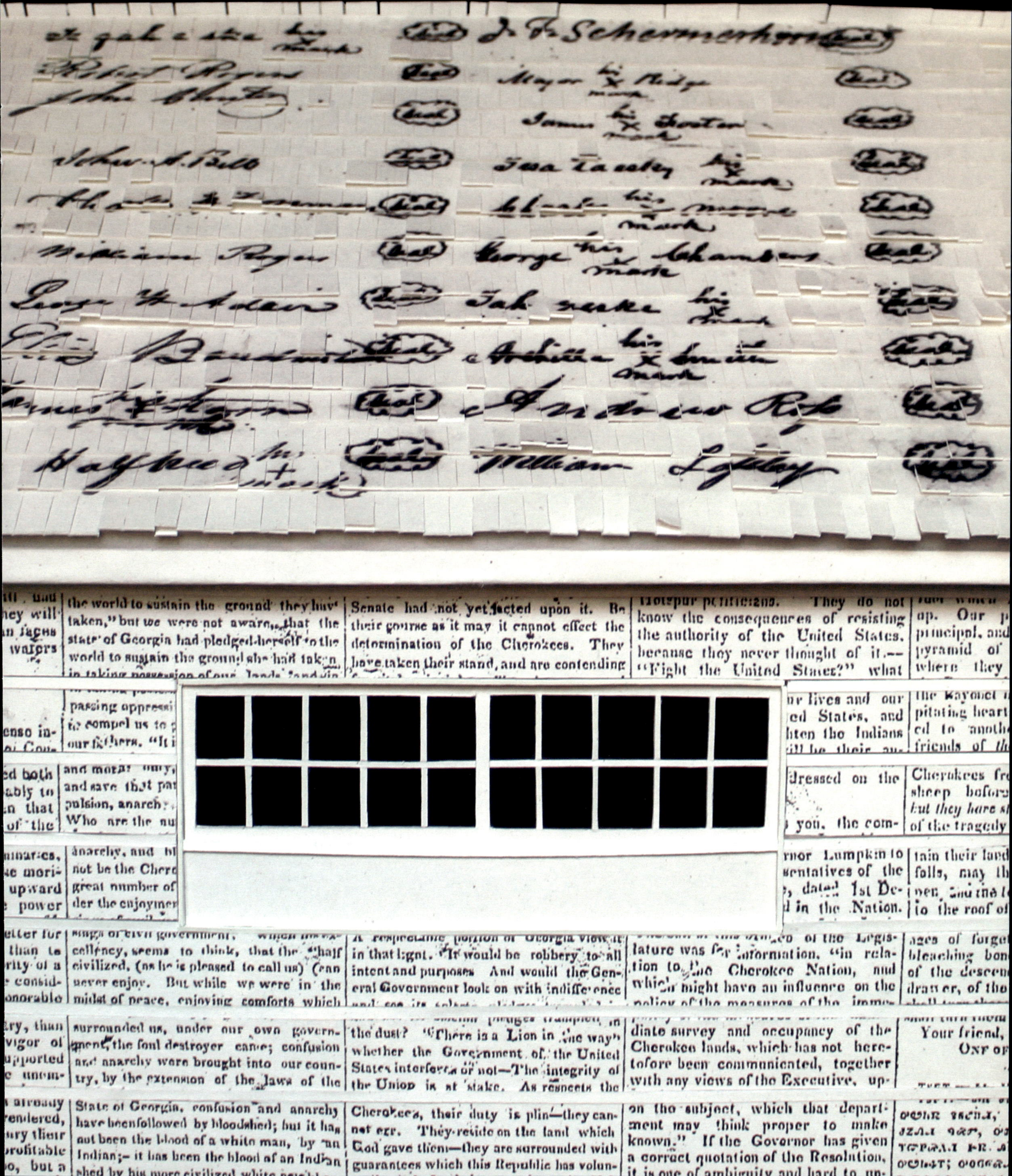
the world to sustain the ground they hav
taken," but we were not aware, that the
state of Georgia had pledged herself to the
world to sustain the ground she had taken
Senate had not yet acted upon it. Be
their course as it may it cannot effect the
determination of the Cherokees. They
have taken their stand, and are contending
know the consequences of resisting
the authority of the United States.
because they never thought of it.—
"Fight the United States?" what
cellency, seems to think, that the "half
civilized, (as he is pleased to call us) can
never enjoy. But while we were in the
midst of peace, enjoying comforts which
in that light. "It would be robbery to all
intent and purposes And would the General Government look on with indifference
lature was for information, "in relation to the Cherokee Nation, and
which might have an influence on the
surrounded us, under our own government, the foul destroyer came; confusion
and anarchy were brought into our country, by the extension of the laws of the
the dust? "There is a Lion in the way"
whether the Government of the United
States interferes or not—The integrity of
the Union is at stake.
diate survey and occupancy of the
Cherokee lands, which has not heretofore been communicated, together
with any views of the Executive, up-
Your friend,
State of Georgia, confusion and anarchy
have been followed by bloodshed; but it has
not been the blood of a white man, by an
Indian;— it has been the blood of an Indian
Cherokees, their duty is plain—they cannot err. They reside on the land which
God gave them—they are surrounded with
guarantees which this Republic has volun-
on the subject, which that department may think proper to make
known." If the Governor has given
a correct quotation of the Resolution,

KENT MONKMAN

b. 1965, St. Mary's, Ontario;
lives in Toronto, Ontario

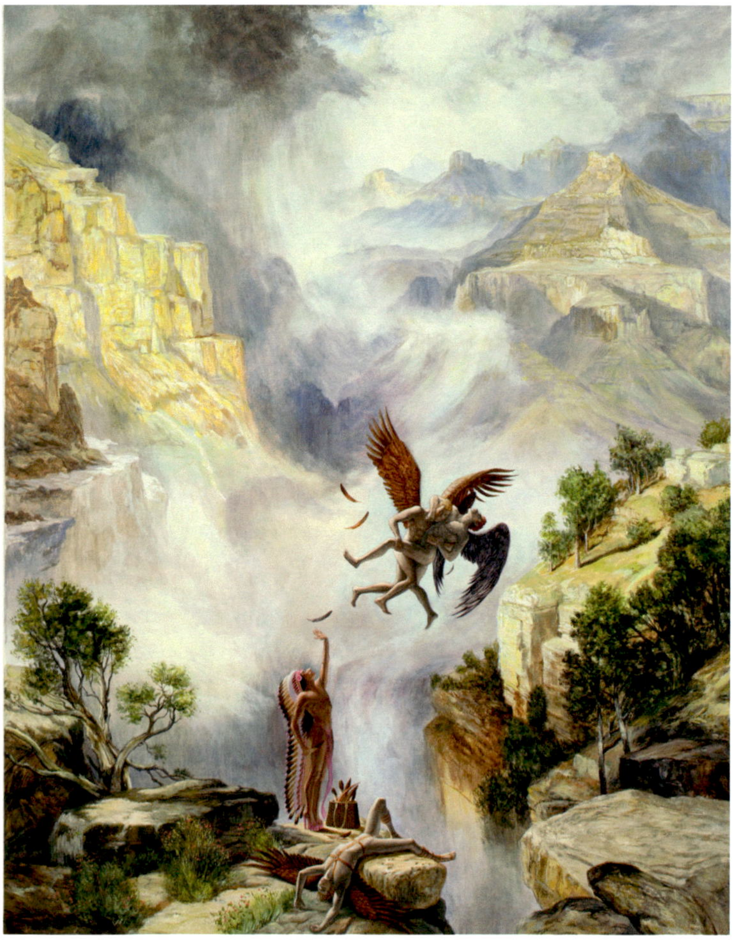

Kiss the Sky, 2010

Acrylic on canvas
59 x 47 x 2 in.
(149.9 x 119.4 x 5.1 cm)
Courtesy of the Kitchener-Waterloo Art Gallery, Kitchener, Ontario

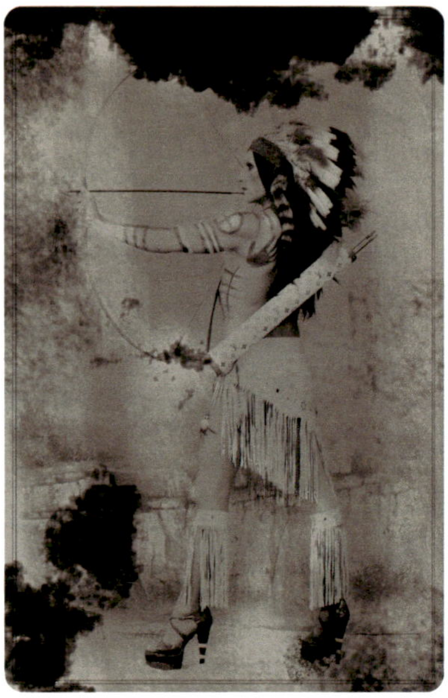

Emergence of a Legend, 2007

(in collaboration with Christopher Chapman and Jackie Shawn)
One of five chromogenic prints on metallic paper
4 ½ x 6 ½ in.
(11.4 x 16.5 cm)
Courtesy of the artist

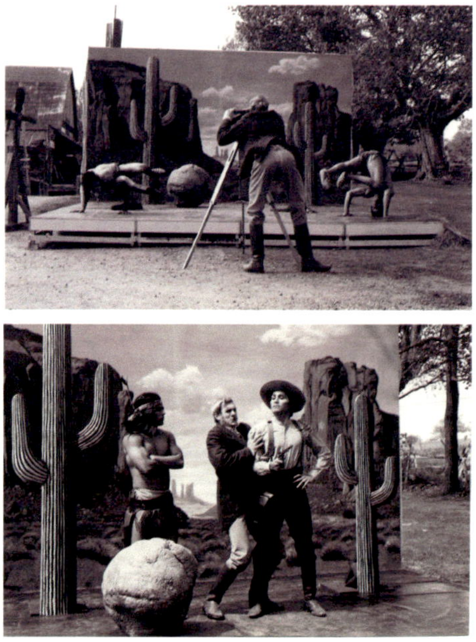

Shooting Geronimo, 2007

Production stills from two channel, black-and-white, super-8 film transferred to DVD
11:11 minutes
Courtesy of the artist

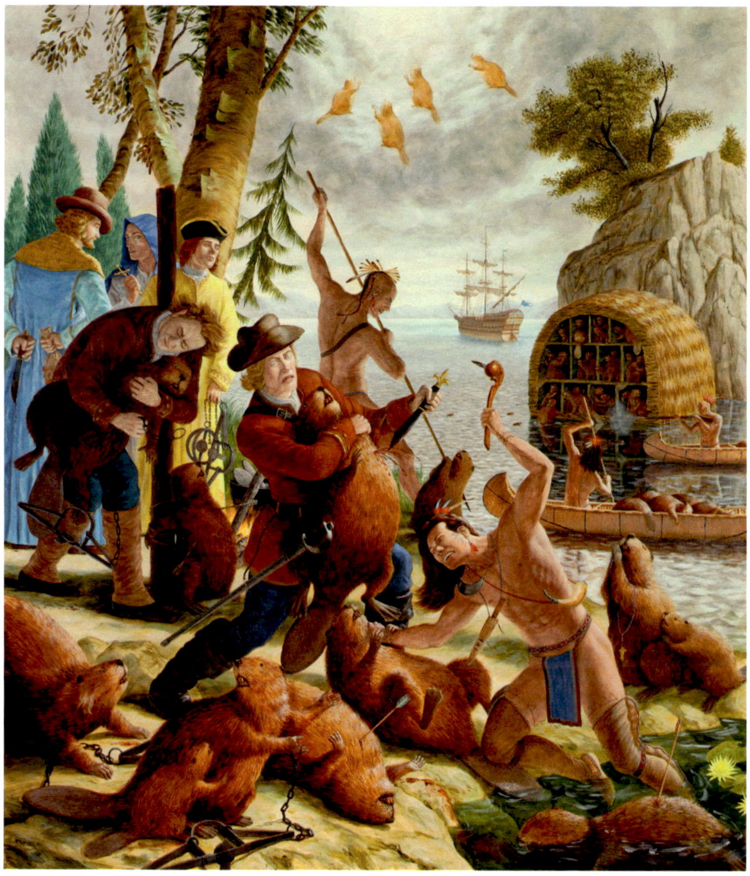

The King's Beavers, 2011
(not included in exhibition)

Acrylic on canvas
96 x 84 x 1 3/4 in.
(243.8 x 213.4 x 4.4 cm)
Courtesy of The Montreal Museum of Fine Arts; Gift of the artist and W. Bruce C. Bailey in honour of Nathalie Bondil to mark the 150th anniversary of the Montreal Museum of Fine Arts
Inv. 2011.401

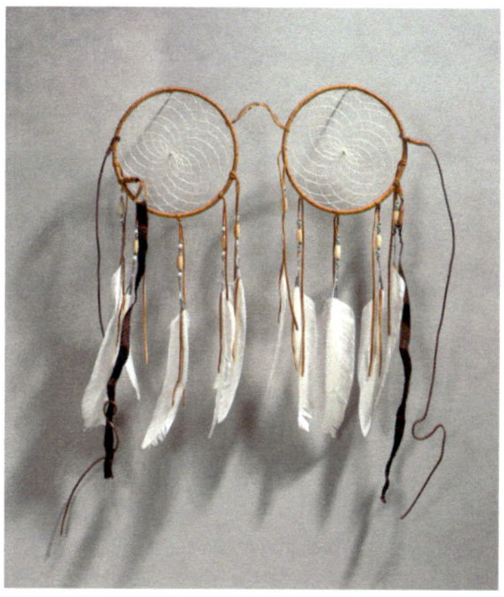

Dreamcatcher Bra, *Racoon Jockstrap*, and *Quiver*, 2007
(worn by Miss Chief Eagle Testickle in various performances)
Cree Leggings, 2011 (bottom right)

Mixed media
Dimensions variable
Courtesy of the artist

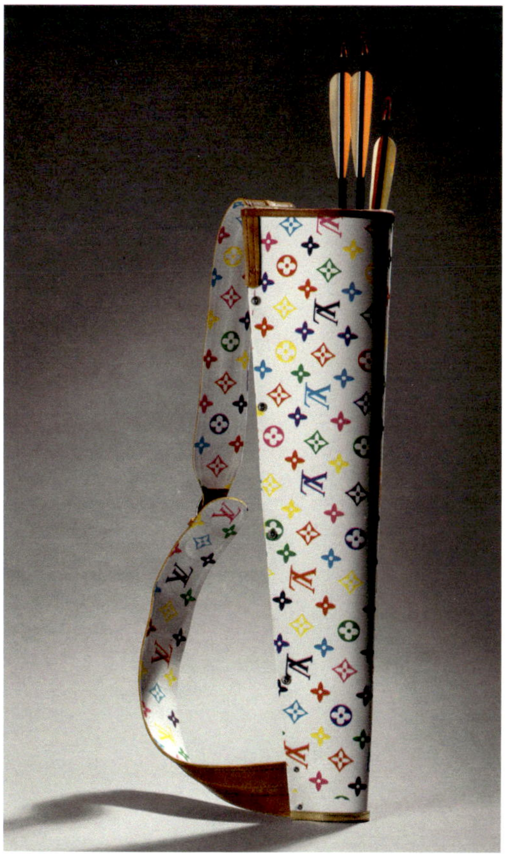

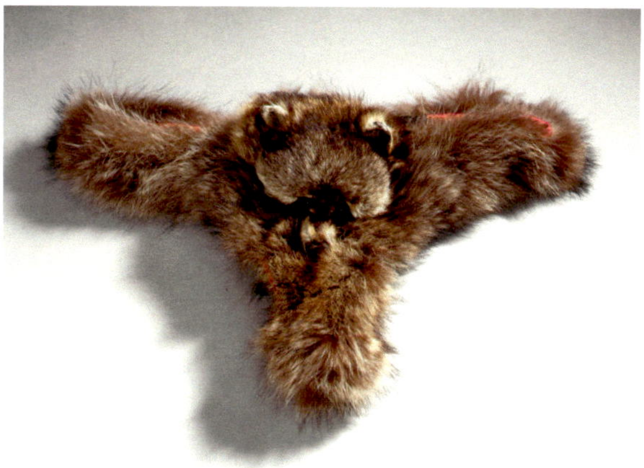

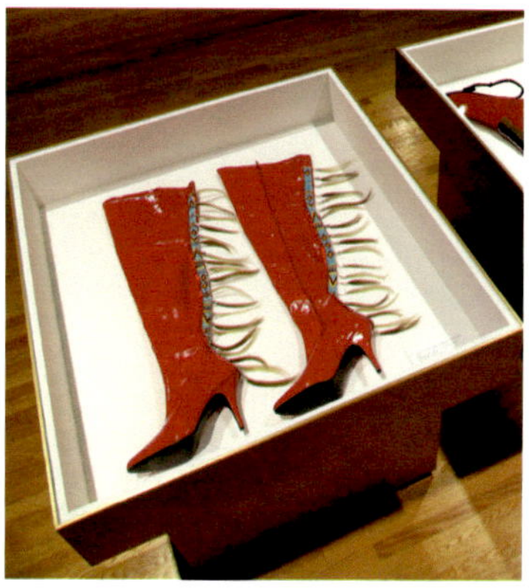

SHELLEY NIRO

b. 1954, Niagara Falls, New York;
lives in Brantford, Ontario

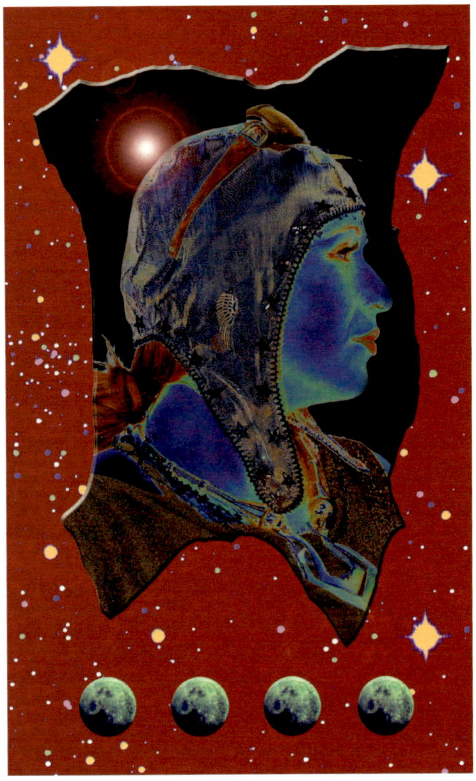

Ancestor

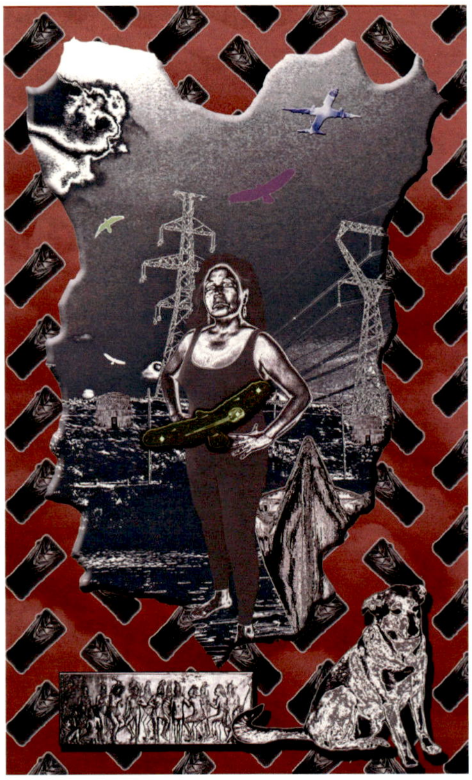

Bagging It

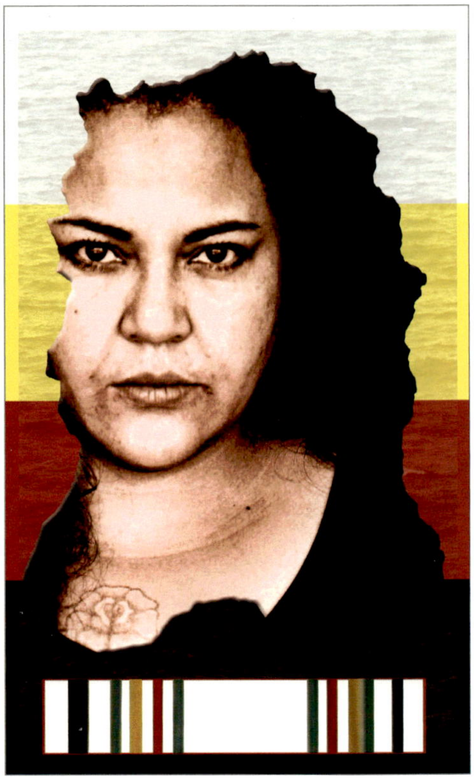

Blanket

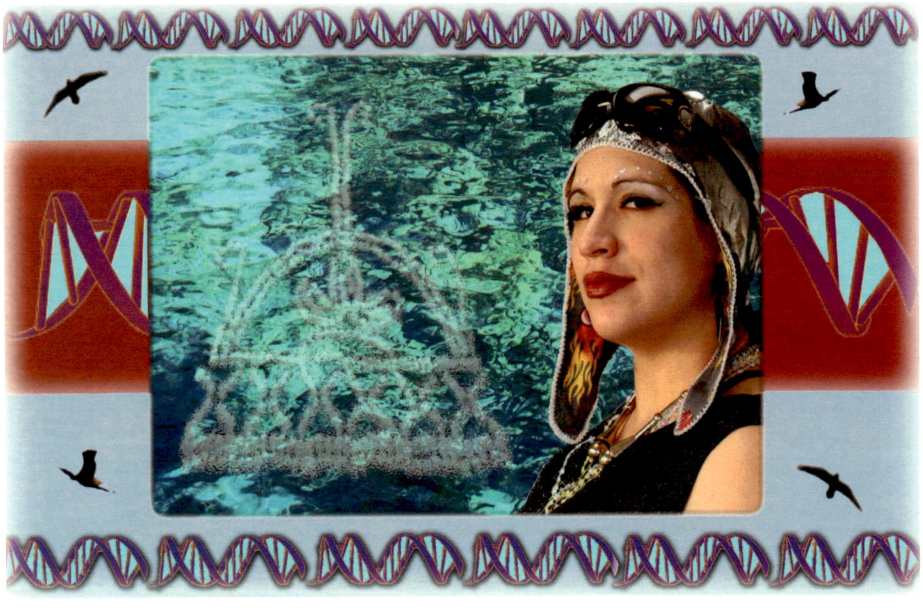

Beginnings

M: Stories of Women Series, 2011

Series of 10 digital photographs
Vertical: 54 7/8 x 34 7/8 in. (139.4 x 88.6 cm);
horizontal: 34 7/8 x 54 7/8 in. (88.6 x 139.4 cm)
Courtesy of the artist

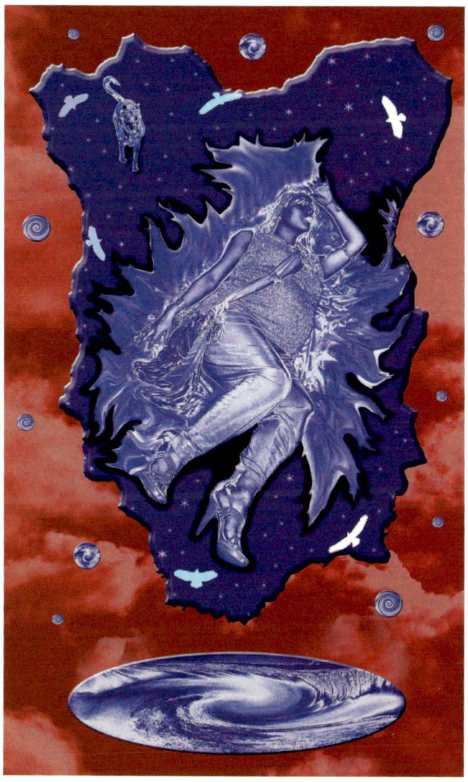

Finding Her Helpers

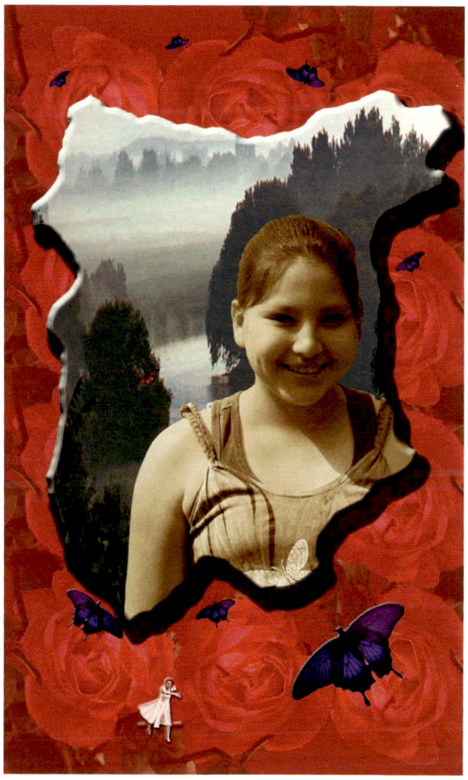

Land of Opportunity

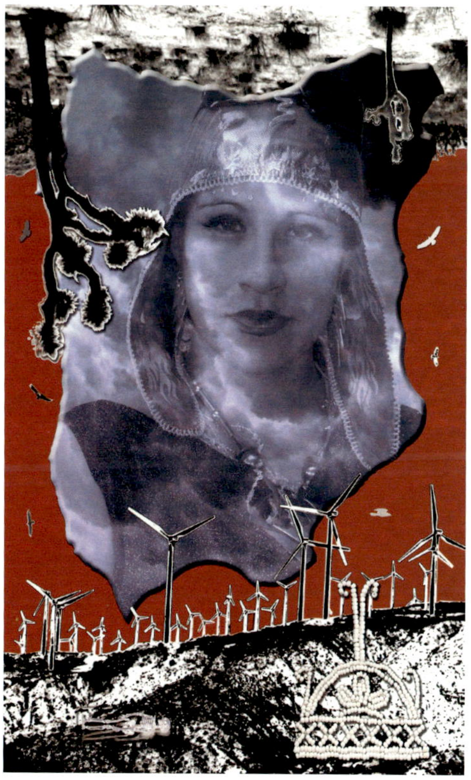

Legacy

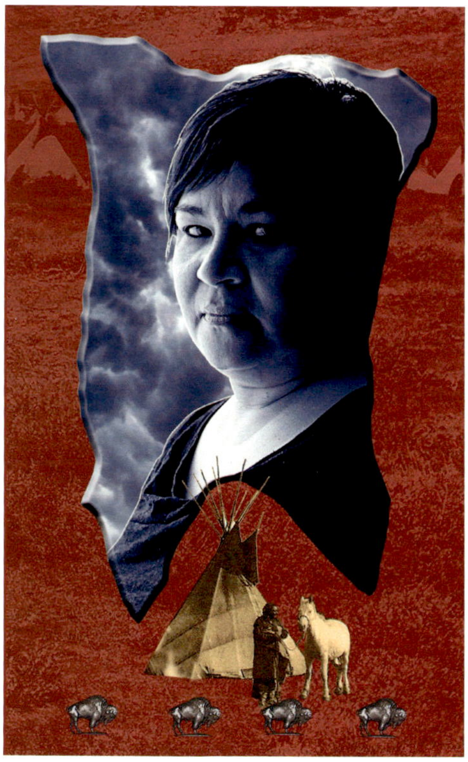

Many Horizons

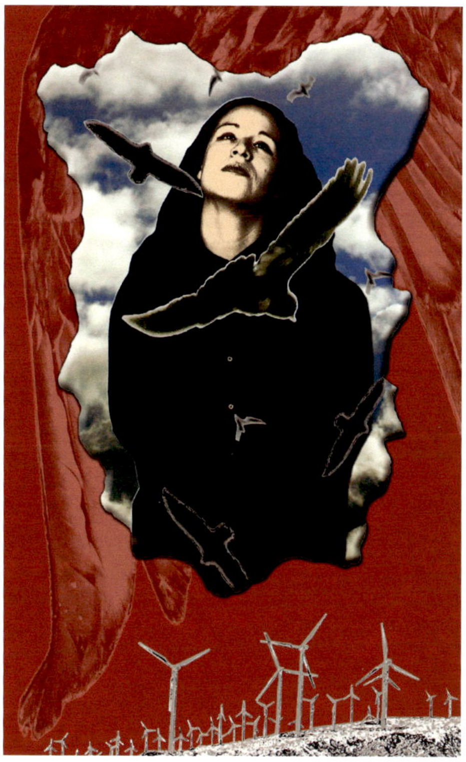

Memories of Flight

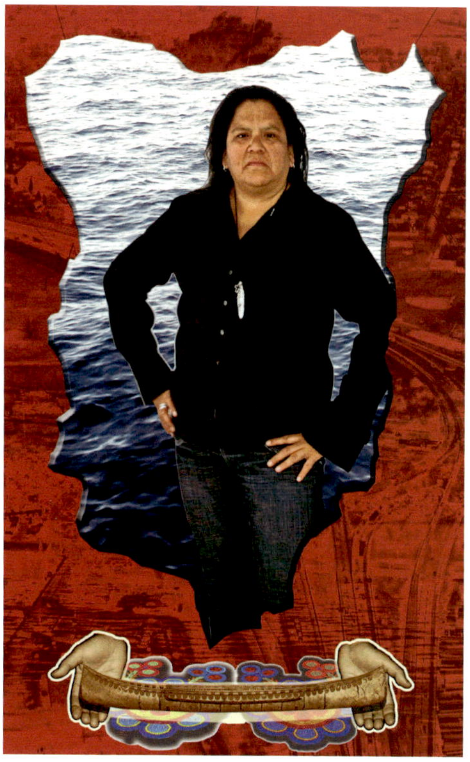

Routes

RON NOGANOSH

b. 1949, Magnetawan, Ontario;
lives in Ottawa, Ontario

Old Soldiers Never Die (War of 1812, World War I, World War 2, Korea), 2009

Mixed media, including recycled aluminum, copper
Diam. 31 ½ in. (80 cm);
depth 11 7/8 in. (30 cm)
Collection of John Cook

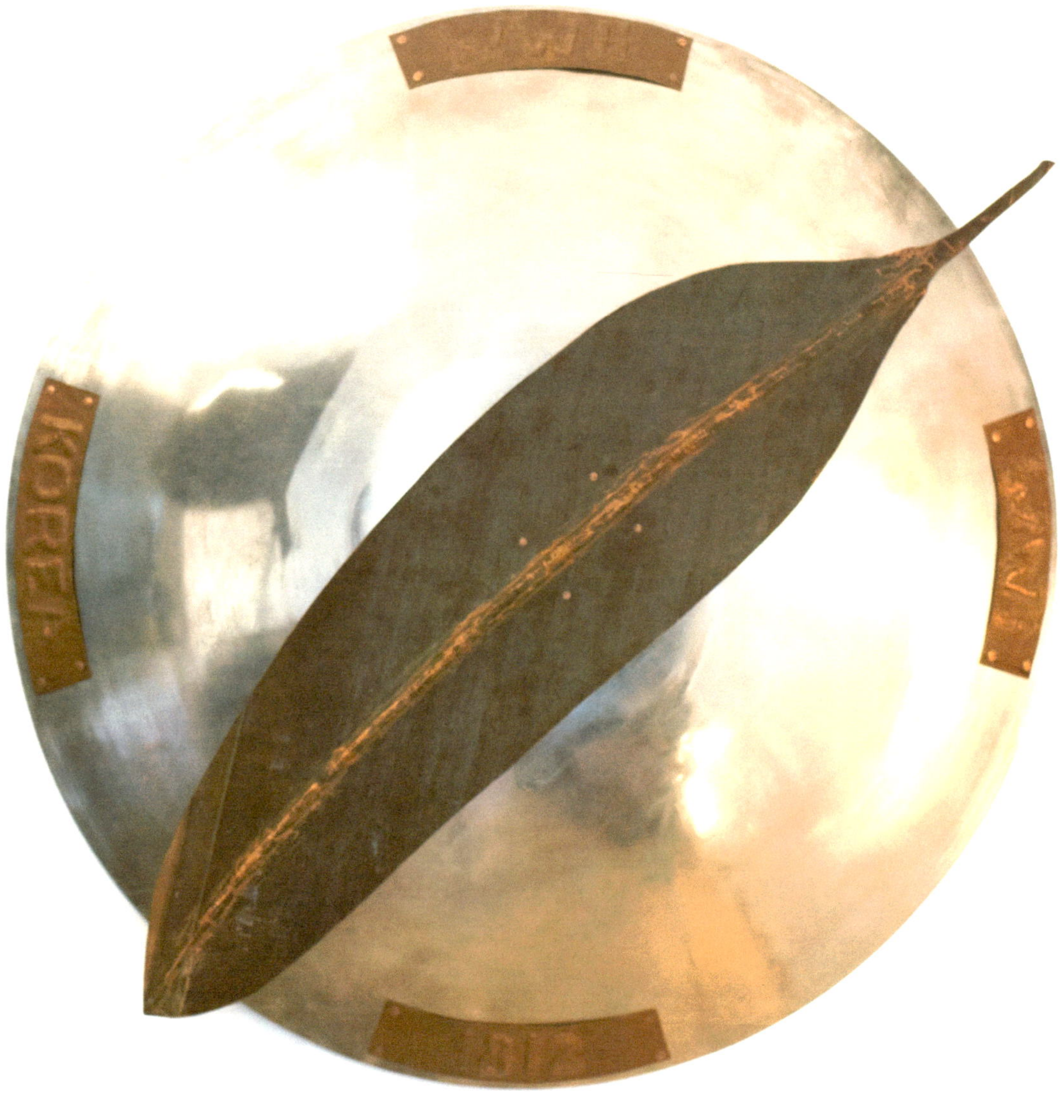

TAMMY RAHR

b. 1958, Rochester, New York;
lives in Santa Fe, New Mexico

Kateri Tekakwitha Blanket, 2011

Pendleton wool, unbleached muslin, canvas, glass beads, German silver brooches, cotton/polyester threads
132 x 60 in. (335.3 x 152.4 cm)
Courtesy of the artist

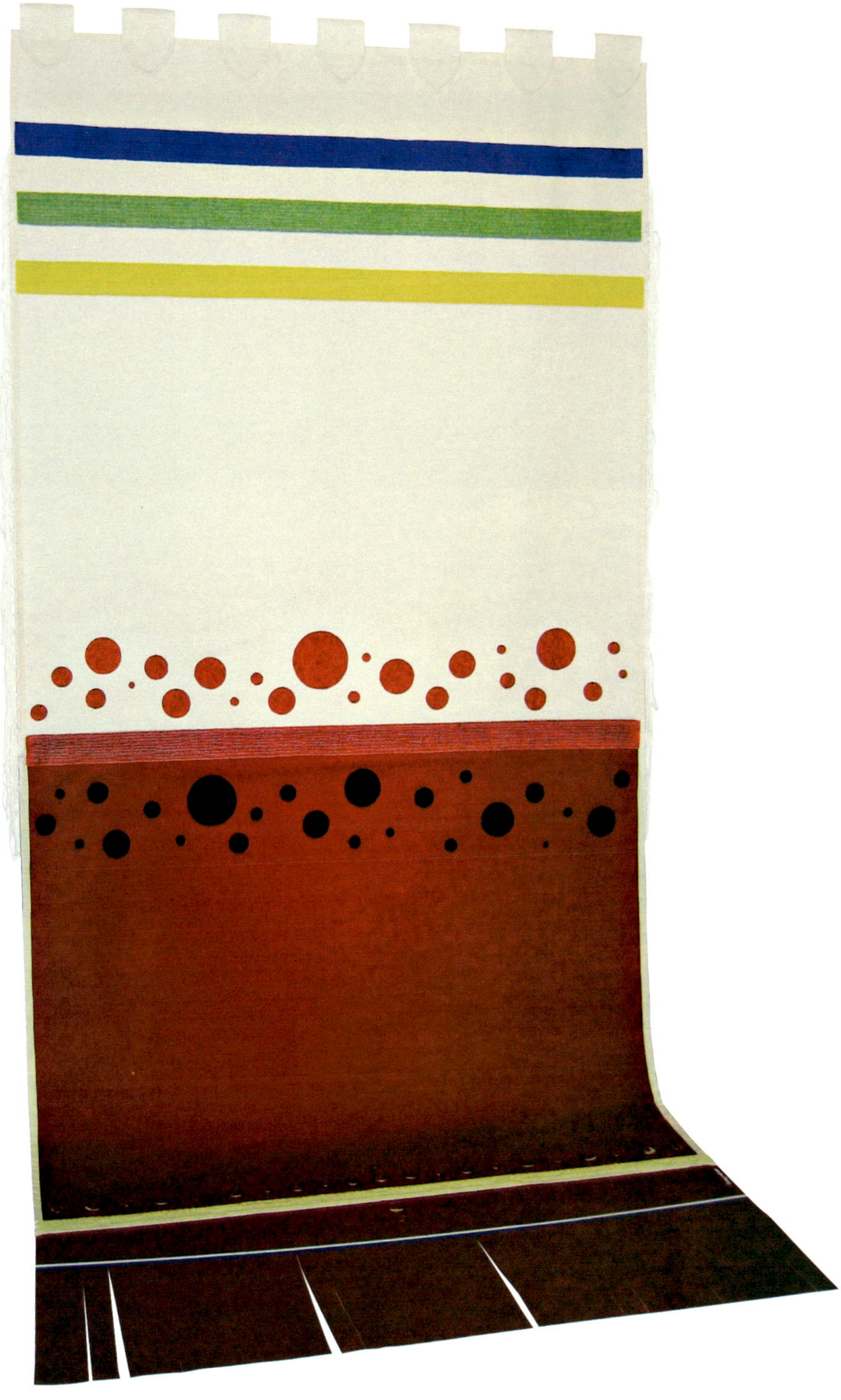

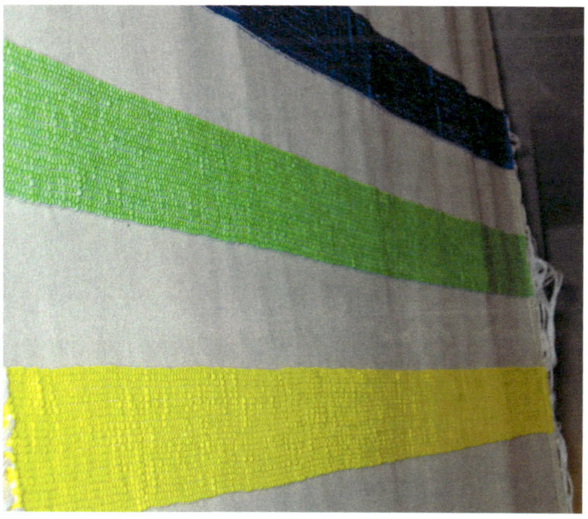

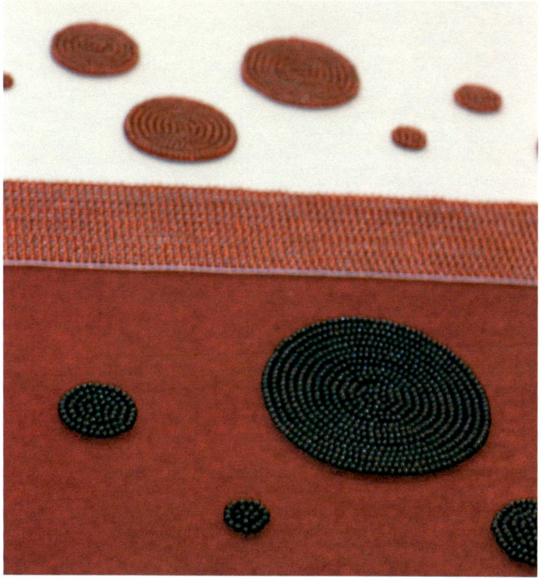

SKAWENNATI

b. 1969, Kahnawake, Quebec;
lives in Montreal, Quebec

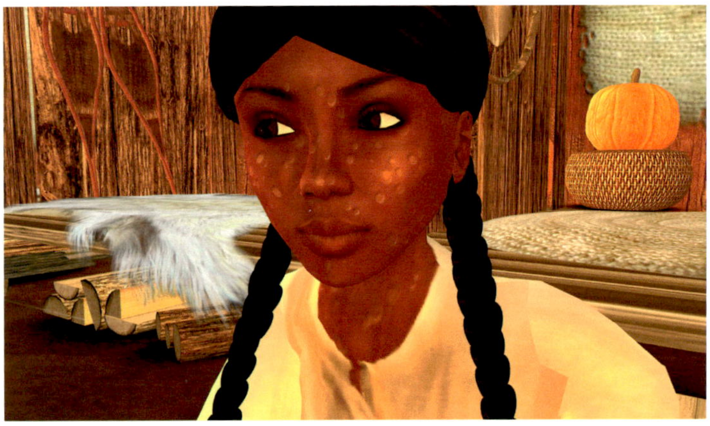

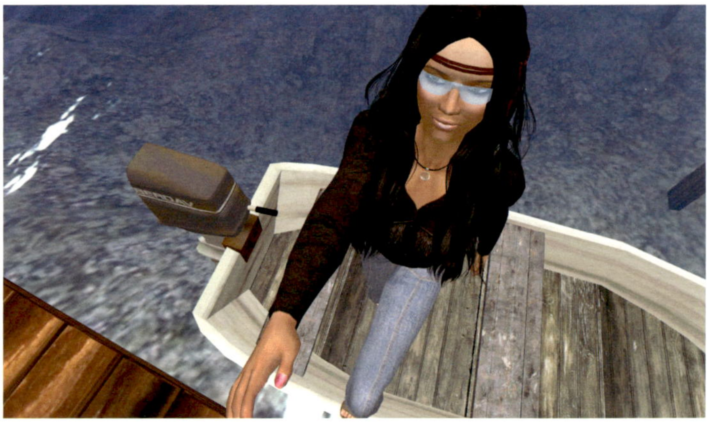

TimeTraveller™: Episode 06,
"Disembarking at Alcatraz," 2012

Production still from
Machinima on Blu-Ray DVD
Approx. 10 minutes
Courtesy of the artist

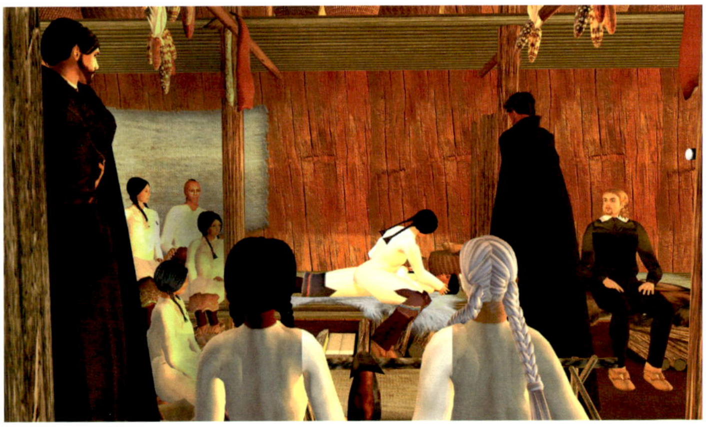

TimeTraveller™: Episode 05,
"Kateri At Home," 2012

Production still from
Machinima on Blu-Ray DVD
10 minutes
Courtesy of the artist

TimeTraveller™: Episode 05,
"Saying Goodbye," 2012

Production still from
Machinima on Blu-Ray DVD
10 minutes
Courtesy of the artist

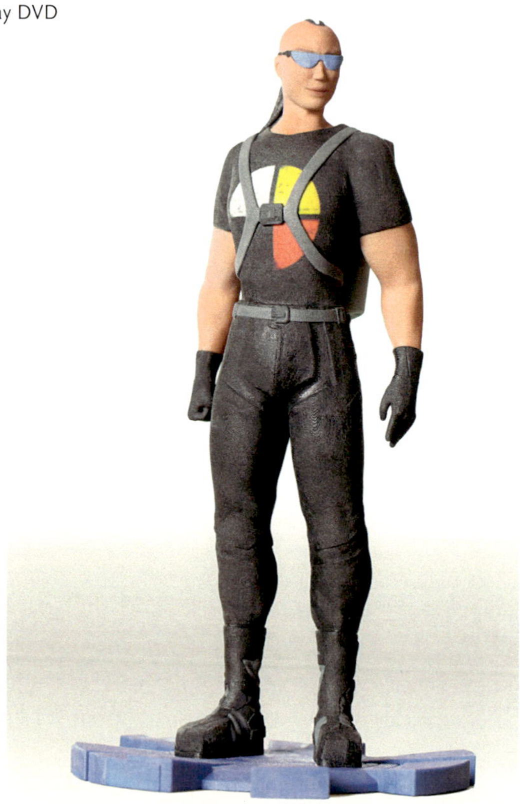

Hunter Mega-Figurine (prototype), 2012

Powdered plaster composite
produced with color 3D Printer
12 x 6 ½ x 6 ½ in.
(30.5 x 16.5 x 16.5 cm)
Courtesy of the artist

TONY A. TIGER

b. 1964, Los Angeles, California; lives in Tahlequah, Oklahoma

Life, Liberty and the Pursuit of Being, 2010

Mixed media on wood
30 x 24 x 3 in. (76.2 x 61 x 7.6 cm)
Courtesy of the artist

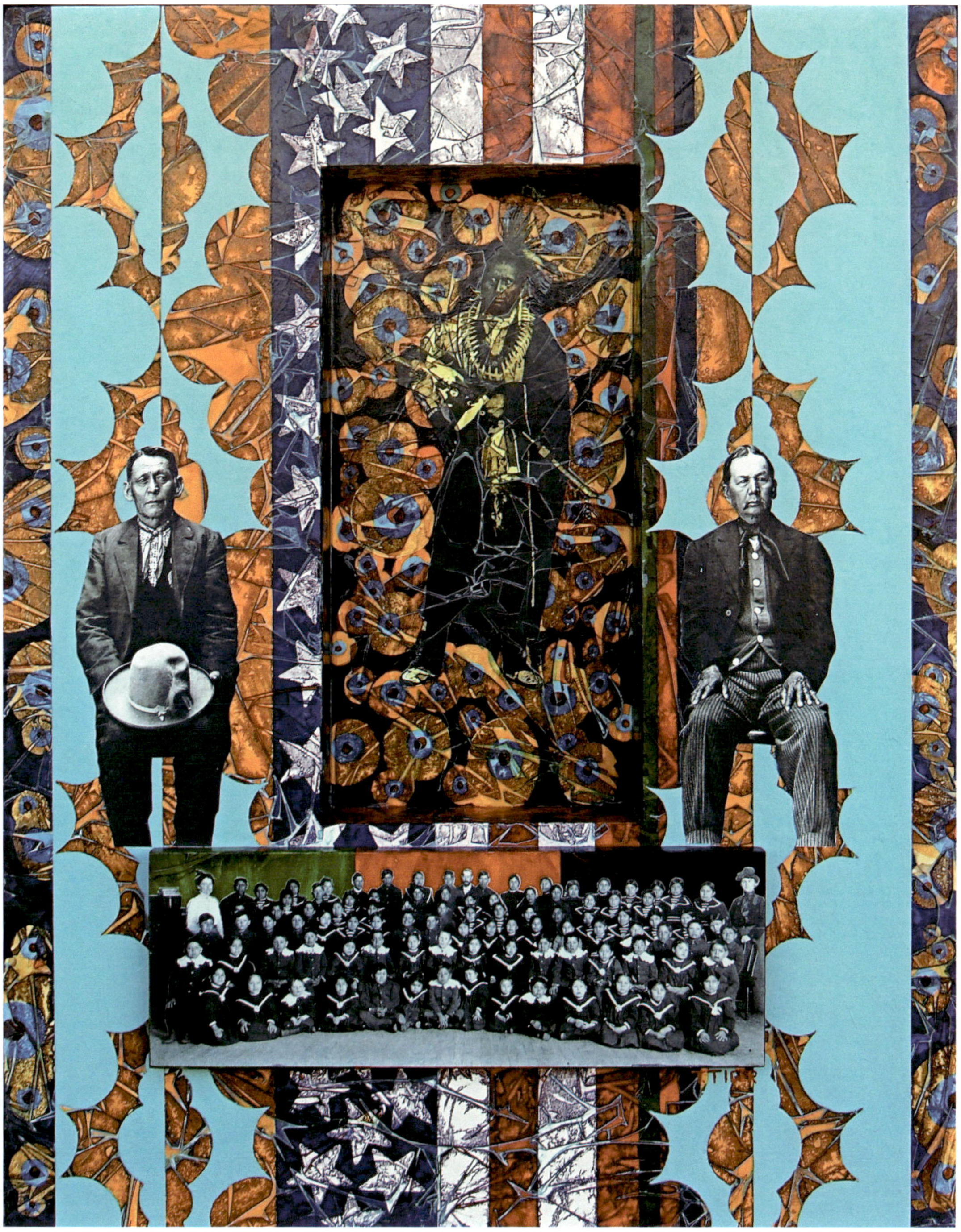

GAIL TREMBLAY

b. 1945, Buffalo, New York;
lives in Olympia, Washington

It Was Never About Playing Cowboys and Indians, 2011

16 mm film, leader, metallic thread and braid
Approx. ht. 24 in. (61cm); diam. 14 in. (35.6cm)
Courtesy of the artist

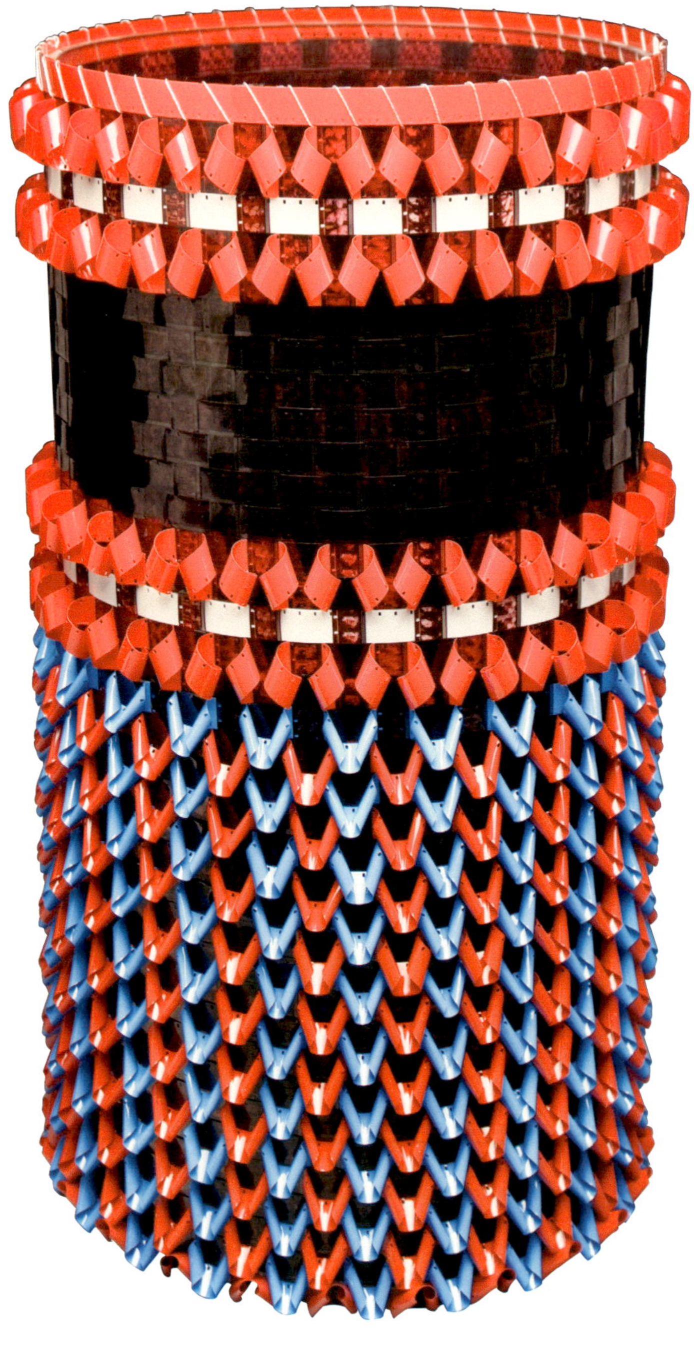

STEPHEN WALL

b. 1950, Roswell, New Mexico; lives in Jemez Pueblo, New Mexico

Techno-Wiindigo 3.5, 2010

Mixed media, including pine and tamarisk woods, wire, recycled electronics, acrylic paint
51 x 13 ¼ x 5 ¾ in.
(129.5 x 33.7 x 14.6 cm)
Courtesy of the artist

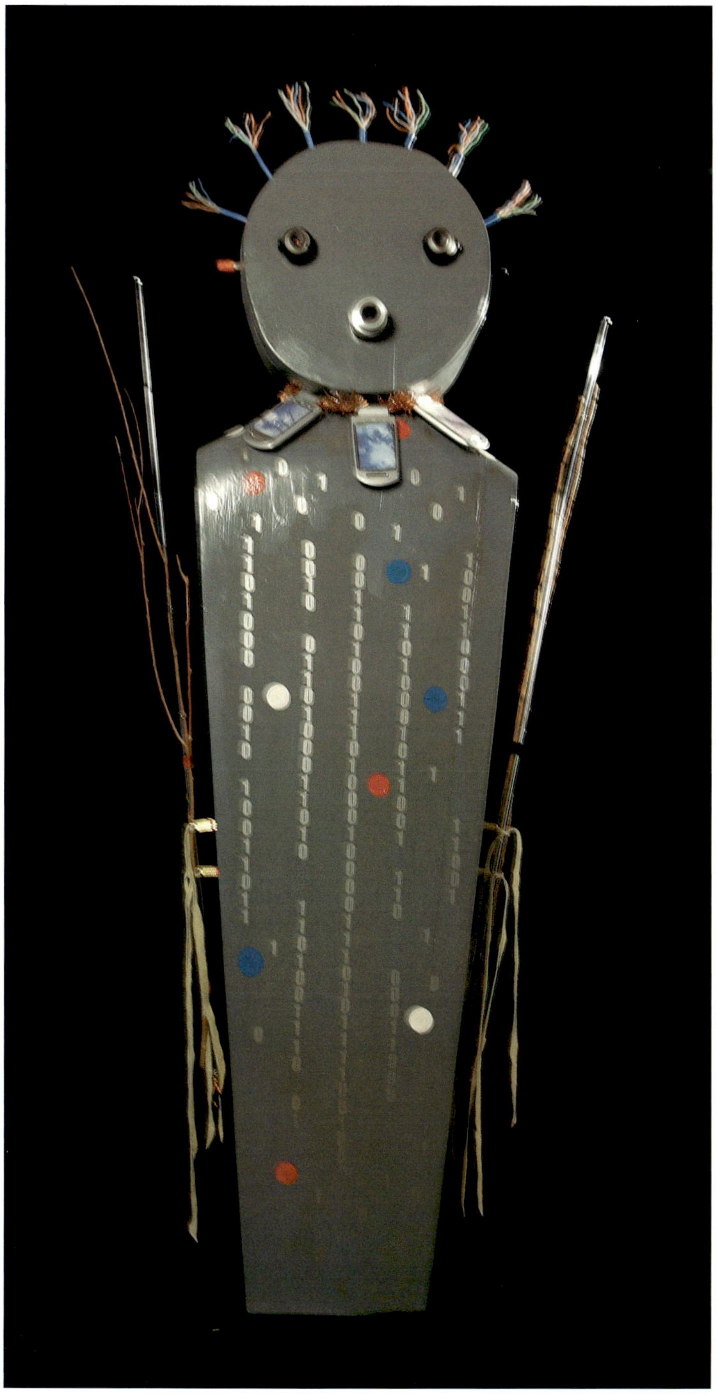

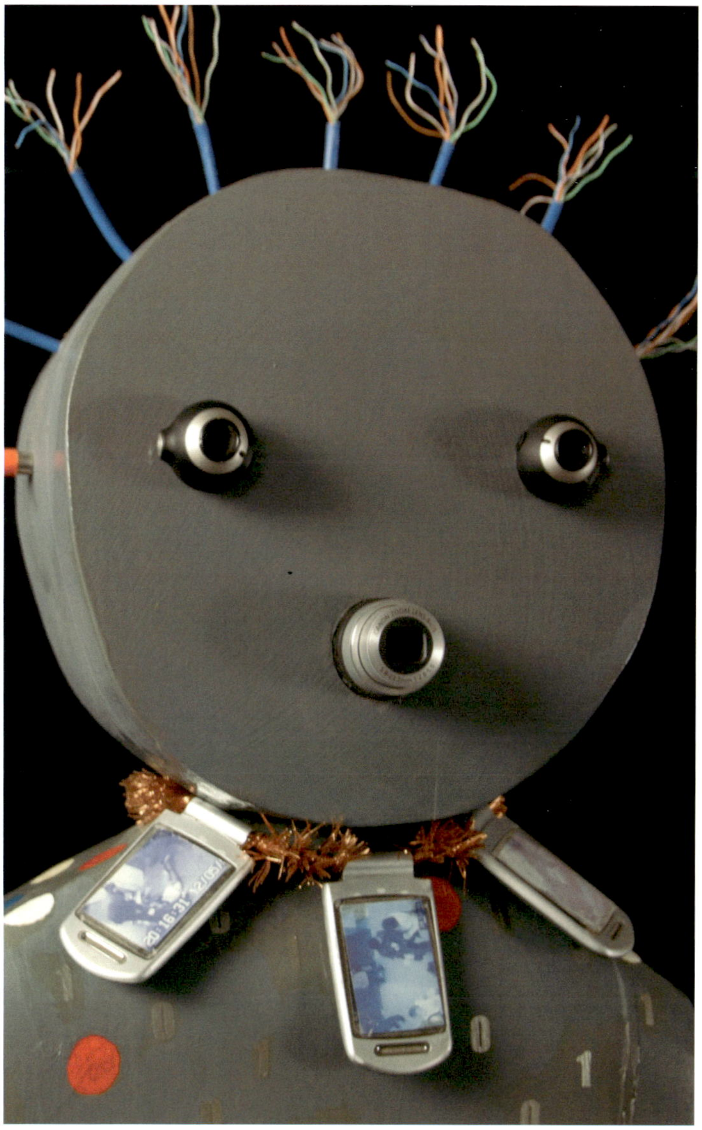

MARIE WATT

b. 1967, Seattle, Washington;
lives in Brooklyn, New York

Ledger: Generations, 2011

Recycled satin bindings
from wool blankets
Each: approx. 17 x 18 in.
(43.2 x 45.7 cm)
PDX Contemporary Art,
Portland, Oregon; courtesy
of the artist

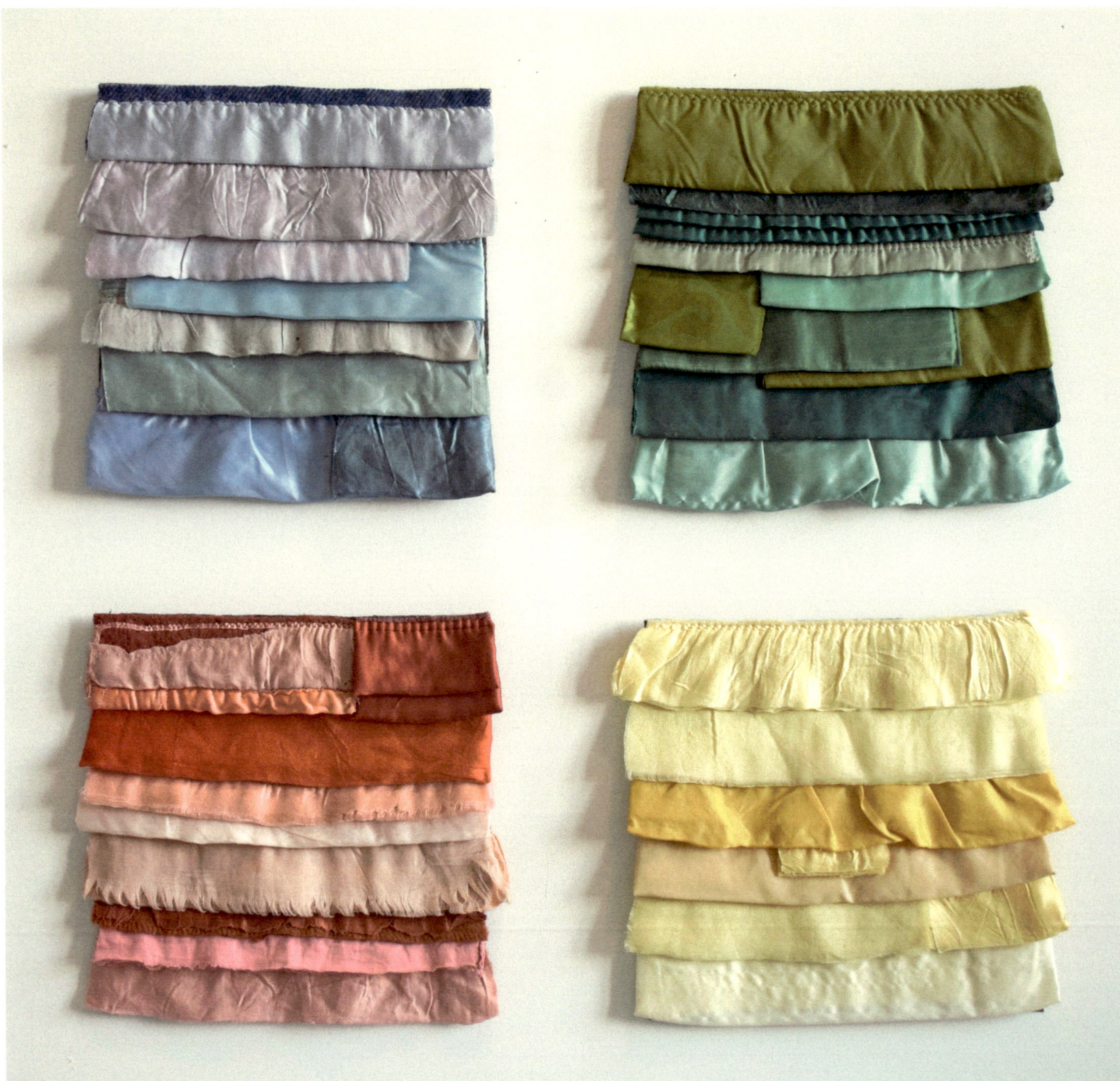

Karen Wright and Jimmie Durham: A Conversation

Karen Wright (KW): I wonder why you say that you are a Cherokee, not an Indian.
Jimmie Durham (JD): A French person will say he is French, not that he is European, nor that he is white.

KW: But you wouldn't say you are a New Yorker, would you? You would say you are an American. There is a different kind of definition going on. You've lived away from America for a long time.
JD: Twenty-five years.

KW: Are you still an American?
JD: I like to think that I'm homeless.

KW: Where did you grow up?
JD: In southern Arkansas. I had a very privileged childhood. We had a movie house close to us that played quite a few silent movies. They were poor so they took what they could get. Silent movies were cheaper, and they got a lot from the 1920s and 1940s, but we didn't know that that was happening. We just thought you go and see movies. I loved Buster Keaton and Laurel and Hardy. I think Laurel and Hardy had sound, but they didn't need it.

KW: I have read that you made art before you could talk.
JD: That is because I was such a late talker. My little sister who is four years younger than me taught me to talk. But I was making toys for myself and for her out of anything that was around—rocks, pieces of wood, nails. There were always a lot of rusty nails. I loved them so much! If you have a big nail, you just have to take a hammer and bend one part of the head of the nail up, and then it becomes the man's hat. He's not a man exactly but a strange kind of being. He only has one kind of leg that is pointed on the end so he has to hop along.

KW: Making things from nothing seems to be a theme of your work—and finding materials themselves seems to be important.
JD: I don't know why, but I'm a good carver. I love to carve stone, and wood, and bones. I like to use my hands, and I have this talent for it. I was in Mexico, the first time, in the early 1960s, and I found a dried mango seed on the street, and I didn't know what it was—I just knew it was magic and beautiful and strange, so I carried it with me, and I went back to the U.S. and I still had this thing. I had no idea what it was. And I painted it. [Laughs] Maybe it wasn't art, but it pleased me just as much as carving pleases me. To find something, or just to have some material like that, it's an incredible thing.

KW: So what did it hold for you? What was the magic of it?
JD: I didn't know what it could possibly be. I still wash them and clean them and dry them.

KW: Does it still have a talismanic quality for you?
JD: I collect them only as material. I don't collect anything except blue and green stones, and I don't try to expand my collection; it just happens. When I find material I like, I put it in my studio, so it's always there as material, not as a collection of something.

KW: I remember you had some beautiful stones, and you said that they speak to you. You don't think of yourself as a collector.
JD: I don't collect. I only get materials and I will use them sooner or later, and sometimes it's later. I have pieces of wood that I have not used yet, that I have been carrying for forty years or more, but I *will* use them.

KW: So it's very different from a collection. It is to be used; it has a purpose.
JD: It gives me a magic studio. Magic, to me, in the sense that at any time I can go into my studio, and if I have to make something, I can make it. I can look around the studio, walk around the studio, start picking up things that I might have forgotten or that I never thought went together, and then I can make a work.

KW: Tell me about the work titled *The Dangers of Petrification* [1996–2007]. It uses stones—which you've used in your work for a long time.
JD: That's a work of two vitrines, and in them I have all kinds of petrified things. A petrified apple slice, petrified bacon, petrified pecorino, and a petrified cloud.

KW: A petrified cloud? Where did you find that?
JD: I explain in the vitrine how it was done. When I find a stone that looks like something I decide *it is that*. I have a petrified oyster for the show [in Berlin]. I found it in a park close to here—a piece of semiclear agate that has the shape of an oyster, that looks like an oyster.

KW: So we can look forward to more rocks?
JD: I've been making a drastic change within the last year. I was in Brazil and have started working with wood again. his is going to sound mystical, but the world of wood keeps getting in my face.

KW: Do you mean carving wood?
JD: I am going back to sculpting, yes.

KW: Will they be totems?
JD: No, they are almost always horizontal. Usually a cross between animal shapes and angular shapes.

KW: Why do you aim for the horizontal?
JD: It gives the material, the piece, more form, more power. I will show one upright piece in Antwerp that I made in the 1970s. Everyone will say it is totemistic but it is not.

KW: We place the binoculars of Indian-ness on you.
JD: This piece stands up because the wood was too thin to show it lying down. In my culture we never had a totem, but we did have—they are not there any more—a dance ground called, in racist American terms, the "stomp ground." It was delineated by poles that had carvings, or sometimes skulls of different animals, on top, and their job was not just to delineate but to connect because we are fanatics of making connections, so I never had thought of that when I make my work. Never enters my mind.

KW: It is the subconscious. Is it true of other artists?
JD: The French really make French paintings. They are not trying to be French when they paint.

KW: Does that frustrate you that we have those Indian binoculars on you?
JD: It can be disturbing sometimes. Especially when people think they know my mental agendas from my artistic agendas. He is an Indian, therefore he cares about nature and the environment. It is exactly the same as saying, "you are afraid of heights; I thought that Indians did high-steel work."

KW: But you yourself have talked about how artists come from place—you have said "Picasso was a Spanish artist." It's a wonderful quote.
JD: Picasso *was* a Spanish artist. He was never a French artist!

KW: And Duchamp was always a French artist with his materiality, which you talk about. You have been accused of getting the reading of his work wrong.
JD: [Chuckles] You're right. There is a love of materiality.

KW: There is the same love of materiality in your work. I think you are Duchampian.
JD: Yes, Exactly!

KW: Is that a good way to think of your work?
JD: Yes, it's not bad. It works.

KW: When you went to Mexico, they saw your love of materials. You inspired a lot of young Latin American artists.
JD: The work I did in Mexico now looks very ideological, but the basis was *always* the material.

KW: You may not have meant to have that element—the political or social element—but it always seems to come out in the work. Tell me about the oil drums that seem to recur in the work.
JD: There is not an easy answer at all to anything. As soon as you say what it contained. . . . All artists like containers for some reason. Most artists like boxes, but I am allergic to angles and squares, so I don't like boxes so much. But I like things that are always around, that pretend to never be around.

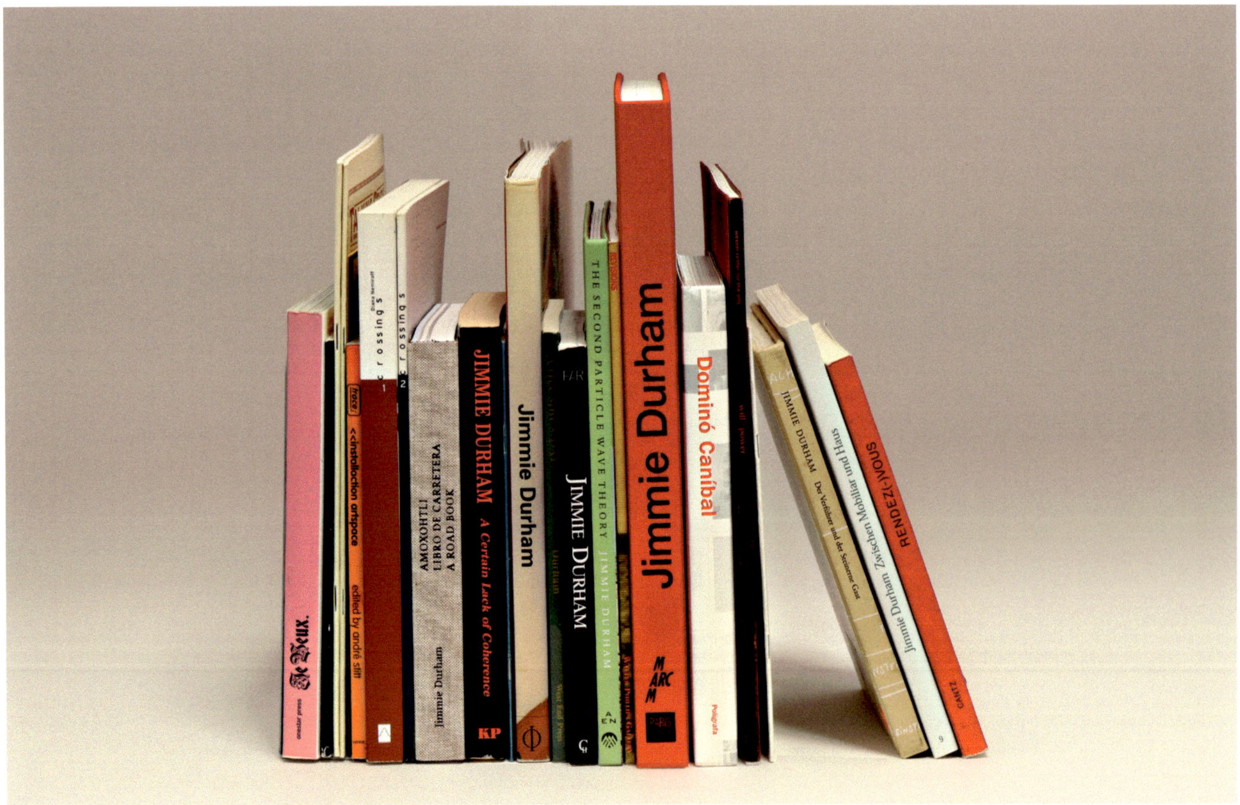

Selection of publications written about and by Jimmie Durham (b. 1940).

KW: You lose sight of them because they are ubiquitous?
JD: I don't do it *for* that but I *like* them for that. In Mexico, just like in the U.S., you cannot separate these things from material. The stuff of the Americas has been so degraded, the plants and the animals, the earth itself has been so degraded in the U.S.—Hollywood-ized, sinfully. So if I wanted to make Pocahontas or La Malinche [1988–91], who was Cortés's interpreter and mistress, in Mexico, which I did—I used local guava wood for her head, I used snakeskin for half of her face, and so on. One of her feet is made of cactus. Because the material is so beautiful and so politicized.

KW: Tell me about the film work with Anri Sala.
JD: That was part of a film [*La Poursuite du Bonheur*, 2002] in 35 mm—a real film. It's about an American Indian artist who makes some art out of garbage and who makes some money and then goes away and lives happily ever after. I got to thinking, I am now in Europe, I can make this film. So I needed an Indian. It just has two actors, one really, and then there is the gallerist. I had met Anri in Japan and I liked him. He doesn't look the least bit Indian, but then I don't either, so that's all right.

KW: Anri Sala makes wonderful films, but they have an almost unbearably slow rhythm to them.
JD: If I watch silly films, like reading a silly book, just to make your mind vacant—a James Bond type of film—then the films from a couple of years ago seem entirely too slow, I want to say, "Come on get on with it, we understand what you are trying to say"—so it affects even me.

KW: Every generation has its rhythm. Will every generation have its artwork? Is Damien Hirst only of this moment?
JD: There is something that I think is important about Hirst's early work. He made a famous piece, of butterflies hatching, and they lay eggs and then more butterflies hatch. This piece, you don't want it to continue forever. You want to know all about the piece. I suppose I would have liked to see all the butterflies.

KW: You will be able to see it soon at the Tate; they are replicating it.
JD: That's not nice. It is not a replicable piece. It should be in the mind. With Duchamp, you want to see the bottle rack, you want to say, "Oh yes, there's that bottle rack, I want to touch that bottle rack." . . . There's a work that I intended to make when I was in Mexico, long before there was a Damien Hirst. In 1974, at the Standing Rock reservation, there was a conference and some French people came out to interview all the Indian big shots. We had just slaughtered a steer to make a big stew and the head was by the river, so I took the television people down to this head which was absolutely full of flies by then and I did the interview there. I don't know why I did it. I was probably showing off. Years later, I got to Mexico and I had a great big flat roof on my house, and the market had cows' heads, steers' heads, all kinds of heads, skinned but everything was there, the horns and all that. I thought I would just stick one on the iron things coming up from the roof and let the flies eat it. But I never did it because I found a very kind-hearted stray dog who did not like to see bones or parts of animals. It would have disturbed him.

KW: When we met in Rome, you told me about the Swiss museum project. Then I saw it in Basel. Can you tell me how the reality of making it differed from the original idea?
JD: Except for my skill, it is exactly what I thought it would be. I had these photos of old masks from when I was in art school in Geneva. My thesis was about the politicization and destruction of folk art. A marginalizing that makes it not serious. I wanted to show these masks because they are astounding—they are not folk art at all, they are art. There are now Swiss masks that are folk art. They are made as folk art—made to be sold to tourists. They have no energy. They have no anything! They are just a sign, and a bad sign at that. I knew that was going to be the center of what I did. I was working mentally on what else is Swiss. I had to make two masks because I wanted some old-looking masks that did not look like tourist masks and I did not have time to find wood and carve them, so I went to an African souvenir shop in Rome and bought two. I brought them home and it takes half a minute to erase what they had done, because it is soft wood, chip away and start over again. One turned out not so bad, but not so good, and the other turned out totally bad. I realized I am not one of these people. I can't make these masks. I can't copy these masks. They are not copiable. I had lived with them all these forty years and I had seen them in use and I could not copy them. Could not replicate them. You have to be inside it or you cannot do it otherwise. And I saw something that I liked about anyone's art. If it is not yours you cannot do it.

KW: Did realizing they were bad feed into the project?
JD: No, because I didn't have time, so I showed these two masks, embarrassingly. The sad thing is that nobody else noticed.

KW: But you knew?
JD: I knew, and I thought everybody would notice, that they would say, "He made two masks because he thought he could make these masks." It was a relief that I wasn't embarrassed.

KW: Hans Ulrich Obrist did not notice?
JD: [Chuckles] I think so much of the world doesn't notice bad copies now, so when we see young artists doing bad copies of 1970s work, we don't notice that either—you and I do, but the people who make it don't notice that they are making bad copies. But I had a lot of funny facts in that show, in the vitrines, and Gianni Jetzer [Director, Swiss Institute Contemporary Art, New York] thought I had made up some of those facts, because everyone thinks I am a funny guy who is ironic and makes up stories—but I never lie. I always see what happens. Fact is much better than fiction.

Oh Kanata: Our Home and Native Land

SHERRY FARRELL RACETTE

> I am, according to the Government of Canada, a real INDIAN. The number that has been assigned me is B047957 and my band number is 99. This has helped me to find my place in society, for without this information, I would, in all probability, not know that I was an Indian, says the government. I spent my youth on the Shawnaga Indian Reservation, attending various and sundry schools, after which I was pronounced CIVILIZED. Upon completing a Graphic Design course in Toronto in 1980, I was officially declared an ARTIST, and let loose upon an unsuspecting world.
>
> Ron Noganosh (Anishinaabe)[1]

Canada is a vast country with a comparatively small population. Due to its rugged terrain, its modest population of 33.5 million is concentrated along the southern border it shares with the United States. Unlike the heavily populated United States, where Native American, Alaskan Native, and Native Hawaiian peoples are often rendered invisible (.9 percent of the total population), in many Canadian cities and towns, Indigenous peoples are the most visible minority. According to the 2006 federal census, the total Indigenous population in Canada is 1,172,790 or 3.8 percent of the total population. This is also the fastest growing sector (twice the national growth rate), and the youngest, with more than half the total Indigenous population under the age of twenty-five.[2]

Canada's national anthem has the phrase, "the true north strong and free," which is sadly ironic for northern peoples. Until the mid-twentieth century when "The North" became a natural resource colony for the rest of Canada, many were able to pursue a subsistence economy of hunting, trapping, and fishing. Northern First Nations and Métis people continually struggle against mega-projects that destroy their hunting territories and frequently displace them from their original homes, seeking at minimum, a share in the economic benefits.[3] Today the Inuit are at the forefront of the global campaign against climate change, as they witness significant shifts in the fragile Arctic environment and suffer the consequences. But while their homelands may be under siege, northern communities are also the bastions of language, artistic traditions, and environmental knowledge.

More Than a Line

The border between the United States and Canada is a drama that unfolded through colonial contests, war, and negotiation.[4] It shifted over time, eventually demarcating the edges of the two nation-states as they are today. Among nineteenth-century Cree, Assiniboine, Dakota, and Lakota peoples, the 49th Parallel from the Red River to the Rocky Mountains was known as the "Medicine Line" because of its power to stop armies, whether Sitting Bull's Lakota fleeing the American cavalry or the Cree and Métis who fled to Montana and North Dakota following their failed resistance against Canada.[5] In the Great Lakes region, the border was more ambivalent—troubling, arbitrary, and invisible—"a line drawn upon the water."[6] For Indigenous peoples, the border was a disruption to be resisted, negotiated or avoided. It severed trade routes and divided territories, nations, and individual communities.[7]

There are fundamental differences north of the line. There are trivial variations in terminology (reservation/reserve, Native American/First Nations) along with the more profound impacts of different colonial histories, legal systems, and government policies that continue to unfold. These differences emerge in contemporary art, juxtaposed with deep similarities and enduring connections. Critical themes and subject matter may be obscure or puzzling to viewers unfamiliar with the cultural, political, historic, and social terrains from which artists draw their inspiration. Powerful visual references might be instantly recognizable in one national context, meaningless in another.

One such visual reference would be a simple pale cream rectangle with green, black, and red stripes, or alternately a red field with black stripes. These are visual signs that might baffle an American viewer. In actual and abstracted form, many artists evoke complicated histories by wielding the graphic image of trade blankets sold by the Hudson's Bay Company, a fur trade enterprise that controlled most of what-is-now Canada for two hundred years. Keesic Douglas's photographic, performance, and video series *Trade Me* (2010) and Rebecca Belmore's video installation *The Blanket* (2011) are two recent works that wrap, shroud, and tangle the body in the same way the fur trade ensnared humans and animals. Although the fur trade was a significant field of encounter in the territories that became the United States, its importance diminished by the early nineteenth century. A gross simplification might state that while the United States used aggressive settlement and military colonization, the world's oldest corporation colonized most of Canada's territory.

The Fur Trade and Colonization

Northern boreal forests were rich in fur-bearing animals: beaver, otter, muskrat, mink, and ermine. Subsequently northern people's initial encounters and earliest relationships were with seventeenth-century fur traders who came from France and Britain to trade and stayed to colonize. By 1821 the Hudson's Bay Company had outmaneuvered and absorbed its various competitors and held an absolute monopoly over trade. Like the British East India Company, it shifted from a trading company to a quasi-colonial administration on behalf of the British crown. Canada, at the time of confederation in 1867, comprised only the small settled eastern regions, until the Hudson's Bay Company transferred its vast territory to the newly created nation in 1870. Indigenous peoples had no role in negotiations and found their lands and destinies transferred without their knowledge or permission.

The extended period of the fur trade—more than two centuries—led to another critical difference between the United States and Canada. The Métis, a large group of mixed-heritage individuals, coalesced in the early nineteenth century into a unique, collective group with a strong national identity. Descended primarily from French and Scottish fur traders who formed marriages and alliances with First Nations women, their language, culture, and governance merged influences. But like the Michif language, which is structurally either Cree or Anishinaabewin with French phrases and nouns, the core of their culture and identity is Indigenous. The Métis straddled the border zones of the Great Lakes and Northern Plains, but their much larger population and two armed resistances under the charismatic leadership of Louis Riel, earned them a place in Canadian history and the Canadian constitution.[8]

Legislated Identities: Status, Nonstatus, Treaty, Registered, Métis, Bill C-31

With the exception of the Grande Paix de Montréal (Great Peace of Montreal) signed in 1701, treaties signed in the later half of the nineteenth century were with the British crown. Following Canadian confederation in 1867, legislation relating to First Nations people and lands was consolidated in 1868 and 1869, and an Act to Amend and Consolidate the Laws Respecting Indians to be Known and Cited as the Indian Act, 1876, was passed into legislation.[9] The Canadian government embarked on a series of treaty negotiations to secure the western and northern territories for settlement. Known as the "numbered treaties" signed between 1871 and 1921, they were negotiated in the name of the reigning British sovereign.

The descendants of treaty signatories and the people they represented are known collectively as "Treaty Indians" with a relationship with the crown articulated through their specific treaty. Although a variety of agreements and land surrenders were also signed with the crown, many areas of Canada—including the province of Quebec—were not covered, and the land has never been officially surrendered. To address the significant number of people excluded from the treaty process, the Department of Indian Affairs embarked on a process of registration, creating an enumerated list of individuals recognized as "Indians" by the federal government. "Status" or "Registered Indians" are those whose names appear on the federal register.

At the time of registration many communities continued their traditional movement and resource harvesting. Some were registered and some were not. The vastness of the land, remoteness of some communities, lack of roads, and negligence resulted in entire communities and groups being left off the federal register. Nonstatus Indians were (and are) First Nations individuals and communities not federally recognized.

To further complicate matters, the Indian Act provided mechanisms for removing individuals from the federal register. The act was highly patriarchal, recognizing descent only through the male line. Women, who married men other than status Indians, lost their status and were "no longer considered an Indian pursuant to the Indian Act." Whether they married a Euro-Canadian, Métis, or a nonstatus Indian, they and their children lost all their rights, including the right to live on their home territory. Men, on the other hand, could marry anyone and pass their status to their wives and children. Men who served in the navy or air force or pursued post-secondary education often lost their status, and individuals also voluntarily "enfranchised" and removed themselves from the register. Individuals leaving or pushed off the federal register joined the ranks of nonstatus Indians and often united with the Métis in a collective struggle for recognition.

The Métis were never recognized as having federal status, and the only existing legislation was the province of Alberta's Métis Population Betterment Act (1938) which defined a Métis as "a person of mixed white and Indian blood," amended in 1940 as "persons with a minimum of one quarter Indian blood who were not status or Treaty Indians pursuant to the Indian Act."[10] Although the Manitoba Act of 1870, negotiated by Louis Riel's provisional government, guaranteed the Métis of the Red River region 1.7 million acres, the aggressive actions of the Canadian military resulted in a large exodus west, north, and south. The federal government refused to negotiate with the Métis during the treaty process and extinguished their Aboriginal title through individual land or money scrip. The process was fraught with corruption, and most of the land passed almost immediately to land speculators. By the early twentieth century, many Métis people were landless noncitizens, denied hunting and fishing rights, excluded from education, caught in a jurisdictional abyss. Pushed off their territories and onto the margins of Canadian society, the term "Road Allowance People" referred to their small camps and settlements on tracts of land set aside for roads by municipal and provincial governments. Many were living in abject poverty.

First Nations people living under the Indian Act received basic Canadian citizenship in 1960, voting for the first time in 1961. The 1970s and 80s were decades of activism across Indigenous Canada that ushered in two profound changes. The first was the repatriation of the Canadian constitution from Great Britain in 1982. Initially excluded from negotiations, a series of constitutional meetings with Inuit, First Nations, and Métis leaders resulted in Section 35 of the Canadian Constitution Act of 1982, which recognized and affirmed "the existing aboriginal and treaty rights" of the "Aboriginal people of Canada" who were defined as "the Indian, Inuit and Métis." In 1985, Bill C-31, an amendment to the Indian Act, attempted to address the gender discrimination embedded within the act, providing a mechanism for restoring rights to individuals and their children.[11] By 2007 an estimated 117,000 persons had been restored to the Indian Register.[12]

The complexities of identity legislation in Canada, its historic omissions and exclusions, and the large population of people of mixed heritage not affiliated with a "tribe," have made Indigenous people in Canada somewhat baffled by the exclusionary definitions and resulting practices emerging from legislation such as the United States Indian Arts and Crafts Act of 1990. Sculptor and writer Jimmie Durham (Cherokee), for example, is embraced in Canada and has been highly influential through collaborations with artists and curators such as Edward Poitras (Cree/Métis), Candice Hopkins (Tlingit), and Richard Hill (Cree).

The Culture Ban, Residential Schools, and "The Sixties Scoop"

The Indian Act remains a very powerful piece of legislation. Throughout its history it has been modified and amended, sometimes with horrific consequences. The act does much more than define who is and who is not "an Indian pursuant to the Act." An overview of amendments reveals its intrusive presence, which at its peak created an oppressive reality with devastating and continuing consequences. Traditional ceremonies were criminalized, beginning with the Northwest Coast Potlatch and Tamanawas ceremonies in 1885, but expanding to include all other ceremonies, dances, and even nonsanctioned public appearances in traditional dress.[13] Freedom of movement, freedom of assembly, traditional leadership and governance, even raising money for legal challenges, were criminalized. To survive, critical knowledge and ceremony went underground. In 1939, the Supreme Court of Canada ruled that Inuit people were under the jurisdiction of the Indian Act, which resulted in ill-considered relocations, mass shootings of sled dogs to curb Inuit mobility, and the removal of children to residential schools.

In 1880 local Indian agents were granted status as justices of the peace and magistrates, enabling them to prosecute, punish, and summon the police. Indian agents had the legislative authority to forcibly remove children and arrest parents who refused to let their children go.

The Residential and Industrial School Era in Canada (1879–1986) was inspired by the American policy of "aggressive civilization" espoused by the Carlisle Industrial School and Haskell Institute, but Canadian schools were a grim shadow of those institutions. The children provided the labor force and lived in overcrowded conditions, underfed, sick, and often abused. In 1907 Peter Bryce, an inspecting physician working for the Department of Indian Affairs, reported appalling conditions and high death rates. Bryce continued to monitor the situation and finally published *The Story of a National Crime: Being an Appeal for Justice to the Indians of Canada* (1920) in an effort to rally public pressure.[14] While health conditions improved, other abuses continued. The last residential school in Canada closed in 1996, the same year the Royal Commission on Aboriginal People released the findings of a major study examining the impact.[15] The subsequent legal struggles and class action suits were finally settled in 2007, with a $2 billion dollar compensation package that offered cash settlements to all individuals who had been forced to attend the schools. Larger compensation packages are promised to those who suffered physical and sexual abuse, which was systemically rampant. In 2008 Prime Minister Stephen Harper issued an official apology, and a nationwide Truth and Reconciliation process is currently underway.

Further complicating the consequences of this era were the provincial social welfare programs that alienated children from their families. In common with Indigenous peoples in Australia and the United States, thousands of children were adopted, primarily in their home provinces, but also by families in Europe and America. Known as "The Sixties Scoop," Ontario Children's Aid agencies alone removed an estimated 16,000 First Nations, Métis, and Inuit children between 1965 and 1984.[16]

The social consequences of these policies have continuing ramifications. Indigenous people in Canada struggle with environmental crises, poverty, and chronic economic underdevelopment. Indigenous people are overrepresented in the criminal justice system, and underrepresented in education, business, and government. One of the most critical struggles today is with the high number of unsolved cases of missing and murdered women, currently estimated at 600, but possibly as high as 3,000, attracting condemnation from both Amnesty International and the United Nations. By contrast, increasing autonomy and cultural revitalization affirm the continuing presence and growing strength of Indigenous people, who may be damaged, but whose surviving languages, religions, stories, and artistic traditions witness their resilience and fortitude.

Artists, Revitalization, and Resistance

The trajectory of Indigenous art history in Canada is a powerful testimony of the role of art and artists in articulating political struggle, opposing erasure, and envisioning a future. For artists living under the oppressive regime of the Indian Act, choices were severely constrained and cultural expressions were outlawed. A light appeared when the 1951 edition of the Indian Act quietly omitted the most oppressive amendments, an unofficial response to political activism and a growing chorus of advocates. Ceremonies came back into sight, drums were heard again, and traditional artists began reclaiming their regalia and artistic practices.

Contemporary First Nations art did not emerge into the national conscience until Expo '67 in Montreal, which coincided with the Canadian centennial. The newly formed Cultural Affairs division of the Department of Indian Affairs engaged in dialogue with artists and selected a group of male artists to create work for the Indians of Canada Pavilion. This group included Jackson Beardy (Cree), Alex Janvier (Dene), Tom Hill (Seneca), and Norval Morrisseau (Anishinaabe), who all went on to become key figures in the development of a contemporary art movement.[17] With the exception of Janvier and Hill, these artists were self-taught and their distinct styles were closely tied to traditional story, belief, and imagery. Drawing on early pictorial forms on rock and hide, they created completely new modes of artistic expression. Also emerging in the 1960s, an Iroquoian sculptural practice similarly drew from the oral tradition, most notably in the works of Stan Hill (Mohawk), Duffy Wilson (Tuscarora), and Joe Jacobs (Cayuga). While this was primarily a "man's world," Daphne Odjig (Odawa/Potawatomi), Ellen Neel (Kwakwaka'wakw), Doreen Jensen (Gixsan), and Freda Diesing (Haida) were respected and influential artists.

For societies bent upon conceptualizing "Indians" as a colorful part of history, contemporary "Native" art challenged the notions of art, craft, and the accompanying spaces of museum and art gallery. Where to put it? What to call it? Initially

Indigenous art and artists were assumed to belong in museum spaces, but artists resisted. Denied access to art galleries, artists claimed the status of "artist" and fought to be considered on the same ground as other Canadian artists, while resisting pressure to conform to mainstream imagery and practices. Acceptance and access on their own terms has been, and continues to be, the focus of arts activism.

In 1973 a small group of artists formed Professional Indian Artists, Inc., on the heels of the first exhibition of Canadian First Nations artists in a public art gallery. The exhibition organized by the Winnipeg Art Gallery, was ironically titled *Treaty Numbers 23, 287, 1171* and featured the work of Daphne Odjig, Jackson Beardy, and Alex Janvier. Although more artists emerged in the following decades, the struggle to gain entry into Canadian art institutions continued. In 1983 a group of artists from around the country met in British Columbia and the following year established the Society of Canadian Artists of Native Ancestry (SCANA). Curator Lee-Ann Martin (Mohawk) recalled:

> SCANA was an organization of Native artists from across the country that wanted to fight for inclusion in art galleries, because . . . in the late 80s and early 90s it was still a huge uphill battle. It's gotten much better—still a long way to go—but Bob [Boyer] really was at the forefront of banging down those doors. I shared that with him. That was my firm belief as a curator. Get contemporary Aboriginal art into those glass towers.[18]

Although SCANA ceased activity in the 1990s, a variety of artist-run organizations emerged across the country, some with fleeting influence, while others had more lasting impact. SCANA's confrontational debates continued, both outside and inside institutions, and the culture of Canadian arts slowly shifted. It was pushed by a series of politically and emotionally charged events. National demonstrations to protest the 1988 *Spirit Sings* exhibition at the Glenbow Museum resulted in the Museums and First Peoples Task Force. The 1990 Oka crisis, a three-month armed standoff between the Canadian army and the Mohawk communities of Kahnesatake and Kahnawake—precipitated by a land dispute with the town of Oka—had a riveting affect, politicizing Indigenous peoples across the country and triggering national soul-searching (and reactionary racism).

In 1992, a landmark year for Indigenous art, there were three major group exhibitions: *New Territories: 350/500 Years After* in Montreal, *Indigena: Perspectives of Indigenous Peoples on Five Hundred Years*, curated by Lee-Ann Martin (Mohawk) and Gerald McMaster (Cree/Blackfoot) for the Canadian Museum of Civilization, and *Land, Spirit, Power: First Nations at the National Gallery of Canada* curated by Diana Nemiroff, Charlotte Townsend-Gault, and Robert Houle (Anishinaabe).

The 1990s also marked a new initiative: the use of the artist-run center as a means of creating Indigenous art spaces, borrowing a strategy that emerged in Canada during the 1960s to develop artistic collaboration and increase opportunities to present contemporary work. The Canada Council for the Arts (est. 1957), which provides critical arts funding to a range of arts and artists, established an Aboriginal Arts Secretariat in 1994 with the initial goal of increasing the number of applications from Indigenous artists and artist groups. As it is a highly competitive process, multiple applications are needed for any sector to receive funding. Nation-to-Nation (Montreal), Tribe (Saskatoon), Urban Shaman (Winnipeg), and Sakewewak (Regina) were all established during this time. Partnerships with other artist-run centers, collectives, and small regional galleries created a vibrant, although marginalized, terrain that nurtured collaboration, creativity, and experimentation. The Banff Art Centre made space for Indigenous arts, and became an important creative laboratory. Most contemporary Indigenous artists in Canada have honed their practice in these spaces, often crafting a network.

A national voice returned in the form of the Aboriginal Curatorial Collective (ACC) in 2006, organized by a founding group of four artist-curators. The current board and membership are national, with a few international members, and the emphasis has shifted to curatorial concerns, exploring Indigenous practice, and continuing to lobby for representation and access.

The importance of Indigenous artists to contemporary Canadian art, and a belated recognition for some, is reflected in a series of of landmark events:

1995	Edward Poitras (Cree/Métis) represents Canada at the Venice Biennale
2002	Brian Jungen (Dunne-za) wins the inaugural Sobey Art Award[19]
2002	Edward Poitras wins a Governor General's Award in Visual and Media Arts
2004	Tom Hill wins a Governor General's Award in Visual and Media Arts
2005	Rebecca Belmore (Anishinaabe) represents Canada at the Venice Biennale
2006	*Norval Morrisseau: Shaman Artist*, solo exhibition at the National Gallery of Canada
2006	Annie Pootoogook (Inuit) wins the Sobey Art Award
2007	Daphne Odjig wins a Governor General's Award in Visual and Media Arts
2008	Alex Janvier and Kenojuak (Inuit) each win a Governor General's Award in Visual and Media Arts
2009	*The Drawings and Paintings of Daphne Odjig: a Retrospective Exhibition* at the National Art Gallery
2010	Robert Davidson (Haida) wins a Governor General's Award in Visual and Media Arts

Recent developments attest to the importance of Indigneous artists to contemporary Canadian art. *Oh Canada*, which opened at the Massachusetts Museum of Contemporary Art in May 2012, included a substantive group of Indigenous artists and authors, and in 2012 an unprecedented number of Indigenous artists—Nadia Myre (Algonquin), Mark Igloliorte

(Inuk), and Sonny Assu (Kwakwaka'wakw)—are among the twenty-five nominees for the annual Sobey Award.

While these are significant achievements, historic concentrations of recognition, and exhibitions are often followed by long periods of drought. Indigenous artists, perhaps, have become too adept at creating strong work and crafting compelling exhibitions on a perpetual shoestring. This has created the perception of a well-developed infrastructure, but in fact it is only patched together, short-term, and tentative. The margin has become productive and vital, but the aesthetic "Road Allowance" is as vulnerable a space as its historic precedents, which were swept away by the bulldozers of development and short-sighted government policies. The current economic and political climate demands vigilance in securing the hard-won gains made by Canadian Indigenous artists to safeguard a place for the next creative generation.

---

1 Ron Nogonosh, quoted in Alfred Young Man, "Towards a Political History of Native Art," in *Visions of Power: Contemporary Art by First Nations, Inuit and Japanese Canadians*, exh. cat. Harbourfront, Toronto, June 1991 (Toronto: Earth Spirit Festival, 1991); online at Centre for Canadian Contemporary Art, Canadian Art Database, http://www.ccca.ca/c/writing/y/young%20man/you001t.html.

2 Thomas Townsend and Michael Wernick, "Hope or Heartbreak: Aboriginal Youth and Canada's Future," *Horizons* 10, no. 4 (2008): 4.

3 Massive hydro-electric development projects devastated northern Quebec and Manitoba in the 1970s, also uranium mining in northern Saskatchewan, the tar sands in the Mackenzie River delta, and diamond mining in northern Cree territory in Ontario. See Paul Joffe, *Sovereign Injustice: Forcible Inclusion of the James Bay Crees and Cree Territory into Sovereign Québec* (Nemaska, Que.: Grand Council of the Crees, 1995); Peter Kulchyski, *È-nakàskàkowaàk (A Step Back) Nisichawayasihk Cree Nation and the Wuskwatim Project* (Winnipeg, Man.: Canadian Centre for Policy Alternatives, 2004).

4 The border originated with the Treaty of Paris in 1783, clarified by the 1794 Jay Treaty's International Border Commission, finally settling into its present form in 1903, when the boundary between Alaska, the Yukon and British Columbia was negotiated.

5 Tony Reese, *Arc of the Medicine Line: Mapping the World's Longest Undefended Border Across the Western Plains* (Lincoln: University of Nebraska Press; Vancouver: Douglas & McIntyre, 2009).

6 Karl Hele, ed., *Lines Drawn upon the Water: First Nations and the Great Lakes Borders and Borderlands* (Waterloo, Ont.: Wilfred Laurier University Press, 2008).

7 Anishinaabe (Ojibway/Chippewa), Haudenosaunee (Iroquois), Blackfoot (Blackfeet in the US), Micmac, Abenaki, Potawatomi, Dakota, Lakota (Sioux), Nakota (Assiniboine) are some of the nations divided by the American/Canadian border.

8 See Jacqueline Peterson and Jennifer S. H. Brown, eds., *The New People: Being and Becoming Métis in North America*, Manitoba Studies in Native History (Lincoln: University of Nebraska, 1985); Jennifer Reid, *Louis Riel and the Creation of Modern Canada* (Albuquerque: University of New Mexico, 2008).

9 Katherine Pettipas, *Severing the Ties That Bind: Government Repression of Indian Religious Ceremonies on the Prairies* (Winnipeg: University of Manitoba Press, 1994), 87.

10 Letha MacLachlan, "The 1990 Alberta Métis Settlements Legislation: An Overview," *Resources: The Newsletter of the Canadian Institute of Resources Law* 33 (Winter 1991): 2.

11 For a discussion of the history of Bill C-31 and continuing challenges see "Native Women's Association of Canada, Aboriginal Women and Bill C-31," issue paper prepared for the National Aboriginal Women's Summit, Cornerbrook, Newfoundland, June 2007, online at http://www.laa.gov.nl.ca/laa/naws/pdf/nwac-billc-31.pdf.

12 Mary C. Hurley and Tonina Simeone, "Legislative Summary of Bill C-31, Gender Equity in Indian Registration Act," Publication No 40-3-C3E, Parliamentary information and Research Service, Library of Parliament of Canada, 2010.

13 Pettipas, *Severing the Ties That Bind*, 88, 122–24.

14 Peter H. Bryce, *The Story of a National Crime: Being an Appeal for Justice to the Indians of Canada* (Ottawa: James Hope & Sons, Ltd., 1922).

15 The report was subsequently published as John S. Milloy, *A National Crime: The Canadian Government and the Residential School System, 1879–1986* (Winnipeg: University of Manitoba Press, 1999)

16 Linda Diebel, "Legal Setback for Ontario Aboriginal Children Taken from Their Families during the 'Sixties Scoop,'" *The Star*, January 25, 2012, online at http://www.thestar.com/news/canada/politics/article/1121500.

17 Myra Rutherdale and Jim Miller, " 'It's Our Country': First Nations' Participation in the Indians of Canada Pavilion at Expo 67," *Online Journal of the CHA 2006 revue en Ligne de la S.H.C* 17 no. 2 (2007): 159.

18 Lee-Ann Martin, "SCANA and Contemporary Aboriginal Art in Canada," video vignette at *Bob Boyer: His Life's Works*, Mackenzie Art Gallery, Virtual Museum website, http://www.museevirtuel-virtualmuseum.ca/sgc-cms/expositions-exhibitions/bob_boyer/en/videos-scana.html.

19 The Sobey Art Award is a prestigious annual prize awarded to a Canadian artist under the age of forty.

A New Day for Contemporary Native Arts

PATSY PHILLIPS

> For some, the almost mythic aura around the early years of the IAIA is overrated, but the undeniable fact is that the Institute opened up a world of possibilities for Indian artists and changed the perspectives of non-Indian curators and critics.
>
> — Richard W. Hill, Sr.[1]

The "world of possibilities" cited by the former Director of the Institute of American Indian Arts (IAIA) Museum, is now a reality. After forty years of change and development, the Museum of Contemporary Native Arts (MoCNA) is defining anew the *possibilities* of Indian art in the twenty-first century. In 2012, my fourth year as Director, I am proud to say MoCNA is heading up many new developments in the contemporary Native arts world. Changing our name in 2008 from the "IAIA Museum" to the "Museum of Contemporary Native Arts," a center of the Institute of American Indian Arts, has had a major impact on advancing our mission, thus advancing contemporary Native arts.

The Museum celebrates its fortieth anniversary in 2012. Originally established to collect and showcase student work, MoCNA evolved to represent a wide range of contemporary Native arts from the best artists in North America. For the past four decades, many individuals have been a part of and contributed to the success of the Museum.

In 2008 MoCNA conducted a major study to analyze perceptions of the Museum's image and identity. Focus groups were held with faculty, students, alumni, staff, museum partners, and supporters. The study showed that the general public was confused by the IAIA Museum name and unclear of its mission. Participants suggested the name did not represent its current work and did not demonstrate its standing on a par with leading museums nationwide. The assessment determined that the new name, Museum of Contemporary Native Arts, would best represent its mission as the only museum in the world dedicated solely to advancing the scholarship, discourse, and understanding of contemporary Native arts.

Today, MoCNA's challenging and thought-provoking exhibitions from Indigenous artists globally reveal the complexity of the field and encourage critical engagement and dialogue in the contemporary arts field. MoCNA's progressive exhibitions and programming invite the viewer/visitor to rethink Native American art. To lead the dialogue and advance the field of contemporary Native arts, MoCNA is producing major publications that address current issues.

In 2011, MoCNA published its first major book in more than twenty years, *Manifestations: New Native Arts Criticism,* edited by Dr. Nancy Marie Mithlo.[2] Representing the voices of eighty American Indians from fifty-one different sovereign nations, *Manifestations* highlights the work of sixty living contemporary Native artists who have made central contributions to the field in the United States and beyond. *Manifestations* also expands the practice of cultural criticism for contemporary Native American art and addresses the most pressing concerns in the field of contemporary Native arts practice including the nature of place, identity debates, pedagogy, vocabulary, professional standing, and our global presence. Through this publication, Native art administrators, curators, writers, and artists are reaching out to national and international audiences, inviting dialogue.

MoCNA also recently published an exhibition catalogue for *Counting Coup* curated by MoCNA Chief Curator, Ryan Rice, with essays by Rice and scholar Dr. Jolene Rickard. This project brought together a remarkable group of eighteen Native artists from the United States, Canada, and Australia. Rice appropriated the phrase "counting coup" from the Plains Indians, using it as a metaphor for equalizing history. The text addresses social consciousness, recognizes and embraces the magnitude of Native creativity, celebrates the enormous contributions made by Native Americans to society, and ultimately honors our ancestors. MoCNA's publications and exhibition catalogues create a "life" beyond the galleries.

The Museum of Contemporary Native Arts has now come of age. As the second part of our mission states, MoCNA is the "global leader in the acquisition, presentation and study of contemporary Native arts . . . challenging pre-conceived notions of contemporary Native arts." Combined with the name change and strategic advice from our constituents, we are actively engaged with national and international audiences to promote contemporary Native arts.

As MoCNA moves forward, we are striving for museum accreditation from the American Association of Museums and recently received a grant from them for a "museum assessment" —a step toward reaching that goal. In 2012 we are showcasing works from MoCNA's collection of 7,500 objects, in celebration of our fortieth anniversary, and we continue to develop and establish relationships with art organizations and museums to create a dialogue with Native and non-Native audiences. As the country's leading museum for contemporary Native arts, MoCNA is beginning a dynamic new chapter in its history.

---

1 Richard W. Hill, Sr., "The Institute of American Indian Arts and Contemporary Native Art," in Lowery Stokes Sims et al., *Fritz Scholder: Indian/Not Indian* (New York: Prestel Publishing, 2011), 133.

2 Nancy Marie Mithlo, ed., *Manifestations: New Native Art Criticism* (Santa Fe: Museum of Contemporary Native Arts, 2011). *Manifestations* was made possible by the Ford Foundation—Working with the Visionaries on the Frontlines of Social Change Worldwide.

Epilogue—Close Encounters: The Next 500 Years

CANDICE HOPKINS, STEVEN LOFT, LEE-ANN MARTIN, JENNY WESTERN

Close Encounters: The Next 500 Years (2011) was the largest international exhibition of Indigenous artists ever mounted in Canada, perhaps anywhere.[1] It was a chance to reflect on the significance of Indigenous artists on the world art stage and here in North America, and to ponder the distances traveled, literally and metaphorically. Indigenous artists are increasingly represented in the largest public and private collections, in exhibitions in major galleries, and at international art shows and bienials. The question remains, however: are their voices being heard amid the self-congratulatory backslapping of the art elite? Is the movement of Indigenous aesthetics and cultural sovereignty getting through? The answer is both yes and no. Certainly the number and impact of Indigenous artists, and the critical dialogue about them, has come to represent a real movement in the art world. Exhibitions such as *Close Encounters* and the *Changing Hands* series prove that. But what is sometimes lost in the (rightful) celebration of these accomplishments is their place as an assertion of cultural sovereignty. Without acknowledging the colonial violence and cultural oppression committed against Indigenous peoples by settler states, there can be no peace, no rapprochement, no moving forward.

The future is past—the exhibition has closed, the publication has been released. Artwork has been purchased or returned; relationships have been solidified. For a dizzying fourteen months, the curatorial collective responsible for the *Close Encounters* project talked of little except the future. Not only was this our curatorial premise, it was the time in which we lived and worked. We brainstormed about the future at meetings, in conference calls and e-mail exchanges; we spoke of the future with artists throughout Canada, the United States, Norway, Australia, and New Zealand (thirty-four artists eventually participated). What if we could organize a large international exhibition of Indigenous artists whose works would speculate upon future possibilities? What if these works could turn upside down moribund notions of Indigenous peoples perpetually frozen in the past? And within this framework, how might we still show respect for our various customary traditions and beliefs—drawn from the past but still relevant in defining our future? What would be the potential legacy of a project of this scope?

There seemed no better place and time to launch the project than in Winnipeg in January, when the city is cold and still, with hours of darkness briefly interrupted by brilliant sunshine reflecting off crisp white snow. The temperature tends to dip below minus 22°F (-30°C) and lingers there for weeks on end. It is under these circumstances that we invited artists from across Canada and such climes as the southwestern United States and New Zealand to join us for an opening celebration in 2011, and they came bundled up and eager to explore this seemingly alien landscape.

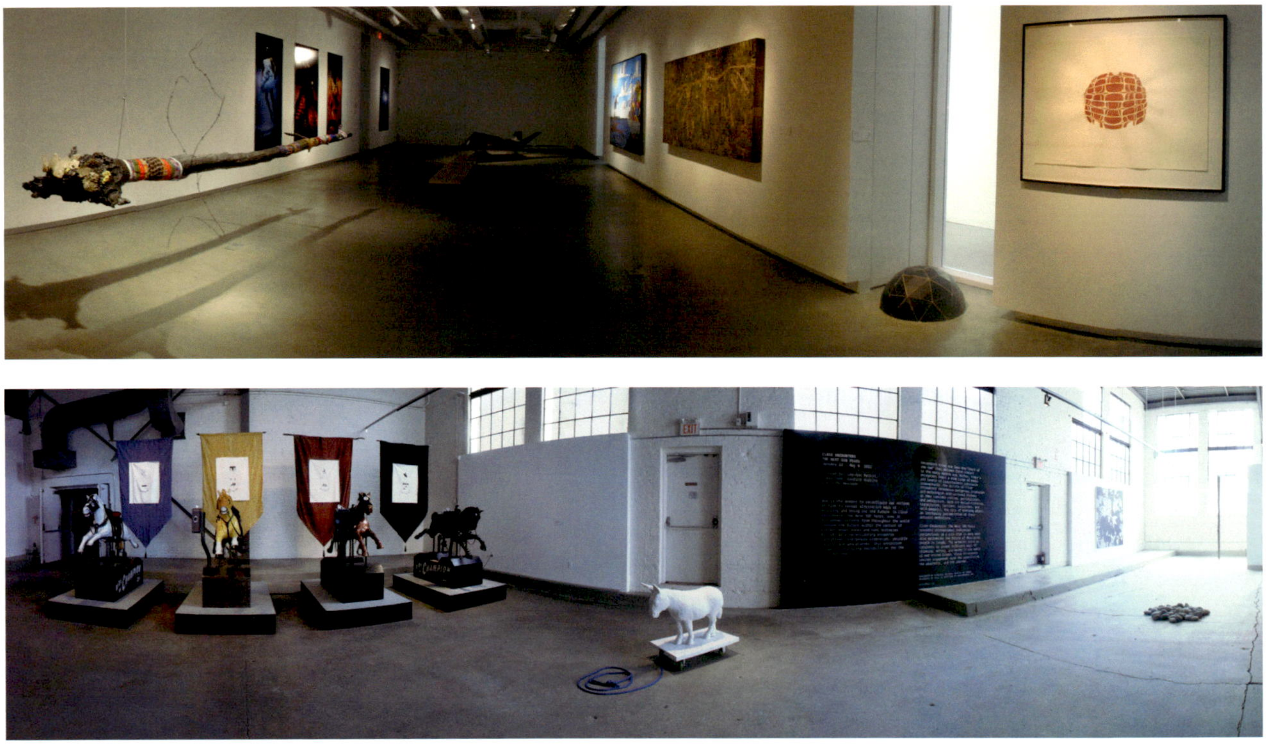

Close Encounters as installed at the Plug In Institute of Contemporary Art, Winnipeg, Manitoba, 2011
Courtesy of the Plug In Institute of Contemporary Art

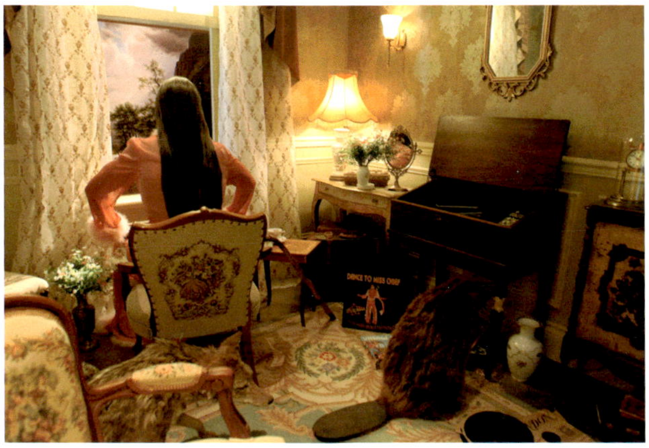

Kent Monkman. *The Collapsing of Time and Space in an Ever Expanding Universe*, 2011 (as installed at the Plug In Institute of Contemporary Art). Courtesy of Plug In Institute of Contemporary Art, Winnipeg, Manitoba.

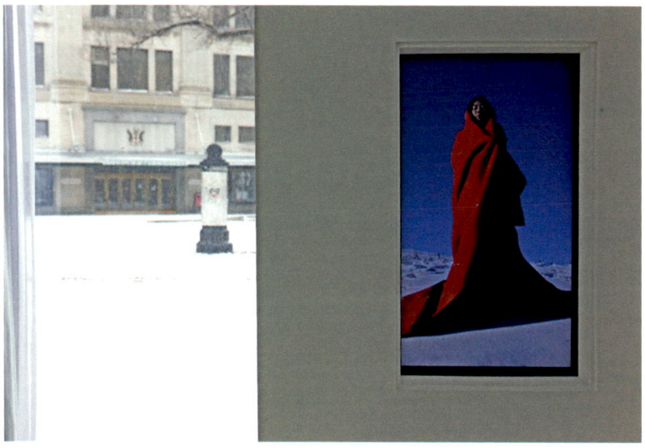

Rebecca Belmore. *The Blanket*, 2010 (as installed at the Plug In Institute of Contemporary Art). Courtesy of the Plug In Institute of Contemporary Art, Winnipeg, Manitoba.

There is a history of close encounters in Winnipeg. This an ancient meeting place where two far-reaching rivers, the Red and the Assiniboine, come together. These rivers form part of a vast network of waterways across North America. They are partial remnants of the long-departed glacial Lake Agassiz which once covered parts of Manitoba, Ontario, Minnesota, North Dakota, and Saskatchewan. The disappearance of Lake Agassiz coincided with major changes in the local and global climate and landscape, but contemporary residents of the area are reminded of its grandeur and power each spring with the threat of another flood season. Dating back as far as 6,000 years, the confluence of the two rivers has served as a location for cultural exchange and trade among Indigenous peoples.

When *Close Encounters* closed in May 2011, the Assiniboine River was at its highest level in recorded history. That winter's above-normal precipitation and high soil-moisture conditions led to what became a one-in-three-hundred-year flood that affected many parts of Manitoba. Yet one revolution of the earth around the sun later, in January 2012, the third warmest on record, Winnipeg saw a month with little snow and an average temperature of 14°F (-10°C), very different from the year before.

Culturally, Winnipeg has also been changing lately. The city has one of the highest Aboriginal populations of any Canadian urban center, and some estimates anticipate that this population will be 77,900 strong by 2017, making up 10.6 percent of the city's entire population.[2] Perhaps because Winnipeg is not (yet) an international art center, it served as a unique location for *Close Encounters* and proved to be an inspiration to many of its participating artists. Faye HeavyShield's installation, *slivers,* investigated the Red and Assiniboine rivers, and Jimmie Durham's sculptural work, *A Pole to Mark the Centre of the World* (at Winnipeg), considered the locality and underlined the importance of exhibitions of this kind occurring outside of the expected centers.

Many of the artworks in *Close Encounters* demonstrated the extent to which notions of utopia—the conception of an ideal society—and apocalypse—the prophesying of future end times—are not limited to Western-European thought.[3] Visions of the future are often couched within ideas of utopia and apocalypse, and this is no different for Indigenous people. The emergence of the Ghost Dance ceremony in North America, for example, demonstrated the degree to which apocalyptic conceptions of mass destruction and future regeneration become more pronounced with the introduction of Christianity and the merging of these ideologies with Indigenous spiritual practices.[4] This ceremony became a poignant historical reference for Rebecca Belmore in her video *The Blanket*. The Ghost Dance, where peace and prosperity would emerge from the ashes of the former world, was a wide-scale attempt—for many, a desperate last ditch effort—to redefine relationships with settler culture and actively bring this new world into being.

Nostalgia and reflections from the future also figured into the exhibition. A once-famous Native artist and entertainer, an aging Miss Chief Eagle Testickle (the alter ego of artist Kent Monkman), was seen looking out the window of her Parisian apartment, shedding tears as she gazed upon an image from her past—a time when she rode horses and chased buffalo freely in the Great Plains of the Americas. Additional clues revealed this to be not just a pastiche of former glory, but also an indictment of colonial history. In the installation *The Collapsing of Space and Time in an Ever Expanding Universe*, Miss Chief seemed to be exhorting: "No matter how much we long for the way things were we can't go back in time and live life the way it once was."

Other works in *Close Encounters* offered a means of tempering the destructive tendencies fueled by these same colonial ideologies: Choctaw-Cherokee painter and sculptor Jeffrey Gibson intuited the future as a place of regeneration and renewal. Crystals and glossy silicone drips, like chrysalides, emerged from the trunk of a suspended tree as though it is in the process of transformation. An act of creation, change, and wonder.

Positioning ourselves in the future enables us to tackle the complicated link between Indigenous people and the past head on. Jimmie Durham, writing in 1990, in words that still ring true today, observed that "there has been no serious treatment of the United States' relation to its 'indigenous populations.'" He found that "Instead there has been a stunning silence."[5] But with time the situation has become even more precarious. In 2009 Canadian Prime Minister Stephen Harper proudly declared at a G20 summit meeting, while listing a series of Canada's assets, that "we also have no history of colonialism." The ignorance of the statement is stunning. What his words make clear is that silence has all but been transformed into outright denial. This is not to say that things have to be this way. Perhaps this in and of itself serves to underscore the importance of exhibitions like *Changing Hands* and *Close Encounters*. Change begins with the ability to articulate what the problem is and the challenges faced.

Jolene Rickard once called sovereignty "a line in the sand." Sovereignty, when viewed from Indigenous perspectives, is predicated on notions of communal responsibility, cultural autonomy, traditional knowledge, and nationhood. It disavows colonialism, by not being predicated on it, but in "relation" to it. Daunting, to say the least, but this establishes a position of cultural self-awareness and philosophical as well as ontological strength. For Rickard, sovereignty as an Indigenous concept "needs to be articulated as a framing device to interpret the work of Indigenous artists. The incorporation of expanded ideas of sovereignty in combination with contemporary analysis of Indigenous art has the potential to shift consciousness within Indigenous communities and surrounding colonial settler nations."[6]

Her statement is a call to continue the assertion of Indigenous sovereignty and a reminder of certain responsibilities that apply to all artists:

- Never build your identity on what an oppressor has done to you.
- Never condemn future generations to ongoing assimilationist agendas.
- Never allow your image to be used as a weapon against you.

These are the tenets of an art history and an art trajectory that reclaim space in the wide universe of cultural knowledge and dissemination. And, it is a challenge to everyone to view art and culture in new ways and to continually aspire to be better for the journey.

In "reading" the works of Indigenous artists, the viewer must always be cognizant of the artists' positioning as creators, interpreters, translators, and purveyors of an inherent and ancient cultural autonomy. To decolonize is to supplant racist patriarchies in favor of multicontextual dialogues, while understanding and acknowledging the place of an Indigenous sovereignty rooted in land, language, culture, and ways of knowing and being. It is a progression—one that is vast and rich and challenging—based on mutual respect and understanding, and a desire to explore the complexities of interrelationships.

Close Encounters was one manifestation of that progression. It showed what Indigenous artists thought about the future in 2011: a future of cultural dialogue that is polycultural, intercultural, and resistant to racist hegemonies. With hope and optimism the exhibition allowed the beauty and the struggle and the veracity of Indigenous art and culture to be brought forward. It was, as with many encounters, a lingering and reflective moment in time. And what of the future?

---

1 *Close Encounters* was organized by Plug In ICA, Winnipeg, Manitoba, and co-curated by Lee-Ann Martin, Candice Hopkins, Steve Loft, and Jenny Western. The exhibition ran from January 22 to May 8, 2011 and occupied five sites within the city. The catalogue, *Close Encounters: The Next 500 Years*, edited by Sherry Farrell Racette, was published by Plug-In Editions.

2 *Manitoba's Aboriginal Community: A 2001 to 2026 Population & Demographic Profile* (July 2005), www.gov.mb.ca.

3 North America was initially regarded as a potential utopia by early explorers (and in many ways it was for first settlers who had been driven by the need for change and the possibilities that this New World offered). This sentiment, however, left little room for the Indigenous peoples already living in these lands.

4 Both the Maori prophet Rua and the Paiute leader Wovoka, whose vision sparked the Ghost Dance movement, were spiritual leaders whose religious movements were influenced by Christianity and merged these ideologies with local spiritual and religious beliefs.

5 Durham, "Cowboys and . . . ," in *A Certain Lack of Coherence: Writings on Art and Cultural Politics* (London: Kala Press, 1993), 176.

6 Jolene Rickard, "Visualizing Sovereignty in the Time of Biometric Sensors: Sovereignty, Indigeneity, and the Law," *South Atlantic Quarterly* 110, special issue (Spring 2011): 478.

ARTISTS' BIOGRAPHIES AND STATEMENTS

multitruths. Such dualities present complex spaces for dialogue and negotiation to address power dynamics of domination narratives—the historical place occupied by Indigenous peoples including both the psychological and daily physical challenges that come with it. My work is grounded in a combination of both Anishinaabek (Ojibway) and Western art practices. Present investigations continue to explore previous interest in the imposed dichotomies that exist within the fourth world, academy, and community. — MH

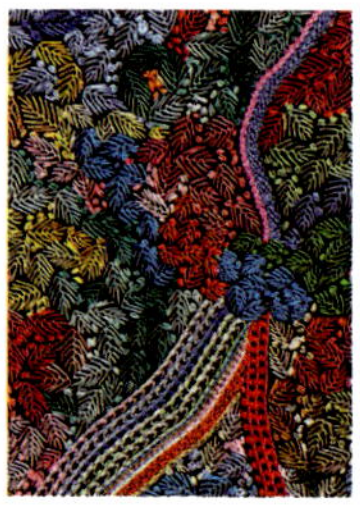

EVA IKINILIK, the daughter of textile artist Ruth Qaulluaryuk, was raised by adoptive parents, Luke Anguhadluq and Marion Tuu'luq. She learned to create embroidered and appliquéd wall hangings by observing Tuu'luq at work and, beginning in the mid-1990s, developed a personal style of tactile, densely patterned mazes of dazzling color. Organically conceived and reflecting the creative process itself, these highly textured works are meticulously and painstakingly executed. Work by Ikinilik was featured in the traveling exhibition *In the Shadow of the Midnight Sun: Sámi and Inuit Art 2000–2005*, organized by the Art Gallery of Hamilton, Ontario (2006–8).

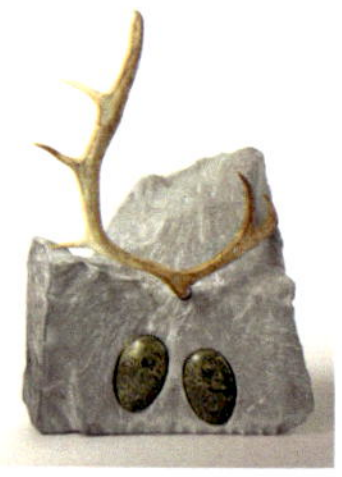

MATTIUSI IYAITUK began sculpting at age fourteen, following in the footsteps of his father, Markusi, and his brother Nutaraaluk, who were both sculptors. Until the late 1970s, he created figurative pieces, but he changed direction after encountering the work of Inuit artist Lucy Tasseor Tutsweetok and British scupltor Henry Moore. In 1984 a Canada Council grant allowed Iyaituk, then a policeman, to give up police work and devote himself to a fulltime career as an artist. In 1996 he became president of the Inuit Art Foundation and remained in that position for sixteen years. He is one of few Inuit artists to have traveled extensively, teaching workshops, for example, in Siberia and China.

Iyaituk works in a variety of materials—soapstone, serpentine, marble, wood, caribou antler, alabaster, and copper—often recording personal experiences in abstract sculptural forms. He has been the subject of numerous articles, and his work has been featured in many exhibitions, both nationally and internationally, including *Inuit Modern, The Samuel and Esther Sarick Collection* (Art Gallery of Ontario, Toronto, 2011). Work by the artist can be found in many public and private collections.

When you look at my sculpture, you don't understand all of it. You have the freedom to dream. I just choose a title for a piece and leave the rest for dreams. I started to do abstract forms in 1979. One day, I was doing a sculpture of a man but I didn't like it. So, I just made forms on one side and that was the beginning. My work is in both worlds because the abstract forms I use are considered by many to be a modern way of doing art, but I combine the abstract forms with the old Inuit technique of inlaying, using materials such as caribou antler, or different colored stones for faces or other details like tools. The inlaying of bone faces is an old form of art used by earlier Inuit sculptors.

Unforgettable fantastic feeling my wife Qumaq and I experienced being near a 400 foot high iceberg in Sisimiut, Greenland was inspired by a cruise to Greenland organized by the Kativik Regional Government. The goal of the trip was to give underprivileged teenagers in Nunavik a chance to travel and learn new skills. My wife Qumaq and I were involved as instructors, but this was also our first trip to Greenland. I gave soapstone carving classes, and Qumaq taught painting and was a counselor. Some time later I made another trip to Greenland, this time monitoring polar bear activity and as Zodiac driver for tourists, taking them to shore or to ice floes. The icebergs in Greenland were amazing, and back in Ivujivik, I felt I simply had to carve my impressions of them in stone. It was consuming. I worked day and night until the work was finished. My work is based on what I've seen or heard, but you can also say that it's the result of my crazy mind. — MI

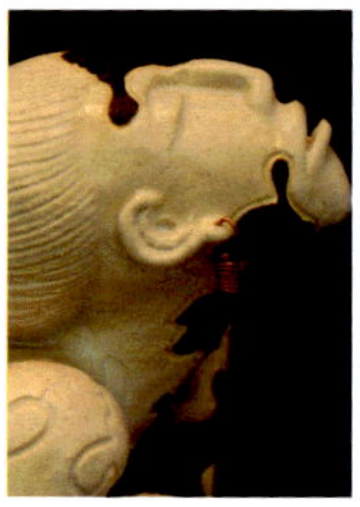

TROY JACKSON is a multimedia artist working primarily in sculpture and ceramic. He earned his MFA (2005) at the University of Arkansas, Fayetteville, and AFA at Bacone College, Muskogee, Oklahoma, where he currently teaches sculpture and three-dimensional design. President of the Cherokee Artists Association, he was recently also elected president of the Tahlequah Art Guild and serves on the advisory board of the Cherokee Art Center.

His expressive and elaborately detailed ceramic sculptures have earned numerous awards throughout the region, including, most recently, a Grand Award at the 16th Annual Cherokee Homecoming Art Show, Tahlequah, Oklahoma; and Grand Award, First Place in Sculpture at the Annual Trail of Tears Art Show, Cherokee Heritage Center, Park Hill, Oklahoma (2011).

Putting The Pieces Together is exactly what I find myself doing to better understand who I am and where I came from. Taking bits and pieces from an Indian culture, fitting them into a white culture, then, attempting to draw some sensible conclusion as to what will be tolerated, not only by my family and friends, but also in this diverse and complicated society we live in. Being part red and being raised white, I find it hard to understand what it would have been like to grow up solely as a Native American—even though I am not exactly sure what that means. At most, I would probably be more proficient in the Cherokee language than I am. Or perhaps the old legends and stories that I find so intriguing when I look them up on the internet would have been passed down to me by a more practical and reliable source, maybe by a wise and knowledgeable grandparent. I am, however, thankful for my upbringing, for access to a higher education, and for an understanding of the diversity that surrounds my daily existence.

As an artist, I work to shed light on the civility of the two cultures, and *Putting the Pieces Together* is part of this effort, an attempt to tie the two cultures together. The humble gesture of a half-red/half-white figure questioningly looking upward, as if seeking answers from a higher power, while holding puzzle pieces gives the impression that something needs to be addressed. The closed eyes of the figure signify an unbiased opinion of an untold story that may reveal something behind the figure being put in this situation. Puzzle pieces seem to share the same anticipation, waiting to be joined together. Webster's Dictionary defines the verb "puzzle" as "to offer or represent to (a person or his mind) a problem difficult to solve or a situation difficult to resolve," making it synonymous with such verbs as perplex, distract, and bewilder. These words describe my thoughts as I, again, take bits and pieces from an Indan culture and put them together with a white culture. — TJ

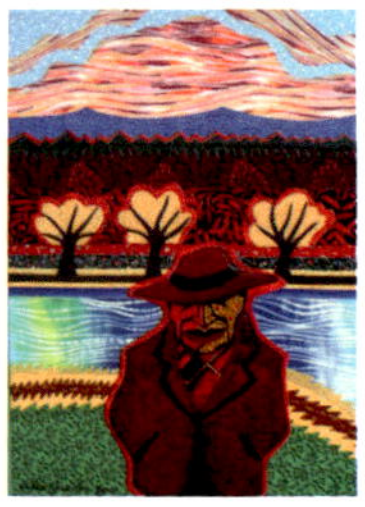

ALEX JACOBS earned an AFA (1977) from the Institute of American Indian Arts, Santa Fe, and a BFA (1986) from the Kansas City Art Institute in Missouri; he also attended Manitou Community College, La Macaza, Quebec. Jacobs is a poet and spoken-word performer, as well as an artist. In his varied career, he has been an ironworker, the editor of *Akwesasne Notes* (a journal devoted to Native American activism), and a disk jockey for CKON Mohawk Nation Radio. His unique, layered figural fabric collages, for which is is perhaps best known, drew inspiration from the quilting traditions of his mother and grandmother and have earned him Best of Classification, Best of Division, and First Place awards in Painting/Graphic/Drawing/Photography at the Southwestern Association for Indian Arts (SWAIA) annual Indian Market, Santa Fe (2006). Jacobs has exhibited in venues across the United States, as well as in Canada and Germany, and his work was included in *Oh So Iroquois* (The Ottawa Art Gallery, Ontario, 2007).

I've always had a political streak thanks to my upbringing at the Mohawk Nation at Akwesasne, straddling the border between the U.S. and Canada. In the 1970s I went off to study at the Institute of American Indian Arts in Santa Fe, New Mexico, and discovered the rich art scene. I started to create art from found objects and materials and assembled them into my own designs. I went on to make my own kind of large soft sculpture, hand-sewing canvas, burlap, construction fencing, vinyl, mesh, mylar into my art, making oversized "vests" and Ghost Dance shirts and medicine bags, often with collaged images and found objects and debris. I became an early member of the international Native journal *Akwesasne Notes* (the largest Indian newspaper in the world) and of CKON–Mohawk Nation Radio, a truly sovereign border station. All of these influences allowed me to create art and poetry and to work and tour the country with cultural networks and organizations. While I worked on earning a New York State Poetry Fellowship in 1995, I was also re-evaluating my own visual art. The themes I had been thinking about finally mixed with the gentle influences of my family, especially my mother, Sarah Jacobs, and grandmother Anna Billings. While my mother created quilts from cotton calicos, I made paper and fabric collages on canvas. My father, Abe Jacobs, who is the subject of *My Father at the River,* worked as a lumberjack for the WPA in the 1930s, cutting roads into the Adirondacks, and my grandmother organized community quilting bees. My mother became a well-known quilter in the North Country winning many awards during her lifetime.

I refer to my collage work as "soft therapy"; the fabric holds family memories and community traditions and speaks directly to people's consciousness. The same applies to my paper cutouts, but on a larger scale. Fabric is internal, it travels within our memories, it is introspective, it is longing, it's happy and as compelling as any family memory. The paper cutouts are quick and immediate, part of the mass-media culture. I use humor and empathy and compassion and narrative, not the politics of guilt or blame. The "soft therapy" of the fabric perhaps speaks to the older generation while the politics of the paper cutouts speak to the younger, but as collage they can be read by anyone and can cut across time and space and history. — AJ

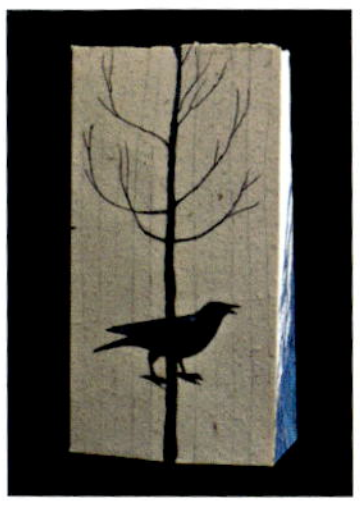

G. PETER JEMISON is a multidisciplinary artist working in painting, mixed media, and video. He received a BS and an honorary doctorate in fine art from Buffalo State College, in New York. Jemison's work has been extensively shown and collected over three decades. He has had solo exhibitions at the Albright-Knox Art Gallery, Buffalo, and the Fenimore Museum, Cooperstown, New York. Additional group exhibitions include *Lifeworlds—Artscapes: Contemporary Iroquois Art* (Woodland Cultural Centre, Brantford, traveling to Frankfurt, Germany, and Zurich, Switzerland, 2003–5), *Oh So Iroquois* (The Ottawa Art Gallery, Ontario, 2007), and *Haudenosaunee: Elements* (Everson Museum of Art, Syracuse, 2010–11), among others. Jemison received the prestigious Jennifer Easton Community Spirit Award Fellowship from the First Peoples Fund in Rapid City, South Dakota (2012). An advocate for his community and culture, Jemison currently manages the Ganondagan State Historic Site in Victor, New York, and represents the Seneca Nation of Indians on repatriation issues; he served on the Advisory Council on Historic Preservation until 2010. Jemison is among the artists featured in *Manifestations: New Native Art Criticism* (Museum of Contemporary Native Arts, Santa Fe, 2011) and in *Iroquois Art, Power and History* by Neal Keating (University of Oklahoma Press, 2012).

Each of the bags in *Changing Hands 3* tells a different story or marks a different mood. I based *Shadow on the Porch* on a photograph I took of shadows cast by a dried hydrangea plant in the late afternoon. The shadow had to bend over the boards and fit within the columns. I liked the contrast of organic lines and the geometry of the porch and columns. Winter was also the inspiration for *Crows in Winter,* with a flock of crows crowding the bag. *Crow in the Shadow* was also inspired by the hydrangea outside my studio. I saw how the shadow of the plant fell within the shadow of the sugar maple on the lawn. Into that mixture of shadows walked a crow searching for food around the porch.

Three of the other bags are more political. *Treaty Indians* is about maintaining our sovereignty as Haudenosaunee (Iroquois) Nations. Generations of our people have fought for our human rights. My wife and I work each year to commemorate the Canandaigua Treaty of 1794, which established peace between the Haudenosaunee and the United States. I have included an image of my wife's mother, Melissa Miller (Mohawk) who taught the Mohawk language and also stood up for the treaty.

Fur Trade III comments on the trade in furs between Native people and Europeans, which changed the economy of both groups. Sadly, rum was one of the trade items, bringing devastation to Indigenous communities all over North America. Greed entered into our societies, and the balance we had maintained with our animal brothers was thrown out of kilter.

Ganondaman combines two artifacts—a horse carved out of moose antler and a figure (Ganondaman) carved out of antler. Both were found on Seneca sites by archaeologists. Putting Ganondaman on the horse seemed a fitting way to capture the scene the Seneca witnessed when Wentworth Greenhalgh and his men rode out from Albany to Seneca country in 1677. Greenhalgh recorded in his diary that there were then 150 houses at Ganondagan where the figure was found. I am also using antler combs of horse and riders to depict that event. — GPJ

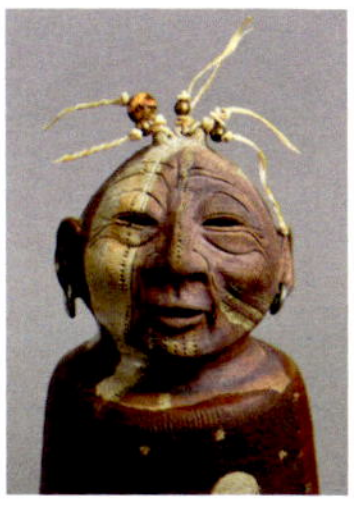

PETER B. JONES Pioneering ceramic artist Peter B. Jones paved the way for several generations of ceramicists working today. Jones traveled to Santa Fe in 1963, at the age of sixteen, to attend the newly opened Institute of American Indian Arts (IAIA), earning an ADA (1968). While there he studied with acclaimed Hopi ceramicist Otellie Loloma, who mentored and inspired him to consider clay in alternative ways, both Native and non-Native. In 1967 Jones interned at the Archie Bray Foundation for the Ceramic Arts in Helena, Montana, where he met prominent ceramic artists Val Cushing, Dave Shaner, and Chuck Hindes. After completing military service, Jones taught pottery at Indian City USA, Anadarko, Oklahoma (1971–74). His work has been included in many exhibitions and publications, among them *Iroquois Art: Visual Expressions of Contemporary Native American Artists* (Amerika Haus, Frankfurt am Main, 1998), *Oh So Iroquois* (The Ottawa Art Gallery, Ontario, 2007), and *Haudenosaunee: Elements* (Everson Museum of

Art, Syracuse, New York, 2010–11). He is a featured artist in *Manifestations, New Native Criticism* (Museum of Contemporary Native Arts, Santa Fe, 2011). His work is in many national and international public collections, and he has received numerous commissions.

Sometimes I will start working on a piece directly in clay. Even without sketches or ideas in mind, something clicks and it takes on a life of its own. *Red Moon* started this way. I made the face, and the face dictated what it should be. It is based on ancient bone effigy works called *September Moon* pieces by archaeologists. The face inspired me to create a harvest moon, or "blood moon." It could also be a woman's cycle, representing life and creation.

Portrait Jar demonstrates the changes happening in our culture. A portrait jar is something that Mound Builders and other cultures created to represent their gods, people, animals, and so on. I chose this kind of vessel to represent our people. It shows a traditional headdress of our people that is morphing into a hybridized representation of a chief's headdress. The three protrusions on the head are button antlers, instead of the traditional deer antlers. In place of the knife sheath that once hung around the neck, there is an iPod with a wire running to the ear bud. Technology is all-invasive, even as we try to maintain our ways. — PBJ

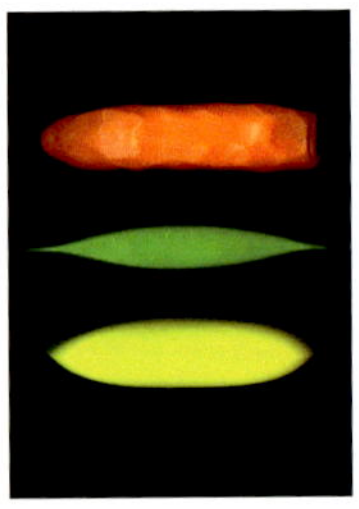

TOM JONES is a photographer who explores contemporary issues of American Indian ancestry and heritage. He earned his MFA (2002) in photography and MA (2002) in museum studies at Columbia College, Chicago, and is currently an associate professor at the University of Wisconsin, Madison. Jones has both curated and juried many exhibitions and is the recipient of numerous awards, including a Visual and Expressive Arts Grant from the National Museum of the American Indian, Smithsonian Institution, Washington, DC.

Selected solo exhibitions include *Honoring the HoChunk Warrior* (Michigan State University Museum, East Lansing, 2004), *Encountering Cultures* (Museum of Wisconsin Art, West Bend, 2009), and *The People of the Big Voice* (Diocletian's Palace, Croatian American Society, Split, Croatia, 2010). He has also participated in numerous group exhibitions, including *Migrations: New Directions in Native American Art* (traveling, University of New Mexico Art Museum, Albuquerque, 2006), *Transitional/Transcultural: New Paradigms for a New Century* (Milwaukee Institute of Art and Design, 2010), and *Counting Coup*, Museum of Contemporary Native Arts, Santa Fe (2011). Jones is a featured artist in *Manifestations, New Native Art Criticism* (Museum of Contemporary Native Arts, Santa Fe, 2011) and recently published *People of the Big Voice, Photographs of Ho-Chunk Families by Charles Van Schaick, 1879–1942* (2011). His work can be found in public collections nationwide.

The three works in *Changing Hands 3* are from my series *I Am an Indian First and an Artist Second.* This series examines the ongoing debate in contemporary American Indian art between artists who claim their Native ancestry and those who prefer to minimize or even deny it. This debate has come to be known as the "post-Indian" issue.

I question whether a denial of one's cultural background is generated by mainstream Western art norms or is a form of identity genocide. Why do some American Indian artists claim Native ancestry (by using Indian symbols or entering shows specifically geared towards Indian artists) while simultaneously rejecting classification as American Indian artists? The series addresses the tensions and multiplicity of identity referents currently at play in the context of our perceived "post-race" country.

In each of the photographs in the series, I use plastic toys—mostly toy Indians, but also corral fencing as a metaphor for current thoughts about ownership of land. I photograph scans of the undersides of these plastic Indians and other toys. From above the Indian figures are fighting with one another, which the viewer cannot see, but with the view restricted to the perspective of the abstracted bases, there emerges a surface rendering of the complexity of Native identity in the twenty-first century. — TJ

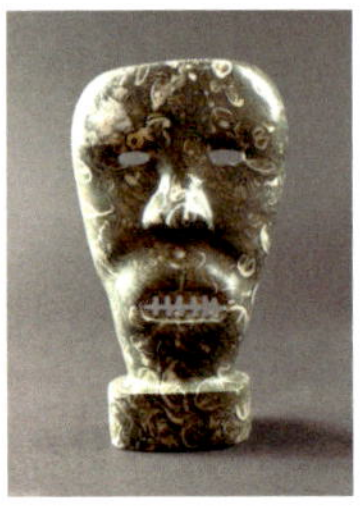

RUBEN ANTON KOMANGAPIK creates work unlike most Inuit art. Although influenced by traditional stories, songs, and legends heard from his grandfather, he has a contemporary sensibility, often combining the more typical materials with precious metals and gemstones or, for example, contrasting the roughness of porous whalebone with the smooth texture of ivory. He completed the jewelry and metalwork program at Nunavut Arctic College, Iqaluit (1995), and has been a full-time artist since the late 1990s. Komangapik has been featured in numerous exhibitions and publications. Recently he was the subject of *Isuma: The Art and Imagination of Ruben Anton Komangapik*, with text by his mother, Dorothee Komangapik.

Ujararuqtuk (Became Stone) was inspired by a mask that was found on Bylot Island, which is across Pond Inlet, Nunavut, where I was born. In the past, people used to get together when the sea-ice formed, after returning from their summer grounds. Everybody celebrated their reunion. The mask is a part of our culture and was used to perform rituals—sometimes to scare kids, to make them accustomed to the feeling of being scared, so they would be able to handle the unexpected. Some of these rituals were erased by Christianity. It was important to me to sculpt and exhibit this piece, to show that the rituals are not forgotten.

The stone I used has marbleized fossils, little creatures once native to the Gaspé Peninsula, where I've been living for the last three years. It's the only place you can find this kind of marble. I chose this rock with its remembrance of ancient times to represent something old and forgotten, just like the ancient rituals my people used to perform. The choice of this rock was important to me, because it reminds us that things are still here and actually not forgotten—just like those fossils. I also feel that I'm giving life back to those little creatures, those fossils, bringing them back to life in my work, like the rituals commemorated by this mask. — RAK

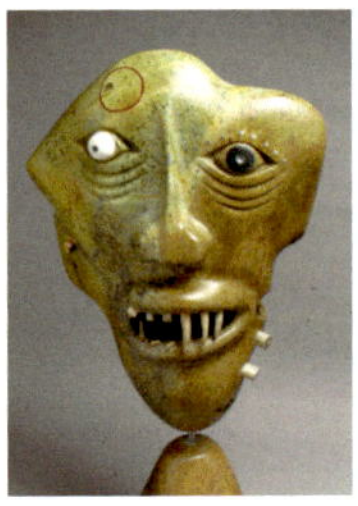

FLOYD KUPTANA was born in the Northwest Territories but spent much of his life as a carver in other areas, until ultimately settling in Toronto in 1996. Though self-taught, Kuptana learned from his cousins, the noted artists Francis and Abraham Angik Ruben, for whom he sanded and polished carvings, and David Ruben Piqtoukin, another cousin and an artist featured in *Changing Hands 2.* Since the early 1990s, Kuptana has developed a personalized carving aesthetic, producing an array of sculptures in a variety of stone materials that are often described as "surrealistic, metamorphic and highly spiritual." His work was included in *Inuit Sculpture Now* (National Gallery of Canada, Ottawa, Ontario, 2006) and in the traveling exhibition *In the Shadow of the Midnight Sun: Sámi and Inuit Art, 2000–2005* (Art Gallery of Hamilton, Ontario, 2006–8). Kuptana was also the focus of a cover story in *Inuit Art Quarterly* (2008).

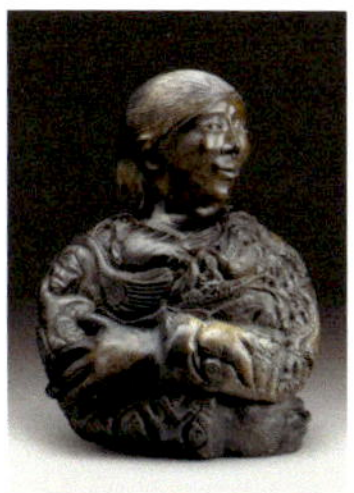

JOHN KUROK learned to draw from his grandfather, John Kurok Sr., and to carve from his father, Mathew Kurok. As a teenager, he learned to make pottery at a local gallery (now the Kangirqliniq Center for Arts and Learning), where art was taught partly as a collaborative process. Kurok's elaborate sculpted clay forms reflect a more animated approach to ceramics, relying less on traditional Inuit iconographies and displaying a greater awareness of the mainstream world. His work has been shown internationally; recent exhibitions include *Rankin Inlet Ceramics* (Winnipeg Art Gallery, 2003) and *Ceramic Work from Rankin Inlet* (Canadian Clay and Glass Gallery, Waterloo, Ontario, 2010).

> *My Dad used to work in clay sometimes*, but mostly he worked in soapstone, and I used to help him. I like working in three dimensions. When I started working with clay, I made all kinds of shapes. Now I work first on paper, drawing and getting the shape of the pot right, and when I have something I like, I make the pot. Then I start to think of what I'll put on it. Sometimes it's a story, but I like it to be abstract. I try to do something different, to put different things on the side of the pot. That way it is more alive. — JK

Collaborating artist: Leo Napayok has been a carver for some time but is a relative newcomer to working with clay. He specializes in low-relief incising as surface decoration and generally works in collaboration with other artists. He is often responsible for the elaborate, almost tapestry-like carvings that decorate Kurok's ceramics.

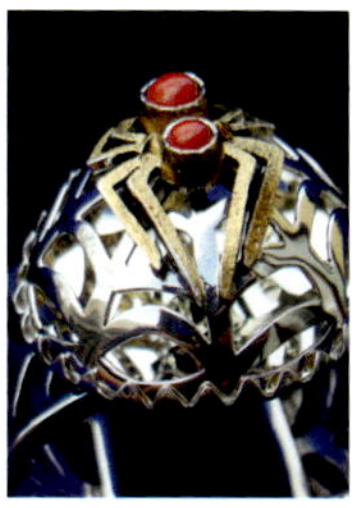

SAMUEL LaFOUNTAIN designs jewelry that shows evidence of the traditional jewelry techniques he learned from his mother, Gloria Goldtooth, combined with an atypical sculptural approach, likely gleaned from his father, noted sculptor Presley LaFountain. Participating in juried competitions at an early age, LaFountain won a First Place in the Sculpture/Youth Division at the Southwestern Asssociation for Indian Arts (SWAIA) annual Indian Market, Santa Fe (1997), when he was eleven years old. He has continued to show work at the various regional Indian Markets and recently earned Best of Classification in the Jewelry/Lapidary Division at the Heard Museum Indian Market and Festival, Phoenix (2012). As an emerging artist, he has had his work included in the *Invitational for Young Native American Artists* (Wheelwright Museum, Santa Fe, 2001, 2003) and *Freedom of Information: FBI, Indian Country and Surveillance* (Athalenia Studios, Santa Fe, 2010).

> *When I was growing up*, I watched my parents and family friends make art. I found myself drawn to the notion of turning my own ideas into wearable art. The process of harmonizing raw materials and contemporary and traditional designs continually inspires me to create the next piece. — SLF

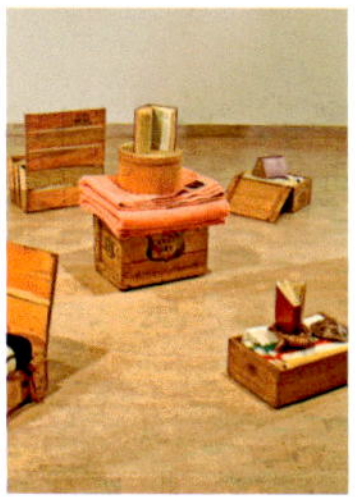

MICHELLE LaVALLEE has explored colonial relations in her curatorial practice and how they have shaped contemporary culture. In her artistic practice, working primarily in acrylics and mixed media, she addresses stereotypical iconographies and broader First Nations social and political issues. Since 2007 she has been associate curator at the MacKenzie Art Gallery, Regina, Saskatchewan, and recently earned her MA (2012) in history and curatorial studies, from the University of Regina, Saskatchewan.

LaVallee has lectured and published extensively on contemporary First Nations art. She is a member of the Aboriginal Curatorial Collective and of the Canadian Artists' Representation/Le Front des Artistes Canadiens. Her work has been included in a number of group exhibitions and is in several private collections.

> *Final Proof* began with my purchase of *The Chronicles of Canada,* a series of thirty-two volumes, published in 1920. Like most history books of the time, not one of these volumes included Aboriginal content. There were minor mentions of the First Peoples here and there, but these were generally offensive, ignorant, and negative. I began to research and gather the missing history. I inserted, replaced, and covered up what I saw as an inaccurate and incomplete history, leaving a few unedited pages as examples of the problem. In one passage, for example, the authors proclaimed that "nowhere was the art of writing sufficiently developed in America to give us a real history of the thoughts and deeds of its people before the arrival of Columbus; the red race which inhabited what is now Canada . . . spent a primitive existence." I intervened by juxtaposing the erroneous text with such evidence as transcribed stories from elders, ledger drawings, petroglyph images, wampum belts. I also included documents recording the discriminatory attitudes, actions, and policies of individuals, the government, and colonial bodies.
>
> Other culturally loaded objects in the installation—I call it an intervention—add further support. I placed the first volume of *Chronicles* atop a ceramic turtle (in reference to Turtle Island), itself standing on Hudson's Bay blankets. These and other elements were packed into worn crates, suggesting both shipping and storage, and posing a question: Is this information being sent off, to be received by someone else, or is it coming from or going to a forgotten warehouse? Interested in broadening awareness, understanding, and appreciation of Aboriginal culture, I am engaging the viewer to reconsider "truths"—historical and contemporary. *Final Proof* also acts as the physical record of my journey to recover concealed histories, to reclaim the past, and remove the stigma of being "Indian" that was once widely disseminated. — MLV

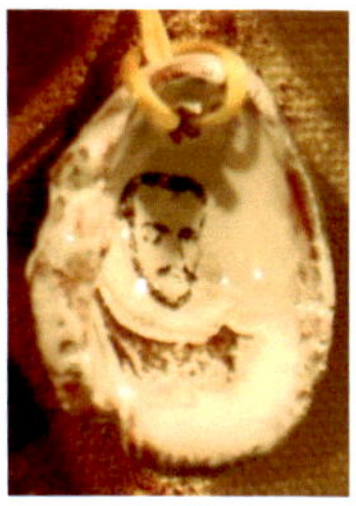

COURTNEY M. LEONARD is a multimedia artist, whose art practice began with ceramics. Her father was an officer in the U.S. Air Force and the family traveled the globe, while her mother instilled in her a sense of the traditions and values that had been passed down from one generation to the next. This background continues to inform her work. Leonard earned an AFA (2000) from the Institute of American Indian Arts, Santa Fe, a BFA (2002) at the New York State College of Ceramics, Alfred University, Alfred, and an MFA (2008) from the Rhode Island School of Design, Providence.

Recent solo exhibitions include *Current Carrier* (Akus Gallery, Eastern Connecticut State University, Willimantic, 2011), and *Catalyst* (Art Space 105, Steel Valley Arts Council, Homestead, Pennsylvania, 2011). She has also participated in group exhibitions, among them *Counting Coup* (Museum of Contemporary Native Arts, Santa Fe, 2011). Her work can be found in the New York State Museum, Albany, New York; Mashantucket Pequot Museum & Research Center, Mashantucket, Connecticut; and the Museum of Contemporary Native Arts, Santa Fe, among others.

Contact 1,609 was made with more than 1,600 thumb prints in clay, each one carrying a miniscule decoration and together mapping New York State and the Hudson River. For me this work became a metaphorical reference to piecing together the fragments of my life, using the traditional utilitarian form of Algonquin pottery as a canvas for these ideas. Its inspiration came—the germ of an idea—in 2007, when I was awarded a grant to travel to the Netherlands to research the historic relationship between Dutch culture and Shinnecock Indian pottery of the early seventeenth century. I toured the Royal Tichelaar Makkum, the delftware factory, which had been established in 1572, thus contemporary with the Shinnecocks of 1609. The factory has many cross-cultural connections throughout the world. (The façade of the Museum of Arts and Design is lined with Makkum tiles.)

Although I had originally planned to merge the process of Dutch delftware decoration onto ceramic forms I was making for an exhibition, using the decoration to present realistic imagery rather than abstract, after my trip, my focus shifted. I am of the Shinnecock Indian Nation of Long Island, so this was always a personal journey, but now I sought to explore memory and language through the lens of personal history. — CML

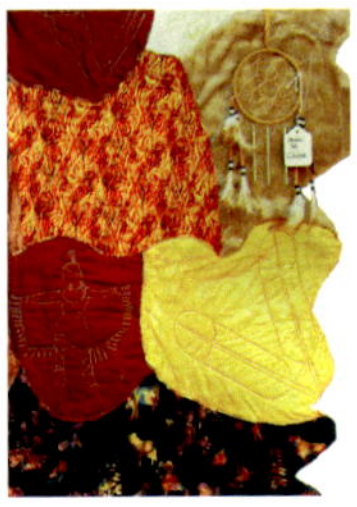

FAYE LONE is a self-taught artist who began her career in the 1980s by making ribbonwork dance regalia for pow-wows. Having learned the art of machine quilting and mastering the "block" technique, she started creating limited-edition quilts that reflected a highly contemporary approach and sensibility, often including historical passages and present-day themes. Lone's artistry has been recognized in various exhibitions, and she has received numerous private commissions. Her work can be found in the Eiteljorg Museum of American Indians and Western Art, Indianapolis; the Smithsonian Institution, National Museum of the American Indian, Washington, DC; and others. Her daughter, Naquaqua Lone, assisted in making the work featured in *Changing Hands 3*.

Constructed Indian grew out of frustration with a curator who was critiquing my work, commenting that she wanted "modern art." My daughter, Naquaqua Lone, who helped with the cutting and layout of the pieces, and I started listing all the things that people usually expect in Indian art. The dreamcatcher, for example, has been appropriated by many sources and is something I often get in the mail. These things are ridiculous in many ways: one I received was an appeal for donations to help the Sioux school. Historically, the dreamcatcher is a Chippewa/Ojibway article. The school has been raising money for decades, and the plight of that area's Natives has not changed. The items are generally not made by Native people, but are probably made in China, which is ironic, since if the charitable organization built a factory for manufacturing these dreamcatchers, they could do more good for the Natives by providing jobs.

I created the outline to suggest the stereotypical Indian head, with a stunted feather headdress and hooked nose, not unlike some sports mascot images The fabric choices match the "Indian" image: fire, animals, fur, leather. I used my original digitized "pow-wow dancer" stitching, which I can do on my computerized long-arm quilting machine, to represent the Indian dancing that is a must for any Native presentation. In the other fabrics, I stitched in words that are often applied to Indians: "savage," "princess," "how," "kimosabe," "heathen," "ugh," "primitive," and so on. The deliberate choice to do a crude zigzag stitch to assemble the pieces was to mimic a "Frankenstein" approach to a "constructed Indian," a careless, insensitive, perhaps immoral collection of parts that were not meant to go together. It reflects the power taken by someone who reduces people to parts that they fit together in an assembled image. The work was cathartic for me and my daughter. — FL

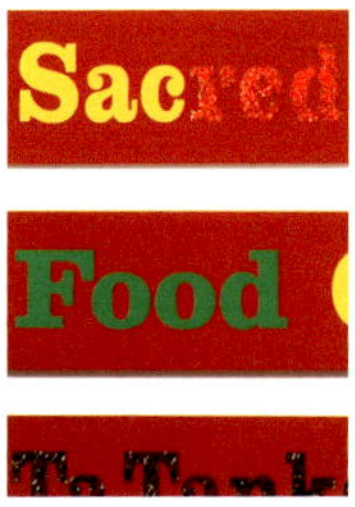

GEORGE LONGFISH has played a leading role in the field of contemporary Native American art as artist, educator, curator, and writer, and continues to serve as an inspiration to generations who have followed. He was the director of the University of Montana graduate program in American Indian art (1972–73)—the first university graduate curriculum program that focused on Native American art in the United States—and professor in the Department of Native American Studies at the University of California Davis (1973–2003). While at UC Davis, Longfish was also director of the CN Gorman Museum (1974–96), where he organized exhibitions that highlighted works by emerging Native artists, including Edgar Heap of Birds, Duane Slick, Kay WalkingStick, and many others.

Longfish earned his MFA (1972) in painting, sculpture, printmaking, and film at the Art Institute of Chicago. While formally influenced by abstract expressionism, his work is equally infused with an innate spirituality that visually confirms an awareness of his cultural roots and of the harsh realities that have continued to confront Indigenous populations. Longfish was accorded a major retrospective exhibition, *George Longfish, A Retrospective* (Montana Museum of Art & Culture, Missoula, 2007–9), and his work has been featured in numerous solo and group exhibitions, including *Indigena: Contemporary Native Perspectives in Canadian Art* (Canadian Museum of Civilization, Ottawa, 1992), *The Decade Show* (New Museum of Contemporary Art, New York, 1990), and *Continuum: George Longfish* (Smithsonian Institution, National Museum of the American Indian, George Gustav Heye Center, New York, 2004). He is also featured in *Manifestations: New Native Art Criticism* (Museum of Contemporary Native Arts, Santa Fe, 2011). Works by the artist can be found in numerous public collections.

For five hundred years a people and its culture have been affected by Columbus's discovery of this new continent. From the beginning, there has been a battle of the bodies and spirits to garner respect for the Native culture from the discoverers and conquerors. Change has had a great effect on Indigenous people who have gone from a culture closely in tune with nature and the environment to participation in the industrial revolution, not to mention the spiritual revolution. Five hundred years later the non-Indians, who have had little respect for human rights, animal rights, or the earth's environment, are having to overcome their own ignorance and come to terms with the alternative concept of making change that doesn't destroy elements of this planet and its people. We have a long history to review—we have been survivors. Much of who we are involves our belief in our intuition, our religion, or that knowingness of Spirit. The most important element of survival is to look at the information of the game you are playing. When you know your information, then you can make choices and decisions. This is freedom. The only time you make a mistake is when you don't look at all the information. The greatest lesson we can learn is that we can bring spirituality and warrior information from the past and use it in the present and see that it still works. — Derived from artist's statement in McMaster and Martin, *Indigena, Canadian Perspectives* (1992).

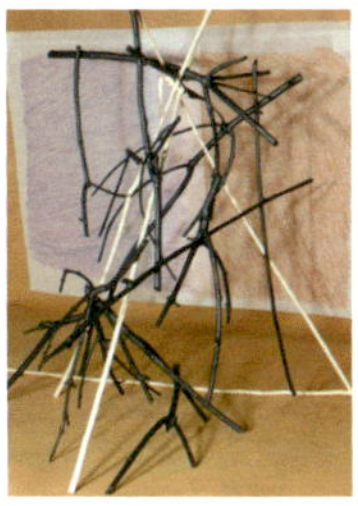

TRUMAN LOWE is one of Wisconsin's foremost contemporary artists and a nationally known sculptor. His recurrent themes are the natural environment and aspects, real and imagined, of his Native American heritage. Philosophical musings, personal history, and tribal legend are woven into abstract, minimal sculptures. Lowe received a BS (1969) in art education from the University of Wisconsin, LaCrosse, and an MFA (1973) in sculpture from the University of Wisconsin, Madison. He served as the university's coordinator of the Native American Studies program (1975–88) and professor of art, becoming elected chair of the art department (1992–95).

Lowe's career has spanned more than four decades. His work has been featured in solo exhibitions since 1977, including a major retrospective, *Truman Lowe: Haga (Third Son)* (Eiteljorg Museum of American Indians and Western Art, Indianapolis, 1994), and a publication was devoted to his life and work, *Woodland Reflections: The Art of Truman Lowe* by Jo Ortel (2003). He has been the recipient of honors and awards that include an Individual Fellowship from the National Endowment for the Arts (1994) and the Eiteljorg Fellowship for Native American Fine Art (1998), among many others. Additional exhibitions include *Land, Spirit, Power: First Nations at the National Gallery of Canada* (Ottawa, Ontario, 1992) and *Shared Visions: Native American Painters and Sculptors of the Twentieth Century* (Thomas Gilcrease Institute of American History and Art, Tulsa, Oklahoma, 1992), to name but a few.

In 2000 Lowe was appointed curator of contemporary art at the National Museum of the American Indian, Smithsonian Institution, Washington, DC, where he conceived and organized *Native Modernism: The Art of George Morrison and Allan Houser* (2004), one of the inaugural exhibitions in the newly opened building on the Mall. He also implemented an ongoing program of contemporary art exhibitions.

> *Mythography I* is a personal examination of the evolving knowledge based on the intersection between mythology and geography. Origin myths describe becoming who we are and can be located in a geographic area that has significant historic importance. — TL

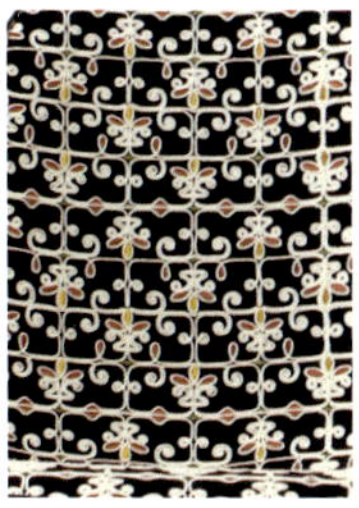

MINDY LAUREEN MAGYAR earned a BS (1997) from Cornell University, Ithaca, where she focused on chemical engineering and American Indian studies. She entered the Foundation Studies Program (2004–5) at Pratt Institute, Brooklyn, and went on to the Cranbrook Academy of Art, Bloomfield Hills, Michigan, where she earned an MFA (2007). This was followed by an MBA (2009) in arts and culture management and entrepreneurship from the Wharton School, University of Pennsylvania, Philadelphia. She worked at the office of executive planning at the National Museum of the American Indian (2009) and is currently a project manager in retail operations at the Smithsonian Institution, Washington, DC. As an industrial designer and artist, Magyar is committed to furthering the field of contemporary Native art and continues to explore the inherent meaning of utilitarian objects.

> *My work incorporates traditional Micmac techniques*, designs, and materials within a contemporary context. I borrow from the semantics of functional objects to share my own experiences and celebrate my culture. — MLM

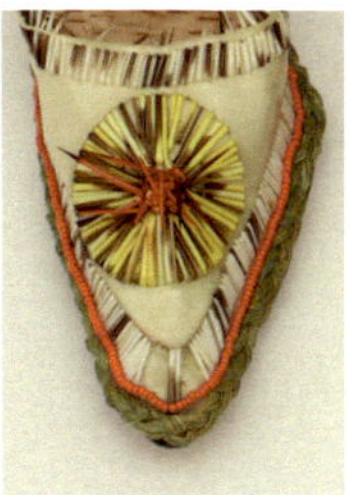

TERESA MARSHALL creates mixed-media sculptures and installations that often address the intentional omissions in the Europeanized versions of North American history. She studied theater arts at Dalhousie University, Halifax, Nova Scotia (1987), and earned her BFA (1990) from Nova Scotia College of Art and Design, Halifax. Since then she has lectured and held artist residencies in venues across Canada. Marshall was a recipient of the Eiteljorg Fellowship for Native American Fine Art (2001).

Marshall's work has been included in both solo and major group exhibitions including *Land Spirit Power: First Nations at the National Gallery of Canada* (Ottawa, Ontario, 1992), *New Territories, 350/500 Years After: An Exhibition of Contemporary Aboriginal Art of Canada* (Maison de la culture, Montreal, 1992), *Topographies: Aspects of Recent B.C. Art* (Vancouver Art Gallery, 1996), *Band Stands: Recent Work by Teresa Marshall* (Thunder Bay Art Gallery, Ontario, 1997), *Teresa Marshall: A Bed to the Bones* (Contemporary Art Gallery, Vancouver, British Columbia, 1998), and *After the Storm* (Eiteljorg Museum of American Indians and Western Art, Indianapolis, 2001), among others. Marshall's work can be found in the collections of the Royal Ontario Museum, Toronto; the Woodland Cultural Centre, Ottawa; the Vancouver Art Gallery, Vancouver, British Columbia; and elsewhere.

> A brief case of history
> from a tenant of time.
> the land is my wardrobe.
> the mountains, my spine.
> The shoes. A reminder of how far I've walked a smile
> in my grandmothers' shoes. — TM

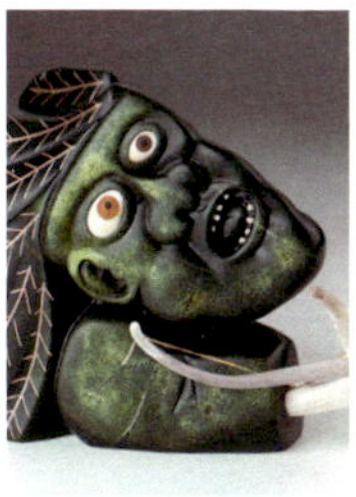

MICHAEL MASSIE practiced drawing as a child by using comic books as references, gradually refining his characterizations. He earned a commercial arts certificate (1982) from the College of Trades and Technology, St. John's, Newfoundland. After a stint as a self-employed sign painter, he returned to his studies, focusing on painting and and printmaking at West Viking College, Stephenville, Newfoundland. He earned his BFA (1991) from the Nova Scotia College of Art and Design, Halifax. Massie's work reflects his mixed Inuit, Métis, and Scottish heritage. His innovative teapots merge contemporary and traditional themes and symbols from Native and European cultural traditions. Massie has participated in exhibitions in North America and abroad, and his work is in many prestigious collections, including the the National Gallery of Canada, Ottawa, Ontario; the Albrecht Inuit Art Collection at the Heard Museum, Phoenix; and the National Museum of the American Indian, Smithsonian Institution, Washington, DC. He has twice been nominated for Canada's prestigious Saidye Bronfman Award for excellence. As an instructor, Massie has conducted jewelry and stone-carving workshops in the Arctic region. He has also served on a number of art committees, including board of directors of the Visual Artists of Newfoundland.

> *When I was looking over this piece of stone*, I was searching for a form that would work with inlaid metal. What I saw were two faces, one on each side of the stone. When I began grinding, the feather shapes just wanted to come out, so I went with them. I still had the inlaid metal—only this time I could use the feathers as the design. Once I had the eyes and feather pattern, I had to then figure out what would make up

the hands. I decided that if the faces are both of one piece of stone, then the hands could perhaps work the same way. So, finding the best-shaped antler, I cut it to length and then began adding the fingernails. Because the two figures had feathers added (one as a parka, the other as a headdress), I felt that a shared bow-and-arrow would give the piece a completed appearance as an overall form.

I thought the two images would work together if I imagined them both out hunting the same thing—ptarmigan to be exact. I thought of how some Inuit in Greenland used to make parkas of feathers, and how the feather headdress is associated more with the First Nations groups in the south. And this is maybe how they met while out hunting—and they talked of how they came to be where they ended up.— MM

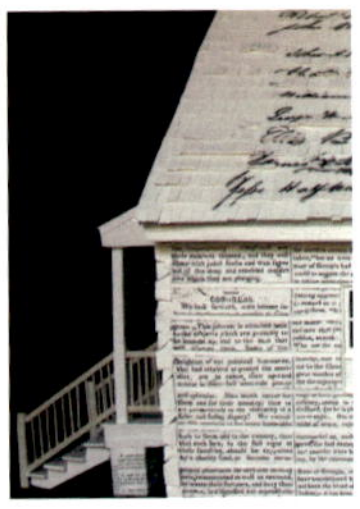

ALAN MICHELSON addresses North American geography, history, and identity in his multilayered, multimedia installations. He studied at Columbia University in New York and earned his BFA (1981) from Tufts University and the School of the Museum of Fine Arts, Boston.

Michelson has had an extensive career as an artist, lecturer, teacher, and writer. His work will be included in the 18th Biennale of Sydney, Australia (2012), with a concurrent solo exhibition at the Milani Gallery in Brisbane. It has also been featured in numerous solo and group exhibitions, including *The Sixth Borough, No Longer Empty* (Governor's Island, New York, 2010), *A Stake in the Ground* (Gallery Art Mûr, Montreal, 2011), *We Are Here!—The Eiteljorg Contemporary Art Fellowship* (Eiteljorg Museum of American Indians and Western Art, Indianapolis; Smithsonian Institution, National Museum of the American Indian, George Gustav Heye Center, New York, 2011–12), *The Value of Water* (Cathedral of St. John the Divine, New York, 2012), and others.

Among his many honors, he is the recipient of a National Endowment for the Arts Visual Artists Fellowship and, most recently, the 2011/2012 Native Arts & Cultures Foundation Artist Fellowship in Visual Arts. He was also the Invited Artist of the Eiteljorg Contemporary Art Fellowship (2011). Michelson's work is in the permanent collections of many institutions, including the National Gallery of Canada, Ottawa, Ontario; National Museum of the American Indian, Smithsonian Institution, Washington, DC; and the Art Institute of Chicago. In 2009 he completed a permanent public art commission as part of Art in Architecture Program, from the U.S. General Services Administration at the U.S. Port of Entry, Massena, New York, for which he received the GSA Design Award, Citation in Art, and the Public Art Network Year in Review (2010).

Phoenix is based on the log print shop in New Echota (now near Calhoun, Georgia) where the *Cherokee Phoenix*, a newspaper published by the Cherokee Nation—and the first paper by a Native American nation and in a Native American language and syllabary as well as in English—was printed from 1828 to 1834. The model is imprinted with text from the December 17, 1831 edition of the newspaper, which was renamed the *Cherokee Phoenix & Indians' Advocate* in 1829. The text describes events leading up the forced relocation of Cherokee under the official U.S. policy of Indian Removal. The Cherokee Nation had selectively adapted to modernity in significant ways, with large prosperous farms, a written constitution, judicial system, and police force, as well as a higher rate of literacy than their non-Native neighbors. They exhausted every political and legal means to retain their lands, and were eventually ousted after a series of legal, legislative, and executive maneuvers by the state of Georgia, the Supreme Court, Congress, and President Andrew Jackson. The unauthorized Treaty of New Echota in 1835—printed on the roof of the model—was the basis for the later U.S. Army–directed removal of some 12,000 Cherokees at gunpoint. Perhaps as many as a quarter of them perished in the brutal forced march to the Indian Territory (present-day Oklahoma). The *Cherokee Phoenix* continues to publish today and is available on the internet and on iPhone. — AM

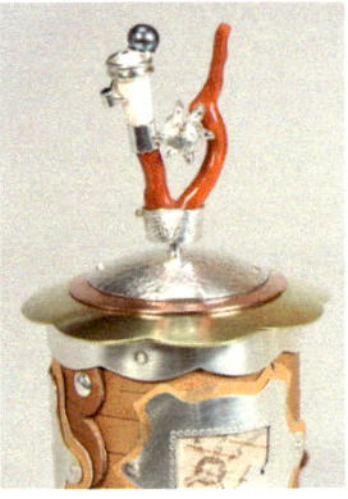

WANESIA MISQUADACE is skilled at birch-bark biting, a traditional art form to which she gives a contemporary context by using the patterns as templates for jewelry and combining the bark panels with metals and stones. She earned an AFA (2002) in three-dimensional studio arts from the Institute of American Indian Arts, Santa Fe, where she studied with Lane Coulter who became her mentor, and she received a certificate in advanced metalsmithing techniques (2009) from the Poeh Center, Pojoaque, New Mexico. Misquadace is currently working toward an MFA in metalsmithing at the University of Wisconsin, Madison. She has further developed her skills by learning master metalwork techniques from her partner, Navajo jeweler Fritz Casuse. Misquadace's work has been featured in the recent exhibition Mni Sota: Reflections of Time and Place (traveling, Native American Community Development Institute, Minneapolis, 2011–12).

Birch bark is the strength of our people. It's used in our baskets and canoes and the bitings as a means to tell our stories. I'm contemporizing the traditional use of birch bark by using silver and wood. It's very organic, and I'm making it my own. Birch bark is so thin, yet so strong. Such is the nature of our Annishinabe ways—our culture is gentle, yet we are strong and resilient.

I first became interested in birch bark biting when I discovered that my mother used to do it. Later, I went out and harvested some and sat outside, peeled the bark that I had just collected into the thin layers, and connected with my mother, who passed away when I was a child. Now, my mother's talent lives on through me and I can pass that tradition on to my son.

Essence of the Lake Canisters takes the traditional art of birch bark biting and combines it with the finest in silver and gold work, and Lake Superior pebbles, as well as diamonds and pearls. The Lake Superior pebbles are considered to be healing stones, and we sometimes call them "Thunderbird stones." Harvesting blueberries is an annual Ojibway tradition. Children are given birch bark baskets with which to gather the berries, collect swamp tea, and enjoy the woods. My first cannister represents my son's first birch bark basket. Spending time in Fond Du Lac with my son and grandmother and harvesting birch bark inspired me to create my most beautiful vessels. As I made them, I remembered these very beautiful and special times. I use my birch bark biting designs, traditional cutouts, and silversmithing to create a new version of our traditional baskets. — WM

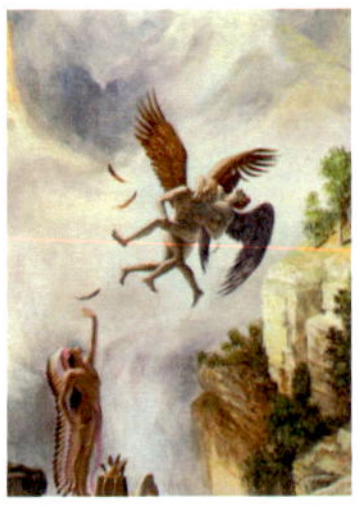

KENT MONKMAN began his career as a painter and illustrator, having studied at Sheridan College of Applied Arts in Brampton, Ontario. Today, he works in a range of mediums, including film, video, performance, and installation, as well as painting, sculpture, and drawing. He explores issues of gender, sexuality, racism, colonialism, religion, and power politics—themes that are significant to Indigenous traditions but also universally understood. By way of his alter ego, Miss Chief Eagle Testickle, Monkman probes below surface appearances exposing individual and cultural biases and values.

Monkman's work has been featured in numerous solo and group exhibitions, most recently *The Art Game* (Art Toronto, 2011), *Shapeshifting: Transformations in Native American Art* (Peabody Essex Museum, Salem, Masschusetts, 2012), and the 17th Biennale of Sydney, Australia (2010), among many others throughout Canada, as well as in New York, London, and other European cities. His performances include *Gone With the Wind* (Museum of Contemporary Canadian Art, Toronto, 2007), *Séance* (Institute for Contemporary Culture, Royal Ontario Museum, Toronto, 2007), *Miss Chief Justice of the Piece* (National Museum of the American Indian, Smithsonian Institution, Washington, DC, 2012), among others. Among his numerous film and video credits are *Shooting Geronimo* (2006) and *Dance to the Berdashe* (2008).

I explore fashion, history, and sexuality in my work, to address Native American experience. The nineteenth century was a period of extreme change, with the ongoing colonization of North America by the French and English. This occupation is well documented in art history, but the dominant version mostly obscures Native Americans and diminishes the complexity of our diverse cultures.

In my paintings, installations, and film/video projects, I revisit the work of nineteenth-century European artists whose subjects were Native American peoples and the North American landscape (Albert Bierstadt, George Catlin, Edward Curtis and others). I challenge the subjectivity of their work and their influence in shaping dominant and narrow perceptions of Indigenous peoples. Artists like Catlin and Curtis reinforced the common belief that Native peoples were a vanishing race, without the capacity to evolve and adapt. They never saw that Native Americans favor innovation and embrace new technologies. Innovation and adaptability are rooted in Native American philosophy, but nineteenth-century artists recognized European influences on Native Americans as evidence of a "dying race."

My work plays with the idea of cultural cross-pollination, as in my *Louis Vuitton Quiver*. My video, *Shooting Geronimo*, is a deconstruction of early Hollywood Westerns as well as the silent film by Edward Curtis, *In the Land of the Head Hunters* (also called *In the Land of the War Canoes*.) Through my glamorous, gender-bending alter ego, Miss Chief Eagle Testickle, I use humor along with multimedia installations and sexy films, to suggest different historical narratives, repositioning First People at center stage. My artworks play with sexual power dynamics as a metaphor with which to challenge historical assumptions of conquest, sovereignty, art, commerce, and colonialism. Much of my work confronts colonized sexuality, exposing the colorful, but repressed sexual diversity present in pre-contact North America.

While my explorations have been grounded in works from the nineteenth century, I also investigate the impact of modernity on Indigenous cultures. In the twentieth century, Native people faced the brutal assault of the modern industrial age, which espoused a creed of deliberate amnesia, turning its back on history and tradition. A culture of amnesia wielded by colonial forces further increased the momentum of erasure and obliteration of Indigenous cultures and languages. — KM

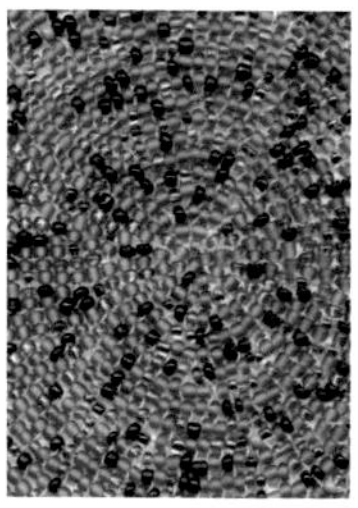

NADIA MYRE is a multidisciplinary artist whose work addresses complex issues of history, memory, and experience. She received her fine arts associate degree from Camosun College, Victoria, British Columbia (1995), and fine arts degree from Emily Carr School of Art, Vancouver (1997). In 2002 she earned an MFA from Concordia University, Montreal, Quebec. Myre's work has been featured throughout Canada and abroad, and her achievements have been recognized by the Montreal Arts Council; Canada Council for the Arts; Conseil des arts et des lettres du Québec; National Aboriginal Achievement Foundation; and the Eiteljorg Fellowship for Native American Fine Art, which she received in 2003. Myre also curated the recent exhibition *A Stake in the Ground* (Gallery Art Mûr, Montreal, 2012). Recent solo exhibitions include *Landscapes of Sorrow and Other New Work* (Gallery Art Mûr, Montreal, 2009), *Nadia Myre: Symbology* (Carleton University Art Gallery, Ottawa, 2011), and *Meditations on Black Lake* (Gallery Art Mûr, Montreal, 2012). Among significant international group exhibitions are *HIDE: Skin as Material and Metaphor* (Smithsonian Institution, National Museum of American Indian, George Gustav Heye Center, New York, 2010), as well as the Biennale de Montréal (2009); Toronto International Film Festival; imagineNATIVE Film + Media Arts Festival, Toronto; and the 18th Biennale of Sydney, Australia (2012).

Her work is in the permanent collections of the Eiteljorg Museum of American Indians and Western Art, Indianapolis; National Gallery of Canada, Ottawa, Ontario; Musée des beaux-arts de Montréal; Musée national des beaux-arts du Québec; and National Museum of the American Indian, Smithsonian Institution, Washington, DC, among others.

Nadia Myre's *Meditations* on *Black Lake* are large, textured tondos in somber blues, blacks, and grays, resembling gongs, planets, mandalas, or darkened pools with ripples extending radially from their centers. Closer inspection reveals a digitized universe of intertwined glass seed beads of varying shapes, sizes, and colors. These pieces are not woven on the loom with a pre-established pattern but are worked in a more organic, instinctual manner. Selecting two to three beads at a time to form a brick stitch, Myre views this act of choosing the colors as akin to painting.

Digitally scanning the beaded works introduces the paradox of a visually smooth, flat distillation of the actual objects' highly textured surfaces. The subsequent increase in scale monumentalizes these modest, craft-based objects. Myre sees the *Meditations* as abstract paintings, signaled by the disjunction between her actual palette and the series' title, which reduces the chromatic subtleties in the works to *Black*, a noncolor, the absence of light, or when made with pigment, the result of all the shades being mixed together. While Western societies associate it with death, mourning, and emptiness, for Myre black also represents awareness gained through reflection—staring into a dark pool, one sees oneself.

Myre began this series as a rumination on her massive, collaborative *Scar Project*, which required her constant presence, as facilitator, mediator, and caretaker. The beaded *Meditations* arose from the weight of this commitment, becoming metaphors both for the existential condition of humanity, and the political realities of Indigenous peoples. As Myre remarked recently, beading in moving meditation creates the potential for insight. Myre describes it as a "connection with the self through gazing at something deeply [in order to] bring yourself to a global consciousness, a deep knowledge that you are intimately connected to everything." — Rhonda L. Meier, from conversations with the artist, January 2012.

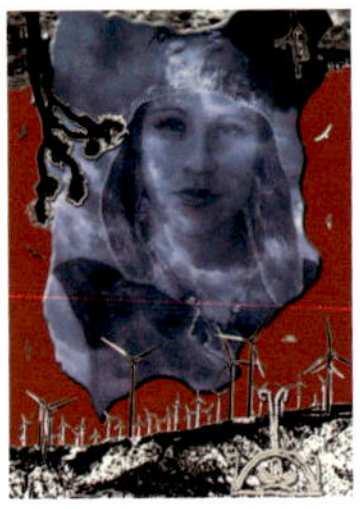

SHELLEY NIRO is a highly accomplished and well-regarded photographer, painter, sculptor, bead worker, multimedia artist, and independent filmmaker, who holds a degree in painting and sculpture from the Ontario College of Art and an MFA from the University of Western Ontario. Niro is probably best known for depictions that challenge the stereotypical images of Native American and Indigenous people as a whole, through masquerade, parody, and more. She wrote and directed her first feature-length film, *Kissed by Lighting* (2009), which premiered at the imagineNATIVE Film + Media Arts Festival, Toronto, and won the Santa Fe Film Festival's Milagro Award for Best Indigenous Film (2009). She has had numerous solo and two-person exhibitions and has participated in group shows over the last two decades, most recently *Oh So Iroquois* (The Ottawa Art Gallery, Ontario, 2007), *M: Stories of Women* (Gallery 44, Toronto, 2011), *Our Language is Beautiful* (Woodland Cultural Centre, Brantford, Ontario, 2011), and *Haudenosaunee: Elements* (Everson Museum of Art, Syracuse, 2011), to name a few. Niro was awarded the Eiteljorg Fellowship for Native American Fine Art in 2001. Her extensive filmography includes *Robert's Paintings*, a documentary on noted artist Robert Houle (2011). Her work can be found in collections that include the Rockwell Museum of Western Art, Corning, New York; Art Gallery of Ontario, Toronto; National Gallery of Canada, Ottawa, Ontario; and Smithsonian Institution, National Museum of the American Indian, Washington, DC, among many others.

Art to me is a body function. It begins with an urge and transfers desire to manifest ideas. Sometimes the ideas come from a place that expresses innermost questions or observations. Mostly it develops out of a need to create and reflect my surroundings. The work is physical. It has to have a concentrated effort of muscle and material. Before I begin the process, the brain dips, dances, twirls, and jumps. It searches the areas in the shadows. There is a crossing of conjecture between body, brain, memory, and pigment. There are no distinct borders. Instead the mind warbles on the periphery of thought.

I am a North American Indian artist from the Six Nations Reserve. I am Turtle Clan. I grew up in houses heated by woodstoves, and which had no indoor plumbing. In some ways it was limiting. However, looking back, it was a great training ground for the imagination. Hearing the wind blow through the cracks in the windows on winters nights, rain hitting the roof of the house, frogs and crickets in the summer singing all through twilight, and the night sky in its mass of stars with its infinite view, made for good opera, drama, and mystery. I was encouraged to listen, look, and learn from what was around and never take anything for granted. — SN

M: Stories of Women, is a series of twelve self-portraits. I used my image to express emotion and anger at the ongoing reality and depiction of Native people in Canada. I am referencing the day-to-day struggle faced by Native people. Using myself as the subject within the work, I will portray, abstractly, innermost feelings as my personal space is impeded by actual happenings exploited by the media. The M of the title could also refer to "Matriarchy." Traditionally, First Nations' economies were controlled by the women. They owned the land and everything that came out of it. In essence, the women were the overseers. This changed, however, when colonialism became the enforced power. — Sally Frater, from a conversation with the artist, 2011.

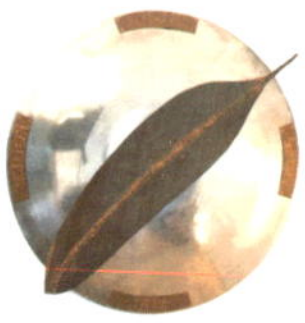

RON NOGANOSH studied graphic design (1980) at George Brown College, Toronto and holds a fine arts degree from the University of Ottawa, with a focus in print and sculpture. Through his work, Noganosh contributes to a national discourse on Native issues with criticism, wit, and humor. He has exhibited around the globe, including venues in Canada, Costa Rica, Denmark, Finland, France, Germany, Japan, Mexico Russia, and the United States. He has had solo exhibitions at The Ottawa Art Gallery, Ontario (also at the Woodland Cultural Centre, Brantford, Ontario, 2000–2001); and at Urban Shaman Gallery, Winnipeg, Manitoba, 2008. He has participated in group exhibitions such as *New Territories, 350/500 Years After: An Exhibition of Contemporary Aboriginal Art of Canada* (Maison de la Culture, Montreal, 1992), *Double Jea: Identité et Culture* (Musée national des beaux arts du Québec, 2004), and *Myths of the Land* (The Ottawa Art Gallery, Ontario, 2008), and others. In addition, his work was shown in the Canadian Pavilion, Shanghai World's Fair, China (2010). The artist's work can be found in the collections of the Canadian Museum of Civilization, Gatineau, Quebec; The Ottawa Art Gallery, Ontario; the Indian Art Centre in Gatineau, Quebec; and the MacKenzie Art Gallery, Regina, Saskatchewan, among others institutions.

Old Soldiers Never Die is the first in a series of large recycled copper and aluminum shields that I created between 2009 and 2011. The piece notes that First Nations people have participated in every war that Canadians have entered—the War of 1812, the First World War, the Second World War, the Korean War—but First Nations veterans were not accorded the same rights, privileges, or recognition that other Canadian veterans received after the wars. First Nations people are loyal to Canada, however, in spite of ongoing discrimination. The beaten copper feather symbolizes two things: First Nations' quest for peace in the struggle to attain equality; and on a global scale, the need for Canada to maintain its stance as an international peacekeeper, rather than making war in Iraq and Afghanistan. This is the first time the piece has been exhibited. I like to recycle found objects in my art, melding them with natural materials like feathers, wood, stone, bone, and metals that come from the earth—copper, aluminum and iron. — RN

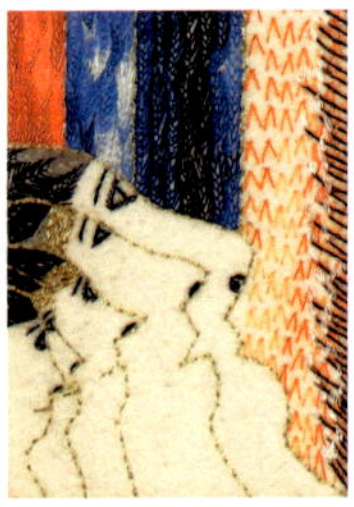

JANET NUNGNIK spent her earliest years learning skills relevant to a semi-nomadic lifestyle. Around age seven, she was removed from her family and sent to school, ultimately completing her education and then reuniting with her parents at Baker Lake in the early 1960s. She learned the art of cloth appliqué and textile embroidery by assisting her mother, Martha Tiktak Anautalik, and working with Inuit artist Jessie Oonark. By the late 1980s, Nungnik was creating her own works on cloth to sell in the southern art markets.

Nungnik has become celebrated for making cut-and-sewn figures that appear against colorful, abstract landscapes and are contemporary both in concept and sensibility. Often, she embellishes her images with glass beads. Through her work, she hopes to teach future generations the importance of respecting the environment and animal life. Her work was included in the traveling exhibition *In the Shadow of the Midnight Sun: Sámi and Inuit Art 2000–2005* (Art Gallery of Hamilton, Ontario, 2006–8).

CHANGES
Time in my lifetime
Thought only five of us existed

The land was there for us
and we were there for it.

Changes happened on and on
Even the blanket didn't stay
the same and our numbers

Moved north to ice
Short summer man in black in
the air.
Letting our hearts free as
Stars must continue to shine. — JN

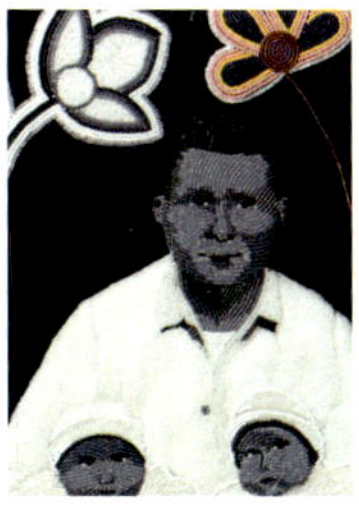

SUMMER PETERS learned traditional-style beading techniques from her mother and grandmother and received her first private commission at age fourteen. She earned a BA in fashion design and merchandising at Collins College, Phoenix. Only recently entering the arena of juried competitions, Peters was awarded Second Place in the Traditional Jewelry division at the Indigenous Peoples Art Market, Mount Pleasant, Michigan (2010), and earned Honorable Mention, Diverse Art Forms at the annual Heard Museum Indian Market and Festival, Pheonix (2012). Her lively beaded creations combine both historic and contemporary elements.

My beadwork is a gateway from present to past. I descend from a long line of Ojibway people of artistic skill and ability. For me, doing beadwork is more than creating a beautiful work of art. It also helps ensure that my people's traditional art will survive and thrive in the centuries to come. Beadwork was the way of life for many women on my Reservation when I was grew. My career as an artist also reflects the values and morals instilled in me from my mother. I hope to show my children that by working hard, they can be self-sufficient.

In addition to keeping Native traditions alive, I also aim to breathe new life into them. My work includes both historic and modern mediums and themes, presenting traditional Native American elements in a contemporary fashion. When I begin a new beadwork piece, I first draw the design with pencil and paper, a creative step I especially enjoy. I then attach the drawing to the fabric and begin beading in the center, working my way outward. I do not use the expected materials, such as leather, as the base for my beadwork. Instead I choose nontraditional materials such as thick interfacing. I have found that these unexpected materials work well for me.

Recently, I introduced a new technique into my routine: capturing the same effect of shading in a drawing with beadwork. The group portrait I created, *1946*, was based on a photograph taken in 1946 of my uncle holding my mother and her twin sister. It is a tribute to the unity and closeness in Native American famlies. This work was a labor of love. Somewhere, I hope my ancestors can see how much I appreciate and honor them with my artwork. — SP

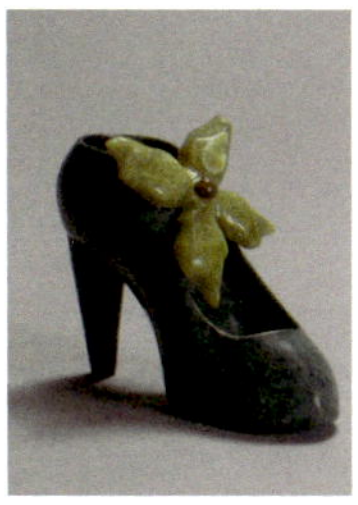

JAMASIE PITSEOLAK is from a family of artists. He is the son of carvers Oopik and Mark Pitseolak, and grandson of noted carver and photographer Peter Pitseolak, who was his first inspiration. Pitseolak began his career at a young age, selling his first works to the Hudson's Bay Company. He studied painting under Peter John Voormeij. Feeling a lack of connection with the more traditional themes of hunters and wildlife generally found in Inuit sculpture, in the late 1990s he began incorporating more unconventional and modern imagery, such as machinery with movable parts, motorcycles, guitars, and other items from everyday life, often with a sense of humor or irony. Using a "collage-like" style rather than working from a single block of stone, Pitseolak painstakingly assembles his sculptures from individually carved pieces.

Pitseolak's work has been included in many exhibitions, most recently *Jamasie Pitseolak: Northern Soul* (Marion Scott Gallery, Vancouver, 2011) and is in many private and public collections, including the Canadian Museum of Civilization, Gatineau, Quebec; National Gallery of Canada, Ottawa, Ontario; and Winnipeg Art Gallery, Winnipeg, Manitoba.

Inuit art is always going to be Inuit art. But as generations come along, this new generation is going to make their own doorways, opening their minds. When I was doing "traditional stuff" I felt limited, but when I started doing different stuff, it opened doors for me. It's kind of second nature. When my mother moved to Kimmirut, we had family there and one day I was visiting a cousin and he had a battery-operated motorcycle. I really liked it; that was almost thirty years ago. I really liked it so I kept visiting him. Come Christmas, his mother decided that I should have it. It's different. It's not just polar bears; it is something that is coming from today. — Derived from Norman Vorano, "Jamasie Pitseolak: Coming from Today," *Inuit Art Quarterly* 23, no. 1 (Spring 2008): 10–16.

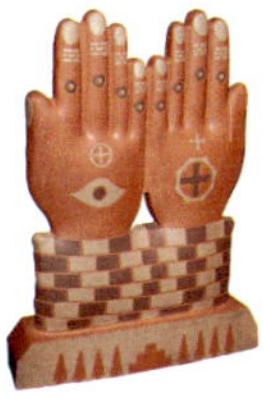

DAVID L. PRUITT attended East Central University, Ada, Oklahoma, and Northeastern State University, Tahlequah, Oklahoma, focusing on drawing and painting courses, until he took a few basic pottery classes and discovered his medium. His work, inspired by prehistoric Southeastern pottery designs, can now be found in a many public, private, and corporate collections. Pruitt has also worked as a master craftsman in wood, making furniture and custom cabinets as well as building homes, and he serves as a construction manager for the Cherokee Nation.

I have no formal education in art, but I have a tremendous passion for it. When I work with clay, my thoughts go to the clay and everything else is forgotten. The anticipation I feel while creating a new piece is part of the lure of clay. I was born and raised within the Cherokee Nation, and I incorporate both ancient traditional designs and contemporary ones. My art connects me to my heritage, but I find inspiration in everything and everyone around me. I've been lucky to have been helped along the way by so many artists who were willing to share. My work is slab or coil built, and I use an earthenware clay body. Surface patterns are textured by incising, paddle stamping, or by pressing walnuts or corn cobs, or are carved by hand. Colored clay areas are painted with slip. — DLP

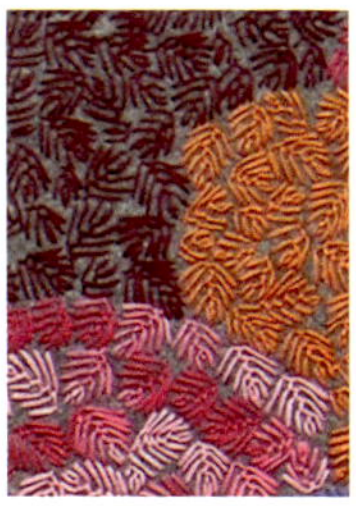

RUTH QAULLUARYUK (NUILAALIK) is the daughter of Baker Lake artist Luke Anguhadluq and the birth mother of Eva Ikinilik. Until the 1950s she and her family lived a traditional nomadic lifestyle, but severe game shortages forced them to relocate to Baker Lake in the mid-1960s. Qaulluaryuk began by making drawings in the community's newly built printmaking studio. To help with the family income, she also turned to sewing, making handcrafted items for sale through newly established, government-operated arts and crafts programs. Over time, she refined her skills as draftsperson and textile artist, becoming renowned for her lyrical and often abstracted depictions of nature, abundant wildlife, and dense, colorful vegetation.

Ruth Qaulluaryuk is concerned with neither the supernatural world nor Inuit folktales, even though she, too, belongs to the group of Inuit who came south to Baker Lake from the Back River region. Based on landscape and foliage motifs, her unique, largely abstract compositions are almost entirely lacking in ethnographic content, thus challenging any too-easy conception of what the phrase "Inuit Art" can mean. In Qaulluaryuk's densely covered and richly colored images, overlapping circles crowd almost humorously in upon one another, usually in combination with patches of leafy textured color. The results are, quite simply, beautiful. Her wall hangings are at once sophisticated and charming, sensuous and, notwithstanding a heavy reliance on repetition of motifs, never merely decorative. — Derived from Kardosh, *Works on Cloth: Imagery by Artists of Baker Lake, Nunavut* (2002).

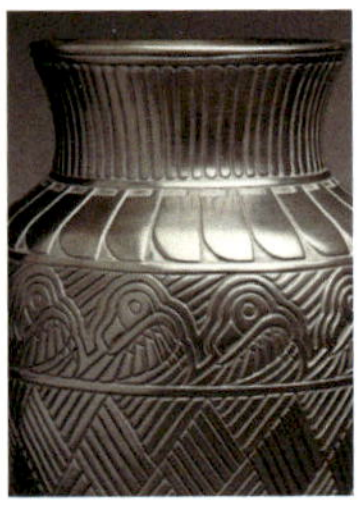

JOEL QUEEN is from a long line of ceramicists, going back at least nine generations. He earned an MFA (2009) and BFA (2005) from Western Carolina University, Cullowhee, North Carolina. He has participated in numerous juried exhibitions and has been the recipient of more than thirty-five awards, including Best of Division in Traditional Carved or Incised Pottery and First Place Ribbon for Incised Pottery at the Southwestern Association for Indian Arts (SWAIA) annual Indian Market, Santa Fe (2009); Best of Show and First Place Ribbons for Traditional Pottery at the Red Earth Festival, Oklahoma City (2009); and Best of Class for Pottery at the Cherokee Art Market, Catoosa, Oklahoma (2011), to name a few. Queen's work is in numerous public and private collections including the British Museum, London; Cherokee Heritage Museum, Tahlequah, Oklahoma; Museum of the Cherokee Indian, Cherokee, North Carolina; and the National Museum of the American Indian, Smithsonian Institution, Washington, DC.

As a member of the Eastern Band of Cherokee Indians, I feel a responsibility to keep Cherokee art alive. I teach others about my art and the Cherokee culture. Prejudice has driven me to educate viewers and has made me passionate about breaking the stereotype that has been placed upon Native art. The simplicity of line is what I look for. Line is what I manipulate. Stone and wood speak to me in a picture, and then I carve that image. Clay binds my images to the functional world, but my goal is to create art that allows people to see the past and the future. — JQ

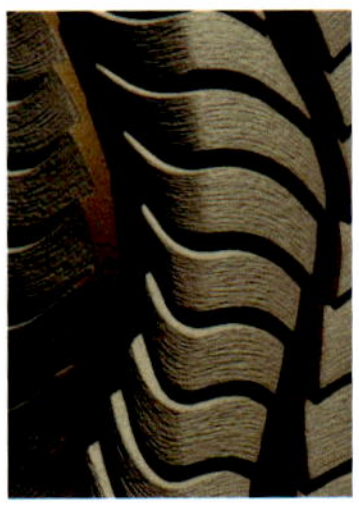

JASON QUIGNO has been sculpting in stone since he was fourteen years old. Whether working in soft soapstone or hard granite, he uses a contemporary and nonobjective style to tell his stories. This skill has garnered Quigno awards at the Heard Museum Indian Market and Festival, Phoenix (2010), and the Southwestern Association for Indian Arts (SWAIA) Indian Market in Santa Fe (2010).

Recent exhibitions include *Works in Stone* (solo exhibition, Central Michigan University, Mt. Pleasant, Michigan, 2007), *Surface Matters* (Poloma Gallery, Ann Arbor, Michigan, 2009), and *Michigan Perspectives* (Grand Rapids Art Museum, Michigan, 2011), among others. His work is in the Grand Rapids Public Museum, Michigan, as well as Okaya City Hall, Nagano Prefecture, Japan. In addition, he has completed major commissions for the Odawa Casino and Resort, Petoskey, Michigan, and the Saginaw Chippewa Tribal Elders Center, Mt. Pleasant, among others. Quigno has lectured at a number of universities including Oakland University, Oakland, Michigan, and Central Michigan University, Mt. Pleasant. The artist has also served as a cultural ambassador to Japan (2002).

I am always striving for simplicity, harmony, and movement in my work. The Anishinaabek have always believed everything is connected and has a purpose. With the *Pillar of Tranquility* I would like to show a small portion of that belief and how truly beautiful it is when all the elements come together and do their part. — JQ

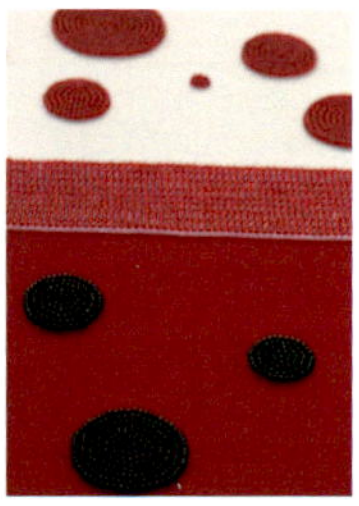

TAMMY RAHR completed a BA (2011) with a minor in Indigenous liberal studies and is working toward an AFA in museum studies at the Institute of American Indian Arts, Santa Fe. Since 1984 she has worked as curator, lecturer, and museum educator, as well as visiting artist and artist-in-residence in various institutions.

Rahr's beadwork, which has earned her numerous awards, has been in numerous exhibitions, including *Mementos & Milestones* (Institute of American Indian Arts Museum Store, Santa Fe, 2009), and *Soul Sister: Reimagining Kateri Tekakwitha* (Museum of Contemporary Native Arts, Santa Fe, 2011). Her work can be found in several public collections including the Museum of Natural History, Cincinnati; Seneca–Iroquois National Museum, Salamanca, New York; and Museum of Indian Arts and Cultures, Santa Fe.

When I was asked to commemorate the life of Kateri Tekakwitha (1656–80), what came to mind was the decimation of Eastern tribes by smallpox. My approach to the subject was the *Kateri Tekakwitha Blanket,* a work that is layered with symbolism. Kateri is mostly recognized for the work she did as a Catholic nun, but I imagined her as much more. I was struck by her youth and her bravery in caring for Mohawk people afflicted with small pox, and also saddened by the conflicts she must have faced with her identity and spirituality. Despite her devotion to the Catholic religion, Kateri was first and foremost a Mohawk woman who died of tuberculosis at the age of twenty-four.

The blanket documents her life and the colonization of the Iroquois. It is divided into fields of red and white, with the white field dominating the red, symbolizing the attempt to conquer by religious conversion and theft of Native lands. It also represents the two smallpox-infected blankets given to the Mohawk. The top part of the blanket resembles a Hudson's Bay blanket, the twenty-four red dots symbolize smallpox, the twenty-four black dots represent the scars that Kateri carried after surviving the disease that left her an orphan. Twenty-four marks her age. The beaded strips, a reference to wampum belts, go off the sides of the blanket, representing an Iroquois concept of creation with no beginning or end. I chose to fringe only part of the blanket, to symbolize a life only partly lived.

The *Kateri Tekakwitha Blanket* contains approximately 40,000 beads and over 50,000 inches of thread. The blanket is backed by "treaty cloth," which is issued by the U.S. Government to Iroquois tribal members every year. It is intended to "pay" for land that was stolen from them during the time of Kateri.

In 2011, Blessed Kateri Tekakwitha became the first Native American woman to become a recognized Saint, and is set for canonization by the Pope in October 2012, in Rome, Italy. — TR

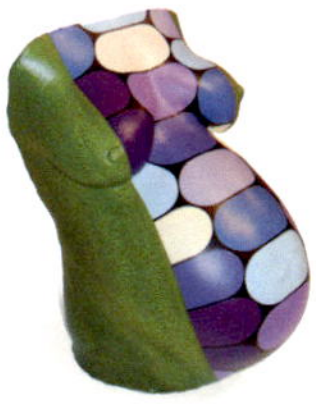

NATASHA SMOKE SANTIAGO was raised in a highly traditional family and remains connected to her Native communities. She learned her artistic practices primarily from family members and friends, and since 2001 her work has been featured in numerous exhibitions, including *Haudenosaunee: Elements* (Everson Museum of Art, Syracuse, New York, 2010–11), *Kanien'kehá:ka Onkwawén:na Raotitióhkwa* (solo exhibition, Language and Cultural Centre, Kahnawake, Quebec, 2011), *Iohskats Ne Onkwawen:na—Our Language is Beautiful* (Woodland Cultural Centre, Brantford, Ontario, 2011), and *Under the Influence: Iroquois Artists at IAIA* (Museum of Contemporary Native Arts, Santa Fe, 2012). In addition she has garnered awards at several juried shows, and her work is in the collections of the Fenimore Art Museum, Cooperstown, New York; National Museum of the American Indian, Smithsonian Institution, Washington, DC; and the Mashantucket Pequot Museum & Research Center, Mashantucket, Connecticut, among others.

I don't remember a time when I was not drawing or painting. Throughout my life, art has been a constant companion, a place to go in times of sadness and times of joy. I have grown organically through self-study and working with mentors. My work reflects my traditions and interests, as well as my family. I work in many mediums and am always looking to the next project. *Calico Corn* reflects the kind of corn we grow in our communities. It is of a type of *oneste* (corn) created by Onkwehonwe and passed down through our families from long ago. I am inspired by the "carries" of life, the pregnant woman and the seed. — NSS

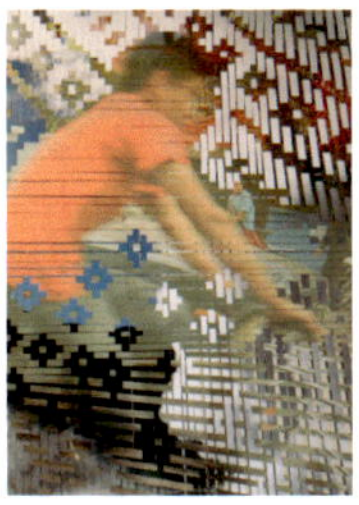

SARAH SENSE weaves photographs with traditional Chitimacha basketry techniques, commenting on complex familial constructs of American history and contemporary society. Sense received a BFA (2003) from California State University, Chico, and an MFA (2005) from Parsons The New School for Design, New York. Since 2010 she has been traveling and researching contemporary Indigenous arts throughout North, Central, and South America, recently publishing her first book, *Weaving the Americas: A Search for Native Art in the Western Hemisphere.* Her solo exhibition premiered at Museo de Arte Contempráneo, Universidad Austral, Valdivia, Chile (2011), subsequently traveling to Galería de Arte Trece, Santiago, Chile, and Legends Santa Fe, New Mexico (2011–12). Other recent exhibitions include *HIDE: Skin as Material and Metaphor* (Smithsonian Institution, National Museum of the American Indian, George Gustave Heye Center, New York, 2010), *Pieces of Home* (Evergreen State College, Olympia, Washington, 2010), *Reimagining the West* (Scottsdale Museum of Contemporary Art, Arizona, 2010), and *In/SIGHT* (Chelsea Art Museum, New York, 2010). Her work can be found in numerous public collections including the National Museum of the American Indian, Smithsonian Institution, Washington, DC; and the Tweed Museum of Art, University of Minnesota, Duluth.

After researching the history of Chitimacha basketweaving, I was inspired to continue the tradition of my ancestors. In 2004, the chairman of the Chitimacha Tribe of Louisiana gave me permission to use nontraditional material in weaving our basket patterns, and since then I have incorporated photographic images into my work. I began by weaving reservation landscapes. The images evolved as I incorporated Hollywood posters, family photo archives, and my personas of "The Cowgirl" and "The Indian Princess." Most recent bodies of work are photos woven over photo silkscreen prints.

In the *Weaving the Americas* series, I have woven together photographs and images of my journey from Canada to Chile. Through my weaving practice, I have met other Indigenous artists and learned about their traditional practices, as I weave a cultural landscape of the Western Hemisphere. In this search for art and culture of the Americas, I interviewed more than sixty artists who practice a variety of different art genres, making my weaving traditional Chitimacha patterns from my ancestry all the more meaningful. — SS

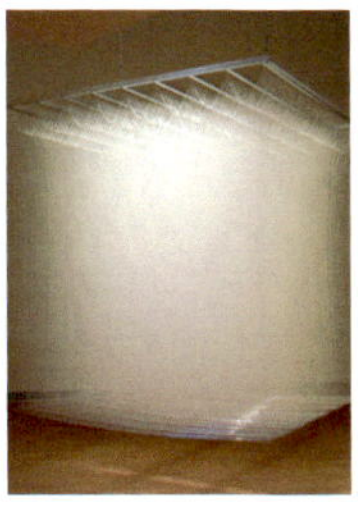

FRANK SHEBAGEGET is an installation artist whose work reflects his interest in the geography of the "Canadian Shield" and the aesthetics of everyday materials. He explores the tense relationships between production, consumption, and the economics of beauty, often by playing with the incongruity of mass production versus the handcrafted object. Shebageget earned an AOCA (1996) in interdisciplinary studies from the Ontario College of Art and Design and an MFA (2000) in sculpture from the University of Victoria, British Columbia. He is currently a member of the artists' collective Enriched Bread Artists in Ottawa.

Shebageget's most recent solo exhibitions include *Model Life* (Surrey Art Gallery, Surrey, British Columbia, 2010) and *Light Industry* (Carleton University Art Gallery, Ottawa, 2010), and he joined with Michael Belmore in a two-person traveling exhibition, *Scout's Honor* (University of Lethbridge Arts Gallery, Alberta, and Museum London, Ontario, 2008–9). His work is in many public collections, including The Ottawa Art Gallery, Ontario; the Canada Council of the Arts—Art Bank, Ottawa, Ontario; the Dorothy Hoover Library, Ontario College of Art, Toronto; National Aboriginal Achievement Foundation, Oshweken, Ontario; and in private collections across Canada.

My previous work mainly used references to Native history—historical information and images—and employed conventional art techniques to manifest contemporary issues. This focus was an attempt to locate positive connections that have been established between Native and non-Native cultures in Canada, without falling into tropes of stereotypical issues about Native culture.

I rely on both repetition and the handmade object, a time-consuming and labor-intensive process. Execution of the work, physically and conceptually, relates to a kind of mass production. The artistic elements form part of a larger critical conversation about the production and consumption of contemporary Aboriginal art. Their implementation simultaneously allows me to use objects and space in a manner that reveals a unique view of my culture. — FS

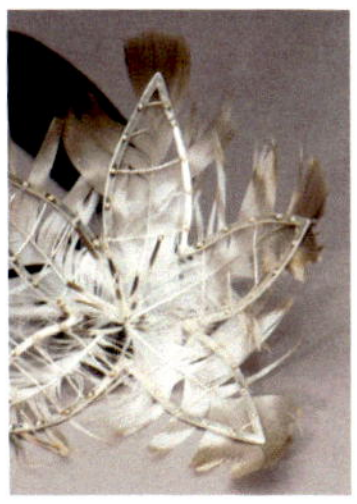

LEAH SHENANDOAH identifies herself as a designer of jewelry and metal objects, singer, composer, and performance and recording artist. She learned jewelry making from her grandmother Maisie Shenandoah and earned a BS (2006) in visual and performing arts/textile design at Syracuse University, New York, and an MFA (2011) in metalsmithing and jewelry design from the Rochester Institute of Technology, New York. Shenandoah often uses Indigenous symbols in her work, along with natural stones, textiles, and materials from around the world, expressing spirituality and her cultural heritage. Her jewelry was featured in the *Go Native Arts Fashion Show* at the Southwestern Association for Indian Arts (SWAIA) annual Indian Market, Santa Fe (2009) and the recent exhibition *Haudenosaunee: Elements* (Everson Museum of Art, Syracuse, New York, 2010–11). Shenandoah's work can be found in the permanent collections of the National Museum of the American Indian, Smithsonian Institution, Washington, DC; and the James Fenimore House, Cooperstown, New York.

Leah is also a gifted vocalist who has recorded award-winning releases with her mother, Grammy Award–winner, Joanne Shenandoah. Leah is a featured singer on *Path to Zero: A Prayer Cycle,* a music CD by Jonathon Elias (2011).

I am a member of the Oneida Iroquois, Wolf Clan, and my art is rooted in my Aboriginal heritage, combining a Native American aesthetic with contemporary design. I consider and incorporate the healing properties of color, matching them with materials that serve my intention, in creations that attempt to capture an emotion. When I'm working I feel myself in a place where time and space do not exist. I consider myself a radical compassionist in a world filled with suffering. I am creating tools for healing, manifestation, and enlightenment.

I made *Haute Couture Hood* to be worn as a hood and breastplate, protection for the sacred spaces of the head and heart. White rabbit fur and white satin lining represent the purity of the "good mind," the Iroquois belief in honoring and respecting Mother Earth and all her inhabitants. The sterling silver beads are etched with Japanese designs of the Edo period, which resemble Aboriginal designs from around the world. By blending designs from different cultures, I am honoring our humanness.

Stars in Her Hair was created to imitate the stars, from which the Iroquois believe we descended. I included earth (porcupine quills) and air elements (hawk feathers) to represent our interconnectedness to the universe. — LS

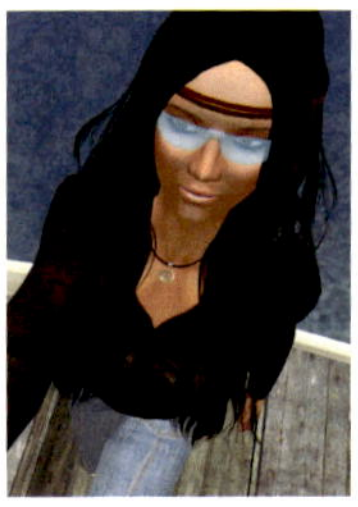

SKAWENNATI is an artist and independent curator with a BFA (1992) from Concordia University, Montreal, where she also received a diploma in institutional administration, specialization in the arts (1995). While a board member at artist-run Oboro, Montreal, she co-founded Nation to Nation (1994), a First Nations artist collective, with fellow artists Ryan Rice and Eric Robertson.

In 1996, Skawennati established the online art space, *CyberPowWow*. Her own new-media artwork, addressing history, the future, and change, includes *Imagining Indians in the 25th Century*, a web-based paper-doll journal; *Thanksgiving Address: Greetings to the Technological World*, a flash movie; and *80 Minutes, 80 Movies, 80s Music*, an ongoing series of music videos. TimeTraveller™ won the imagineNATIVE festival's Best New Media Award (2009). Skawennati also received an Eiteljorg Contemporary Art Fellowship (2011) from the Eiteljorg Museum of American Indians and Western Art, Indianapolis.

TimeTraveller™ is a multiplatform project that includes a website (www.TimeTravellerTM.com), a ten-episode machinima series (in-progress), a prototype action figure, and an Alternate Reality Game (forthcoming). Together they tell the story of Hunter, an angry young Mohawk man living in the twenty-second century. Despite his impressive range of traditional skills as hunter, warrior, and ironworker, Hunter is unable to find his way in an overcrowded, hyperconsumerist, technologized world. In an act of desperate clarity, he has decided to use his "edutainment" system—his TimeTraveller™—to embark on a technologically enhanced vision quest that immerses him in historical events featuring his ancestors. Along the way, he meets Karahkwenhawi, a young Mohawk woman from our time, who also gets a pair of TimeTraveller™ glasses. Together they criss-cross time and Turtle Island, discovering the complexity of history, and of truth itself. — S

The artist gratefully acknowledges the support of the Social Sciences and Humanities Research Council; Fonds de recherche sur la société et la culture; Hexagram Research Institute at Concordia University, and Canada Council for the Arts.

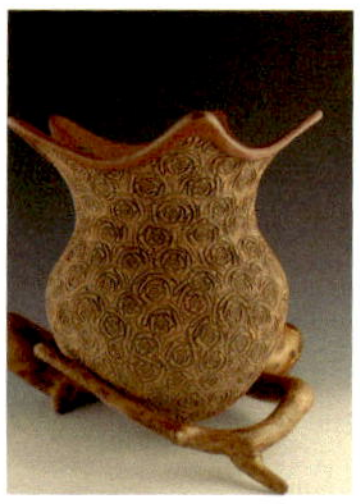

JAMIE ZANE SMITH belongs to a family of musicians and artists but found his form of expression in ceramics. Perhaps his biggest influence and inspiration has been his uncle, the noted ceramicist, Richard Zane Smith, who was featured in *Changing Hands 1* and with whom Jamie apprenticed for a year (2008). Putting himself through college by working as a concrete and stone worker, Smith studied ceramics at Western New Mexico University, Silver City, and earned a BFA (2007). He is currently a resident potter at La Vista CSA Farm, in Godfrey, Illinois, near an ancient Mound Builder site in Cahokia. In his work, Smith concentrates on retaining an integral sense of form inspired by ancient sensibilities but with a dynamic connection to today's world. Recent exhibitions include *Living Wyandot* and *Double Vision: Reinterpreting a Classic Zuni Jar* (King Galleries of Scottsdale, Arizona, 2009).

A major theme of my work is the celebration of Indigenous ancestry and the teachings of the natural world. Both spring from the same source and are centered around the heart. At the heart is the desire to fulfill the creator's intent. We strive to connect to our roots and to create beauty in our world. It is my goal to sustain the soul so I can succeed as well as a healthy oak tree or dogwood in creating valuable fruit. When I look at ancient pottery and other decorated wares, I see this familiar ideal woven into the design of everyday functional objects, like the design woven into pinecones. The object of my work is to refer to the original source from which life was born and acknowledge the significance of the seed planted within.

I see a parallel between ancient cosmic symbolism and patterns of growth occurring organically in other life forms such as trees. At a rudimentary level there are common structural patterns that underscore our relationship with arboreal beings. It is not too terribly profound to look up at tree branches and notice a similar structure of veins in a human lung. Similar to the exchange of oxygen and carbon dioxide is the communication of consciousness between humans and plants occurring on a cellular level. Even though we might not consider it on a daily basis we could not survive without it. — JZS

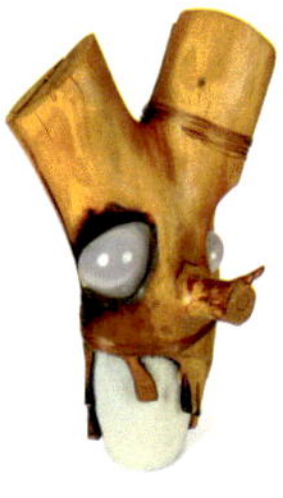

ROBERT TANNAHILL is part of a second generation of Native glass artists. He often uses cultural history as the reference and basis for sculptural forms. He studied art history and English literature at the University of Toronto, earned a degree (1998) as glass major at Sheridan College, School of Craft and Design, Oakville, Ontario, and received his MA (2001) from the Department of Ceramic and Glass, University of Art and Design, Helsinki, Finland. Tannahill has received numerous awards and grants including several from the Ontario Arts Council as well as a Métis Nation of Ontario Cultural Grant (2007) and Abraham and Malka Green Sculpture Award (2009). Tannahill's work has been exhibited both nationally and internationally. Recent solo exhibitions include *Yskin (Alone)* (Gallery Septaria, Helsinki, Finland, 2003), *Portraits* (Gallery Happihuone, Helsinki, Finland, 2004), and *Mohawk Mothers, Scottish Fathers* (Gallery AyrSpace, Ayr, Ontario, 2010), among others. Recent group exhibitions include *Fusing Traditions: Transformations in Glass by Native American Artists* (traveling, Museum of Craft and Folk Art, San Francisco, 2002–5), *Masterworks Southwest* (traveling, Ontario Crafts Council, 2010), *Sculptures by Robert Tannahill and Mirta Virtasalmi* (Lighthouse Festival Theatre, Port Dover, Ontario, 2011), *FACE IT!* (The Canadian Sculpture Centre, Toronto, 2012), and many others.

The *False Face* series is my interpretation/reinvention of the ceremonial "False Face" masks traditionally made by the Iroquois. For me, my *False Faces* echo or give a voice to the Mohawk ghosts I never heard when I was growing up. In my family history, the traditions have long been forgotten. By blowing glass inside the wooden masks, I aim to reanimate those stories hidden in time and reawaken the spirits of the pre-Columbian forest. — RT

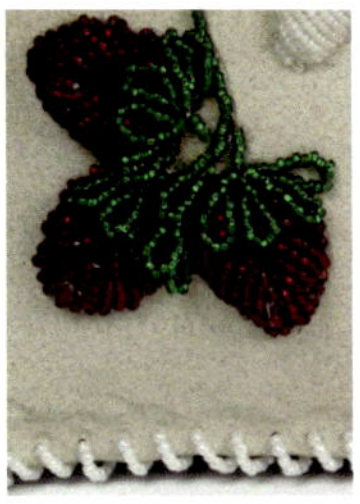

TAMMY TARBELL earned her BFA (1980) from Syracuse University, New York, and has continued her art practice since then. She has entered work in various juried competitions and has won numerous awards including Artist's Choice at the Southwestern Association for Indian Arts (SWAIA) annual Indian Market, Santa Fe (2004). The artist also received an Excellence in Iroquois Arts Award from the New York State Governor's Office (1996) at the Iroquois Indian Museum, Howes Cave, New York.

Tarbell's work has been featured in solo and group exhibitions, including *Tammy Tarbell-Boehning, Iroquois Art: An Exhibition of Her Work* (Iroquois Indian Museum, Howes Cave, New York, 1996), *Where We Stand: Contemporary Haudenosaunee Artists* (Fenimore House Museum, Cooperstown, New York, 1997), *Haudenosaunee: Elements* (Everson Museum of Art, Syracuse, New York, 2010–11), *Lifeblood: Women in Haudenosaunee Art* (LeMoyne College, Syracuse, 2011), and many others. Her work is in permanent collections around the United States: Governor's Collection of Contemporary Native American Crafts, New York State Museum, Albany; Frances Lehman Loeb Art Center, Vassar College, Poughkeepsie, New York; Iroquois Indian Museum, Howes Cave, New York; National Museum of the American Indian, Smithsonian Institution, Washington, DC, and others.

I am a woman of the Mohawk Nation, Turtle Clan. My artwork is used as a tool to educate others about my heritage. Our artists are like ambassadors—we are the visual voice, telling the stories, legends, and history through our art. It is so much easier to make the work than to put it into words. The pieces I make are intended to uplift and I like to use clay with other mediums, such as glass beads, because beadwork is another passion for me.

Strawberry Whimsey combines the beauty of glass beads with clay. It relates to the tradition of creating "whimsies" made of cloth, stuffed with horsehair, and then beaded. These were once sold to tourists at Niagara Falls. This piece gives the impression of being a cloth pillow until closer inspection reveals that it is actually made of clay. Aha. . . I fooled you! Mission accomplished! — TT

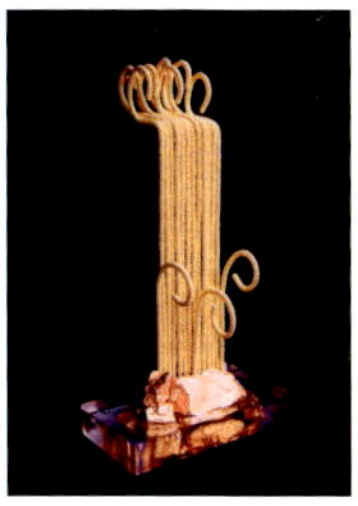

SAMUEL THOMAS, armed with magnifying glass, sketchbook, and painstaking patience, set out to resurrect centuries-old beadwork styles. His recovery of several "lost" techniques has garnered respect for Iroquois beadwork. He has also helped revive bead traditions in Kenya, Africa, under a Chalmers Art Fellowship from the Ontario Arts Council (2003). This project resulted in a beaded *Tree of Peace* displayed at the United Nations headquarters (2007). Recent exhibitions include *Across Borders: Beadwork in Everyday Life* (traveling, McCord Museum, Montreal, and Castellani Art Museum of Niagara University, New York, 1999–2003) and *Oh So Iroquois* (The Ottawa Art Gallery, Ontario, 2007). As curator, Thomas has organized *Ska-Ni-Kwat: The Power of the Good Mind* (traveling, 2003–7) and *Through the Voices of Beads* (traveling, Royal Ontario Museum, Toronto, through 2015). In addition, Thomas has earned more than ninety national and international awards. His work can be found in the permanent collections of the British Museum, London; Canadian Museum of Civilization, Quebec; Royal Ontario Museum, Toronto; Rochester Museum and Science Center, New York; National Museum of the American Indian, Smithsonian Institution, Washington, DC; and museums, galleries, and private collections in North America and Europe.

Niagara: the sound of thundering waters, the magnetic attraction of one of nature's most majestic sights, one of the world's most iconic landmarks, "power" in its truest form. To the Haudenosaunee peoples, the true power of *T:gana wen'h ta'h—The Place Where the Water Comes Over*—has been revered, respected, held sacred, admired for countless centuries. For the First Nations people, Niagara Falls has been a major source for oral narratives involving giant serpents, mythological sea creatures, and Thunder Beings, among others. The narrative that inspired the creation of this piece originates in the age-old traditional prophecies that foretell of a time coming when the world will change drastically. It will be a time when birds will disappear from the skies, fish from the waters, animals from the forests, a time when we have lost our languages, forgotten our ceremonies, and lost our identity as Aboriginal peoples; a time when "the place where the water comes over" flows in reverse, thus ending life as we know it.

Prophecy II was created not as an omen, but as a reminder that we need to be more respectful of the earth, nature, the environment, the places we hold sacred, and especially each other. When we choose to neglect nature's power, there will be repercussions; nature has the power to unleash divine chance. Human interaction with nature will determine the future for all people. — ST

The artist gratefully acknowledges the support of the Ontario Arts Councils, Aboriginal Artists Material and Supplies Assistance.

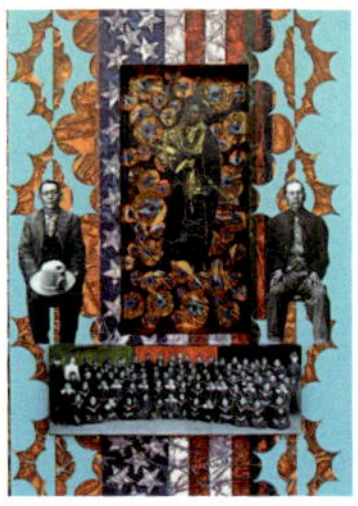

TONY A. TIGER earned an associate of arts degree from Seminole State College, Seminole, Oklahoma, a BFA from Oklahoma State University, Stillwater, and an MFA from the University of Oklahoma, Norman. He has had solo exhibitions at the Southern Plains Indian Museum Anadarko, Oklahoma (2010); and the East Gallery, Oklahoma City (2010); and he has participated in group exhibitions at the Goddard Art Center. Ardmore, Oklahoma (2011); and the Southeastern Indian Artist Association at the Five Civilized Tribes Museum in Muskogee, Oklahoma (2011), among many others. He is the recipient of numerous awards in juried competitions, and his work is in many public and private collections.

Tiger is currently director of art at Bacone College, Muskogee, Oklahoma, which his grandfather attended in the 1920s. He has curated many exhibitions at the college, most recently *Perceptions of Being* (2009), *Ruthe Blalock Jones Retrospective* (2010), and *Exploration of Identity* (2010). He is also co-curator of *H2OK: Native Response to Water Issues in Oklahoma* (2012) and is active in the Southeastern Indian Artist Association.

The last few years have challenged the idea of what "art" means to me as an artist in the twenty-first century, an artist who happens to be an American Indian, with a Master of Fine Arts degree. From an early age, I heard people at school and in the community say "an Indian person who has the ability and skill to create and re-create artwork about Indian culture could make a living at selling the art to the tourists and collectors." I found myself drifting into this melancholy kind of art-making, for monetary gain, selling my artistic soul for fashion. Many fine Native artists must create and sell this kind of work to put food on the table for their families.

The economic downturn of recent years actually had an upside for me. I began creating art, not for the market per se, but art that expresses my time as an artist and an American Indian in the twenty-first century. My art is now fueled by this rediscovery of being. We are more then mere reflections in a mirror. We are soul and spirit. I create art with various mediums and dimensions—paint, paper, wood, metal, and photographs. Each creation expresses something about the relationship of mankind in the world around us, the mystery of life, and how each part represents an equally dynamic expression of the whole. *Life, Liberty and the Pursuit of Being* suggests the importance of understanding the past so that one may travel forward with wisdom, knowledge, and understanding. — TAT

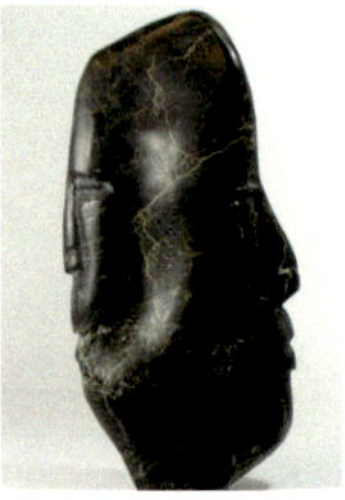

JUTAI TOONOO, a painter and stone sculptor, is the son of noted Inuit artists Sheojuk and Toonoo. He, along with his siblings—renowned sculptors Oviloo Tunnillie and Samonie Toonoo—learned to carve from their father and other family members. In the early 1980s, Jutai decided to take a break from carving and work in an office, but by the 1990s he had returned to his tools after completing a course in jewelry making and metalwork at the Nunavut Arctic College, Iqaluit (1995). Toonoo belongs to the "middle generation" of Inuit artists who straddle the traditional and modern worlds of the Arctic, negotiating an identity that is simultaneously introspective and worldly. He departs from ethnic expectations, using traditional Inuit stones in new and unexpected ways. Recent solo and group exhibitions include *Continuum* (Inuit Gallery of Vancouver, 2011), *Stone and Paper: Cape Dorset 2011* (Native Art Gallery, Oakville, Ontario, 2011), *Jutai Toonoo: Body Contemplation* and *Dorset Now* (Feheley Fine Arts, Toronto, 2012), and many others . His work is in the collections of the Winnipeg Art Gallery, Manitoba; Art Gallery of Ontario, Toronto; National Gallery of Canada, Ottawa, Ontario; and Canadian Department of Foreign Affairs and International Trade, Ottawa.

When I carve, I am giving part of myself. I put so much energy and passion into the carving that I am working on that I am physically and mentally drained when the carving is finished. I do not like wearing a protective mask when I'm carving, so I also know that the dust that I'm breathing in is killing me. Each carving that I make takes so much out of me. — Derived from Norton and Reading, *Cape Dorset Sculpture* (2005).

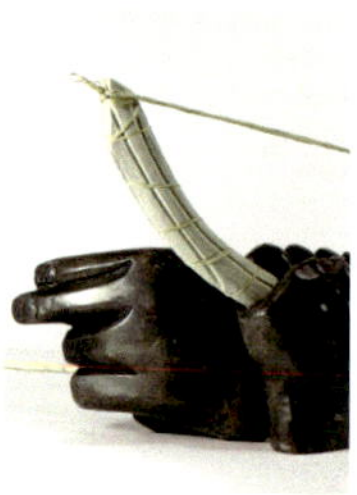

SAMONIE TOONOO is the son of graphic artist Sheojuk Tunnillie and noted sculptor Toonoo Tunnillie and younger brother of Oviloo Tunnillie and Jutai Toonoo, also accomplished artists. Samonie began carving in his early twenties focusing on more typical style of wildlife and figurative subjects. This soon developed into sculptures that embodied more abstract concepts.

Work by Toonoo has been exhibited in solo and group exhibitions, including *Samonie Toonoo: Sculpture* (Albers Gallery, San Francisco, 2005) and *Samonie Toonoo* (Feheley Fine Arts, Toronto, 2009). Group exhibitions include *Small Sculptures by Great Artists* (Feheley Fine Arts, Toronto, 2010), *Continuum* (Inuit Gallery of Vancouver, British Columbia, 2011), *Stone and Paper: Cape Dorset 2011* (Native Art Gallery, Oakville, Ontario. 2011), and *Small Treasures 2011* (Inuit Gallery of Vancouver, British Columbia, 2011).

Samonie's figures are unlike any other carver's work in Cape Dorset. He often combines several materials in one piece—carving a face from antler, for example. Samonie's works often have a deeper spiritual meaning, reflecting what he describes as a strong connection to a world beyond the here-and-now. He believes that powerful spirits are always here to protect us in need. — Derived from the artist's page, Coastal Peoples Gallery, Vancouver, British Columbia

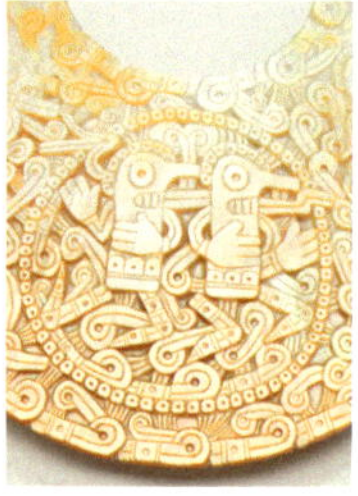

DAN TOWNSEND was born and raised in the Everglades and Keys regions in Florida. A self-taught artist, he was first inspired by his grandmother and as a child carved coconut shells. As he learned more about his cultural history, he began to create works that comprised patterns based on early Southeastern iconography. While his earliest works were intended for use by community elders, it was they who convinced Townsend to pursue a full-time career as an artist. He has been featured in several publications including *Native Peoples Arts & Lifeways* (November/December 2005) and the *Tulsa Indian Art Festival* journal (2007). Townsend served as an artist-in-residence at the Art Institute of Chicago (2005), during the run of the exhibition *Hero, Hawk and Open Hand, American Indian Art of the Ancient Midwest and South.* His work can be found in collections throughout the world and continues to be used in a number of tribal communities for ceremonial teaching.

Each time I create a piece of medicine work, there are always two created. The two characters in the center are referred to as the "Birdman morphing into the Warbird." They are also considered to be the twins—lightening and thunder. All the swirls and "J" motifs are considered breath scrolls, words, songs, prayers, medicine, chants, wind, smoke (after prayer has been breathed on the tobacco it is delivered to the fire, and then thus it becomes the smoke that goes up to master breath, the creator). This piece is the little brother of the piece worn by the speaker of the house when the Creek Council house is in session in Bruce, Florida, the Muscogee Nation of Florida. — DT

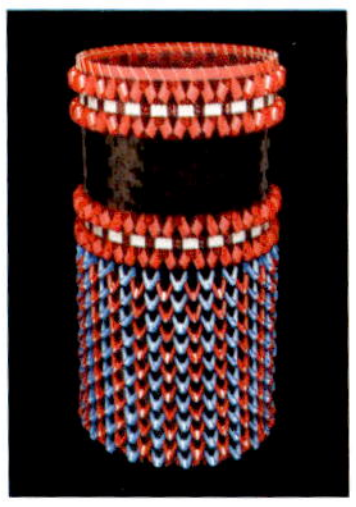

GAIL TREMBLAY is an accomplished artist who works in a wide range of disciplines. She is also an educator, author, and poet. In her art practice, Tremblay often draws upon the traditional culture of her heritage while using contemporary materials such as recycled film to weave baskets or create multimedia installations. She earned a BA (1967) in drama at the University of New Hampshire, Durham, and an MFA (1969) in creative writing at the University of Oregon, Eugene. For the past twenty years Tremblay has been on the faculty of Evergreen State College, Olympia, Washington, where she teaches programs in the visual arts. She is a recipient of numerous awards and honors including the Governor's Art Award (2001) for the State of Washington and is past-president and member of the national board of the Women's Caucus for Art.

Tremblay's career as an artist has spanned more than three decades, and her work has been featured in innumerable solo and group exhibitions that include *Iókste Akweriá/It is Heavy on My Heart* (installation and film baskets, Lewis and Clark College, Portland, Oregon, 2004), *Women Only! In Their Studios* (curated by Eleanor Flomenhaft, traveling, 2006–8), *Recycled Images/Iroquois Forms* (Froelick Gallery, Portland, Oregon, 2009), *Show of Hands: Northwest Women Artists 1880–2010* (Whatcom Museum, Bellingham, Washington, 2010), *Emergence From Place* (Clatsop Community College, Astoria, Oregon, 2012), and many more. Tremblay has also written and published many articles in the field of contemporary Native art and has curated and co-curated a number of exhibitions. She is one of the featured artists in *Manifestations: New Native Art Criticism* (Museum of Contemporary Native Arts, Santa Fe, 2011). Her work is in many public and private collections including the Portland Art Museum, Oregon; National Museum of the American Indian, Smithsonian Institution, Washington, DC; and Microsoft Corporation, Redmond, Washington.

I use nontraditional materials to weave traditional Onondaga and Micmac basketry forms that comment on Indigenous life in the twenty-first century. I began making "film" baskets in 1985 when I was teaching film theory with filmmaker Marge Brown at Evergreen State College. It was she who suggested that I do a film project. I asked our students for out-takes from their projects and wove my first "film" basket, which I presented to Marge at the end of the quarter. Film was an interesting material, and I enjoyed the notion of recycling it and gaining control over mediums that had historically been used by Hollywood and documentary filmmakers to stereotype American Indians. I relished the irony of making film take on the traditional fancy stitch patterns of our ash-splint and sweetgrass baskets. I developed complex patterns and began to use leader as well as exposed film. I also began to use recycled footage from films being thrown away by libraries, which allowed me to choose certain images that suited my themes. I enjoy creating titles to contextualize these baskets and often choose materials to ironic purpose. The choice of weaving stitches, many of which have names, is also deliberate.

The "film" basket that I created for *Changing Hands 3—It Was Never About Playing Cowboys and Indians*—was made from a documentary titled *Play and Cultural Continuity, Part VI: Montana Indian Children*. The content of the film focuses on various kinds of play: girls learning to put their dolls in cradle boards, children learning to do beadwork, and other activities that maintain Indian culture. I chose a porcupine-point stitch in red and blue at the bottom of the basket to refer to the prickly nature of Indian–White relations in America, where, for generations, non-Indian children have played cowboys and Indians. I chose to use red ribbon stitch at the top to praise Indian children for playing games that help them to preserve their culture. — GT

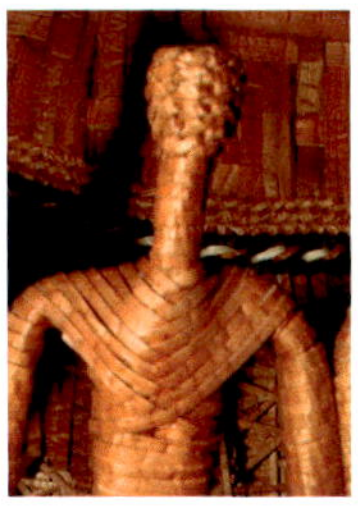

DAWN WALDEN makes cedar baskets that bridge two worlds, drawing from her Ojibway heritage while looking to the future. Trained in commercial art technology at Ferris College, Grand Rapids, Michigan, and with forty years of self-study in ethnobotany, Walden is also recognized as a wood and stone sculptor. Her earliest lessons were from elder master carvers and weavers from whom she learned to weave black ash and birch bark at the age of nine. Later she mastered cedar bark, cedar root, and bear grass construction while living in the Pacific Northwest. In 2006 she become interested in "stretching the traditional into the contemporary," looking for other basketry forms to explore. She is dedicated to preserving age-old Ojibway tools and techniques and uses natural materials that give her baskets their character. Walden sketches before starting a basket, each of which takes months to complete.

Walden is a member of and instructor for the National Basketry Organization; Michigan Basket Makers Association; Ancient Arts Technology; Northwest Native American Basketry Association; the Seattle Basketry Guild; and the Oregon Basketry Guild. Her work has been published numerous times and can be found in many public and private collections including Arkansas Museum of Art, Little Rock; Boston Museum of Fine Arts; Racine Museum of Art, Wisconsin; and the Sara and David Lieberman Collection.

Dawn Walden's cedar baskets are elegant representations of the dualities of life.Following the traditions of her Ojibway ancestry, she personally collects and processes the cedar. After she had completed the ardous process, she begins each basket with the traditional, uniform weaving technique. Yes this orderly structure is only visible from the interior of the basket. The exterior surface is defined by a second weave that is entirely random, a weave that is her own creation and sets her apart from the rigors of tradition. The arbitrary weave was inspired by the construction process of a bird's nest. After discovering that a bird was borrowing her cedar strands as they dried in the sun, she began incorporating this random weave into her work. Walden feels that the combination of these regular and random techniques is an appropriate meditation on the "random order" of life. — Derived from artist's page, Jane Sauer Gallery, Santa Fe, New Mexico

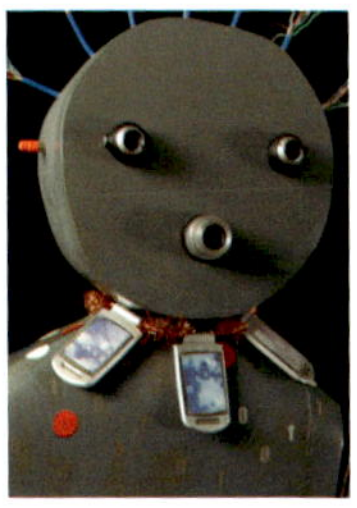

STEPHEN WALL works in a wide range of media but focuses on stone sculpture and silversmithing, finding a balance between his visions and the materials he uses to interpret them. Since graduating from Fort Lewis College, Durango, Colorado (1972), Wall has held numerous positions in both legal and social agencies serving his community. He is currently the faculty chair of Indigenous liberal studies at the Institute of American Indian Arts (IAIA), Santa Fe. In addition to these commitments, Wall serves on the board of the Southwestern Association for Indian Arts (SWAIA), Santa Fe.

Exhibitions include *Native Views: Influences of Modern Culture, A Contemporary Native American Art Exhibition* (traveling, 2004–7), and *The End of the Trail* (Institute of American Indian Arts Museum, now the Museum of Contemporary Native Arts, Santa Fe, 2007). Wall has won a number of ribbons and other awards at juried competitions both for his jewelry and sculptures, including First Place, Mixed Media at the Southwestern Association for Indian Arts (SWAIA) annual Indian Market, Santa Fe. His work can be found in the collection of the Museum of Indian Arts and Culture, Santa Fe (a collaboration with sculptor Laura Fragua-Cota).

Over the past several years I have been working with the combination of natural materials, such as stone and wood, and cast-off and recycled electronic devices. *Techno-Dodems,* the fusion of modern technology with Neolithic sensibilities, were the first of this experimental series. The *Techno-Dodems* and the natural materials used to create them represent the Earth and our ultimate reliance on the Creator and the Gifts that have been given to us. The materials from the Digital Age represent the efforts of humanity and show how far we have advanced as a species on this planet. The melding of the two materials brings to mind the ultimate fact that as advanced as our technology has become, we are still dependent on the Gifts from the Creator.

There is also the reality of dark forces that exist in world. While the *Techno-Dodems* represent the Gifts from the Creator, the *Techno-Wiindigo* series is a reflection of the dark forces. Wiindigo is the cannibal in Anishnaabe mythology, a spirit who brings fear and sorrow to families and communities. Similarly, aspects of technology have taken on a spirit of their own. Like the Wiindigo who seduces people into his lair only to be killed, the spirit of surveillance technology is seducing people into a false sense of security while taking away their privacy and freedoms. *Techno-Wiindigo 3.5* represents the cannibalizing of our society through the use and abuse of surveillance technologies. — SW

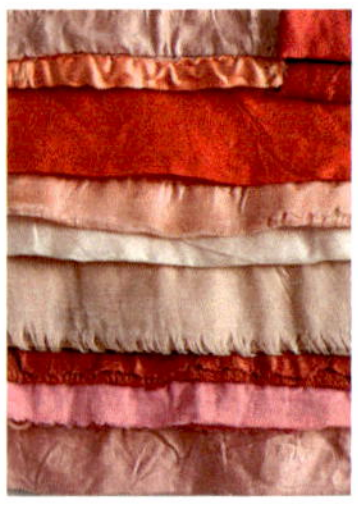

MARIE WATT is a multidisciplinary artist whose work draws from Indigenous design principles, oral tradition, biography, and history. Her practice consists of a vocabulary of natural materials, including stone, cornhusks, wool, and cedar, as well as forms such as blankets, pillows, and bridges that are universal to human experience. Watt received an AFA (1994) in museum studies from the Institute of American Indian Arts, Santa Fe, and subsequently graduated from Yale University School of Art with a MFA (1996) in painting and printmaking.

Her exhibition history is extensive, the most recent solo exhibitions include *Forget-Me-Not* (traveling, Holter Museum of Art, Helena, Montana, 2009–11), *Marker* (PDX Contemporary Art, Portland, Oregon, 2010), *Lodge* (Hallie Ford Museum of Art, Willamette University, Salem, Oregon, and the Tacoma Art Museum, 2012), and *Cradle* (Greg Kucera Gallery, Seattle, 2012), among many others. Recent group shows include *Counting Coup* (Museum of Contemporary Native Arts, Santa Fe, 2011), *Close Encounters: The Next 500 Years* (Plug In Institute of Contemporary Art, Winnipeg, Manitoba, 2011), and *Shapeshifting: Transformations in Native American Art* (Peabody Essex Museum, Salem, Massachusetts, 2012). Her work has been acquired by more than thirty public and private collections including the Eiteljorg Museum of American Indians and Western Art, Indianapolis; Museum of Fine Arts, Santa Fe; National Gallery of Canada, Ottawa, Ontario; Seattle Art Museum, Seattle; and the National Museum of the American Indian, Smithsonian Institution, Washington, DC.

I am interested in how woolen blankets are markers for memory and story. I also find these objects personal. In my tribe, and other Native communities, we give blankets away to honor a person for being witness to an important life event. It is as meaningful to give a blanket away as it is to receive one. In the ledger pieces, I am attracted to the way the satin binding of a blanket begs to be touched, but also reveals a history of use. It is a dream catcher and ledger of secrets. The word "ledger" refers to a journal of accounts. *Ledger: Generations* is an account or inventory of blankets and their bindings broken into four categories or color fields—red, yellow, green, and blue. — MW

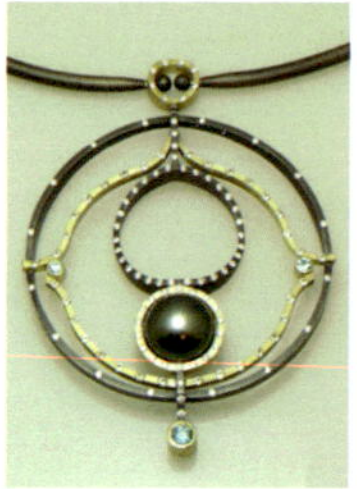

ROBIN WAYNEE began to develop her jewelry-making skills at a young age, learning from her father, the sculptor/jeweler Robert Lone Eagle Waynee. In 1999 she obtained an apprenticeship with Ryan Roberts in his Santa Fe studio, studying advanced jewelry techniques. Over the last decade, Waynee has continued to work from her home studio, refining her design idiom and honing her skills. Her attention to detail, sculptural approach, and intermixing of materials has been recognized with numerous awards at the Southwest Association for Indian Arts (SWAIA) annual Indian Market, Santa Fe, and the Heard Museum annual Indian Market and Festival, Phoenix. Since 2010 she has won successive Saul Bell International Design Awards, earning a First Place award in the silver category (2010), the First Place award in the gold category (2011), and both First Place in the gold category and Grand Prize (2012).

My designs are hand-fabricated and usually one of a kind. I primarily work in 18K gold and often include precious and semiprecious stones. I consider my designs to be very "gem oriented." The design process begins on paper, usually centering on a single gemstone. When I move on to create the actual piece, it is built from scratch in the most literal sense. I use 24K gold grain and then add the alloy, melt it down, and pour an ingot. This allows me to create sheet metal, wire, tubing, whatever I need, in whatever size or thickness I need.

I feel my style is at first glance simple and elegant, but will reveal subtle complexities. I prefer a shape with clean flowing lines, but this sometimes creates a challenge in the quest to be original. It is important to me to focus on every detail of the piece, from the meticulous selection of accent stones, hidden hinges, and clasps, to an unusual way of setting a stone. My goals as an artist are to continue to expand my knowledge and skill level in the jewelry field, and the wonderful thing is that there is a lifetime of knowledge to explore.

When I considered collaborating with another artist I wanted to work with someone who used similar materials but had a different aesthetic. Not knowing much about her personally, I thought Keri Ataumbi's jewelry had a lighthearted, realistic natural quality that was appealing. And as soon as we met and talked, I knew we could come up with something wonderful! I learned new techniques, challenged myself by working out of my comfort zone and came out of it with a wonderful friend to boot. — RW

Collaborating artist: Keri Ataumbi was a featured artist in *Changing Hands 2.*

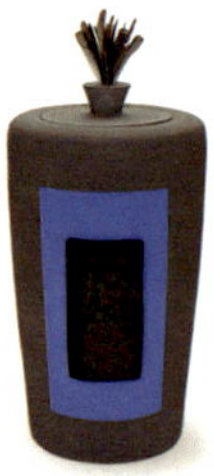

JASON WESAW began exploring his creativity at a young age, always curious about his Indigenous heritage. First through music and photography, and subsequently through the study of ceramics, Wesaw has devoted his life to the study and preservation of his people's history and culture. Using native clay from the Michigan lakes region, the artist works in a variety of ceramic techniques to create wares on a variety of scales that resonate as both historic and highly contemporary. Though very involved in his community, Wesaw has participated in a number of juried regional markets and has been artist-in-residence at the Eiteljorg Museum of American Indians and Western Art, Indianapolis (2008 and 2011).

My process for creating is born from time spent praying, singing, exploring, and photographing. Imagining the way of life my Potawatomi ancestor's lived five hundred years ago and how that same knowledge is still alive in me. A language of blood, laughter, and memory. Communicating through the movement of my fingertips and hands, shaping and molding the earth, giving it a new form. I find influence on the streets of Chicago as easily as I do sitting by the lake where my people have lived since the beginning of time. I follow my traditional tribal ways, yet I absolutely love all the conveniences of modern-day life. Attempting to bridge the gap between expressions both contemporary and traditional, my ceramic art lies somewhere in between. This work is not mine alone. It is a compilation of the gifts and teachings I have been given by my elders, a lot of hard work, a nd my humble desire to leave a legacy for the generations to come.

The Doorway: Lidded forms are intriguing because of the simple mystery of what it may contain inside. A closed vessel, similar to the human body, has a true beauty that comes from the inside, the place where its spirit is contained. For a Native person, the knowledge of our history and culture can bring enlightenment. There is a doorway leaving the drab, gray existence that comes from a lack of identity, through which, we can attain levels of knowing we never imagined possible.

Four Directions: As tribal culture evolves and the world changes around it, there are truths that remain a constant. The power of a feather and the teachings of the Seventh Generation bring us back to the essence of what we have always been: spiritual beings living in a physical world.

Spirit—Spring: Birth, renewal, purity, and possibility. The southern direction, where the young spirits stay. What does spirit look like? It is not known, but it can be felt. This is a representation of the spirit felt during the time of year we call spring.

Spirit—Universal: Time does not concern itself with us. We are a part of a continuum, interrelated with all of creation, from the most seemingly insignificant grain of sand to the mystery and awe of the Milky Way. This is a representation of the spiritual connection to everything in this world and beyond. — JW

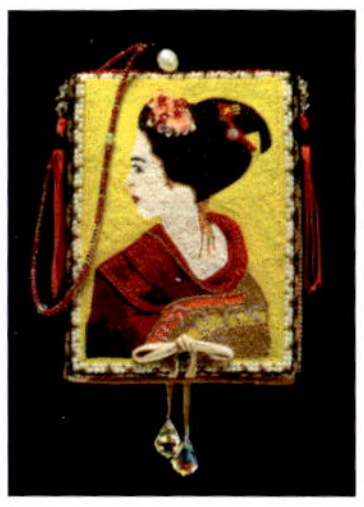

KENNETH WILLIAMS JR. began his career at an early age, experimenting as a self-taught artist who learned by observing family and friends. He is the brother of noted ledger artist Dallin Maybee. He completed his BA in museum studies at the Institute of American Indian Arts, Santa Fe (2007) and while there took beadwork classes from noted beadwork artist Terri Greeves, whose work was featured in *Changing Hands 2*. Since 2003 he has been participating in the Southwest Association for Indian Arts (SWAIA) annual Indian Market, Santa Fe, and since 2006 at the Heard Museum annual Indian Market and Festival, Phoenix. Williams's work has been widely exhibited and garnered many awards. It is in many prominent collections including the Nerman Museum of Contemporary Art, Overland Park, Kansas; Ralph T. Coe Collection, Metropolitan Museum of Art, New York; Wheelwright Museum of the American Indian, Santa Fe; and Utah Museum of Natural History, University of Utah, Salt Lake City, among others.

I am a beadworker. I was born into this artistic tradition and have had the benefit of generations' worth of knowledge and experience passed down to me. Beadwork is something I grew up with, both familiar and comforting. Yet I am mostly self-taught. I began experimenting with beadwork when I was six years old, while living on my father's Reservation. Mostly through trial and error, I started making basic necklaces and earrings, along with small pouches, which I sold locally. As a teenager, I moved away from New York State and lived closer to my mother's family, who were master beadworkers. Under their influence and with their support, I was inspired to start bigger projects. Both my late uncle, Robert Spoonhunter, and my aunt, Agnes Spoonhunter Logan, were role models who encouraged me to pursue beadwork as a serious life endeavor. I resolved to focus on refining my work—not just as a potential career, but also to uphold my family's reputation.

I went on to study at the Institute of American Indian Arts in Santa Fe and learned about contemporary beadwork from Teri Greeves who encouraged me to discover my "own" style. In many ways, she really broke me out of my shell. I newly realized how my personal contemporary style could also reflect hundreds of years of traditional beadwork aesthetics. Thanks to her, I gained confidence in myself and my work, came to recognize who I am, where I've been, and to see that my future is full of new possibilities. — KW

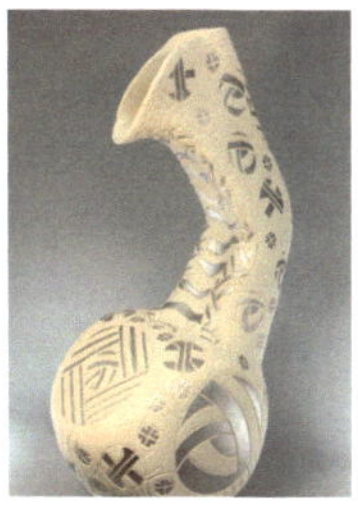

STEPHEN WOOD is a multimedia artist who combines traditional techniques and modern influences. His paintings have sometimes been referred to as "Indian Pop Art with a twist." He earned a BFA (2004) from Northeastern State University in Oklahoma and, in addition, has studied pottery techniques and glassblowing. He has taught filmmaking under the aegis of the Philbrook Museum in Tulsa, Oklahoma, and art at an alternative high school. Solo exhibitions include *30: A Collection of New Works by Stephen Wood* (Wheelwright Museum of the American Indian, Santa Fe, 2010). Among his recent group exhibitions are *Pop: Popular Culture in American Indian Art* (Heard Museum, Phoenix, 2010) and *Works on Paper by Contemporary Native Artists* (Ekaterinburg Museum of Fine Arts and State Museum of Novosibirsk, Russia, 2012). Wood has been the recipient of numerous awards for painting and pottery at juried markets and festivals, including the Best of Division, Non-Traditional Pottery, Heard Museum annual Indian Market and Festival, Phoenix (2009).

I intended *Song of Creation* to be an abstract interpretation of the creation of life and the universe. The circular forms that travel over and up the piece to me represent both atoms and planets, relative to each other in scale. They spin and form along what seem to be chaotic lines but on further inspection are actually balanced and reflect each other. I wanted the silver to create a sense of light. I wanted the lines and forms to dance with each other, creating a sense of movement. I knew this had to be a very large piece to convey what I wanted, which was that it look unbalanced, as though it could tip over at any moment. The neck is larger than it should be to create tension between the piece and the viewer. — SW

SUGGESTED READING

Abbot, Lawrence, ed. *I Stand at the Center of the Good: Interviews with Contemporary Native American Artists.* Lincoln: University of Nebraska Press, 1994.

Baker, Joe, and Gerald McMaster, eds. *Remix: New Modernities in a Post-Indian World.* Washington, DC: Smithsonian Institution National Museum of the American Indian, 2007.

Blomberg, Nancy, J., ed. *[Re]inventing the Wheel: Advancing the Dialogue on Contemporary American Indian Art.* Denver: Denver Art Museum, 2008.

Bordewich, Fergus M. *Killing the White Man's Indian: Reinventing Native Americans at the End of the Twentieth Century.* New York: Doubleday, 1996.

Devon, Marjorie, ed. *Migrations: New Directions in Native American Art.* Albuquerque: University of New Mexico Press, 2006.

Dubin, Margaret. *Native America Collected, The Culture of an Art World.* Albuquerque: University of New Mexico Press, 2001.

Falvey, Emily A., ed. *Counting Coup.* With essays by Ryan Rice and Jolene Rickard. Exh. cat. Santa Fe: Museum of Contemporary Native Arts, 2011.

Hessel Ingo. *Inuit Art: An Introduction.* New York: Douglas & McIntyre, 1998.

Hopkins, Candice, and Kerry Swanson. *Shapeshifters, Time Travellers and Storytellers.* Exh. cat. Toronto: Royal Ontario Museum, 2008.

Kan, Sergei A., and Paul Turner Strong. *New Perspectives on Native North America, Cultures, Histories, Representations.* Lincoln: University of Nebraska Press, 2006.

Kardosh, Judy. *Works on Cloth: Imagery by Artists of Baker Lake, Nunavut.* Vancouver, BC: Marion Scott Gallery, 2002.

Martin, Lee-Ann. *Au Fil de Mes Jours.* Quebec: Musée National des beaux-arts des Québec, 2005.

McMaster, Gerald, ed. *Reservation X.* Ottawa: Canadian Museum of Civilization, 1998.

———, ed. *Inuit Modern: The Samuel and Esther Sarick Collection.* Toronto: D&M Publishers Inc., 2011.

McMaster, Gerald, and Lee-Ann Martin, eds. *Indigena: Contemporary Native Perspectives in Canadian Art.* Vancouver and Tortola, BVI: Craftsman House, 1992.

McNutt, Jennifer Complo, and Ashley Holland, eds. *We Are Here: The Eiteljorg Contemporary Art Fellowship 2011.* Indianapolis: University of Washington Press, 2011.

Mithlo, Nancy Marie, et al. *Manifestations: New Native Art Criticism.* Santa Fe: Museum of Contemporary Native Arts, 2011.

Myre, Nadia. *Baliser La Territoire: Manifestation d'Art Contemporain Autochtone/A Stake in The Ground: Contemporary Native Art Manifestation.* Exh. cat. Montreal: Art Mûr, 2012.

Nemiroff, Diana, Robert Houle, and Charlotte Townsend Gault. *Land Spirit Power: First Nations at the National Gallery of Canada.* Ottawa: National Gallery of Canada, 1992.

Norton, Derek, and Nigel Reading. *Cape Dorset Sculpture.* Seattle: University of Washington Press; Vancouver, BC: Douglas and McIntyre, 2005.

Ortel, Jo. *Woodland Reflections: The Art of Truman Lowe.* Madison: University of Wisconsin Press, 2003.

Ostorowitz, Judith. *Interventions: Native American Art for Far-Flung Territories.* Seattle: University of Washington Press, 2009.

Racette, Sherry Farrell, ed. *Close Encounters: The Next 500 Years.* Winnipeg: Plug In Editions, 2011.

Rice, Ryan. *Oh So Iroquois.* Exh. cat. Ottawa: The Ottawa Art Gallery, 2007.

———. *Anthem: Perspectives on Home and Native Land.* Ex. cat. Ottawa: Carleton University Art Gallery, 2008.

Rushing III, W. Jackson, ed. *Native American Art in the Twentieth Century: Makers, Meanings, Histories.* Abingdon: Routledge, 1999.

Russell, Karen Kramer, et al. *Shapeshifting: Transformations in Native American Art.* New Haven: Yale University Press, 2012.

Sweet, Jill D., et al. *Staging the Indian: The Politics of Representation.* Saratoga Springs: Tang Teaching Museum and Art Gallery of Skidmore College, 2002.

Williams, Dana Alan, and Pierre-Léon Tétreault. *New Territories 350/500 Years After: An Exhibition of Contemporary Aboriginal Art of Canada.* Montreal: Ateliers Vision Planetaire, 1992.

PHOTO CREDITS

Every effort has been made to properly credit the works illustrated in this publication. All photographs were taken by the artist, unless otherwise noted below.

Illustrations to The Native American Art Market: From Curiosity to Commodity
A pair of Micmac moccasins from Captain Farquharson's Invercauld Trust
Courtesy of Sotheby's, New York

Illustrations to Transformations: A New Era in Contemporary Inuit Art
Estelle Marcoux Komangapik

Illustrations to Karen Wright and Jimmie Durham: A Conversation
Ed Watkins

Illustrations to Epilogue—*Close Encounters: The Next 500 Years*
Scott Benesiinaabandan

Barry Ace: Rosalie Favell
Adam Alorut: Brad van der Zanden, Feheley Fine Arts
Joe Baker with Le Décor Français: Ed Watkins
Kelly Church: Jeff Strand
Hannah Claus: George Khayat
Bonnie Devine: Srimoyee Mitra
Jeremy Frey:
Point Basket – Ari Plosker; ©2012 Ari Plosker, All Rights Reserved
Urchin – Julia Clark, Abbe Museum
Billy Gauthier: Kenji Nagai, Spirit Wrestler Gallery
Jeffrey Gibson:
Column – Barb Choit
Everlast – Ed Watkins
Richard Glazer-Danay: *Mohawk Ironworkers Headdress* – David Barbour
Shan Goshorn: Robert Hawks, Tulsa OK
Karen Goulet: *Xander's Morning Star* – Brian Basham Photography
Cody E. Harjo: Steven Lang
Carla Hemlock: *Treaty Cloth Shirt* – Greg Horn
Donald "Babe" Hemlock: Greg Horn
Rosemary Rickard Hill: Deniece Woods
Robert Houle: Keesic Douglas
Tom Huff: Jack M Hardendorf
Eva Ikinilik: Paul Conroy, Marion Scott Gallery/Kardosh Projects
Mattiusi Iyaituk: Paul Conroy, Marion Scott Gallery/Kardosh Projects
G. Peter Jemison: Kevin Vickers and David Mitchell
Peter B. Jones:
Portrait Jar: New Indian – Warren Wheeler
Red Moon – James M. Via
Ruben Anton Komangapik: Estelle Marcoux Komangapik
Floyd Kuptana: Brad van der Zanden, Feheley Fine Arts
John Kurok: © National Gallery of Canada
Samuel LaFountain: *Black Jade Bracelet* – Ed Watkins
Courtney M. Leonard: Dianne Stromberg; Courtesy of the Museum of Contemporary Native Arts
George Longfish: Bo Byrnes
Truman Lowe: Tonia Lowe and James Paige
Theresa Marshall: Ed Watkins
Michael Massie: Kenji Nagai, Spirit Wrestler Gallery
Wanesia Misquadace: Phil Karshis
Kent Monkman:
The King's Beavers – Photo MMFA, Christine Guest
Kiss the Sky – Robert McNair
Cree Leggings – Paul Smith.
Dreamcatcher Bra, Racoon Jockstrap, and *Quiver* – Brian Boyle
Janet Nungnik: Paul Conroy, Marion Scott Gallery/Kardosh Projects
Summer Peters: Brandt Photography
Jamasie Pitseolak: Paul Conroy, Marion Scott Gallery/Kardosh Projects
David L. Pruitt: Cora Lathrop, Tahlequah, Oklahoma
Ruth Qaulluaryuk: Paul Conroy, Marion Scott Gallery/Kardosh Projects
Joel Queen: Addison Doty
Jason Quigno: Jim Gebbin
Tammy Rahr: Teresa Fields-Athabascan ©2011
Frank Shebageget: David Barbour
Leah Shenandoah:
Rabbit Fur Purse and *Haute Couture Hood* – Joanne Shenandoah
Stars in Her Hair (Headpiece) – © Leah Shenandoah
Skawennati: *Hunter Mega-Figurine* (Prototype) – David Ward
Jamie Zane Smith: Charles S. King
Robert Tannahill: Miia Virtasalmi
Tammy Tarbell: Tim See
Jutai Toonoo:
In Tune with Nature – Brad van der Zanden, Feheley Fine Arts
Two Guys Growing Apart – Dorset Fine Arts
Samonie Toonoo: Dorset Fine Arts
Dan Townsend: Jordanross Inge, Dallas, Texas
Gail Tremblay: Michael Ryan
Stephen Wall: John Hagen, Haines, Alaska
Robin Waynee:
Rolling Pearl Necklace – Robert Railey
Wasp Necklace – SWAIA
Kenneth Williams Jr.: *The Beauty of a Maiko* – Maggie Nimkin
Stephen Wood: Amber Watson

INDEX

Catalogue references are indicated in bold.